Local government
and strategic choice

Local government and strategic choice

AN OPERATIONAL RESEARCH APPROACH
TO THE PROCESSES OF
PUBLIC PLANNING

J. K. FRIEND *ohn imball* *and* W. N. JESSOP

TAVISTOCK PUBLICATIONS

First published in 1969
By Tavistock Publications Limited
11 New Fetter Lane, London E.C.4

Printed in Great Britain
In 'Monotype' Plantin 10 on 12 point
by Spottiswoode, Ballantyne & Co. Ltd.,
London and Colchester

This book was written under the auspices of
the Institute for Operational Research
56/60 Hallam Street, London W.1 and
42B New Union Street, Coventry, Warwickshire

Maps 1–6 and *Figure 8* are reproduced by
courtesy of Coventry City Council. All other
maps and diagrams were drawn by S. Wyatt.

SBN 422 73050 5

Contents

The origins of the book   *page* xi

Acknowledgements   xv

Synopsis   xix

PART I   AN APPRAISAL OF PLANNING IN A MAJOR LOCAL
         AUTHORITY

  1   An introduction to Coventry and its Council   3
  2   Four years of planning in Coventry   7
  3   Planning and the mechanisms of decision   47
  4   Information and uncertainty in planning   69
      References for Part I   98

PART II   PLANNING: A PROCESS OF STRATEGIC CHOICE

  5   The nature of planning   101
  6   The operational problems of the planning process   115
  7   Planning in its organizational context   120
      References for Part II   136

PART III   TOWARDS A TECHNOLOGY FOR STRATEGIC CHOICE

  8   An approach through case examples   139
  9   Case one: land allocation in a redevelopment area   142
 10   Case two: priorities within a changing town   162
 11   Case three: strategy for a sub-region   214
 12   A general appraisal of the technology   231
      References for Part III   239

PART IV   THE ORGANIZATIONAL CHALLENGE

 13   Organizational choice in local government   243
 14   A case example in organizational choice   250
 15   Prospects for public planning   287
      References for Part IV   290

Index   291

Maps

1   Policy Map of Coventry   *facing page* 22

2   Desire lines 1981 – journey to work trips   *page* 80
        Source: *The Coventry Road System* (Coventry City Council, 1963)

3   1957 Development Plan pattern – outline plan   82
        Source: *The Coventry Road System* (Coventry City Council, 1963)

4   Modified Development Plan pattern (inverted 'Y') – outline plan   82
        Source: *The Coventry Road System* (Coventry City Council, 1963)

5   Saturated roads 1981, under 1957 Development Plan pattern   85
        Source: *The Coventry Road System* (Coventry City Council, 1963)

6   Saturated roads 1981, under modified Development Plan pattern
        (inverted 'Y')   85
        Source: *The Coventry Road System* (Coventry City Council, 1963)

7   Boundaries of area A   143

8   Sub-divisions of area A   143

9   Area A in relation to its surroundings   153

10 Area A and surroundings: options for future land use   153

11 Outline map of Fluxton   163

12 Fluxton: sector Z   164

13 Sector Z: location of decision problems   168

14 Adminster and its sub-region   216

15 Administrative map of Newbound   251

The origins of the book

A Note by Neil Jessop

Director of the Institute for Operational Research

This book is the outcome of a research project of a somewhat unusual kind: one whose scope encompassed the entire range of policy-formation within an English local authority during a four-year period, and which sought to bring together the complementary approaches of operational research and the behavioural sciences.

Access was virtually unlimited. The opportunities made available to the research team included freedom to attend all committee meetings, interdepartmental discussions, and even party political groups. The local authority was the City Council of Coventry, a city whose post-war reconstruction achievements have attracted wide interest in many countries. Throughout the research we were conscious of the unique nature of the opportunities afforded us, and the need to make the outcome of the project something more constructive than a critical case-history. We have used our experience, therefore, to make a general analysis of the governmental planning process from which there emerge certain propositions for innovation and change. In putting forward these propositions, we realize that we are entering the field of controversy. It is, however, desirable that as much debate as possible should be stimulated on the processes through which public policies are formed, and it is first and foremost as a contribution to this debate that I would wish this book to be judged.

The project was the outcome of certain developments in the world of operational research. In May 1963, discussions in London between the Operational Research Society and the Tavistock Institute of Human Relations* culminated in the setting-up of an Institute for Operational Research, as an autonomous unit within the matrix of the latter body, with the purpose of developing operational research against a background of the human sciences. Operational research, in its origin an application of scientific method to the decisions of warfare, has, since the Second World War, become widely accepted in industry as an activity which can assist managers by giving them a qualitative and logical basis for many of their more difficult decisions.† In any healthy subject, criticism is liable to

---

* Established in 1947 as an independent not-for-profit association undertaking research, consultancy, and teaching in the field of the behavioural sciences.

† See for, instance, *A Manager's Guide to Operational Research*, by B. H. P. Rivett and R. L. Ackoff (New York: Wiley, 1963).

develop as practices become established. At the time immediately preceding the setting-up of the Institute for Operational Research, it was realized by many engaged in 'O.R.' that its greatest successes lay in fields where objectives were clearly defined, while its conspicuous failures arose where organizational objectives, values, and human relationships were both complex and obscure. Was it therefore any accident that operational research was scarcely practised in, for example, the management of social services where the word 'service' itself can carry moral or political overtones? Nevertheless, such fields of management were important to the ordinary citizen and raised questions on which he could, on occasion, be highly vocal. Perhaps it might be worth while seeking to extend the scope of operational research to include problems of social policy, especially within the public sector. To do this, operational research must be broadened and changed; and in particular it would be necessary to take more account of the human sciences. These ideas found a wide currency in the early sixties; they found particular expression in the convening by the Operational Research Society of an international conference on *Operational Research and the Social Sciences* in Cambridge in 1964,* and they provided the impetus for the foundation within the Tavistock Institute of the new Institute for Operational Research.

As the newly appointed Director, I was immediately concerned with the setting-up of a 'portfolio' of projects which would allow the Institute to develop a wide range of field experience within its chosen area of concern.† The 'Coventry Project' was one of the earliest of these to be launched. Indeed, some informal discussions took place in Coventry in the very month the Institute itself was formed. One accidental but helpful factor was that for some years I had worked for an industrial firm in Coventry and seen something of the city's development. From the start, the focal points of the proposed project were 'policy' and 'planning'. Clearly, operational research might well be applied to the *execution* of policies and plans and produce good effect in terms of economy. But how could more understanding and more conscious control be brought to bear upon the interplay of diverse and often intangible objectives? How did one relate technical management, as expressed in the specialist and co-ordinative activities of officials, to policy management, the responsibility of part-time, unpaid lay persons who were nevertheless held accountable by their local electorates?

Early discussions helped to shape a proposition for research of a scale which required the support of a foundation, and accordingly an approach was made to the Nuffield Foundation at a comparatively early stage. Discussions with the Town Clerk of Coventry, Mr (now Sir) Charles Barratt, and with other representatives of the City Council, led to a final proposal to the Foundation‡ which the trustees

* Proceedings published in *Operational Research and the Social Sciences*, edited by J. R. Lawrence (London: Tavistock, 1966).
† See 'Institute for Operational Research: The First Four Years' (Tavistock Institute of Human Relations, 1967).
‡ 'Policy Research for Local Government: The Development of a Planning Process' (I.O.R. internal document T.217, 1963).

accepted in November 1963, making available a grant of £42,000 spread over a period of four years. In the following month, Coventry City Council formally accepted the terms and objectives of the proposed research and the project was launched in December 1963 with a general meeting of councillors and officials in the ancient guildhall of St Mary, where the purpose of the research was explained and discussed. Perhaps the spirit in which the City Council approached this venture can best be summed up by the words of the Town Clerk on that occasion, which were reported in the *Coventry Evening Telegraph* the next day: 'I don't think anyone cares two hoots where this research leads to so long as it is to something good.' Whether these expectations were fulfilled is a matter which the reader of this book must judge for himself.

Acknowledgements

The possibility of writing this book would never have arisen but for a readiness to take risks on the part of two very dissimilar groups of people – the Trustees of the Nuffield Foundation, and the City Council of Coventry.

It is of course in the nature of the contribution which the independent charitable foundations make to our society, that they may sometimes undertake the sponsorship of research whose outcome is potentially of much value, but whose success is particularly difficult to guarantee in advance. However, in the case of the research which is reported in this book, the normal element of risk was increased by the fact that the applicant body, the Institute for Operational Research, was at the time only a few months old and had no established staff other than the Director himself. Furthermore, the nature of the research which was proposed – involving a fusion of two very different research traditions, the behavioural and the operational, in a particularly challenging field environment – had no obvious parallels either in the United Kingdom or elsewhere. Our indebtedness to the Nuffield Foundation is all the greater, not only because of the readiness of the Trustees to accept these initial risks in our particular case, but also because of the tolerance they have since shown in awaiting an outcome whose final shape remained in doubt until the closing stages.

The risks accepted by Coventry City Council were of a rather different kind. Having agreed to provide us with a field base for our study of planning and policy-making in local government, the members and officers of the Council showed remarkable generosity in giving us virtually unlimited access to their most intimate processes of decision-making. Our repeated appearances as observers in the committee rooms were accepted without demur, and our clear impression was that, in the cut and thrust of debate, few if any concessions were made to our presence. Even more generous, in terms of acceptance of risk, were the opportunities we were given to penetrate behind the scenes in departmental meetings and in the meetings of party political groups, where many of the strategies for the formal meetings of committees and of Council itself were first worked out. The facilities we were given to attend the private group meetings of both the opposing political parties, Labour and Conservative, must surely have been unique, and we owe a very substantial debt to the leaders and ordinary members of both the local party organizations.

In acknowledging the help we have received from the City Council, it would be invidious for us to single out for special mention any of the many individuals concerned. Although several of the people we met expressed an enthusiastic attitude to our research from the start, there were also of course some sceptics, and we wish not only to thank the more optimistic for their often much-needed encouragement, but also the sceptics for their forbearance over a period of years in which it was by no means clear what the outcome of the research would be.

The departments with which we had closest contact, and to which our greatest debt is due, included those of the Town Clerk, Sir Charles Barratt; the City Treasurer, Mr J. D. Hender (previously Dr A. H. Marshall); the City Architect and Planning Officer, Mr T. W. Gregory (previously Mr A. G. Ling); the City Engineer and Surveyor, Mr N. Rayman (previously Mr Granville Berry); the Director of Education, Mr W. L. Chinn; the Transport Manager, Mr N. McDonald; and the City Estates Surveyor, Mr A. J. Vickers. The heads of other departments also gave unstinted help when required, and it was only the limited extent of our own resources which prevented us extending our network of working relationships more widely within the Council's organization.

Our debts to the elected members of Council are equally deep, and it would be invidious for us to single out the names of any of those now serving, apart from the present leaders of the local Conservative and Labour groups, Councillors G. S. N. Richards and G. M. Park. However, we would wish especially to acknowledge the help given by two former members, Mr S. Stringer – who was leader of the Council during the formative period of our research – and Mr G. E. Hodgkinson – who was Chairman of the Planning and Redevelopment Committee and whose name is particularly associated with the post-war reconstruction of the city. While acknowledging this special debt to two former elected members of Council, it is also perhaps in order that we should acknowledge the particularly valuable help and encouragement we received during our research from two former officers of the Department of Architecture and Planning; Mr M. Reece, now Deputy County Planning Officer of East Sussex, and Mr E. Osborn, now of the Research and Intelligence Unit of the Greater London Council.

Our indebtedness as authors also extends to the contribution that has been made to this research by other members of the Tavistock Institute of Human Relations, within which the Institute for Operational Research forms one of five autonomous units. In particular, Dr Hugh Murray of the Human Resources Centre played a major part in the formulation of the original research proposal, in clearing the ground for our involvement with Coventry, and in the earlier stages of the research itself. Without his energetic participation in this crucial formative period, it is at least open to question whether the conditions for a fruitful relationship with Coventry could in fact have been created.

The content of the book has also been influenced, perhaps much more profoundly than he himself would wish to admit, by the contribution of Dr Paul Spencer, who served for three of the four years as a full-time member of the research team, and whose name does not appear as a joint author of this book only because of his secondment, during the final year of the project, to the research team of the Royal Commission on Local Government in England. In particular, our appreciation of Coventry's processes of decision-making in Chapter 3 owes much to Dr Spencer's analysis of the structure of local government in Coventry. It is our hope that much of his work in this field will in due course be published separately; so, we hope, will several other contributions by him which are at present assembled together in an internal project document.*

Among the many other colleagues who have assisted us from time to time, special mention must be made of Messrs John Stringer, John Luckman, James Morgan, and Brian Smith (now manager of the London Hospitals Computer Centre) whose advice was especially welcome at crucial stages in the preparation of this book. A great deal of advice and encouragement was also freely given by several people in the academic world who were active in related fields, including especially Professor Russell Ackoff of the University of Pennsylvania, Dr J. D. Stewart of the Institute of Local Government Studies at Birmingham University, and Mr K. R. Carter of the Town Planning Department of Lanchester College of Technology in Coventry. Another informal relationship which we have particularly appreciated during our time in Coventry has been that with the Director and Staff of the Local Government Operational Research Unit, which has played a key role in furthering the practice of operational research at many levels of British local government since the early nineteen sixties.†

The very diversity of people to whom we feel indebted must of course imply that only the authors themselves are responsible for the form in which this research is presented and the viewpoints that are expressed.

And our final word of thanks must go to Mrs Betty Fox for cheerfully and skilfully typing innumerable drafts of the manuscript – ably assisted in the later stages by Miss Elizabeth Williams – and to our respective wives and families for putting up with the many disturbances and inconveniences created by our involvement in what we now look back on as an exceptionally stressful, but also in the end an exceptionally rewarding, assignment.

* 'The Nature of the Planning Process in Coventry' (I.O.R. internal document T.930, 1967):

Part I: Community and the Social Network.
Part II: The Self-Fulfilling Prophecy and the Self-Defeating Prophecy in Local Planning.
Part III: Financial Planning and the 'Long Term Capital Works Programme' in Coventry.
Part IV: A Model for the Planning Process in a Changing City.

† See *Operational Research in Local Government*, by R. A. Ward. London: Allen and Unwin, 1964.

Synopsis

THE THEME

This book is about decision-making in local government. It addresses itself in particular to those more strategic levels of choice which tend to be linked with the terms 'planning' and 'policy-making', and to impinge on the future physical and social development of local communities in a variety of ways which may be only imperfectly understood.

Much attention has been focused in recent years on the basic challenge of planning in a democratic society; how can those who are elected to exercise choice on our behalf preserve and extend their capacity to choose discriminatingly, when the sheer complexity of the issues facing them tends all the time to make them increasingly dependent on the skills and judgements of their professional advisers?

The theme which we shall develop is that it is possible, given sufficient persistence and ingenuity, for local government to develop ways of meeting this challenge more effectively than at present. It can never be a simple matter to reconcile the basic principle of democratic control with the use of techniques which match the complexity of contemporary planning problems, but we believe it is far from impossible and our aim is to offer a few pointers to how we believe it can be achieved in practice.

Any organization tends to develop certain methods to assist it in taking decisions which, even if they are ill formulated, can be thought of collectively as forming a 'technology of choice'. We shall argue that the planning process, in local government or for that matter in any other sector of the governmental system, requires a technology of choice that explicitly recognizes the particular types of challenge posed at this level; these include the difficulty of isolating one decision from another, the difficulty of appreciating what range of solutions may be possible, the difficulty of making value judgements when confronted with a wide range of social effects, and the difficulty of striking a balance between the pressures for early commitment and the flexibility to adapt to unforeseen circumstances. We shall also argue that, if such a technology is to be consistent with the principle of democratic control, new approaches will be necessary to problems of internal organization and communication within local authorities.

After some initial analysis based on our field experience, leading to the development of some general concepts concerning the nature of the planning process, we will develop our theme primarily through the use of case example. This, we hope, will demonstrate the feasibility of the approaches we propose, both to the development of a more explicit 'technology of strategic choice' and to the creation of appropriate organizational forms; and we hope it will encourage local authorities, and other organizations concerned with the public planning process, to experiment with new ways of meeting the challenges that face them in their own particular environments.

THE RESEARCH

The research project on which this book is based was designed to extend the application of operational research, itself a subject of quite recent origin, into new and comparatively uncharted areas.

Operational research has been defined in many different ways, but perhaps the most satisfactory definition describes it as the attack of modern science on problems of decision-making arising in the management of organizations. By this definition, operational research is not a pure science; it is an application of science

Figure 1

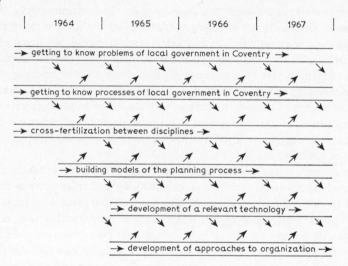

to the practical end of assisting decision-makers. In effect, it sets out to provide a more explicit 'technology of choice', to amplify the capacity of people in organizations to make purposive selections between alternative courses of action.

The research was begun in December 1963 and officially came to a close in December 1967. It is not easy to chart its course in detail over these four years, even in retrospect, because the object of the project was to break completely new ground and there was no ready-made strategy which could be adopted at the outset and pursued consistently to a conclusion. However, *Figure 1* attempts to give a broad indication of the way the research developed over its four-year term.

In this diagram, we have indicated six parallel streams of activity, some developing at a later stage than others, but each continuing until the end of the project in 1967 and each exerting a continuing influence on each of the other streams.

Initially, it was necessary for the team to spend most of its time simply learning about the problems of local government in Coventry (stream 1) and the processes through which these problems were tackled (stream 2). We were fortunate in that we were present in Coventry during a period of much activity in the fields of planning and policy formation: in particular, we were able to witness a comprehensive review of the city's development plan, and the consideration of radical changes in such fields as education, transport, and capital budgeting. We were equally fortunate in the degree of access we were given to the many different settings where these problems came up for consideration, and where contributions to the overall decision process were made; these settings ranged from official meetings of the committees of Council to unofficial discussions in departmental offices and debates in the private group meetings of the local Labour and Conservative parties. It was through these opportunities that we were able to develop, gradually through the course of our research, an appreciation of the problems and processes of local government in Coventry as they appeared from many different viewpoints within the local authority itself.

However, the team meanwhile was also concerned with another type of learning activity (stream 3), in that its membership was drawn from a range of disciplines from mathematical statistics to social anthropology, and brought to the project a range of research experience varying from the study of industrial operations, on the one hand, to the study of networks of community relationships, on the other. The members of the team did, however, all share what might be called a 'systems approach' or, in other words, a common philosophy of attempting to obtain a balanced view of operational or social systems as a whole rather than concentrating on detailed study of particular component parts; and it was this common denominator which provided the basis for the emergence during the course of the project of a research outlook in which it would, we believe, be particularly difficult to isolate the distinctive influences of the operational research and the social science traditions.

Through these processes of learning (streams 1 to 3), the team was able gradually to develop certain conceptual models of the nature of the planning process (stream 4); in effect, these 'models' consisted of generalized descriptions of the process which provided us with insights into its basic relationships and how these relationships might be expected to respond to different forms of change. We were able continually to test these conceptual models against our experience in Coventry, and to use them as a basis for developing ideas both about a relevant 'technology of strategic choice' (stream 5) and about appropriate organizational forms (stream 6).

It was only during the last year or two of the research that these last two streams of activity began to crystallize into the forms described in Parts III and IV of this book. This means that, by the conclusion of the research project itself, the process of practical testing of the technological and organizational guidelines described in this book had only just begun; but at the time of writing some modest experimentation is already under way in their application to practical situations, and our hope is that this book will stimulate further experimentation in a field of considerable importance both to government in all its forms and to the individual in his various relationships with the local community of which he or she forms a part.

THE STRUCTURE OF THE BOOK

Of the four main parts into which this book is divided, the first relates directly to our field experience in Coventry. In the second part, a more general analysis is presented of the nature of the planning process in any governmental setting, and the characteristic types of operational and organizational problem to which it gives rise. In the third and fourth parts, we use the medium of case examples to suggest how the planning process can be made more effective, first through the development of an appropriate technology of choice, and secondly through the adaptation of organizational forms to allow the technology to become a workable instrument of democratic control.

The book therefore follows basically the same sequence as that in which we have described the interacting streams of the research itself. Although each part of the book builds to some extent on the content of the previous parts, an attempt has been made to write each part in such a way that it can be read independently if desired. For instance, those who are already well acquainted with the problems and processes of planning and policy-making in local government, or whose interest is in other contexts of planning, may prefer to miss Part I at a first reading; those who are more concerned with practice than with theory may choose to miss Part II; and those whose special concern is with problems of local government organization may prefer to turn first to Part IV. There are, of course, certain cross-references between one part and another, but these have been kept to a minimum.

Because we believe that much of what we say has relevance to planning not only in British local authorities but also in local government overseas, and at other levels of the governmental system, we will try to avoid assuming any specialist knowledge at any stage of the book, whether of the formal structure of local government in Great Britain, or of the role played by the party political system, or of such particular aspects as the statutory requirements of town planning and of local government finance. We will therefore include concise introductions to these matters at appropriate points in the book, but only in so far as they have relevance to the development of our general theme.

We will also avoid making assumptions as to any specialist knowledge of the methods of operational research; and we will throughout adopt the policy of introducing the approach and philosophy of operational research (as modified through the contribution of the social sciences) through example rather than through formal exposition.

SYNOPSIS OF PART I

After a short introductory chapter giving some necessary background information on Coventry and its Council, we will proceed in the second chapter of Part I to make a general appraisal of all the many activities we have witnessed during our four years in Coventry, contributing to an overall picture of a planning process which is essentially continuous but also continually evolving over time. These activities include financial planning, the planning of physical development, the planning of land use, and the planning of manpower, all of which affect every service of local government to some degree; we also discuss certain more specialized planning activities such as those concerned with the development of the education service and of the public transport system. We discuss briefly the relationships of these local planning activities to the processes of regional and national planning, and conclude the chapter by stressing the many strands of interdependence between these different aspects of a total planning activity.

The following chapter examines the mechanisms of decision-making in Coventry in both their formal and informal aspects, and describes the difficulties that we saw to arise in adapting them to the challenges of strategic planning. Analyses are made of the distinctive contributions of the professional officers, the committees and their chairmen, and the party political groups. Certain organizational changes in Coventry during the period of our research are interpreted as responses to a growing awareness of the difficulties of coping adequately with the more strategic aspects of the decision-making process.

In the final chapter of Part I, we examine in more detail the structure of two of the most important planning proposals that were formulated by the planners in Coventry in connection with their review of the city's development plan, and that had an important influence on the processes of policy formation during the period of our fieldwork. These concerned the selection of a preferred target for future shopping capacity in the city centre, and of a preferred design for the city's network of primary roads. In both cases, we examine the many kinds of information contributing to the selection of the proposals finally submitted, and the levels of discretion which they imply. From this basis, we develop one of the basic themes of the book: that any difficulties in making a choice between alternative solutions to a given planning problem can be seen as reflecting uncertainties of three different kinds; uncertainties in knowledge of the present and future environment, uncertainties as to intentions in related fields of choice, and uncertainties as to appropriate value judgements. We relate these three classes of uncertainty to the demands which we often heard in Coventry for 'more research', 'more coordination', and 'more policy guidance' as ways of overcoming difficulties in reaching clear decisions; and we argue that the choice between these three modes of action is always liable to reflect the personal and group biases of those who may be concerned.

SYNOPSIS OF PART II

In Part II we proceed to develop a more general analysis of the nature of planning as a continuing dynamic process, and those special characteristics of this process which distinguish it from other activities of government. This we do by presenting a series of models based on the idea of a continuing 'dialogue' between government and community, taking place at many levels both within and beyond the framework of local government with which we are especially concerned. Through these models, a picture is built up of planning as a *process of strategic choice*, requiring a capacity to anticipate the future and yet also to adapt to the unforeseen.

As a result of this general analysis, we go on to identify, in the second chapter of Part II, five basic types of *operational problem* which are characteristic of the planning process in any organizational setting; these relate to the finding of feasible solutions to problems involving many related choices, the expression of preferences between alternative solutions given only imperfect information as to their effects, the exposure of latent uncertainties, the choice of exploratory actions to improve the basis of decision, and the balance to be struck between pressures for early commitment and flexibility of future choice.

In the third chapter of Part II, we identify in a similar way six basic types of *organizational problem* which relate to any planning process which is made more complex by a need to cut across organizational boundaries, either within an authority or between one authority and another. These problems concern the development of machinery for mobilization of joint planning activities, the source of authority for this function of 'strategic control', the maintenance of sufficient levels of information flow, the means of providing an adequate level of democratic guidance, the development of common language, and the need to take into account the personal and group motivations of all participants.

SYNOPSIS OF PART III

Part III puts forward some possible lines of solution to the operational problems which were isolated in Part II. It does this through the medium of a series of linked case examples, concerning different aspects of planning in a fictitious town set in a fictitious sub-region. Each of these case examples is, of course, influenced by actual planning problems which we encountered during our fieldwork in Coventry. However, use of the fictional form enables us to bring together key features from different practical situations; it also allows us to develop the case examples in such a way as to show how any 'technology of strategic choice' must be responsive to changes over time in the pressures to which the decision-makers are subjected by events within the communities they represent.

The first case example concerns a problem of urban renewal in a limited area close to the centre of our fictitious town. It shows how this problem may have to be viewed in relation to certain associated problems in neighbouring areas, and introduces certain aspects of our proposed 'technology of choice' which we believe can be of value even in a situation where measurement is impractical and clear logic is all-important. The second case example moves to another sector of the same town, where a problem of priorities has arisen concerning different types of public development, including housing, schools, shopping, and drainage. In this example, the technology is extended to permit explicit measurement of a range of social costs and benefits, and it is shown how the selection of a set of actions in response to immediate pressures can be related to a desire to keep as many options open as possible for future choice. This case example is considered at some length, since we believe it is at this level of the planning process that some of the most immediate opportunities for application of a new approach to decision-making can be expected to arise.

The third case example opens up some prospects for a more systematic approach to the guidance of a co-ordinated planning activity at the sub-regional level, including such problems as the choice of locations for residential and industrial development, the choice of preferred rates of expansion for two centres, and the choice of a design for an integrated transportation system. In this case example, the pointers we provide are necessarily of a broad and relatively non-specific nature, but we argue that the need for a new approach to the technology of choice is just as strong as in the more well-defined situations of the first two case examples.

Part III concludes with a brief chapter referring back to the five types of operational problem defined in Part II, and reviewing how far these problems have been met through the technology suggested in the case examples.

SYNOPSIS OF PART IV

In Part IV we consider the broader problem of how local authorities can adapt their internal organizational structure to the challenges posed by the planning process as we have defined it. We begin by considering the opportunities for change which have been opened up in the United Kingdom by the work of the Royal Commissions on Local Government in England and in Scotland, and of the Maud Committee on local authority management.

Then, in the following chapter, we go on to develop, from the basis of our own research into the planning process, some suggestions as to how local authorities can adapt their internal organization to deal more effectively with the challenges of strategic choice. While recognizing that each local authority must be free to choose its own solution, we wish to avoid arguing purely in terms of generalities, and we therefore again adopt the technique of presentation through case example. We consider a fictitious situation in which, during the period of change which is expected to follow the recommendations of the Royal Commissions, a new local authority has been formed to cover the whole area embraced by our fictitious case examples in Part III, and faces the challenge of creating a new organizational structure to deal with the problems that lie ahead. We follow the various organizational choices which will face the leaders of the new authority, from the initial setting-up of a central control structure, through the development of a flexible system of policy groups and associated planning teams, to the creation of means by which all elected members can be helped to play a creative part in the affairs of the new council. We consider the corresponding pattern of organization at officer level, and indicate a need for some means of scanning the ongoing activities of the local authority to explore the changing needs for connection between its various parts, and to allow it to respond in an adaptive way to the challenges of strategic choice. We give examples of ways in which the flow of information between departments can be organized, with particular reference to what we call 'soft' information, relating to problems of departmental choice where firm commitments to particular lines of solution have not yet begun to develop. We discuss the human problems of freedom of access to information of this kind, and of making any new organizational forms acceptable to those who will be asked to make a contribution to them; and we suggest that carefully controlled experimentation may be necessary to overcome legacies of mistrust between elected members and officers, and sectional rivalries between one department and another.

In our final chapter we argue that, even though we have set our case examples in a period of future time when the opportunities for innovation may be very much greater than they are now, there is a great deal that local authorities can do in the meantime to put to the test our own and possibly other suggestions as to how the processes of strategic choice might be more effectively controlled within the spirit of a democratic system of local government. We argue that challenges also arise which are of a national rather than a local order, in particular in the provision of central support for the processes of local experiment, and in the development of methods for co-ordinating the planning activities of different local authorities, in association with all other agencies that have a contribution to make to the fabric of national planning.

PART I

An appraisal of planning in a major local authority

1. An introduction to Coventry and its Council

THE SETTING OF THE RESEARCH

Our analyses in subsequent chapters of the problems of strategic choice in local government, and our suggestions as to ways in which those concerned might be helped to deal with these problems more effectively, are founded on four years of field experience in Coventry, during which we were given generous opportunities by the City Council to study the processes of planning and policy-making at many levels of organization, formal and informal.

In deciding to concentrate our fieldwork on a study in depth of one local authority rather than a more extensive survey of many, we had to accept a risk that the planning problems of the authority concerned might be in many ways atypical of those of local government in general. There is, of course, much in Coventry which is by no means typical even of the dozen or so other urban local authorities in the United Kingdom in the same medium-to-large population bracket of 200,000 to 400,000. Coventry is perhaps exceptional most of all in the rapidity of its growth during the present century, and in the problem which it faced of rebuilding its city centre almost from scratch after the devastation of the second world war: however, these special circumstances did themselves make Coventry a particularly relevant setting in which to study the developing processes of local authority planning, in so far as the City Council had already encountered in an accentuated form many of the problems of peripheral growth and of urban renewal which are now being faced, in varying degrees, by cities and towns throughout the United Kingdom.

Our object in Part I, in which we draw together some salient points from our field experience in Coventry, is to emphasize those aspects which we believe to be of general relevance to local government as a whole, rather than those we believe to have more localized relevance to Coventry itself.

To set the scene for the remainder of Part I, we shall of course require to sketch in a certain amount of background information about Coventry and its Council; but with our wider objectives in mind, we will compress this initial introduction into as short a space as possible. There are a number of other publications [1, 2, 3] in which fuller information on the particular local circumstances of Coventry can be found.

THE CITY AND THE CITY COUNCIL

Coventry, situated in the very centre of England, has been an important manufacturing centre since medieval times. Its growth during the present century – as reflected by an increase in population from 70,000 in 1901 to an estimated 333,000 in 1966 – has been at a consistently higher rate than that of any other major city in the United Kingdom; the persistence of this trend has been attributed by local observers largely to an internal momentum which has allowed the city to foster a succession of new technological developments – from the bicycle through the motor-car to the aerospace and telecommunications industries – which have all in their turn played a part in drawing a continuing influx of skilled craftsmen from many other parts of the British Isles and overseas. It is only since the middle nineteen-sixties that the continued economic growth of Coventry has begun to be called seriously into question, because of a combination of economic circumstances and of national policies designed to steer industrial development into less prosperous regions.

Although the centre of Coventry lies only 18 miles from the centre of Birmingham – England's second city with a population of just over the one million mark – the two cities are separated by a rural belt which has been rigorously protected through the machinery of development control. Administratively, Coventry in fact forms an island of independence within the surrounding County of Warwickshire: under the existing system of local government in England and Wales, the city is constituted as a County Borough, which means that the City Council controls the full range of local government services, from the management of schools to the collection of refuse, and from the construction of new highways to the provision of welfare services for the elderly and infirm. In the administrative County of Warwickshire, on the other hand, the control of these various services is divided between the County Council itself and an assortment of Borough, District, and Parish Councils. Because of the continued growth of Coventry, the administrative boundary between City and County has had to be modified six times since the city was originally granted County Borough status in 1888, and this has increased the total area of the city from just under 1,500 to just over 20,000 acres.

THE INTERNAL ORGANIZATION OF THE LOCAL AUTHORITY

Since the time of the latest boundary revision in 1965, the City Council of Coventry has had a total membership of 54 councillors and 18 aldermen. It is presided over by a Lord Mayor whose role, as elsewhere in England, is essentially a ceremonial one.

It is not among the objectives of this book to give a detailed explanation of the formal structure of local government in Coventry, except in so far as it impinges on the activities of planning with which we are particularly concerned. Although we will wish to discuss in later chapters the impact on planning of the processes of local election and of the Council's internal mechanisms of decision, we will find it sufficient at present to outline the broad structure of committees (in which the Council vests its authority for the control of particular services) and of departments (through which these services are operated). In *Table 1* we record the basic

Table 1
Committee and departmental structure of Coventry City Council as at beginning of municipal year 1965/66

COMMITTEE (no. of members, frequency of meetings, in brackets) *Departments for which responsible in italics*		Total no. of employees as at 31.3.65
A. COMMITTEES WITH A DEGREE OF OVERSIGHT OVER ALL LOCAL AUTHORITY SERVICES		
Policy Advisory Committee (8 members, monthly)		
Establishment and General Administration Committee (11 members, monthly)		
Finance Committee (11 members, monthly)		
Finance Department		315
Planning and Redevelopment Committee (16 members, monthly)		
Department of Architecture and Planning (planning staff only)		97
B. OTHER COMMITTEES RESPONSIBLE FOR PARTICULAR DEPARTMENTS (in descending order of total employees)		
Education Committee (22 members + 12*, monthly)		
Education Department		7735
General Works Committee (11 members, monthly)		
City Engineer's Department		1757
Transport Committee (11 members, 2-monthly)		
Transport Department		1550
Health Committee (11 members, monthly)		
Health Department	1170	
Public Health Inspector's Department	59	1261
City Analyst's Department	32	
Watch Committee (11 members, 2-monthly)		
Police Force		713
Estates and Parliamentary Committee (11 members, monthly)		
Town Clerk's Department	333	
City Estates Department	28	549
Department of Architecture and Planning (architectural and quantity surveying staff)	188	
Waterworks and Fire Brigade Committee (11 members, 2-monthly)		
Waterworks Department	308	511
Fire Brigade	203	
Parks and Allotments Committee (11 members, 2-monthly)		
Parks Department		403
Housing Committee (11 members, monthly)		
Housing Department		331
Welfare Committee (9 members + 4*, 2-monthly)		
Welfare Department		208
Catering Committee (11 members, 2-monthly)		
Catering Department		173
Libraries, Art Gallery and Museums Committee (11 members, 2-monthly)		
Libraries, Art Gallery, and Museums Department		169
Markets and Baths Committee (11 members, 2-monthly)		
Markets Department	70	
Baths Department	76	162
Weights and Measures Department	16	
Children's Committee (7 members + 4*, 2-monthly)		
Children's Department		147
Airport Committee (11 members, 2-monthly)		
Airport Department		20
Civil Defence Committee (11 members, 2-monthly)		
Civil Defence Department		14
		Total 16115

* plus additional members co-opted from outside Council (numbers exclude Mayor and Deputy Mayor serving *ex officio*)

committee and departmental structure of Coventry City Council as it stood in the
Spring of 1965, reflecting a pattern which had then remained essentially stable over
a number of years. In addition to the committees shown, there were at that time a
number of joint committees and sub-committees, together with two special committees concerned with international friendship links. Certain significant changes
have taken place since 1965, and in 1968 the Council approved a reduction in the
number of full committees from 24 to 15. However, the structure shown in *Table 1*
provided the basic framework for the activities of the local authority during the
period of our research; as we shall see later, many of the subsequent changes can
be interpreted as attempts to reduce the fragmentation of control which such a
structure implies.

Table 1 groups together first those committees with a degree of general oversight
over all the services of the local authority, and then those other committees whose
responsibilities relate more exclusively to the control of particular services. This is
a significant distinction, whose implications we will discuss more fully in Chapters
2 and 3.

Generally speaking, the committees which we show as meeting at monthly
rather than two-monthly intervals tended to be those with a wider range of
responsibilities to discharge. Although it will be seen that many committees were
associated with the work of particular departments with matching titles, it will
also be noticed that two of the committees in the first group had no direct departmental responsibilities, while a few in the second group carried direct responsibility
for more than one department. Some of the committees in practice carried out
much of their business through sub-committees: this applies particularly to the
Education Committee, not surprisingly in view of the exceptionally large and
intricately structured department for which it was responsible.

In listing the number of members and employees for each committee, we have
made our first reference to the all-important distinction between those people who
serve local government in an unpaid capacity as elected members of Council, and
those who serve in a paid capacity as officers – a category which includes many different types of employee at a wide range of different levels of expertise and responsibility. We will have a good deal to say later about the relationships between these
two groups of participant: for the time being, we simply note the important distinction that the departments are mutually exclusive, in that no officer can have a
direct allegiance to more than one department, while the committees may have a
substantial degree of overlap, in that any elected member can serve as a member of
two or more committees. Indeed, the standing orders of Coventry during the
period in question required that each elected member must be a member of at
least two and at most four 'standing' committees (a definition which included all
but two of the committees listed in *Table 1*). As we shall see later, such a requirement can play an important part in relation to the mechanisms of political control.

2. Four years of planning in Coventry

SOME LANDMARKS OF PLANNING IN COVENTRY, 1963–1967

Table 2 gives a broad impression of the main streams of activity, both within the local authority and beyond, which can be said to have made some direct contribution to planning in Coventry during the period of our research. (We will leave open the question of how exactly 'planning' should be defined until we come to our more general exploration of the planning process in Part II). *Table 2* also picks out a few of the more significant landmarks during the years in question, including the approximate dates of local and national elections and the dates of issue of certain key documents which formed a basis for important planning decisions both at local and at national levels. Of course, the date of issue of the actual document is only of limited significance in each case, since it may represent only one focal point in a more diffuse process of planning choice which may have begun much earlier and extended much later over time.

In this chapter, we will consider more closely each of the various streams of activity which we identify in *Table 2*, taking them one at a time. Our objectives will be, first, to draw attention to the continuing process of evolutionary change underlying each stream, and, second, to explore the rich pattern of interconnection which exists between one stream and another. By so doing, we will aim to lay some foundations for the more generalized analysis of the planning process which follows in Part II, and for the subsequent development of an appropriate technology in Part III.

THE ELECTORAL CYCLE

Table 2 begins with a reference to the annual cycle of municipal elections, since it is through this mechanism that the City Council derives its authority for all the various planning decisions it must take on behalf of the local community. Although the electoral system for urban government in England was not originally conceived in terms of party politics, and indeed still does not formally recognize their existence, it is significant that political organization has now become a reality in all major cities; and in fact it can be argued that it is only through the imposition of party discipline that an elected council can become effective as a controlling body for so complex an entity as an urban local authority.

In Coventry, there are only two parties which have recently been represented on

Table 2

	1963	1964	1965	1966	1967

A. ACTIVITIES AND LANDMARKS OF PLANNING WITHIN COVENTRY CITY COUNCIL
Electoral cycle   *Labour   *Labour   *Labour   *Labour   *Conservative
Financial planning cycle
  annual rate estimates)   )   )   )   )
5-year capital programme)   )   )   )   )
Planning of development
  work
    ....continuing development of outer areas of city....
    ....continuing redevelopment of city centre and other areas of renewal....
    ....development of main arteries (roads, sewers, etc.)....|
    ....special development projects, e.g. swimming pool, college of art....
Land-use planning
  review of Coventry
       City Region)
  review of Coventry
       Road System)
   review of Work in Coventry)
    review of Shopping in Coventry)
          review of Population and Housing)
    ....other reviews of selected topics....
    ....review of land use by sectors....
          FIRST REVIEW OF CITY DEVELOPMENT PLAN)
    ....continuing public discussion of implications of development
                   plan review....
          ....district and action area studies....
Manpower planning
    ....continuing reviews of establishments, salaries and conditions, training....
Planning of public services
    ....departmental planning, e.g. schools, water supply
                 systems....|
    ....cross-departmental planning, e.g. transportation, housing policies....

B. OTHER LOCAL AND REGIONAL PLANNING ACTIVITIES
    ....continuing planning by public authorities, e.g. rail, gas electricity, coal....
    ....planning by independent bodies, e.g. University, industrial firms....
      economic planning studies for West Midlands region)   )
    appointment of West Midlands Economic Planning Council)

C. SOME LANDMARKS OF NATIONAL PLANNING
Electoral cycle   ....Conservative   *Labour   *Labour
'Traffic in Towns' report)
    report on future of Development Plans)
          White Paper on Town & Country Planning)
  severe restraints on local authority investment)   )
          white papers on transport policy)   )
    ....periodic directives from departments of central government....

	1963	1964	1965	1966	1967

Key: * dates of elections
) dates of issue of key planning documents

the City Council; the Labour Party, which held power continuously from 1937 to 1967, and the Conservative Party which gained power in the municipal elections of that year.

The changing composition of the Council is shown in the following table, which is simplified to the extent that it shows only the results of the annual municipal elections each May, without detailing the changes due to the retirement of particular members between elections.

As is normal in local government elections in the United Kingdom, not much more than half the electorate voted in any one year: the votes cast for parties other than Labour and Conservative were in Coventry consistently low and have here been ignored. The decrease in the Labour vote in 1965 and 1966, and the increase in the Conservative vote in 1967, must be related not only to local factors but also to national ones: as *Table 2* records, the general election of 1964 saw the Conservative government at Westminster replaced by a Labour one, and the changing relationships of the two parties at national level undoubtedly had some effect on the incentives to vote in local elections. This was apparent not only in Coventry but also in other cities throughout the country.

The changing pattern of votes was not in Coventry reflected immediately in the composition of the Council because of the particular way in which the electoral cycle operates in English urban government. The City of Coventry is divided into 18 (previously 16) wards, each of which is represented by three councillors, who

Table 3

Year of election	1963	1964	1965	1966	1967
Total Labour vote	46,448	43,248	30,835	32,579	41,492
Total Conservative vote	37,049	37,939	39,704	39,649	59,458
Total Labour + Conservative vote	83,497	81,187	70,539	72,228	100,950
Labour Councillors elected	10	10	8	10	5
Conservative Councillors elected	6	6	10	8	13
Total councillors elected	16	16	18*	18*	18*
Total Labour councillors	31	31	32	30	23
Total Conservative councillors	17	17	22	24	31
Total councillors after elections	48	48	54*	54*	54*
Labour Aldermen elected	—	6	—	—	0
Conservative Aldermen elected	—	2	—	—	9
Total Aldermen elected	—	8	—	—	9*
Total Labour Aldermen	13	13	15	15	7
Total Conservative Aldermen	3	3	3	3	11
Total Aldermen after elections	16	16	18*	18*	18*
Total Labour members	44	44	47	45	30
Total Conservative members	20	20	25	27	42
Total Council after elections	64	64	72*	72*	72*

* Total reflects increase in number of wards from 16 to 18 at time of boundary revision in April 1965.

retire in rotation after serving a fixed three-year term: thus only one-third of councillors will normally be standing for re-election in any particular year. The membership of the Council is completed by the election of one alderman for every three councillors. These aldermen, who serve a six-year term, are elected indirectly by a vote of councillors, half of them retiring every third year.

As can be seen from a study of *Table 3*, the aldermanic elections in 1964 and 1967 were used as a means of strengthening the control of whichever political party could command a majority of councillors (as is also the normal practice in other urban local authorites). Each year, immediately after the municipal elections, we saw how the majority party was able further to strengthen its control by the use of its voting powers to weight the allocation of committee places in its own favour and to appoint committee chairmen and vice-chairmen from its own ranks.

The figures in *Table 3* provide an illustration of the general point that the procedures for electing councillors and aldermen may in certain circumstances allow the composition of a council to respond only slowly to the changing voting patterns of the electorate. Directly and indirectly, this very slowness of response has provided one of the principal conditions for the growth of long-term planning activities in Coventry.

FINANCIAL PLANNING

Coventry is typical of other all-purpose local authorities in the United Kingdom in that it derives its total income in approximately equal proportions from three main sources; grants from central government, direct charges for certain local services, and local taxation. Grants from central government were at one time geared directly to actual expenditure at local level, according to a fixed proportion which varied from one local authority service to another; however, most of these proportional grants had, by the time we came to Coventry, been replaced by a single block grant calculated according to the needs of the local authority (as measured by the size of its population, giving special weight to certain age-groups) with corrections to make good any particular deficiencies in local resources (as measured by property values). The levels of government grant are therefore largely beyond the control of the local authority itself and, during our period in Coventry, they only entered into the financial planning process to the extent that predictions had to be made as to how much would be made available by central government from one year to the next.

A City Council can of course exercise a greater degree of control over the direct charges it makes for the use of particular services. In Coventry, the main sources of direct income from users included the rents charged to tenants of municipal housing and of municipally owned shop and office developments, the fees charged for use of municipal car parks, the rates charged for water supply, and the fares charged for use of the public transport service. In the case of most of these services (notably, as we shall see later, in housing and in public transport) the structure of internal accounting – and the political climate – imposed constraints which meant that the service had to be virtually self-supporting financially; in these circumstances, the level of charges of course became a critical factor in planning the future development of the service concerned.

The third source of income – that from local taxation – of course attracted a great deal of public attention in Coventry, particularly when it came up for review each year only two months before the annual municipal elections. The present system of local government in the United Kingdom allows only one form of local taxation, which is levied on occupiers of property and is known as the rate levy, because it is strictly proportional to the notional rental value of each building as assessed by an independent agency of central government. The only direct fiscal choice faced by the local authority relates once a year to the level of the rate for the following year – expressed as so many shillings and pence per pound of assessed annual property value. However, in Coventry a good deal of planning activity was devoted each year to drawing up detailed estimates of expenditure and of direct income for the coming year for each local government service which impinged directly on the rate fund, and then assessing the rate levy that would be required to meet these estimates. During our years in Coventry, this figure invariably turned out to be unacceptably high, and so there followed an extensive process of bargaining involving all the various committees and departments of the City Council, with the chairman of the Finance Committee and the City Treasurer (as head of the Finance Department) occupying key roles in the negotiations.

During the period of our research, we saw a good deal of dissatisfaction expressed, both locally and nationally, with the rate levy as a sole source of local taxation. Criticism was directed in particular at its inflexibility, its harsh impact on those with small incomes, and the imbalance between the rapid rate of increase in the costs of providing services, on the one hand, and the relatively slow growth of the tax base – the rateable value of property – on the other.

This is borne out by the following table of changes in Coventry over the period from 1963 to 1967.

Table 4

Financial year	Rateable value (millions of pounds)	% increase from previous year	Rate levy	% increase from previous year
1963–64	£12·20 m		10s. 6d. in the £	
1964–65	£12·40 m	1·6	11s. 4d. in the £	7·9
1965–66	£13·05 m	5·2	12s. 0d. in the £	5·9
1966–67	£13·33 m	2·1	13s. 0d. in the £	8·3
1967–68	£13·62 m	2·2	⎧ 13s. 0d. in the £* ⎫	⎧ 0·0* ⎫
			⎨ 13s. 3d. in the £* ⎬	⎨ 1·9* ⎬
			⎩ 13s. 5d. in the £* ⎭	⎩ 3·2* ⎭

* Differentiation between residential, mixed and other property following a new central government scheme for relief to domestic ratepayers.

THE ANNUAL RATE ESTIMATES

In *Figure 2*, we show in diagrammatic form the way in which the overall rate estimates for the year 1965–66 were distributed between the spheres of responsibility
of different committees. This chart emphasizes in particular the heavy demands of
the Education Committee (with its responsibility for schools and colleges of further
education throughout the city), followed by the General Works Committee (with
its responsibility for roads, drainage, and other engineering works and services).

In *Figure 3* we use a different form of chart, based on a logarithmic scale, in
order to provide a basis for comparing the rates of increase in the estimates of
various committees from year to year. The significance of the logarithmic scale is
that similar rates of growth for different committees appear as parallel lines whatever their respective levels of expenditure may be: this effect can only be achieved,
however, at the expense of distorting the overall relationships of scale that are
shown in *Figure 2*.

Figure 2

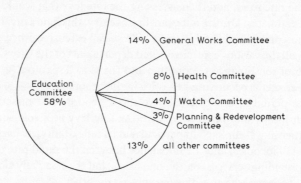

For the sake of clarity, *Figure 3* omits a number of committees whose annual
estimates cluster around the £200,000 line, and one or two other committees whose
estimates were a good deal lower. In the case of those committees with the highest
levels of expenditure, *Figure 3* shows a fairly steady pattern of growth, at a level
roughly equivalent to an annual increase of 10 per cent; this apparent steady rate of
increase does, however, mask certain much less regular movements for particular
expenditure headings within committees.

Each of the more erratic changes lower down the chart has its own particular
interpretation. The abrupt rise in the estimates for the Markets and Baths Committee in 1966 reflects the cost of building a swimming pool of international
standard in the city centre (financed, like many other capital projects, by loans
whose servicing is charged against the rate fund). The equally abrupt fall in the
estimates of the Estates and Parliamentary Committee largely reflects an increased
income in direct rentals from tenants of newly occupied commercial properties in
the city centre. The constant annual estimate for the Housing Committee reflects

Figure 3. Annual rate estimates of selected committees, 1964–1969

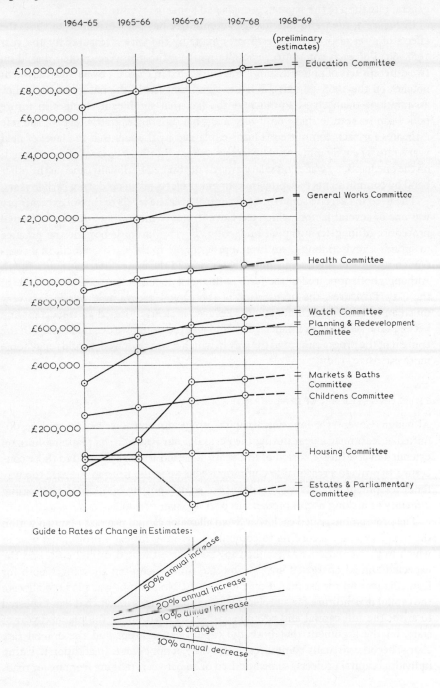

a constraint imposed by the Council on the annual transfer of money from the general rate fund to the separately-managed housing revenue account.

In *Figure 3*, the trend line for each committee has been extended to show the effects of a set of provisional estimates made by the City Treasurer for the year 1968–69. For each committee, two alternative estimates were quoted, based on two different sets of policy assumptions (indicated in *Figure 3* by a pair of adjacent notches on the 1968–69 axis). What is significant is not the nature of the policy assumptions themselves, so much as the fact that significant changes in future policy can be seen to make only very marginal differences in the level of the rate estimates for each committee. This is explained by the fact that the level of next year's rate is heavily influenced by factors outside the direct control of the Council: on the one hand, by wage and salary awards negotiated nationally, and on the other hand by commitments to capital investment projects taken on during earlier years.

The need to exercise some forward control over the levels of capital expenditure was one of several factors which led Coventry over the years to develop a formal procedure of long-term capital budgeting. Every March, it became the practice to submit a revised long-term capital programme to the City Council, in a companion volume to the document which presented the annual rate estimates [4, 5]. Although both appeared in the form of financial documents issued in the name of the City Treasurer, the preparation of the capital programme was in fact very much an interdepartmental activity. Because it clearly formed an important link between the activities of financial and land-use planning, we decided that both the content of the programme, and the way in which it was reviewed, would repay some more intensive study.

THE LONG-TERM CAPITAL PROGRAMME

Although Coventry's long-term capital programme was reviewed and resubmitted at least once a year during the period of our research, its planning horizon extended over a future period of five years, a period which appeared to those concerned to provide a reasonable compromise between the need to prepare the way for development projects well in advance of actual construction, and the increasing difficulty of making useful predictions over a longer period.

The programme issued each year listed all major capital projects planned within the next five years according to committee, quoting for each project the year in which implementation was planned to start, the estimated capital cost, and the expected annual charge (if any) to the rate fund, including allowances both for loan charges and for estimated operating costs. No attempt was made to allocate the capital expenditure for a project over the actual years in which it was expected to arise: the full capital and revenue cost was shown under the planned year of start, on the argument that both the capital expenditure and the annual rate charge become virtually committed at this time, if not before. In addition to listing individual capital projects (some hundred or so per year, ranging from major road, housing, and drainage projects whose capital cost is measured in millions of pounds down to local paving works costing a few thousands), each programme also included certain bulk allocations of capital for items such as minor school improvements, purchase of buses, and acquisition of land in areas of urban renewal.

Each programme was divided between rate-supported capital expenditure on the one hand and self-supporting services on the other, the latter category being dominated by expenditure on new housing development. In *Figure 4* we show the total estimated capital costs for each of the five capital programmes issued during the period 1963 to 1967, first for the total of all rate-supported schemes and then for the total of all housing schemes.

Figure 4. A comparison of successive capital programmes in Coventry, 1963–1968

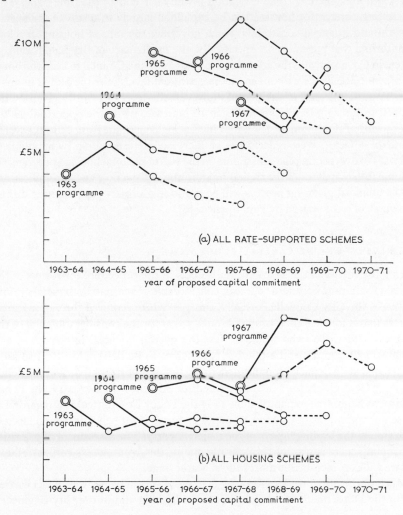

For each successive programme, *Figure 4* uses a progression from a continuous through a broken to a dotted line in order to reflect the increasing tentativeness of those estimates which refer to the more distant periods of future time. It will be noticed, from the first diagram in particular, that the successive estimates referring to the same financial year are liable to fluctuate considerably (and most often to escalate upwards) as the year in question draws nearer: for instance, looking up the vertical axis for 1967–68, it will be noticed that the value of projects expected to start in that financial year increased from an estimated £2,600,000 in 1963 to an estimated £11,000,000 in 1966, before settling down to a level of £7,300,000 at the beginning of the year of implementation itself.

The chart for the housing schemes does not show the same runaway character-istics, although there is some escalation at the later end of the time-scale. This contrasting pattern for housing can be explained largely in terms of the special physical and financial constraints which governed the rate of housing develop-ment during that period: more specifically, the inadequacy of the mains drainage system in Coventry, and the effect of past pledges by the Council to keep the hous-ing account in balance without any increase in rent levels over the period in ques-tion. Towards the end of the period, however, the level of priority given by the Council to housing development began to increase, while the opportunities for other forms of development fell under increasing constraint from central govern-ment: these factors were reflected by an increased determination by members to find ways of overcoming the constraints on the size of the total housing programme.

Some fuller analyses of the capital programme in Coventry and its implications for the financial planning process will be found in a project paper written during the course of our research by Paul Spencer [6].

THE REVIEW OF THE CAPITAL PROGRAMME

During the period of our research, the defects in the procedure for review of the capital programme became a source of considerable concern to both members and officers of the City Council. Formally, this procedure required the various com-mittees to put forward their proposals once a year for the consideration first of the Finance Committee (who would review the overall financial implications, and would usually recommend a number of schemes to be deferred in time so as to avoid too heavy a financial commitment in the first few years) and then of the Policy Advisory Committee, for a final assessment of priorities. In Coventry, the Policy Advisory Committee (renamed since 1967 the Policy Committee) was regarded as the senior committee of Council, its membership of eight being drawn exclusively from among the leading figures of the majority party. The assessment of priorities for capital schemes was, of course, only one of this committee's responsibilities and we will consider its role more fully at a later stage.

Much of the initial work of drawing up a first list of schemes was in fact carried out in the Department of Architecture and Planning and in the City Engineer's

Department which, because of their responsibility for the execution of capital schemes, were in the best position to judge the various constraints on the practicability of carrying out particular schemes at particular times and in particular sequences. When the full draft programme was assembled and submitted to Finance and Policy Advisory Committees, complaints were often heard, from both officers and members, that it was impossible to handle such a complex array of information in such a way as to see what opportunities might exist for choice between alternative policies.

Accordingly, certain procedural changes were put into effect in 1966 and 1967: a new form of presentation was adopted for the programme, with less emphasis on classification of projects by committees and more emphasis on the relatedness of different schemes; a special sub-committee was formed, with a membership of five drawn jointly from Finance and Policy Advisory Committees, in order to keep the programme under more frequent review; a four-monthly cycle of meetings was agreed; and a decision was made to modify the strict allocation of projects to the five years of the programme by the introduction of a new category of priority known as the 'reserve'. It was agreed that the first three years of the programme should be drawn up on the basis of realistic expectations – including only projects for which resources and approvals from central government were expected to be forthcoming – while the 'reserve' category would include other projects which the Council would wish to bring forward to the first three years should subsequent events make it possible. A combined list of projects for the fourth and fifth years would be regarded as a more tentative guide for longer-term planning activities concerned with the definition and acquisition of sites.

Because of this change in procedure, it is not possible in *Figure 4* to show the full five-year programme for 1967 on a basis which would make it comparable with earlier years. It is nevertheless apparent that the Council met with some success in that year in curbing the runaway characteristics of the programme for rate-supported schemes. Introduction of the 'reserve' category led, as expected, to a reduction in the number of schemes included in the first three years of the programme; but the contrast with earlier years is to some extent accentuated by changes in national economic conditions, which led in 1965 and 1966 to a severe tightening of central government constraints on local authority investment.

THE PLANNING OF DEVELOPMENT WORK

The long-term capital programme in Coventry served as a basis for the planning of many kinds of activity that are necessary before the construction of a building or engineering project can be started: these include the choice of a site or alignment, the acquisition of the necessary land, the preparation of sketch plans, working drawings, and cost estimates, the application to departments of central government for authority to raise a loan (this being the principal mechanism of central control over the design, costing, and timing of local government schemes), and finally the negotiation of tenders and signing of contracts. These procedures involved close working collaboration between a number of different departments of the local authority, including in particular the Department of Architecture and Planning, the City Engineers' Department, the Town Clerk's Department, the Finance Department, and the City Estates Department.

The continuing programme of development work in Coventry could be divided broadly into four categories. These include the development of the outer areas of the city for residential and related uses; the renewal of outworn areas nearer to the centre of the city; the extension and reinforcement of the various networks of arteries which help the city to function as a connected system (ranging from main roads above ground to main sewers below ground): and lastly a residual class of developments whose purpose is to fill certain more specialized types of public need. In Coventry, the most significant projects under this last heading during the period of our research included a central swimming pool, a college of art, and a centre for outdoor recreation in the grounds of an historic abbey just outside the boundaries of the city. All these projects were planned with an eye to the needs of the surrounding region as well as the city itself; however, there were a number of other major developments with more localized catchment areas, including new secondary schools, police stations, and multi-purpose community centres to serve existing residential areas which were seen to be deficient in social facilities.

Under the procedure adopted in Coventry in 1966, the approved capital programme, which is published annually, not only includes a complete list of all development projects planned for the next five years, but also incorporates a cross-referencing system to show how these schemes interconnect with each other. As an illustration of these interconnections, we show in *Figure 5* the pattern of relationships that was seen by the Department of Architecture and Planning to exist between a number of housing, road, and school schemes in an area scheduled for new residential development on the outskirts of the city.

Figure 5 shows that each of the future phases of the housing development was seen to be related to the south link road scheme, which in turn was seen as related to certain other longer-term road and bridge developments. A primary school scheme was seen as linked to a particular phase of the housing development, and a secondary school scheme to a neighbouring road scheme. Executive responsibility for these various projects was divided between three different committees – Housing, Education, and General Works – and the diagram gives some indication of the extent to which their responsibilities were interdependent in this particular local setting.

It was an awareness of this kind of interdependence between developmental activities which led the City Council, some years before our research began, to vest virtually all responsibility for redevelopment schemes in the inner areas of the city in a single committee known as the Planning and Redevelopment Committee. In this way, more integrated control was established over the various interdepartmental activities concerned with acquisition of land and property, relocation of occupiers, and phasing of linked development projects within these inner areas. However, integration of control at local level did not always suffice to overcome all difficulties of co-ordination between projects. This was particularly so where the responsibilities of different departments of central government were concerned.

Figure 5

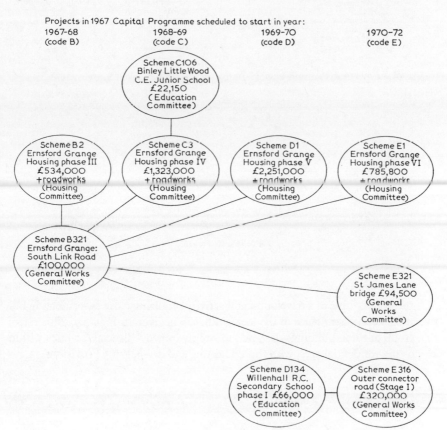

Projects in 1967 Capital Programme scheduled to start in year:

| 1967-68 (code B) | 1968-69 (code C) | 1969-70 (code D) | 1970-72 (code E) |

Scheme C106
Binley Little Wood
C.E. Junior School
£22,150
(Education Committee)

Scheme B2
Ernsford Grange
Housing phase III
£534,000
+ roadworks
(Housing Committee)

Scheme C3
Ernsford Grange
Housing phase IV
£1,323,000
+ roadworks
(Housing Committee)

Scheme D1
Ernsford Grange
Housing phase V
£2,251,000
+ roadworks
(Housing Committee)

Scheme E1
Ernsford Grange
Housing phase VI
£785,800
+ roadworks
(Housing Committee)

Scheme B321
Ernsford Grange:
South Link Road
£100,000
(General Works Committee)

Scheme E321
St James Lane
bridge £94,500
(General Works Committee)

Scheme D134
Willenhall R.C.
Secondary School
phase I £66,000
(Education Committee)

Scheme E316
Outer connector
road (Stage I)
£320,000
(General Works Committee)

In one instance, the committee had to meet the cost of erecting temporary buildings to accommodate shop and office tenants whose permanent premises were already in course of erection, because work on these had been halted by the financial controls of one ministry, even though there was no deferment in the road scheme (controlled by a different ministry) through which these businesses were being displaced.

Figure 6 gives an example of a set of related projects contributing to the continuing process of central area development. This example differs from that of *Figure 5*, first, in the integration of committee responsibility and, second, in the lack of any differentiation of priority between projects; this is because this particular group of projects were all placed in the 'reserve' category of the 1967 capital programme (hence the prefix R in the reference number of each scheme).

Figure 6

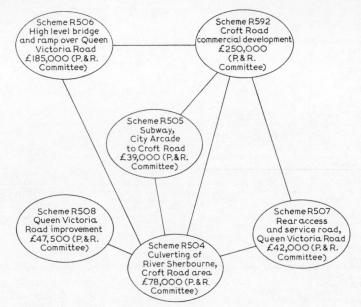

A further example of a developmental activity requiring close co-ordination between the component parts of the local authority is given in *Figure 7*. This refers to a group of three buildings designed to supply improved social facilities within an existing residential area, with shared heating and car-parking provision.

Figure 7

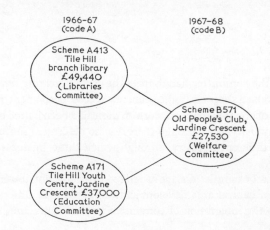

The involvement of many committees in the planning of multipurpose developments of this kind led to some discussion in Coventry as to whether means might not be found in the outer areas of achieving the same level of internal co-ordination as in the inner redevelopment areas, where control of all development was vested in a single committee. However, at the same time there was an awareness that any solution short of a total integration of responsibility for all development work would have its own particular snags; the concentration of powers in the Planning and Redevelopment Committee within the areas of comprehensive development had itself been found to create problems of inter-committee co-ordination at the geographical boundaries of these areas, and there was concern that such problems might become more frequent as the priorities for urban renewal began to shift from the inner areas of the city to other more isolated pockets in the surrounding districts, and the geographical boundaries between the responsibilities of Planning and Redevelopment and other committees became less clear-cut.

LAND-USE PLANNING AND THE DEVELOPMENT PLAN

Perhaps the most significant of all the planning activities in Coventry during the period of our research was the first review of the city's Development Plan. In order to understand the special significance of this review for the planning of land use within the city, it is necessary to go back to the Town and Country Planning Act of 1947, which laid down that each local authority designated as a planning authority (i.e. each County Borough or Administrative County) should prepare for the area under its control a comprehensive development plan, which should thereafter be reviewed at five-yearly intervals in order to ensure that it kept pace with changing circumstances.

The form and content of the development plan to be submitted was carefully prescribed in the legislation; from each urban planning authority, a 'Town Map' was required to show the proposed future use of all land within the city boundary according to certain broadly defined categories (such as residential, industrial, and public open space), together with a 'Programme Map' showing intended priorities of development over successive five-year periods for the next twenty years. Certain supporting information was also required in tabular form, relating to the expected changes in the size and geographical distribution of the population over this twenty-year planning period, the areas proposed for comprehensive redevelopment or for compulsory purchase for particular public purposes, and the proposed provision of facilities for particular public services such as education and health. The declared purpose of the development plan was to provide a general framework for the control of private development according to the machinery embodied in the 1947 Act, and to give the community at large a clear indication of any future intentions for development by the public sector. It was envisaged that the proposals of each authority would not be endorsed by the responsible department of central government until opportunities had been given for a full public discussion of their implications, and for the hearing of any specific objections by interested parties.

Coventry finished preparing its Development Plan in 1951, and submitted, together with the required maps and written statement, an extensive written analysis to explain the reasons for the particular set of proposals put forward. The plan was, however, not finally approved by the Ministry of Housing and Local Government until 1957, by which time a number of amendments had become necessary. The primary reason for this delay was that the machinery of ministerial investigation of proposals, and submission to public inquiry, was inadequate to deal expeditiously with the many plans submitted by different local authorities at about that time. It was therefore not until 1957 that Coventry's first Development Plan became available as an official standard against which to judge the merits of planning proposals submitted by private developers.

THE DEVELOPMENT PLAN REVIEW

The first quinquennial review of the Development Plan should in theory have taken place in 1962, but when our research began in late 1963 the review process was still some way from completion. A number of preliminary studies had however by this time been completed, and a series of public meetings had been held in order to explore the views of the public as to what features of the city they would most wish to see improved. Although the response to these meetings inevitably included a large number of minor and localized grievances, a good deal of useful comment of more general significance was also obtained. During the period of our study, work on the Development Plan Review steadily intensified; in the process, it gradually came to be agreed that the original Development Plan had become so out of date that what was required was not so much a review of the earlier proposals as a completely new plan. It was in this spirit that, after several postponements of the deadline date, the 'Coventry Review Plan' [7] was approved in draft by the City Council in March 1966 and submitted for public consultation. After the results of these consultations had been assessed, certain amendments were made and these were approved by the Council in the following July.

By this time, however, the form and purpose of the development plan procedure as laid down in the 1947 Act was coming increasingly into question, both in Coventry and elsewhere. Recognizing that the accepted form of the Town Map was unduly restrictive and rigid as an instrument of land-use planning, the Department of Architecture and Planning in Coventry decided during 1965 to adopt as their main working framework a form of 'Policy Map' showing only broad intentions as to future patterns of communications and of land use within the city, as opposed to detailed designations of land to particular uses. We reproduce as *Map 1* one of the several versions of the Coventry Policy Map that were issued, as a basis for public discussion, at different stages of the review process. This form of presentation in fact corresponded quite closely to that of the 'Urban Structure Map' which was commended in the 1965 report of the Planning Advisory Group, a national

Map 1. Policy Map of Coventry

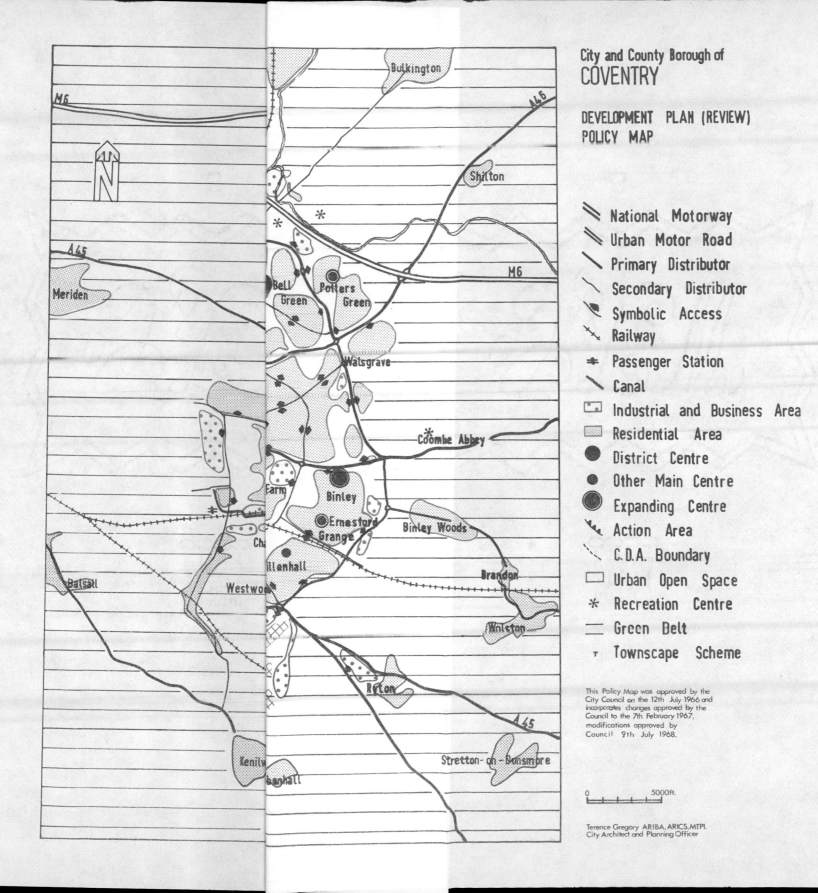

City and County Borough of
COVENTRY

DEVELOPMENT PLAN (REVIEW)
POLICY MAP

- National Motorway
- Urban Motor Road
- Primary Distributor
- Secondary Distributor
- Symbolic Access
- Railway
- Passenger Station
- Canal
- Industrial and Business Area
- Residential Area
- District Centre
- Other Main Centre
- Expanding Centre
- Action Area
- C.D.A. Boundary
- Urban Open Space
- Recreation Centre
- Green Belt
- Townscape Scheme

This Policy Map was approved by the
City Council on the 12th July 1966 and
incorporates changes approved by the
Council to the 7th February 1967,
modifications approved by
Council 9th July 1968.

0   5000ft.

Terence Gregory ARIBA, ARICS, MTPI.
City Architect and Planning Officer

committee which had been set up by the Minister of Housing and Local Government to consider the whole future of the development-plan machinery [8].

During 1965, 1966, and early 1967, the planners in Coventry found themselves increasingly subject to two conflicting pressures: the pressure to push ahead with the formal submission of Development Plan Review proposals under the existing procedure, in order to provide a more up-to-date frame of reference for development control decisions than the 1957 plan, and the temptation to wait for another year or two, by which time they might expect that the recommendations of the Planning Advisory Group for a more flexible planning system would have become embodied in new legislation.

A decision was eventually taken to proceed with the former course, and a formal submission of the review plan, including a Town Map and a Programme Map in accordance with the existing legislation, was eventually made in May 1967. This submission in fact coincided quite closely in timing with the change of political control on the Council. Despite the fact that certain aspects of the plan had been criticized by the Conservative Party while in opposition, the need for a more up-to-date framework for land-use planning was acknowledged and the submission was allowed to proceed while further reviews were carried out of some of the more controversial proposals. It was expected that the holding of a public inquiry – the procedure through which an inspector appointed by the Ministry of Housing and Local Government hears and assesses objections lodged by interested parties – would take place during the summer of 1968; but to allow more time for objectors to prepare their cases, this was later postponed until the autumn of that year.

The processes of study and of external and internal consultation which preceded the submission of Coventry's Development Plan Review are described by the planners themselves in a document 'Coventry 66: The Making of a Development Plan' [9], which was prepared by the Department of Architecture and Planning from material that had originally been assembled for an exhibition of plan-making techniques at the Ministry of Housing and Local Government in London.

As a research team, we were given an opportunity to attend many of the internal meetings – at departmental, interdepartmental, and political levels – where the various proposals of the Development Plan Review came up for discussion. This experience we found to be of particular value in giving us insights into the kind of technology that would require to be developed to assist the processes of strategic choice in local government. Our research was also considerably assisted by the thoroughness with which the planners laid the basis for their final proposals, through a series of published studies of various particular topics issued at intervals over the years.

STUDIES FOR THE DEVELOPMENT PLAN REVIEW

Starting in 1957, immediately after the approval of the original Development Plan, a series of over 50 documents was issued by the Department of Architecture and

4

Planning relating to various topics of relevance to the Development Plan Review. Some of these were brief duplicated reports relating to particular matters such as caravan sites, lorry parking, and public conveniences. However, there were other documents in the series which, because of their basic significance for the review as a whole, were produced to much higher standards of presentation, and made publicly available in order to stimulate wider discussion of the emerging principles of the review plan itself. The dates of issue of these particular documents can be seen as landmarks of the planning process in Coventry, and have been included as such in the overall picture of *Table 2*. We will therefore now make some brief comments on the significance of each of them in turn. Later, in Chapter 3, we will single out two of these documents in particular for closer examination of the many different kinds of information on which they draw, and the many different kinds of assumption on which their conclusions rest.

The document 'Coventry City Region' issued in April 1963 [10] took a broad look at Coventry in relation to its national setting, and developed a case for regarding Coventry as the primary centre for a region of roughly ten miles radius, including such towns as Rugby in the East, Nuneaton and Bedworth in the North, and Warwick, Leamington, and Kenilworth in the South, all with populations between the 20,000 and 60,000 levels. This case rested on analysis of commuter travel, shopping visits, local press sales, and visits for entertainment. The document also made a general exploration of the pressures for growth, the comparative advantages and disadvantages of cities of different sizes, and the options of peripheral, fragmentary, satellite, and linear expansion. Inevitably, this document raised many questions which concerned the future policies of Warwickshire County Council, and its publication was therefore considered in some quarters as something of a provocative act.

At about the same time, the City Council issued another planning report, in two volumes, on the Coventry Road System [11], as the culmination of an extensive programme of research by a roads study team drawn jointly from the Department of Architecture and Planning and the City Engineer's Department. Within this programme, a series of traffic surveys was carried out and their results analysed by computer in order to help in the selection of a preferred broad pattern for the future system of primary roads. This was intended to serve as a basis not only for the more detailed design work on the road network itself, but also for the formulation of local land-use plans. There was some pride in Coventry that this was one of the first instances of application in the United Kingdom of the transportation study techniques then becoming increasingly accepted in the United States. This document, and the subsequent activities to which it gave rise, attracted much concern in Coventry during the whole period of our research. We will consider its conclusions in more detail in Chapter 4.

The document 'Work in Coventry' issued later in the same year [12], examined future employment opportunities in the light of the broad analysis of Coventry's potential for growth in the 'Coventry City Region' report. In particular, it reported on a survey carried out with the co-operation of many medium and large firms in the city, the objective of which was to obtain information on employment, products and processes, traffic generation, and future expansion plans, which could be evaluated together with known land-use information. Taking into account the existence of national policies to restrict the growth of employment in the West Midlands Region, a local policy of controlled expansion was recommended to the Council in preference to the alternatives of total restriction on the one hand or of maximum encouragement to growth on the other. Attention was drawn to Coventry's abnormally high ratio of manufacturing employment to service employment (including work in shops and offices) and it was suggested that future expansion should be particularly encouraged in this latter sector. Estimates were made of land-use requirements for various types of industry, and the question of choice of locations for future expansion was discussed briefly in the light of the recently formulated road proposals.

The next document in the series, entitled 'Shopping in Coventry' [13], was the first to be issued after our research team had become resident in Coventry in 1964, and we were therefore able to observe more fully the processes of discussion which followed its publication, in committee, in the Council Chamber, and in the columns of the press. Many of the recommendations concerned detailed standards of design, location, and ancillary facilities to be applied in the planning and control of new shopping developments throughout the city; however, perhaps the most critical single recommendation concerned the question of how much land should be safeguarded for future expansions of the central shopping area, in the light of the estimates of population growth put forward in the Coventry City Region report. We will discuss this particular proposal in some detail in Chapter 3.

A further major report, on Population and Housing in Coventry, was in preparation throughout 1964 and 1965, and we were able to attend two of the internal meetings in the Department of Architecture and Planning where draft versions came up for review and revision. However, because of the priority given during 1965 to the completion of the review plan itself, the document 'People and Housing' did not appear in final form until April 1966 [14]. The first part of the report developed some more detailed projections of demographic trends than had been possible at the time of the City Region report: changes in population structure were predicted according to age and sex, so as to provide a basis not only for housing estimates but for the planning of other facilities to serve the needs of particular age groups of the population. The second part of the report related specifically to the housing problem; after reviewing the existing stock of dwellings within the city and the expected losses through urban renewal and road projects, an estimate was made of the required future stock and recommendations were made as to locations and densities of development to meet as much of the estimated population growth as could reasonably be accommodated within the existing city boundary.

We have by now perhaps said enough about the five main studies of particular topics for the Development Plan Review – dealing with regional considerations, roads, employment, shopping, and housing – to indicate the existence of some close interrelationships between them. In preparing each document, the planners in fact found it necessary to take some account of the effects of the proposals they had already set out in preceding documents; and, in retrospect, they were very ready to speculate as to whether or not they had carried out their studies in the best possible sequence. Indeed, the hope was expressed by many of those concerned that in future they would be able to move closer to the ideal of a process of continuous review, in which major studies of this kind would come to be supplanted by a series of marginal adjustments to previous predictions and proposals as circumstances required.

During 1965, the attention of those responsible for the Development Plan Review turned from the formulation of broad principles towards the application of these principles in formulating land-use plans for specific localities within the city. For this purpose, it was decided to divide the city into seven zones: the central area, an inner zone of comparatively early development whose boundaries were defined by a triangle of railway lines, and five outer radial sectors. Proposals for residential and industrial development, road alignments, district shopping and social centres, schools, open spaces, and other amenities were developed in detail in a series of draft sector reports with accompanying maps and, at a final stage, locations where some degree of conflict arose between different requirements were discussed in a series of internal meetings in the Department of Architecture and Planning. As a research team, we were given the opportunity to attend these meetings, together with another series of internal meetings which was held at about the same time to consider any final revisions to those parts of the review plan submission dealing with the general topics of transportation, housing, industry, shopping, and social and public services.

CONSULTATIONS FOR THE DEVELOPMENT PLAN REVIEW

Before the publication of the Development Plan Review proposals in 1966, an extensive series of consultations took place with the representatives of other departments and committees of the Council. The proposals were also discussed, on a sector-by-sector basis, in a series of meetings with the councillors representing the various wards of the city. External consultations took place with representatives of several departments of central government, with the Warwickshire County Council, with statutory undertakings such as British Rail and the Regional Gas and Electricity Boards, with the local Chamber of Commerce, and with several other interested parties including many of the major local industrial employers.

The draft review plan was made available for public inspection for six weeks in the spring of 1966, as a result of which 321 written or verbal objections were received from particular individuals or businesses affected by the proposals, together with 18 petitions on behalf of wider groups. An analysis of these objections and petitions was placed before the Council in July, together with the comments of the various public and private agencies which had been individually consulted.

More than half of the objections and petitions related to the effects on property of the Council's proposals for the road system, and a high proportion of the remainder related to the proposals to designate certain new areas of comprehensive urban renewal. Informal reaction from the Ministry of Housing and Local Government (as the authority responsible for final approval or rejection of the plan) was to commend the overall balance of the proposals but to express reservations as to their financial implications bearing in mind expected levels of future investment in the public sector as a whole. It was suggested in particular that a slower phasing of the proposed road developments might be desirable, together with an increased emphasis on the participation of private developers in the proposed urban renewal programme.

During the course of 1966 and 1967, a succession of public meetings was held to discuss the Review Plan with various groups of people within the wider community who had special reason to be concerned with the effects of particular proposals. Many of these meetings took place against a background of increasing political tension, with the approach of the key municipal elections of May 1967. It was not surprising in these circumstances that the proposals of the Review Plan came increasingly to be judged in a party-political light, and that the road proposals in particular became one of the main issues of the campaign.

SEQUELS TO THE DEVELOPMENT PLAN REVIEW

Among the many interlocking themes of the Coventry Review Plan, special attention was drawn by the planners to four outstanding problems – the problem of population growth in relation to limited land availability, the problem of coping with increasing traffic flows, the problem of improving the quality of the urban environment, and the problem of renewal of outworn areas. It was argued that none of these problems could be completely solved by the proposals of the Review Plan on their own, and that the first three problems in particular would require further study in a wider context.

So far as the traffic problem was concerned, it was argued that a full solution could not be achieved solely by implementing the proposed changes to the city road pattern, and that the related problems of traffic management and public transport would have to be considered in the setting of a long-term programme of research into the transportation problem as a whole; and in fact, by the time the Review Plan was finally submitted, a long-term transportation study of this kind (which we will consider later in this chapter) had already got under way.

So far as the problem of growth was concerned, the population projections for Coventry were such as to suggest that all the land available for residential development within the city would be used up by 1975. It was therefore argued that a full solution to the problem of growth could only be sought in the framework of a collaborative planning study in conjunction with Warwickshire County Council. During 1965 and 1966, consultations on these lines were held between the representatives of Coventry and the County, with the active support of the then Minister of Housing and Local Government. There were, however, some fears on both sides that the other side might acquire a dominating position in the joint body set up to sponsor the study: as an alternative to the idea of the comparatively compact 'Coventry City Region' as a natural planning unit, the County Council put forward the idea of a unit of 'Greater Warwickshire', which would have included the whole of the administrative county and also the County Borough of Solihull. Although the City Council in Coventry eventually agreed to join with Warwickshire and Solihull in the sponsorship of such a team, support was withdrawn when the national government found itself unable to offer any financial assistance because of prevailing economic circumstances. By the end of 1967, however, the question had again been re-opened and agreement was reached during 1968 to proceed with the formation of a joint planning team, on the basis of equal financial contributions from Coventry and Warwickshire and a lesser one from Solihull.

The third crucial problem highlighted in the Review Plan, that of environmental improvement, was also the subject of special study extending beyond the review period itself. One of the main proposals in the report of the Planning Advisory Group had been that planning authorities should supplement the broad indications of developmental policy given in their 'structure maps' by preparing, as circumstances required, a succession of more detailed 'district plans' for particular areas, affording more specific guidance for development control and for environmental and traffic improvements. To explore this concept, the Coventry planners embarked on a pilot study in 1965, selecting a district of the city known as Stoke with a population of some 50,000 and a wide cross-section of different kinds of housing development and community structure. It was intended that other similar studies should follow, and that within the districts selected a series of more localized 'action area' plans should be formulated; an action area having been defined in the Planning Advisory Group report as any area where particularly challenging problems of development, redevelopment, or improvement were expected to arise within the next ten years or so.

The study of the transportation system, the proposed sub-regional planning study, and the district and action area studies, all provide instances of a continuing planning activity, with a common thread of land-use planning but also with many wider implications than those of land use alone. Although we were fortunate in being present in Coventry at a time when a major review of the development plan was in progress, the time-scale of change in the processes of land-use planning is such that it was not only the first review to be carried out in the city under the quinquennial review procedure but also the last: by the time the review plan was submitted, legislation was already pending to bring the processes of local land-use planning more closely in line with the more flexible ideas put forward in the Planning Advisory Group report.

MANPOWER PLANNING

In this chapter, we have so far ranged over the activities of financial planning, planning of developmental work, and land-use planning, all of which cut across the full range of local government services, and so impinged to some degree on all departments and committees in Coventry. Before turning our attention to the more specialized planning activities associated with the running of particular local government services, there is one other type of planning activity which still requires to be mentioned at the more general level: the activity of planning the future development of the human resources of the Council as a whole. While we were in Coventry, this was part of the special province of the Establishment and General Administration Committee, acting on the advice of the Establishment and Management Services Division of the Town Clerk's Department.

The activity of manpower planning was rather less in evidence during our research in Coventry than the activities of financial, developmental, and land-use planning. The explanation for this can be found in part in the comparatively rigid allocation of the Council's resources of manpower between the various departments, each of which had inherited a tradition of self-sufficiency and a distinctive career structure for its professional staff. This meant that the scope for transfer of manpower and re-allocation of tasks between departments was always somewhat limited, and consequently the activity of manpower planning tended to be more often in evidence in a departmental than in an interdepartmental context: among the few instances of planning at the interdepartmental level was the preparation of a scheme for the recruitment and training of administrative staff, including a certain number of graduate trainees, with a view to the provision of a satisfactory long-term career structure.

At the departmental level, comprehensive reviews were carried out from time to time of the organization and grading of posts within particular departments, and occasionally these reviews were accompanied by a redefinition of the functional boundaries between one department and another. In the case of those departments most heavily engaged in developmental activities, we saw that the size of the long-term capital programme became a crucial factor in assessing whether any changes were required in the current levels of establishment, while the extent to which established posts remained vacant in turn influenced the rate of progress in fulfilling the programme.

THE PLANNING OF THE SCHOOL SYSTEM

In turning our attention from the more centralized planning activities of Coventry City Council to those concerned more specifically with the development of particular public services, perhaps the most obvious starting-point is the education service, because of its dominant position both in terms of manpower and in terms of total expenditure.

Of the many internal planning problems that occupied the education service during the period of our research, two of the most persistent concerned the building of new schools and the organization of secondary education within the city. The second of these problems was to some extent a by-product of the first, in that the difficulty lay not so much in the choice between alternative systems of secondary education in the longer term – the Council had been committed for many years to the goal of comprehensive or non-selective secondary education throughout the city – but rather in finding an acceptable interim solution to reduce the anomalies of a situation in which shortages of funds were preventing the early realization of this goal.

Although we had the opportunity to see the way in which Coventry's school building programme came up for formal review every year as a component of the City Council's five-year capital programme, it soon became apparent that in the case of schools the Council's own review process was of much less significance than the procedure of submitting projects for inclusion in the national school building programme of the Department of Education and Science. Under this procedure, each local authority was called upon at approximately yearly intervals to submit a list of projects which it wished to be added to the end of a three-year rolling programme, and the relative merits of these projects were then assessed against those of projects submitted by other local authorities, with a particularly detailed investigation of marginal cases. The procedure has been discussed more fully by Griffith in his study of relationships between central and local government [15].

During the years 1963 to 1967, a good deal of effort was devoted within the City Council to the pleading of Coventry's claims for more favourable treatment in the school building programme; a series of deputations of members and officers was sent to London, a succession of documents was prepared setting out Coventry's special circumstances, and a number of steps were taken to publicize the gravity of the problem within the city itself. The substance of Coventry's case was that those concerned with the selection of projects for inclusion in the national programme were applying unduly crude yardsticks to the assessment of need, and did not appreciate fully the special problems created by Coventry's exceptionally high rates of birth and immigration, or by the deterioration of the temporary school buildings erected after the wartime bombing of the city. Among the effects of the inability of the City Council to gain approval for the level of school building which was locally believed to be necessary, was the general acceptance by most councillors of the policy that any cuts in the Council's five-year capital programme should be sought elsewhere than in the projects submitted by the Education Committee; the battlefront for allocation of resources to the school building programme was seen to lie at the level of interface between local and central government, not at the level of local competition between the claims of different public services.

At the time of our arrival in Coventry, progress towards a fully comprehensive system of secondary education was only about half complete. This meant that, in many areas of the city, children were still required to submit to a selection procedure at the age of ten to determine their suitability for the small proportion of 'selective' places in those secondary schools (some independent, some run by the local authority) where a more academic pattern of education could be provided. The division of the city into a number of zones, such that children in some zones would automatically proceed at the age of eleven to comprehensive schools with new buildings and up-to-date facilities, while children in adjoining areas who failed the selection procedure would have to be content with more limited opportunities in older 'secondary modern' schools, usually accommodated in less attractive premises, inevitably caused a good deal of friction within the community. The persistence of national constraints on the rate of school building eventually made it apparent that sufficient comprehensive schools to cover the whole city could not be provided within the foreseeable future, and the desire to remove some of the more invidious characteristics of the interim situation led the Education Committee in Coventry, shortly before our research began, to set up a special sub-committee to investigate whatever possibilities might exist for reorganization of the secondary education system to provide greater equality of opportunity within the constraints of the existing buildings.

We were given the opportunity to attend several meetings of this sub-committee, which issued its final recommendation in 1966. The sub-committee had a number of possible precedents to consider in the shape of schemes which had already been tried out in other parts of the country; but it was agreed that there were many inter-related variables to be examined before attempting to select a scheme which would be appropriate to the special needs of Coventry.

It became apparent to us that the sub-committee faced a design problem of comparable complexity to those faced by the land-use planners, though with a very different pattern of choices, constraints, and objectives. Among the factors discussed were options of altering the age of transfer from primary to secondary education, options of introducing an extra tier of 'middle' schools for some intermediate age-group, options of combining pairs of nearby schools administratively to provide equivalent facilities to the new comprehensive schools, options of converting single-sex to mixed schools, and options as to ways in which existing arrangements for the purchase of places at Coventry's two independent grammar schools might be modified. The appraisal of these various options was made more difficult at the time by a state of uncertainty about the government's future intentions as to the raising of the school-leaving age, and also as to the future structure of primary education (at that time under review by an independent commission). The search for an acceptable solution was also complicated by the need to take into account not only the objectives of the City Council itself, but also the special interests of a number of other parties, including the teachers' organizations, the Roman Catholic and Anglican Churches, and the independent grammar schools.

By the end of our research, the problem of organization for secondary education had also attained a good deal of prominence at a national level, following the election of a Labour government in 1964 and the consequent request to all local authorities to prepare plans for as rapid a transition as possible to a fully comprehensive system. In Coventry, as on the national scene, controversy between political parties tended to take the form of disagreement about the pace of change, the relative priorities of primary and secondary school building, and the future of existing grammar schools, rather than any questioning of the ultimate desirability of the comprehensive principle as such.

OTHER DEPARTMENTAL PLANNING ACTIVITIES

It was once put to us as an interesting phenomenon that, whereas the planning of the secondary education system could be taken as a good example of the kind of problem where the political objectives of elected members were always liable to come to the fore, there were certain other strategic problems – such as that of planning the future water supply of the city – which tended to be seen as essentially non-political, in that members were quite content to accept the proposals of the officers without question.

Certainly, when in 1965 the Waterworks Department submitted a major report on the future water needs of the city, and the measures through which it was recommended that these needs should be satisfied, it passed through the Council with very little controversy. So far as the local representatives were concerned, the problem of water supply, unlike that of secondary education, was essentially a 'technical' rather than a 'political' one. However, in this case it was evident that the matter could only be regarded as non-political in the limited sense that whatever conflicts of interest were involved happened to be external rather than internal to the local authority; because the water requirements of Coventry could only be met through the extension of existing arrangements to draw water from the Severn Valley, well beyond the borders of the city itself, the choice of any particular plan for future water supply could not be 'political' in the sense that it impinged in different ways on different sectors of the community within the city boundary. However, in so far as Coventry was one of a number of Midland water authorities contributing to a major reservoir scheme in mid-Wales designed to regulate the flow of the River Severn, the planning of Coventry's water supply did in fact have some political implications for certain Welsh rural communities, and during our research these implications did find some expression through the activities of Welsh nationalist groups. This serves to illustrate a more general point that a local planning activity that is not seen as a political issue locally may nevertheless sometimes generate external conflicts of interest and so become a matter of political controversy when viewed within a wider context.

One other department of Coventry Corporation whose internal planning problems were particularly in evidence during the period of our research was the Transport Department, whose main responsibility was to operate the city's bus system as a self-supporting undertaking. As in other cities, the public transport undertaking in Coventry had for many years been suffering from a decline in commercial viability, which was attributed principally to the steady spread of car-ownership. Furthermore, the department's inability to offer sufficiently high wages to compete with those available in local industry had led to a chronic instability in the work force, a strained state of labour relations, and a declining standard of service to passengers.

Coventry's efforts to put the transport undertaking on a more stable footing from the point of view of labour and finance were not assisted by the sudden imposition of a six months' 'freeze' on prices and incomes in the summer of 1966. At that point in time, the Council had only recently granted a substantial pay award, agreed after prolonged and difficult negotiations with the local trade union branch, but was still awaiting approval for a related increase in fares. This presented a further short-term set-back to the finances of an undertaking whose forward estimates were already causing considerable concern to the City Council. So far as the long-term future was concerned, it was argued by the Transport Manager that Coventry faced a choice between a rapid run-down in the services provided and a policy of sustained support for the undertaking, perhaps through a contribution from the rate fund account. It was argued that this should be regarded not as a subsidy but as a recognition of the potential contribution of public transport to the solution of the city's wider transportation problem.

During 1966 and 1967, the elected members showed themselves increasingly prepared to make cautious departures from the principle that the transport undertaking should continue to pay its way at all costs. This, however, was only one aspect of a wider trend, whose somewhat erratic progress we were able to observe during the period of our research, towards the growth of an interdepartmental planning activity relating to an integrated system of transport facilities for the city as a whole.

THE PLANNING OF THE TRANSPORTATION SYSTEM

We have so far in this chapter touched on two of the main problems which led to the acceptance of a need for a comprehensive transportation planning activity in Coventry: the problem of maintaining a viable system of public transport, and the problem of selecting a design for a primary road pattern for inclusion in the city's Development Plan. Other problems in the field of traffic and transport with which Coventry had been concerned for some time included the development of car-parking facilities – particularly within the central area and the main industrial zones – and the design of schemes for the improved management of traffic flows; both problems were seen as requiring something more than a localized approach, and it was argued that all these issues should be seen as part of a wider problem of designing an integrated transportation system for the city.

Although the need for a unified transport policy had been stressed on several occasions by several of the officers concerned, it was not found easy to obtain agreement on an appropriate organizational framework, and it was only after

Figure 8

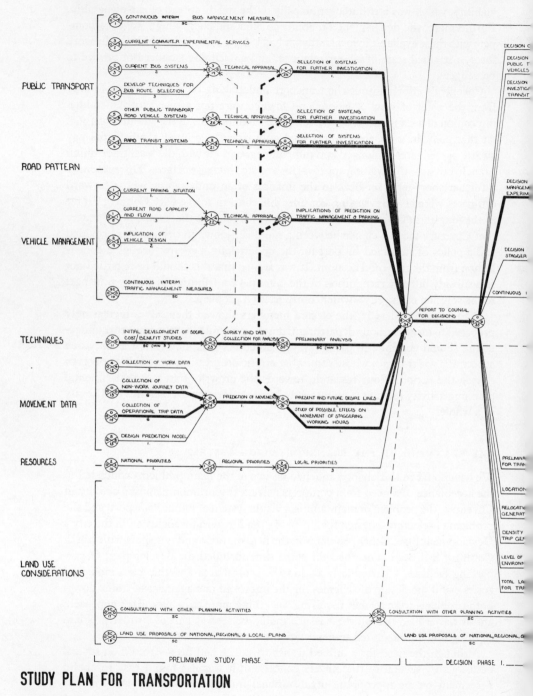

STUDY PLAN FOR TRANSPORTATION
DRAWING A - NETWORK ANALYSIS

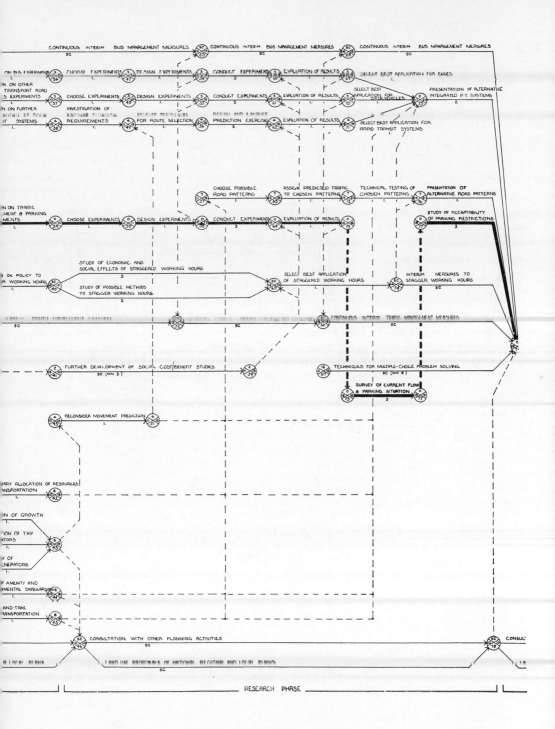

Figure 8—continued

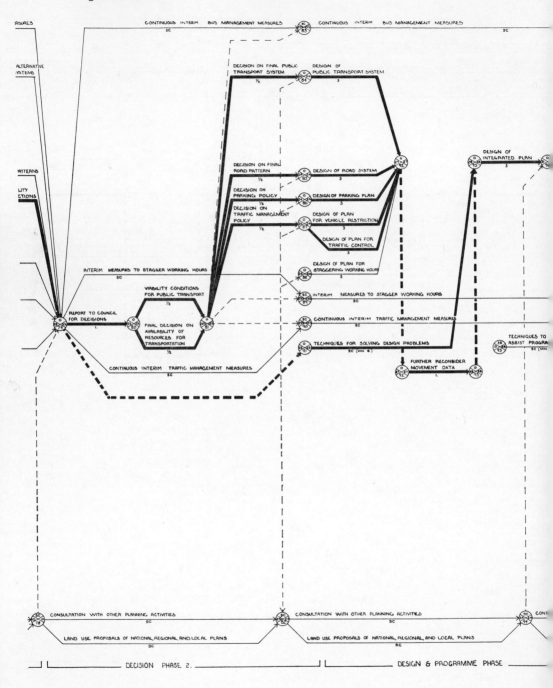

36

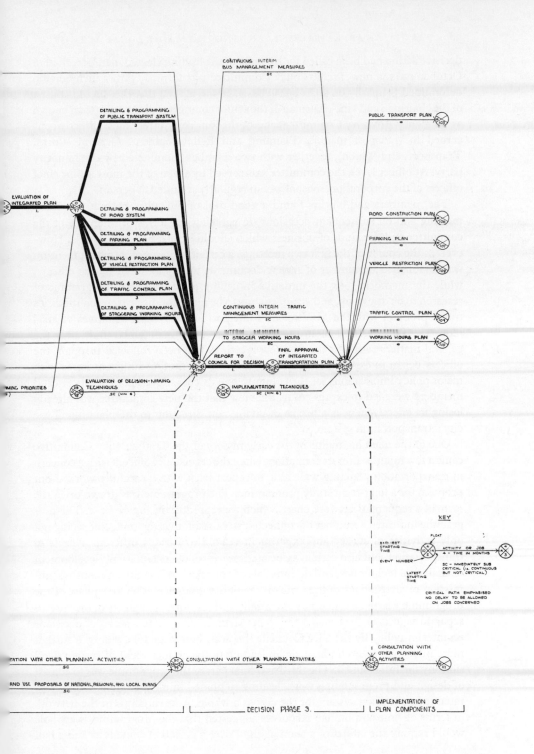

CONTINUOUS INTERIM
BUS MANAGEMENT MEASURES
SC

DETAILING & PROGRAMMING
OF PUBLIC TRANSPORT SYSTEM
3

PUBLIC TRANSPORT PLAN
105

EVALUATION OF
INTEGRATED PLAN

DETAILING & PROGRAMMING
OF ROAD SYSTEM
3

ROAD CONSTRUCTION PLAN
106

DETAILING & PROGRAMMING
OF PARKING PLAN
3

PARKING PLAN
107

DETAILING & PROGRAMMING
OF VEHICLE RESTRICTION PLAN
3

VEHICLE RESTRICTION PLAN
108

DETAILING & PROGRAMMING
OF TRAFFIC CONTROL PLAN
3

DETAILING & PROGRAMMING
OF STAGGERING WORKING HOURS
3

CONTINUOUS INTERIM TRAFFIC
MANAGEMENT MEASURES

TRAFFIC CONTROL PLAN
109

INTERIM MEASURES
TO STAGGER WORKING HOURS

WORKING HOURS PLAN
110

REPORT TO
COUNCIL FOR DECISION

FINAL APPROVAL
OF INTEGRATED
TRANSPORTATION PLAN

MING PRIORITIES

EVALUATION OF DECISION-MAKING
TECHNIQUES
SC (MIN 6)

IMPLEMENTATION TECHNIQUES
SC (MIN 6)

KEY

FLOAT

EARLIEST
STARTING
TIME

ACTIVITY OR JOB
4 – TIME IN MONTHS

EVENT NUMBER

SC – IMMEDIATELY SUB
CRITICAL (i.e. CONTINUOUS
BUT NOT CRITICAL)

LATEST
STARTING
TIME

CRITICAL PATH EMPHASISED
NO DELAY TO BE ALLOWED
ON JOBS CONCERNED

TATION WITH OTHER PLANNING ACTIVITIES
SC

CONSULTATION WITH OTHER PLANNING ACTIVITIES
SC

CONSULTATION WITH
OTHER PLANNING
ACTIVITIES
SC

111

AND USE PROPOSALS OF NATIONAL, REGIONAL, AND LOCAL PLANS
SC

DECISION PHASE 3.

IMPLEMENTATION OF
PLAN COMPONENTS

37

decisive action had been called for by some of the leading elected members that, in October 1965, a new Traffic Policy Committee was formed, with a membership determined primarily on an *ex officio* basis. It was agreed that this should consist of the chairman and vice-chairman of the senior committee of Council (then known as the Policy Advisory Committee) and of the four committees most directly concerned in transport matters (Planning and Redevelopment, General Works, Transport, and Watch), together with two members nominated by the minority party. At officer level, the committee was served by seven of the most senior chief officers of the corporation, most of whom regularly attended in person.

The members and officers found a good deal of difficulty, both at the initial meeting and on subsequent occasions, in agreeing the terms of reference of the committee and the kinds of business which should be placed on its agenda. However, in the course of the first two meetings a certain amount of initial momentum was established; a number of review documents were submitted by the officers, while the members took the initiative in calling for a long-term programme of research to be drawn up, and arrangements to be made for discussions on the city's traffic problem with the Minister of Transport and the representatives of local industry. This early momentum was not, however, maintained and, after the general matters raised in the first few meetings had been followed through, the officers began to experience increasing difficulty in finding sufficient items with major policy implications for the committee to discuss. Several of the officers and members were led to express to us the view that the new committee was already losing its effectiveness as a means of giving new direction to the planning of the city's transportation system.

One of the main highlights in the early history of the Traffic Policy Committee came a few months after its formation, when the seven chief officers with a concern in transportation planning were able to report back with a carefully worked-out proposal for a long-term study programme. The programme was drawn up in the form of a sequential network chart, which we reproduce in *Figure 8a–d*. The programme indicated a number of connected streams of investigation, embracing not only activities of survey and experiment related to various different aspects of transportation, but also certain associated processes of consultation, development of analytical techniques, and (at intervals of approximately eighteen months) submission of alternatives to the Council for policy guidance. The first phase of the programme was to be concerned essentially with exploratory studies of the various separate aspects of the transportation problem, leading up to a series of decisions on interim policy by the City Council; this was then to be followed by a further more intensive research phase, again leading to the endorsement of certain decisions by the full Council. The third and final part of the programme was to consist of design and programming work, leading to phased implementation of an integrated transportation system for the city as a whole. A full analysis of the network in terms of time and human resources suggested that the programme as a whole would require the efforts of a team of eight over a period of some four and a half years. It was suggested that this team should be specially recruited and should include planners, engineers, transport engineers, and economists.

The Ministry of Transport expressed interest in the novel features of the proposed research programme, and agreed to provide financial support for the initial phase. The research team was recruited and started work in late 1966, reporting to a steering group which included five chief officers of the City Council: the Town Clerk, the City Treasurer, the City Architect and Planning Officer, the City Engineer, and the Transport Manager.

A somewhat fuller account of the growth of the transportation planning activity in Coventry appears in a project paper 'Transport Planning and City Government', written in early 1967 as one of the interim products of our total research programme [16].

OTHER CROSS-DEPARTMENTAL PLANNING ACTIVITIES

The field of transportation planning undoubtedly provided the most outstanding example during our four years in Coventry of the growth of an interdepartmental and inter-committee approach to the planning of a particular set of related public services. However, we were also able to observe a growing recognition of the need for a co-ordinated approach in certain other areas of planning which were seen to cut across several committee and departmental boundaries. This search for coordination in forward planning was evident in relation to social welfare and recreational policy, and also particularly in relation to housing, a field which concerned not only the Housing Department itself – whose responsibility related mainly to management of the Council's own housing stock – but also the City Estates Department with its responsibility for operating the Council's home loans scheme, the City Engineers' Department with its responsibility (during most of the period of our research) for the Council's direct labour building force, the Public Health Department with its responsibility for questions of unfitness of housing and control of multi-occupation, and the Department of Architecture and Planning with its dual interests in housing design and overall land-use planning.

We have already made reference, in the course of our discussion of Coventry's long-term capital programme, to the constraints imposed on the rate of housing development by the twin limitations of housing finance and of the city's overloaded drainage system. These constraints, and the possibilities of overcoming them, came up for discussion at frequent intervals while we were in Coventry. On several occasions, the problems of housing development were referred to the Policy Advisory Committee, partly because its status as senior committee of Council made it the only obvious forum for the discussion of matters cutting across the responsibilities of several committees, and partly because of a recognition that the planning of future housing development had many local political implications which could not realistically be discussed without involving the leadership of the majority party of the Council.

5

During these periodic discussions of housing policy in the Policy Advisory Committee, a good deal of consideration was given to the possibility of overcoming the financial constraint by the encouragement of private and institutional housing associations, and the possibility of speeding up the development of the drainage system by the recruitment or hiring of additional engineering staff. Also, as a means of ensuring that the Council had an adequate building organization of its own to sustain an ambitious programme of housing development, a decision was made in early 1967 to replace the City Engineer's Direct Works Section by a separate Public Works Department, accountable to a new Public Works Committee. This decision was strongly criticized by the Conservative opposition, who pledged themselves before the key 1967 election to disband the new department, on the grounds that the corporation's building programme could be more effectively handled by private enterprise.

The coming to power of the Conservative Party in Coventry led to a number of early changes in housing policy, including the introduction of a scheme for the sale of council houses to sitting tenants, and a proposal for a substantial increase in the level of rents, accompanied by a rent rebate scheme for those with low income. Although the implementation of these changes was a matter purely within the province of the Housing Committee, the proposals themselves were submitted to Council through the agency of the Policy Committee (the successor to Labour's Policy Advisory Committee) since they were seen to be items of major significance for overall Council policy.

By the end of 1967, the problems of local housing policy, and in particular of housing finance, had become a matter of intense political controversy in Coventry – a situation which was mirrored in several other parts of the country where there had also been a change of political control after the municipal elections of that year.

RELATIONSHIPS WITH OTHER PLANNING AGENCIES

Many of the planning activities which we were able to observe in Coventry transcended not only the boundaries of departmental and committee responsibilities within the local authority, but also the boundaries between the responsibilities of the City Council and those of other public agencies having specific fields of interest within the city. Although the patterns of interdependence between planning agencies were thrown into particularly sharp relief during the processes of consultation leading up to the presentation of the Development Plan Review, they were also in evidence in other contexts: for instance, in meetings of the Welfare Committee it was frequently argued that the provision of old peoples' homes by the local authority and of geriatric beds by the Regional Hospital Board were related to overlapping areas of need and therefore required to be considered in closer co-ordination than existing arrangements made possible.

In the field of transport, we saw a good deal of concern among members of the City Council that British Rail should have reached a decision to close the local

North-South railway line through Coventry to passenger traffic just at a time when major roadworks and extensions of public transport facilities were being proposed by the local authority to meet the predicted increases in commuter traffic on the same North-South axis. Another action by the rail authority which had an important impact on the plans of the City Council was the introduction in 1966 of fast and frequent new services linking London to Birmingham, Manchester, and Liverpool through Coventry: as predicted, this resulted in an increased demand for parking facilities in the vicinity of the station while, at those points in the city road network where the main line was traversed by level crossings, there was an immediate rise in the degree of traffic congestion, so adding urgency to local demands for replacement of these crossings by bridges.

Another instance of disturbance to the pattern of communications within the city arose when the Ministry of Transport decided, in the interests of road safety, to close many of the existing accesses and crossing-points on the congested trunk road, the A45, which carried most of the through traffic between London and Birmingham. One section of this road fell within the boundaries of Coventry and this already had the effect of imposing a barrier to movement between the southern suburbs and the city centre; the proposal to impose further restrictions on movement across this barrier aroused some strong opposition from residents of the districts concerned, and a number of instances were quoted both in the committee rooms and in the Council Chamber itself of the social consequences of this further severance of one neighbourhood from another within the city.

There were of course a number of other corporate bodies, public and private, whose planning activities within Coventry were of concern to the City Council in that they created prospects of major changes in existing patterns of land use, employment, or traffic generation. For instance, within the public sector, the West Midlands Gas Board announced its intention to close its manufacturing plant on the North side of Coventry, a decision which was seen by the city planners as opening up new possibilities for redevelopment and environmental improvement in a hitherto underprivileged neighbourhood.

Shortly before our research started, a somewhat similar situation of change had been created by the decision by another public agency – the National Coal Board – to close an uneconomic coal mine just inside the city boundary. This was seen by the City Council as creating an opportunity for developing a new industrial estate, to accommodate small firms dislocated by central area redevelopment; and subsequently, the purchase from the Coal Board of an estate of 400 houses, originally built for the local mining community, was seen by the Council as an opportunity both to enlarge the total stock of municipal housing and to undertake much-needed environmental and structural improvements.

Another interaction between the planning activities of the City Council and the National Coal Board was of a very different kind. Despite the closure of the last remaining coalmine within the city itself, the Coal Board continued to mine underneath the city from another colliery just outside the boundary, and at one time the

City Council was seriously concerned by an announcement that this activity was to be extended in a way that appeared to threaten the foundations of many of the new buildings in the central area, including the new cathedral itself.

So far as manufacturing industry was concerned, national restrictions on growth in the West Midlands Region meant that there were no instances of large-scale movement of new industry into Coventry during the period of our research; however, several large firms were involved in negotiations with the City Council on such matters as extensions of buildings and car-parking facilities on existing sites, and rationalization of activities dispersed between two or more sites. It is perhaps significant that the most important single change on the industrial front during the period of our research was not the establishment of a new industry but the closure of an existing one, when a large aerospace establishment had to close as a result of cancellation of a major defence contract, and its premises were converted for use as a trading estate.

THE DEVELOPMENT OF THE UNIVERSITY OF WARWICK

Of the various corporate bodies whose plans were bound up with those of the local authority during our four years in Coventry, the most significant in many respects was the new University of Warwick, established in 1964 on the southern fringes of Coventry, on a rural site straddling the administrative boundary between the City and the County of Warwickshire. The university's development plan envisaged an ultimate student population of 15,000, and it was estimated by the city planners that a further permanent population of perhaps 10,000 would ultimately be directly associated with the running of the university in one way or another. It was argued that the growth of a new community of this size could inevitably be expected to make a significant impact on the future development of the city as a whole, quite apart from its special contribution to the cultural life of the community. Discussions within the local authority related in particular to the university's impact on the three sectors of housing, transport, and further education, so we will comment on each of these aspects in turn.

The university's demands for residential accommodation, in so far as they extended beyond the limits of its own site, were recognized as being of an unusually specialized nature, relating in particular to lodgings for students and lower-density private housing for academic staff. Although the planners in Coventry were concerned to meet the latter demand so far as possible within the boundaries of the city, the only available land for new development near the university site was also in demand for the building of higher-density council housing to meet the general housing needs of the city, and it was argued by the elected members then concerned with housing policy that the provision of housing of this character would help towards a closer integration of the university with the social life of the city. One suggestion was that some of the land should be used to build exceptionally large houses for the local authority; these would initially be allocated to the larger families on the waiting list, but would provide space for student lodgers as the families concerned grew up. The planners made a number of attempts to define plans for the development of this area, but a good deal of difficulty was experienced in finding solutions of such a kind as to be fully acceptable to the Council. A more radical reappraisal of the future of the area took place in 1967, after the change of political power with its reversal of previous housing policies.

So far as transport was concerned, it was widely recognized that the university would need to be served by a major new road in view of the heavy traffic it was expected to generate. However, the choice of route concerned not only the City Council and the university authorities, but also the adjoining County Council, who would have been responsible for building its southern section. Two alternative routes were proposed, and despite a careful evaluation of their implications for traffic, environment, and construction cost, agreement between the three parties proved particularly hard to reach. A significant factor was that the proportion of the road within the city boundary, and hence the allocation of construction cost, differed appreciably between the two schemes. Uncertainty over the outcome of this issue continued during 1966 and 1967, and created further difficulties in the formulation of a satisfactory brief for housing development in the area adjoining the university site.

As was only to be expected, the development of the new university also had important implications for the City Council's system of further education, which already included one recently-established institution of higher education – the Lanchester College of Technology – occupying a strategic site in the central area of the City. In the City Council, there was a good deal of support for the idea of integration of the Lanchester College within the framework of the new university, and we were able to witness some prolonged and difficult negotiations on possible ways of achieving this aim. Although an acceptable scheme for integration was in the end agreed at local level, this was subsequently rejected in higher quarters. Although the scheme could have set an entirely new pattern for relationships between academic and technical education, this was felt to be premature, and in fact would have been in conflict with the 'binary' system of universities and polytechnics which was then emerging through the processes of national policy formation.

COVENTRY AND THE GROWTH OF REGIONAL PLANNING

We have already traced the emergence of a demand for a sub-regional planning activity in the area surrounding Coventry, starting with the issue by the City Council of the 'Coventry City Region' report in 1963 [10]. However, while this demand was emerging locally, a demand was also emerging nationally for closer regional co-ordination between the various departments of national government, and for a greater degree of autonomy in the regions in matters of economic planning. For most purposes of central and regional planning, Coventry was considered as an eastern outlier of a West Midlands Region centred on Birmingham, and the first development in the move to regional economic planning which directly affected Coventry was the publication in 1965 of *The West Midlands: a Regional Study* [17] under the auspices of the Department of Economic Affairs. Although this report was most closely concerned with the problems of growth and dispersal created by the Birmingham conurbation, it also identified the existence of a 'Coventry belt' whose problems were seen as relatively self-contained, and whose boundaries corresponded quite closely with those which had earlier been defined for Coventry City Region.

When steps were taken in 1965 to set up Regional Economic Planning Councils to cover all areas of the country, Coventry City Council was invited to put forward a nomination for appointment to the West Midlands Council, and a leading elected member was proposed and subsequently appointed. The new Council issued its first full report in early 1967 [18], taking as its starting-point the analysis presented in the earlier West Midlands Study report, but taking into account the reactions to its publication from various interested parties within the region. This report contained no specific suggestions for the future of the 'Coventry belt', pointing out that this area was intended to be the subject of a separate sub-regional study by a team drawn from the local planning authorities concerned. This provided some interesting evidence that, at the sub-regional level, the activities of local physical planning and regional economic planning were seen as merging together in one overall planning activity.

THE RELATIONSHIPS OF LOCAL AND NATIONAL PLANNING

The influence of national decisions on local planning activities has been referred to at many points in this chapter. At the foot of *Table 2*, we chose to make reference to only a few of the many landmarks of planning at national level which were of particular relevance to local planning in Coventry. In a number of cases, reports issued by central government commended changes of a kind which had already been discussed and partially implemented in Coventry: this applied to the 1963 (Buchanan) report, *Traffic in Towns*, the 1965 report of the Planning Advisory Group on the Future of Development Plans, the 1965 circular from the Department of Education and Science calling on local education authorities to produce schemes for rapid progress towards a comprehensive system of secondary education, and the 1966 White Paper on transport policy.

These instances of the interplay of local and national planning activities represent only a few salient points in the continuing stream of communication we were able to witness between the various departments of Coventry City Council and the various associated departments of central government. Periodic directives from government departments on particular issues were balanced by continuing feedback of information on their local effects, either through direct channels or through the medium of representative groups such as the Association of Municipal Corporations or the Association of Education Committees. Much of this continuing dialogue took the form of negotiation on specific applications by departments of the local authority for approval of particular schemes in accordance with the various mechanisms of central government control. Perhaps the strongest impression to emerge from this dialogue was of the extent to which the difficulties of inter-departmental planning within the local authority were mirrored in the problems of co-ordination between the departments of national government itself; from our local vantage point, the deficiencies in communication and co-ordination at national level in fact appeared at times to be a good deal more marked than any of those arising within the more limited compass of the local government system within the city.

PERSPECTIVES OF PLANNING IN COVENTRY

We began this chapter with an attempt to compress into a single chart (*Table 2*, p. 8) an impression of all the main types of planning activity which we were able to observe taking place during our research in Coventry. Then, in discussing each of these activities in turn, we were able to explore some of the many threads of interdependence between them: for instance, the interactions between land-use and developmental planning, between the planning of public transport and that of the road system, between the planning of a new university and the planning of the city's housing system; and between different aspects of governmental planning at local, regional, and national levels. Together, these various activities can be seen as strands of one continuing planning process, with a great complexity of inter-actions and involving many different groups of participants, each tending to have a different perspective of the total dynamic process. It was apparent to us that there were in fact substantial areas of overlap between the various aspects of planning which we had observed, in that any particular problem could appear as a com-ponent in many different planning activities. For instance, the problem of align-ment for a new road to serve the university could be seen either as a part of the city's transportation planning activity, or as a part of its land-use planning activity, or as a part of the university's corporate planning activity; while the problem of devising a new pay structure for transport employees could be seen either as a part of the local authority's manpower planning activity, or as a part of its financial planning activity, or again as a part of an interdepartmental planning activity for the city's total transportation system. Among the perspectives of planning which we encountered most frequently within the local authority itself were those which we show diagrammatically in *Figure 9*.

In this diagram, the perspective of planning for any specific type of public ser-vice is shown as having some degree of overlap with each of four other perspectives of planning which are essentially resource based, and which also have substantial areas of overlap among themselves. Although this form of graphical representation has its limitations as a means of giving expression to the complex set of relationships which exist within the total planning process, it is possible nevertheless to develop it further, for instance to show the areas of overlap between particular service-based planning perspectives such as those related to health, welfare, and housing, or to show interactions of local authority planning with different aspects

Figure 9

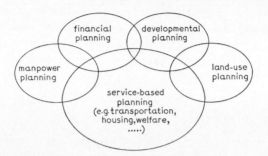

of national planning, and of corporate planning within the private sector. We will make further use of graphical representations of overlapping planning perspectives in Part III, when we come to consider how a body of technique can be developed to meet the requirements of the planning process, and again in Part IV, when we will argue that the design of organizational forms for planning requires a very different approach from that normally used to define hierarchical management structures.

3. Planning and the mechanisms of decision

Any form of planning activity by a local authority must take place within a procedural setting which is laid down in the standing orders of Council, and in the more specific instructions to individual committees. Although each local authority has a measure of autonomy in developing these procedures within the legal constitution of the local government system, no local rules of procedure can in themselves do more than provide a basic framework within which groups and individuals can act. Inevitably, certain patterns of behaviour and expectation evolve which tend to become an integral part of the local government system even though they have no official procedural basis. Such conventions may change gradually over time, but tend nevertheless to acquire some degree of permanence in so far as they may not always merely reflect the idiosyncrasies of particular individuals or groups, but may also to some extent represent responses to the intrinsic requirements for effective communication and control. One important set of conventions concerns the role of party politics in the decision-making process; this is nowhere recognized in the official rules of procedure, but in cities such as Coventry it is central to any understanding of the way in which the local authority actually works. The influence of convention is not, however, confined to political activity in this narrower sense of the conflict between organized parties; rather, it extends in some measure to all relationships between groups and individuals within the local government system.

We have already seen something in Chapter 2 of the formal mechanisms of local government election, and noted the convention that the triennial aldermanic elections are used to provide a more secure base of power for whichever political party commands a majority of councillors at the time. In this chapter, we shall be more concerned with the mechanisms which have evolved for reaching decisions on particular matters which come to the attention of the local authority once the composition of the Council has been determined. We shall start by considering the formal procedures which govern all matters for committee or Council decision, whether or not they can be regarded as matters of 'planning' or of 'policy' as these terms are generally understood; we shall then turn to consider some of the difficulties that have arisen in Coventry in coping with issues of this more strategic nature within the provisions of the formal framework, and the attempts that have been made to find ways of dealing with these difficulties both through the further

47

development of informal conventions, and also sometimes through the incorpora-
tion of changes in the formal rules of procedure.

THE FORMAL PROCESSES OF DECISION-MAKING

The formal sequence of steps in the decision-making process in Coventry is similar
to that in any other all-purpose local authority in the United Kingdom. It can be
summarized diagrammatically as shown in *Figure 10*.

Figure 10

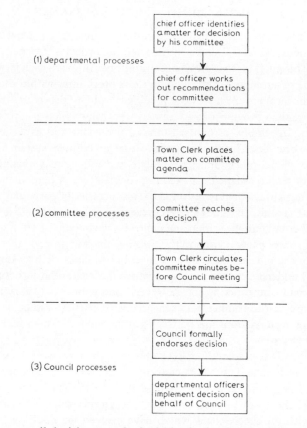

(1) departmental processes

chief officer identifies
a matter for decision
by his committee

chief officer works
out recommendations
for committee

(2) committee processes

Town Clerk places
matter on committee
agenda

committee reaches
a decision

Town Clerk circulates
committee minutes be-
fore Council meeting

(3) Council processes

Council formally
endorses decision

departmental officers
implement decision on
behalf of Council

Of course, not all decisions reached within the local authority need to proceed
formally through each of these stages before they can be implemented. Many of the
more routine decisions fall purely within the discretion of the chief officer of a
department or his subordinates, while other decisions may require endorsement
by a committee although not by the full Council. However, from our perspective
of the planning process, we are inevitably more concerned with decisions that
require the endorsement of the Council than with those that can be settled at a lower
level.

In some cases, the formal processes of decision may become more complicated because of the involvement of more than one chief officer, or a requirement for formal approval of a proposal by more than one committee; for instance, in

Figure 11

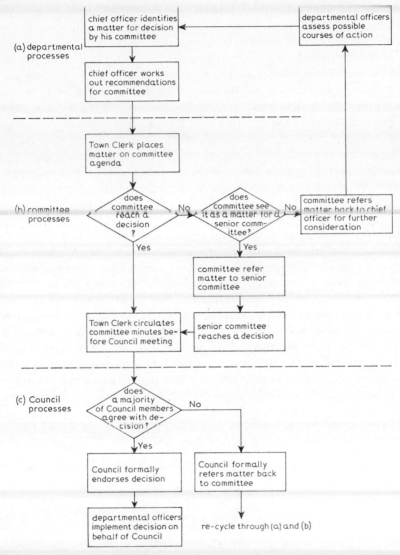

Coventry any proposal for expenditure which was not covered by agreed estimates was required to be submitted not only through the appropriate spending committee but also through the Finance Committee. Also, a committee might consider in the

course of discussion that a matter fell outside its strict terms of reference and should be referred elsewhere – in many cases to the Council's senior committee of arbitration, the Policy Committee (or Policy Advisory Committee as it was known until the final year of our research).

Reference to a senior committee – whether this might be the central Policy Committee or some other body such as the more specialized Traffic Policy Committee whose formation we discussed in Chapter 2 – was, in Coventry, only one of a number of ways in which the automatic progression of an issue through the various steps shown in *Figure 10* might be broken. Still within the provisions of the formal system, we may expand *Figure 10* to show a choice of alternative routes through the decision-making process as indicated in *Figure 11*.

In *Figure 11*, the basic sequence of steps that was set out in the previous diagram is reproduced again on the left-hand side, but this time with allowance for the possibility either that the committee may find itself unable to reach any decision, or that the majority of Council members may disagree with whatever decision the committee asks it to endorse. If the committee fails to reach a decision, two possibilities are shown: that the matter may be referred to a senior committee because it raises issues which the committee does not feel competent to settle on its own, or that it may be referred back to the chief officer to be raised again at a later meeting after further assessments within his department.

Assuming that a decision is eventually reached, either by the committee in question or by a senior committee, the decision will then be minuted and submitted to the full Council at its next meeting for endorsement by a majority vote of Council members or – in the case of a decision taken under delegated powers where Council endorsement is unnecessary – to give other members of Council an opportunity to ask any questions about the matter concerned. In Coventry, the recognized procedure was that, at the monthly Council meeting, all committee minutes requiring approval were submitted *en bloc*, one committee at a time; any member of Council then had an opportunity to move the reference back or amendment of any particular minute and his motion, if seconded, was then accepted or rejected through a show of hands by the Council as a whole. However, the vote in the Council Chamber was only rarely a free one; and it is at this level of the Council meeting especially that it becomes impossible to appreciate the true structure of the decision-making system without taking into account the realities of political control.

THE POLITICAL SIGNIFICANCE OF THE COUNCIL MEETING

As we reported in the previous chapter, the City Council in Coventry was during the period of our research divided without exception between the members of the opposing Labour and Conservative parties. Although we were given equal facilities by both parties to observe their internal decision-making processes, the observational phase of our research had virtually drawn to a close by the end of 1966, and our interpretations of the political processes in this chapter are therefore based primarily on the conditions of relative stability which existed prior to the 1967 local election which brought the Conservative Party to power. However, what we have been able to see of the transitional situation in the months following the change of power has not led us to question the validity of our interpretations in any fundamental way.

With the exception of the Lord Mayor, who has the responsibility of presiding at Council meetings and who by convention dissociates himself from party politics during his year of office, all councillors and aldermen who owe allegiance to the majority party consider themselves collectively accountable for the policies of the Council, and therefore for any decisions which are endorsed within the Council Chamber. It was not in practice difficult in Coventry for the members of the majority party to secure and maintain an effective measure of control over the activities of each committee; they could do this, first, by weighting the allocation of committee places in their favour, within the limits allowed by standing orders of two to four places on standing committees per member, and, second, by appointing the chairman and vice-chairman of each committee from within their own ranks. However, because it could never be practicable for a majority party to lay down precisely in advance its policies on every issue which was likely to arise in committee, there were inevitably some occasions when a committee reached a decision which other members of the majority party subsequently regarded as mistaken and wished to see reversed.

In Coventry, as elsewhere, a practice had developed whereby all members of the majority party met as a group prior to the monthly Council meeting, in order to screen the minutes of the various committees, and also to formulate their tactics for any other items to be dealt with on the Council agenda. This group meeting normally took place on the evening immediately preceding that of the Council meeting, by which time members had had a chance to read through the Council agenda together with the various committee minutes to be submitted. One of the most important functions of this pre-Council meeting was that it gave any member of the majority party an opportunity to draw attention in private to any committee decision which he felt did not accord with the policies of the group. If, after debate, the group as a whole resolved that they could not support the committee decision in question, then it was a simple matter for the committee chairman, on the instructions of the group, to rise in the Council meeting the following evening and ask that the matter concerned in that particular minute be formally referred back to the committee for further consideration.

The members of the minority party also invariably met as a group to discuss their tactics for opposition on the evening before the Council meeting. Because they could not in any normal circumstances expect to command a majority vote for any motion they might raise in the Council Chamber, their direct influence on the decision-making processes of the Council was inevitably slight; however, it was within the public arena of the Council meeting, rather than in the private setting of the committee room, that the minority party could best hope to exploit any weaknesses in the position of the controlling group, particularly as they were aware that any points of controversy would be fully reported in the local press on the following day. Concern as to what might be exploited by the opposition in the Council Chamber could therefore often have an important indirect effect on the decisions of majority party members in committee and in their pre-Council group meeting.

THE FORMAL AND INFORMAL PROCESSES OF DECISION

The majority party's ultimate sanction, to call for withdrawal of a committee decision in the Council meeting, tended in practice to be applied only sparingly. To make sure that officers' recommendations and committee decisions on politically controversial matters were not likely to prove unacceptable at this final stage, a number of informal practices of consultation had grown up at earlier stages of the decision-making process. In *Figure 12* we indicate how the more important of these informal practices (which we distinguish by the use of thinner lines) relate to the more formal process of decision as represented in *Figure 11*.

At the departmental stage, *Figure 12* shows how, on politically delicate matters, a chief officer might be able to ask his committee chairman for guidance as to what kinds of solution were likely to be unacceptable to the majority party group. Then, at the committee stage, there was a possibility that a matter might be regarded by one or more of the members as so politically delicate as to require discussion in the full majority party group before a formal committee vote was taken: in these circumstances, the majority party would have an option either of placing the matter on the agenda for its next pre-Council meeting, or else discussing it on a separate occasion when they might expect to be able to give fuller consideration to its implications.

For a matter to be referred from the formal setting of a committee to the informal setting of a party group required an indirect approach, and this as we saw could be simply achieved through a proposal in committee to leave the matter in the hands of the chairman and vice-chairman for further consideration; it would then be up to the chairman to raise the matter for discussion at an appropriate meeting of the party group before allowing it to be brought up again for formal decision in committee. This practice of referring matters for full debate within the party group is indicated at the point marked 'N' in *Figure 12*, and is shown to lead to the further possibility that, if the full party group found itself unable to reach agreement, it might then refer the matter to a smaller sub-group for more detailed consideration and subsequent reporting back to the full membership. This smaller sub-group, known as the policy committee or policy group of the majority party, could again claim no official standing in the Council's decision-making structure; it is not to be confused with the official Policy Committee of the Council. Although many of the same leading members of the majority party might in fact serve on both bodies, there was a critical distinction between them in that meetings of the former group

Figure 12

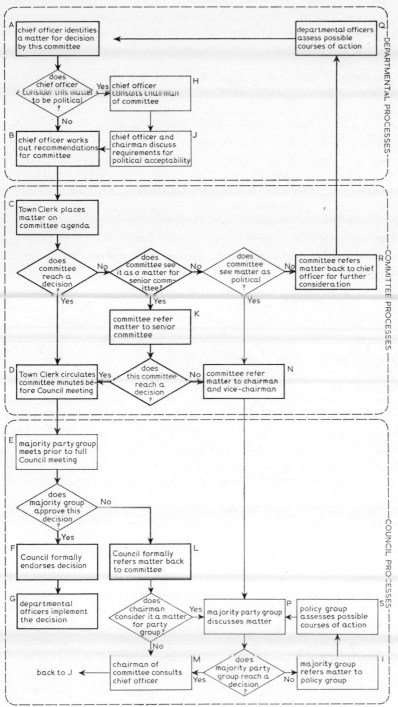

were not attended by officers of the Council. Like the full party group meeting itself, it therefore provided a forum for a more uninhibited discussion of political implications, but only at the cost of being deprived of expert advice on more technical considerations.

Although *Figure 12* shows a number of possible routes which an issue might take through the decision-making system, we do not claim that it gives an exhaustive picture and we will wish to discuss certain other variations later in this chapter. The diagram does, however, bring out the crucial point that, in any realistic consideration of the ways in which decisions are made, it is impossible to separate the formal processes of local government from those less formal practices which have arisen through convention, and which to a large extent serve to make good the shortcomings of the formal system as a practical instrument of control.

The system of decision-making which we illustrate in *Figure 12* involves the participation of many different individuals, some of whom might appear at several different stages or even possibly in two or more distinctive roles (as in the case of the elected member who might participate first as a committee member and then again as a member of the majority party group). We will now take a closer look at each of the main groups of participants in turn, with particular emphasis on its distinctive contribution to the solution of those more strategic problems of decision arising from the various planning activities we reviewed in Chapter 2.

THE ROLE OF THE CHIEF OFFICER

The role of the chief officer of a department is particularly influential within the uppermost section of *Figure 12*, which outlines the departmental processes leading up to the submission of a matter to committee. Of course, the chief officer does not concern himself purely with committee work, but also tends to become involved to some extent in the making of a wide range of decisions relating to the day-to-day management of his department. Some of these decisions may never come to the attention of committee members at all, or may only be brought to their notice in the setting of a periodic report on administrative actions taken within the department. However, the more strategic problems with which we were especially concerned in our research inevitably required to be submitted for committee discussion at some stage, although – as we shall see – the chief officer often had a considerable range of discretion in judging when this stage could be said to have arisen.

Normally, a chief officer would attend regularly the meetings of the committee to which his department was primarily accountable, and possibly certain other committees as well. The chief officer therefore tended to be exposed more fully to the views of elected members than were most of his subordinate officers within the department, and he thereby tended to develop an implicit understanding for the kind of issue on which his committee expected to be consulted, and the extent to which they were prepared to let him act on his own authority.

Much of the groundwork in the preparation of proposals for committee was of course in the hands of less senior officers of the department concerned, who tended to be more closely involved in the execution of departmental work programmes. However, it was always the chief officer who bore the final responsibility for deciding what course of action should be recommended to committee, and it was he whose signature appeared on any document which was circulated to members.

In controlling the flow of information to committee, the chief officer was often faced with a wide variety of choice. Sometimes, as we have suggested, he might have a choice as to whether a matter should be taken to committee at all; in other cases, he could choose whether a matter should be brought forward for early decision, or alternatively whether it should be held back until the ground could be better prepared; furthermore, as we indicated in *Figure 12*, the option was always available to him of raising a particular matter privately with his chairman before the committee met, for an informal discussion of its political implications. Other crucial choices for the chief officer concerned how fully he should try to brief committee members in advance of the meeting itself, by sending out background information with the agenda papers, and how far he should emphasize particular aspects of the problem in his verbal presentation in the committee meeting itself. His discretion was also involved in deciding in what circumstances to select and present a single recommendation to committee, and in what circumstances to put forward a range of alternatives; but, all the time, it was necessary for him to use this discretion with an awareness that among his long-term objectives must be the need to retain the committee members' confidence, and not to seem to be encroaching too far upon their jealously guarded freedom of choice.

In Coventry, we were able to see much evidence of the powerful position which a chief officer could achieve through his control over the flow of information to committee, provided he used his power with due discretion. The level of trust between chief officer and committee in fact varied widely, and it was not surprising that some officers would from time to time be accused of frustrating the will of the elected members by deliberately withholding information or putting forward an unnecessarily narrow range of alternatives. The officers for their part would argue to us that, because committees could be so capricious and unpredictable in their behaviour, it was particularly important to avoid misleading their members by giving them more information than they could absorb, or by failing to give them firm guidance towards a particular course of action.

THE ROLE OF THE CHAIRMAN

The relationship of the chief officer to his chairman we saw to be a particularly significant one for the whole decision-making process. On the one hand, by interpreting the climate of opinion in the majority party group, the chairman would often be able to guide the chief officer towards the submission of recommendations which would be politically acceptable, or at the very least to advise him that certain obviously unacceptable solutions should be discarded. The chairman for his part would have the opportunity to learn, through his frequent informal contacts with the chief officer, a good deal more about the problems of managing the department than would the other members of his committee; this would be of value to him in his role as spokesman for the department in his party group meetings, in the Council Chamber, and in contacts with the public and the press.

A competent chairman, combining a shrewd political sense with a clear understanding of the problems of managing the public service for which he was responsible, could therefore provide a crucial link between the departmental process, the political process, and the community at large. Potentially, this made the role of committee chairman a very powerful one; but, in Coventry under the control of the Labour Party, the power which any particular individual could acquire through this role was deliberately restricted by a standing order which limited tenure to a period of not more than three consecutive years, after which a retiring chairman could normally expect to be replaced by his vice-chairman. For this reason, the role of vice-chairman in Coventry tended to be of some significance in itself, not only as a means of providing cover during the absence of the chairman, but also as a means of maintaining a smooth succession at the end of the three-year cycle.

THE COMMITTEE MEETING

In local government, the committee meeting is the only official occasion at which officers and elected members meet together around a table, and it is at this stage that the recommendations of the officers – if acceptable – become translated into formal decisions of the members. However, despite the formal significance of the occasion, it was evident to us that, particularly where the more strategic decisions were concerned, the committee meeting tended to play a strictly limited role in the actual processes of decision-'making', which extended well beyond the formal procedures of decision-'taking' enshrined in standing orders. During our period in Coventry, many of the more significant matters of Council strategy, such as the capital programme, the Development Plan Review, and the future of the public transport undertaking, were brought to committees on several different occasions and, although it was apparent that the discussion in committee often fulfilled a useful purpose in helping officers and members towards a better understanding of each other's points of view, it was comparatively rarely that a committee seemed able to address itself successfully to the task of making a balanced selection between alternatives.

To some extent, we saw this as an inevitable outcome of the contrast between the complexity of choice presented by major strategic planning problems and the limited options for acceptance or rejection of recommendations permitted by conventional committee procedures. Although on some occasions we saw attempts made to put forward a range of alternative solutions rather than a single recommendation, officers would very often tend to present their alternatives in such a way as to imply an obvious preference between them.

The more intricately structured proposals, such as those for the 1966 Development Plan and the five-year capital programme, tended to present no options for decisive action at the committee stage other than wholesale acceptance, marginal adjustment, or outright rejection – with the last course necessitating a delay while the officers worked out further proposals, possibly with further political consultation through the chairman. Although we did see some instances where members of committee were able to suggest marginal adjustments which could be successfully incorporated, there were other cases when the officers were able to argue that the proposed amendments could not be made without throwing the whole balance of the proposal concerned into question.

Inevitably, these limitations to the effectiveness of the committee as a decision-making body meant that the reality of the decision-making process tended to become largely concentrated within the departmental offices, with the chairman being consulted on any issues seen by the chief officer to have political implications, and any particularly contentious matters being brought in advance to the full majority party group. Certain of the proposals in the Development Plan Review were in fact presented in advance to both political groups, as well as to a series of informal meetings of ward representatives.

This tendency to develop channels other than that of the committee meeting for the discussion of major strategic issues did not, however, mean that the value of the committee meeting itself had become negligible. At the very least, the formal accountability of the chief officer and chairman to the full committee could always be seen to provide some important safeguards against negligence or abuse; and we saw a number of occasions, particularly in the discussion of matters of more localized or tactical significance, where ordinary members of committee were able to make a decisive contribution, sometimes through providing a community-based viewpoint as opposed to the more specialized professional viewpoint of the departmental officers, and sometimes by being able to raise particular points of local knowledge which had been overlooked in the technical assessments within the departments. The points at which these latter contributions arose tended to be determined very much by chance, depending largely on whether or not a particular committee happened to include a representative of a particular ward, or an employee of a particular firm, or a resident of a particular neighbourhood.

It became evident to us, however, that the significance of the committee meeting should not be judged solely according to its direct contributions to the decision-making process. Attendance at committee could also be regarded as the principal means through which councillors could gain an understanding of what was involved in the running of public services; it was here that new members were brought face to face with the difficulty of sharing limited public resources between many community needs, and with the various forms of constraint imposed by central government departments; and it was here that they could develop a familiarity with the various mechanisms, such as the rate estimates and the capital programme, through which departmental claims for resources had to be justified.

Attendance on two or more committees meant that every member of Council was given some opportunity to appreciate factors such as these from the point of view of more than one public service; and, although it could be argued that committee attendance over a period of years was not the only way or necessarily the most effective way of acquiring such experience, our impression was that the committee experience of members made a substantial contribution to the level of realism in the all-important policy discussions of the majority party group, and also to the level of effectiveness of those members who in the course of time were selected to serve as committee chairman or vice-chairmen.

So far as the members of the minority party were concerned, there were not many occasions when their attendance at committee could be seen to have any direct influence on the processes of decision. With only a minority of members on any one committee, the opposition would rarely find itself in a position to sway a committee vote; and, as most committee meetings were held in private, there was little political capital to be made from formal expressions of dissent in the committee room. However, it was apparent that attendance at committees could at least provide the opposition party with an important channel through which to keep itself informed about the course of events within the local authority, and thus had the indirect effect of providing both for more effective opposition in the Council Chamber, and for more effective government than would otherwise have been possible in the event of a change in power.

THE ROLE OF THE POLITICAL GROUP

As we saw in discussing the significance of the monthly Council meeting, the pre-council group meeting of all members of a political party (whether it be the majority or minority party on the Council) could fulfil the important function of giving the rank-and-file member a feeling that he had some say in the matters he was required to support or oppose in the Council Chamber; and so far as the majority party was concerned, we saw that the group meeting could also fulfil a more positive role in relation to the policy-forming machinery of the Council, by providing a forum for the debate of particularly controversial issues at the stage before a formal committee decision was reached.

Within the unofficial setting of the group meeting, we were able to see the elected members giving much less inhibited expression to their views than in the committee room or the Council Chamber; and it was here that we heard the most persuasive advocacy of the interests of particular sectors of the community – whether schoolchildren, old people, ratepayers, tenants of municipal housing, or residents of some particular neighbourhood or street. There was a constant sense of the direct exposure of the elected member to the many conflicting pressures of the electorate and, for this reason, the resolution of conflicts through discussion within the party group often appeared to us to embody a higher level of realism than did attempts to reach decisions involving similar conflicts of interest either in the committee meeting or in the departmental office. However, at the same time we were able to see some of the risks involved in referring the more complex strategic issues for discussion within the unofficial framework of the party group: there was always a strong possibility that, meeting in a politically charged atmosphere and deprived of the guidance of their professional advisers, the members might find themselves becoming committed to resolutions which would subsequently prove difficult to translate into practical courses of action.

Although means were constantly being sought in Coventry for promoting more purposive discussion of strategic planning problems within the Council's official decision-making system, the key issue always remained whether this could be achieved in such a way as to convince the rank-and-file members of the majority party that they could retain adequate control as a group over the decisions for which they would all ultimately be held accountable at the annual municipal elections.

CO-ORDINATION AND THE ROLE OF THE SENIOR COMMITTEE

In our representation of the committee processes in *Figure 12*, one of the options which we considered was that a committee might refer a matter which it found difficult to resolve on its own to another 'senior' committee, which in most circumstances would be the central Policy Committee of the Council. However, during part of our time in Coventry, it was the practice for matters of transportation to be referred not to this committee but to the more specialized Traffic Policy Committee, formed in 1965 as a meeting-ground for chairmen and vice-chairmen with a common concern in this particular sector of the Council's activities.

Neither of these committees, however, dealt exclusively in matters referred upwards by other committees. Many of the strategic problems which we discussed in the previous chapter, such as that of the housing development programme or that of public transport policy, could be seen in advance to cross the boundaries of responsibility of individual specialist committees, and for this reason tended to be brought directly for discussion in the Policy or Traffic Policy Committee as soon as the need for committee guidance had been identified by the officers. Because the attendance at such meetings tended to include many of the more influential members of the majority party, as well as many of the more senior officers of the corporation, the full implications of the problems concerned tended to emerge more clearly than in the meetings of the more specialist committees: however, whenever the field of choice was a complex one, members still tended to experience considerable difficulty in giving clear-cut guidance on the courses of action to be followed. Consequently, many of the more strategic items tended to end up by being referred either to the officers for further technical appraisal or alternatively to the majority party group for a fuller and less inhibited discussion of their political implications. Some of the strategic problems which combined high levels of both technical and political complexity would tend to come up for discussion many times both in the departmental offices and in the majority party group. From our position as observers, it was apparent to us that processes of decision-making and policy formation were in fact taking place in both settings in parallel, in the sense that alternative courses of action were all the time being formulated, compared, and rejected, while group commitments were gradually shifting and becoming more clear cut.

We were led therefore to see the principal role of the senior committee as that of providing a channel of communication between those taking part in these two separate policy-forming processes, the departmental and the political; and we observed that the effectiveness of this channel tended to vary according to whether the particular members and officers who came together in the committee room were also those who made the leading contributions in the departmental discussions or in the political group meetings. In those cases where the flow of communication between the department and the party group was most clearly inadequate, it was not surprising that when officers and members eventually come together around the committee table – often only at a stage when the formulation of a proposal by the officers was well advanced – there were sometimes some painful mutual adjustments to be made.

In 1967, a decision was taken to give the main Policy Committee, whose role had until then been officially regarded as an advisory one, more explicit powers to lay down policy directives for other committees to follow. The committee began to meet at more frequent intervals, and a number of decisions of policy were initiated at Policy Committee level in relation to fields such as housing, education, and car-parking. The chairman, as unofficial leader of the Council, was himself given powers to settle any more limited matters of dispute between committees. It was not surprising that this change in the role of the Policy Committee was resisted by some members of the specialist committees directly concerned, who complained that they had not been adequately consulted in advance on matters which directly affected the discharge of their own responsibilities. By the end of 1967, the new role of the Policy Committee had become a matter of considerable controversy between the two political parties in Coventry.

There were times when the Traffic Policy Committee, working in a more limited field than the main Policy Committee and including an *ex officio* representation of all relevant chairmen and vice-chairmen, appeared to show promise of becoming an effective vehicle for the co-ordination of policies in a sector of the Council's affairs in which many committees and many departments had a common interest. However, the somewhat variable level of achievement of this committee in practice bore out our general conclusion that the effectiveness of any channel for communication between officers and members, at whatever level of seniority, must be dependent not only on the members' depth of appreciation of the problems concerned, but also on the provision by officers of an adequate flow of relevant information as to alternative courses of action and their implications.

THE RESOURCE-CONTROLLING COMMITTEES AND THEIR CHAIRMEN

In our introduction to the Council's internal organization in Chapter 1, we listed three committees other than the main Policy Committee which exercised a degree of oversight over all services of the local authority: Establishment and General Administration, Finance, and Planning and Redevelopment. In Chapter 2, we touched on the roles of these three committees, and of the Policy Committee itself, in the four central activities of manpower, financial, developmental, and land-use planning: and we drew attention to the interdependence of these four planning activities as aspects of the total activity through which resources were procured and deployed for the future benefit of different sectors of the local community.

It is possible to draw a number of parallels between the roles of the four committees concerned, as shown in *Table 5*. Each committee could in effect be seen as controlling its own distinctive form of resource budget, which served as a framework for the total forward planning of the resource concerned. In each case, the committee's responsibilities extended not only to the periodic review and revision of the budget with which it was concerned, but also to the adjudication of claims for the allocation or re-allocation of resources during the interval between such periods of more general review. In each case, claims might from time to time be received on behalf of any of the local authority services, having been submitted either in the name of the specialist committee concerned or, in the case of claims for changes in departmental establishments, directly in the name of the chief officer of the department. The need to adjudicate between such claims inevitably gave the committee responsible for the resource budget a direct interest in ensuring that the resources it allocated would be used to good effect, and we were able to see the various ways in which this requirement was met; through the development of work study, organization and methods, and staff-training activities in the case of the departmental establishments, of cost-control systems in the case of the rate estimates, and of various types of town-planning standard in relation to the development plan. It was only in the case of the capital programme – in effect serving as the 'budget' for allocation of developmental priorities – that the controlling committee appeared to lack suitable mechanisms for ensuring that the priorities allocated (in the form of statements as to the year in which construction of particular schemes should start) were likely to be put to good effect in practice. In the case of this budget alone, the Council had not during our period in Coventry succeeded in developing procedures for monitoring achievement against intention with the result that the capital programme tended to develop the runaway characteristics which we illustrated in *Figure 4*.

In Coventry, we were able to see how both the Planning and Redevelopment and the Finance Committees exercised certain of their more routine control functions through sub-committees, meeting at fortnightly and weekly intervals respectively. In the case of these two committees and also the Establishment and General Administration Committee, we saw a good deal of evidence that the processes of repeated involvement in the adjudication of claims tended to give the elected members concerned a much broader view of the activities of the Council than was available to those who belonged only to the more specialist committees; also, it was evident to us that the chairman of a resource-controlling committee, through his

Table 5   *A comparison of resource-planning activities*

Planning activity	*Manpower planning*	*Financial planning*	*Developmental planning*	*Land-use planning*
Corresponding resource budget	Departmental establishments	Rate estimates	Capital programme	Development plan
CONTROLLING COMMITTEE	ESTABLISH-MENT & GEN. ADMIN.	FINANCE	POLICY	PLANNING & REDEVELOP-MENT
Nature of principal resource controlled through budget of this committee	Manpower	Money	Priority (i.e. position in the queue of development projects)	Land
Claims against budget submitted on behalf of:	all departments	all committees	all committees	private developers plus all committees
Means of ensuring effective use of resource by claimants	O & M, work study, training facilities	accountancy, etc.	—	application of design standards, etc.

Principal relationships between resource-planning activities	*Manpower planning*	*Financial planning*		
	revenue implications of changes in establishments, rates of pay and allowances			
		Financial planning	*Developmental planning*	
		revenue implications of loan charges and running costs of capital projects		
			Developmental planning	*Land-use planning*
			developmental implications of proposed changes in land use	
	Manpower planning		*Developmental planning*	
	staffing requirements of departments concerned in implementing capital programme			
		Financial planning		*Land-use planning*
		implications of land-use changes for rateable value, etc.		

more intimate involvement in the processes of reviewing his budget and his more frequent contacts with his chief officer, could be in a particularly strong position to contribute to the formulation of the overall policies of the Council.

In 1967, a decision was taken in Coventry to bring all four resource budgets within the general area of responsibility of the Policy Committee. However, it was not initially clear to us how significant the effects of this change would be in practice; it was only to be expected that much of the reality of control over the shaping of each resource budget would continue to be concentrated in the hands of the chairman of the committee responsible for adjudication of claims, advised by his own particular chief officer, because of their more intimate understanding of the structure of the budget concerned. At the time the change was introduced, all the chairmen of the resource-controlling committees were in fact also members of the central Policy Committee; however, the crucial question appeared to be one of how far a full understanding of the mechanisms and constraints of each of the four budgets could be expected to develop within the group setting of the Policy Committee itself.

CHANGES IN THE PATTERN OF INTERLOCKING MEMBERSHIPS

Because of the central role of the four resource-controlling committees, and the interconnections between their functions which we describe at the foot of *Table 5*, it was not surprising that the pattern of cross-membership between them often

Figure 13

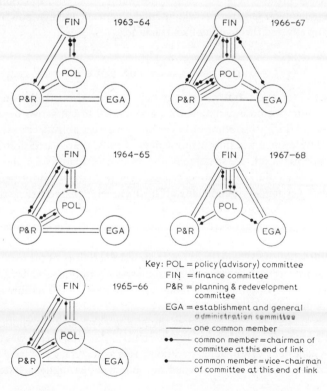

Key: POL = policy (advisory) committee
FIN = finance committee
P&R = planning & redevelopment committee
EGA = establishment and general administration committee

——— one common member

●●——— common member = chairman of committee at this end of link

●——— common member = vice-chairman of committee at this end of link

appeared to exert a particularly significant influence on the overall planning process. On the one hand, we were able to witness a number of instances where the
degree of co-ordination in forward planning was clearly assisted by the interlocking
of memberships within this central group, and especially by the cross-representation of chairmen on each others' committees; but on the other hand we also saw
a number of contrasting instances where lack of such cross-representation led to
misunderstanding and conflict between the committees concerned.

During the four years of our research, the pattern of cross-representation in the
four central committees was never a stable one, and the pattern of change over this
period is shown diagrammatically in *Figure 13*. Of the various changes from one
year to another, most of those which concerned chairmen and vice-chairmen
could be explained by the local standing order by which chairmen were required
to retire after a three-year term (the Policy Committee was exempted from this
rule, so as to allow it to function as a continuing instrument of political control).
With only one exception, the bonds between committees shown in *Figure 13* were
in fact provided by members of the majority party; although the minority party
was by convention allowed some representation on all committees with the exception of the Policy Committee itself, representation of the minority party within the
central group of committees tended in practice to be of a fragmentary character
with few cross-linkages. The result was, inevitably, that co-ordination between
opposition policies for land use, developmental, financial, and manpower planning
could only be effected through unofficial channels.

DEPARTMENTAL CO-ORDINATION AND THE ROLE OF THE TOWN CLERK

Just as many of the more strategic issues which we were able to follow in Coventry
cut across committee boundaries, so they also tended to cut across departmental
boundaries, and during our research in Coventry we were able to witness a number
of gradual developments in informal practices of collaborative decision-making at
interdepartmental level. Most notably, the raising of matters for discussion in
Policy and Traffic Policy Committees tended to be preceded by informal consultations between departments, and many of the documents placed before these committees carried the signatures of three, four, or even more chief officers. The most
frequently recurring names were those of the Town Clerk, the City Treasurer, the
City Architect and Planning Officer, and the City Engineer, each of whom headed
a department which had some direct concern in the activities of the local authority
as a whole as well as in the provision of certain specific public services, and each of
whom played an important role in relation to one or more of the resource-planning
activities identified in *Table 5*.

In the debate in Coventry as to how the processes of departmental co-ordination might be made more effective, one constantly recurring theme was the role of
the Town Clerk. The Clerk, in his traditional role as secretary and legal adviser to
the Council, had always been accorded the somewhat ambiguous status of 'first

among equals' of the chief officers of the corporation. In 1954 however, following a study of the Council's internal administration by a Treasury organization and methods team, the Council accepted a proposal that they should confer on the Town Clerk new responsibilities as the corporation's Chief Administrative Officer. Among other responsibilities, the Clerk was expected to 'take a continuing interest in the effectiveness and economy of all the administrative arrangements throughout the Corporation's administration and ensure that administrative activities with which two or more departments are concerned are effectively co-ordinated' and in addition 'to maintain a broad view of the balance and effectiveness of arrangements made to carry out the policy laid down by the Council and to bring to the notice of departments (and if necessary committees) the need for any change'.

However, this potentially more powerful role also had its ambiguities, because of the explicit accountability of each chief officer to his own controlling committee, and the difficulty of defining any clear dividing line between matters of 'policy' and matters of 'administration'. A further attempt in 1966 to define the powers of the Clerk in relation to co-ordination went some way towards the separation of his interdepartmental role from the more traditional duties of his department, which now became the direct responsibility of his deputy under the new title of Associate Town Clerk.

Among the consequences of the newly defined role of the Town Clerk was the consolidation and more formal recognition of a number of practices of interdepartmental co-ordination which had been developing at an informal level over the years. In particular, the Clerk himself became acknowledged as leader of a small co-ordinating group of chief officers including also the City Treasurer, the City Architect and Planning Officer, and the City Engineer; while at a less senior level the practice of holding fortnightly interdepartmental meetings to control the implementation of the city's redevelopment programme was continued, with any items which were seen to have policy implications being referred upwards for consideration by the 'board of chief officers'. One significant new development was the formation of the transportation study team as an independent unit with no direct departmental affiliations; when this team started work, it was this same team of four chief officers, with the addition of the Transport Manager and a representative of the Ministry of Transport, who formed the basis of the steering group which was set up to maintain a continuing review over its progress.

In 1967, on the vesting of new powers in the Policy Committee, the powers of the Clerk were further increased by giving him the formal right to scrutinize all matters submitted for inclusion in committee agendas, and to refer those which appeared to have major policy implications directly to the Policy Committee. The Clerk was thus officially placed in a more strategic position in the total decision-making process, so that the formal processes which we originally outlined in *Figure 11* were in effect modified by the insertion of an additional channel for direct submission of items to the senior committee of Council.

PLANNING AND ORGANIZATIONAL CHANGE

All these various developments in the processes of decision-making, in so far as we were able to observe them during the period of our research, we were able to interpret as forms of response to a growing awareness of the need to adapt existing organizational forms to the increasing complexities of planning in a large local authority. Members and officers alike were only too ready to acknowledge the difficulty of developing satisfactory processes for coping with decision-making at the more strategic level, and to concede the imperfections of the existing mechanisms for interdepartmental co-ordination, of the committee meeting as a vehicle for policy exploration, and of the political group meeting as a setting for resolution of long-term planning problems.

However, the willingness of both officers and members to countenance change was limited by many factors, including above all the rifts created by the fundamental distinction between the salaried professional and the elected layman. On occasion, this could lead to mistrust of members by officers, arising from a fear that their judgment might be distorted by their political motivations or by an unbalanced appreciation of the practical implications of major policy decisions; and also to mistrust of officers by members, arising from a suspicion that the officers had the ability to manipulate the flow of information in such a way as to reduce the members' effective powers of strategic choice. Despite the considerable evidence we saw of mutual confidence between officer and member, both in the committee room and in less formal settings, relationships across the interface between the two sides were not often completely free from these elements of mistrust, which would always combine to limit the scope for effective change in the decision-making system, and to ensure that many of the most crucial contributions to the policy-forming process continued to be made behind the closed doors either of the departmental office or the party political group.

We have no reason to believe that this observation applies uniquely to Coventry, and, indeed, the experience of certain other local authorities in attempting to introduce innovations in internal organization within the last few years suggests that it may have a more general validity throughout British local government.

THE CITY COUNCIL AND THE RESEARCH TEAM

In this chapter, we have attempted to appraise the internal processes of decision-making in Coventry from the basis of the opportunities we were given to observe them at first hand over the four years from 1964 to 1967. However, our role was not always a purely observational one during this time. From the start, we had many opportunities for personal discussions with key officers and elected members, most of whom were prepared to talk very freely not only about their own problems but also about their relationships with other participants in the decision-making process. After the first year or so of our fieldwork in Coventry, the flow of communication between Council and research team became less one-sided, as we reached a stage of being able to discuss with both officers and members some of the concepts which were then beginning to emerge from our research programme These discussions gave us the opportunity to test the extent to which our perceptions of the problems of strategic planning were in accord with the perceptions of the participants themselves. Some of our more important discussions involved not individuals but representative groups; groups of officers drawn from within particular departments, groups of chief officers convened on an interdepartmental basis, mixed groups of officers and members, and groups of elected members on their own, drawn from both the political parties represented on the Council.

These encounters were of much value to us as a research team, but of course they meant that on occasions we found ourselves drawn from our role of observers of the system to a role of more active involvement in its evolution. It is difficult to judge how far our informal exchanges of views on topical matters such as the structure of committees and the mechanisms for review of the capital programme may have made a contribution to the course of events in Coventry, because there was sometimes a close accord between the conclusions of our analyses and the views of the people most directly concerned; however, there were two particular occasions when the advice of the Institute was sought more explicitly on matters of current concern to the Council. The first occasion concerned the Traffic Policy Committee's request for the drawing up of a co-ordinated programme for transportation research, and in this case we were able to suggest to the chief officers concerned how the principles of network analysis might be used to formulate a long-term programme embracing many elements of policy decision and many activities designed to improve the basis of those decisions; the draft network diagram then developed by the Institute formed the basis of the more detailed programme subsequently developed by the officers and approved by the City Council and the Ministry of Transport. We will refer to and expand upon the main principles of the methodology then adopted in Chapter 11, when we come to discuss a fictitious case study in sub-regional planning.

The second occasion on which the advice of the research team was sought on a particular topic was when the need for improved machinery for co-ordination in policy planning came up for discussion in late 1965 and early 1966. The research team was then able to suggest some general principles which might be relevant to the development of any future system of co-ordination between committees and departments, with stress on the need for more explicit machinery for the co-ordination of information in support of the interdepartmental planning activity. These suggestions, together with some previous proposals by the Town Clerk as to possible improvements in the system of interdepartmental co-ordination, formed the basis of the proposals for the new role of the Town Clerk which were put forward and approved by the Council in March 1966.

In both these instances, events after the intervention of the research team took a course which we would have found it difficult to foresee in advance; however, in following the repercussions of these limited interventions in the internal processes of the City Council, we were able to obtain certain insights into the problems and pressures of the decision-making system at a more intimate level than would have been possible through observation alone. This experience in itself we feel to have been of considerable value to us in formulating the more generalized suggestions for future evolution of the processes of local planning which we develop in Parts II, III, and IV.

4. Information and uncertainty in planning

So far, our concern has been to build up a picture of the planning activities of Coventry City Council in breadth, first from the point of view of the range of problems encountered and then from the point of view of the processes through which these problems were tackled. However, to obtain a fuller understanding of the difficulties facing the decision-makers, we will now find it necessary to select a few of the more far-reaching problems which came up for discussion during the period of our research, and to analyse them in rather greater depth.

In this chapter, we shall take two of these problems in particular, one concerned with the future of Coventry as a shopping centre and the other concerned with the design of the city road network, and make an analysis of the many different types of information which were assembled by the officers concerned, and the many kinds of assumption which they found it necessary to introduce, in order to provide a basis for decision by the City Council. From this basis, we shall go on to develop a classification of certain distinctive types of uncertainty with which all those engaged in any planning activity must be able to contend. The concepts of uncertainty which we develop in this chapter will help us in Part II in our discussion of the general requirements for an effective planning process, in Part III in our development of a relevant technology, and in Part IV in our discussion of appropriate organizational forms.

In Chapter 2, we saw that many of the dominant strategic problems which faced Coventry City Council during the period from 1963 to 1967 became woven into the fabric of the Development Plan Review, and we described how, during the course of the review process, the Department of Architecture and Planning – in collaboration with other relevant departments – brought out a series of survey documents on important topics such as roads, employment, shopping, and housing, with a view not only to discussion and formulation of policy within the Council, but also to the encouragement of wider public involvement in the planning process.

Each of these survey documents could be seen as making a direct contribution to the decision-making process in that it presented a set of recommendations relating to the future development of the city, even though many of these recommendations concerned matters of principle rather than detail and were put forward essentially as elements in a proposed brief for the preparation of more localized land-use plans. In each case, the authors of the document took a good deal of care to explain the data and the assumptions on which their final recommendations were based. This explicitness of presentation was of considerable value to us as a research team, in that it gave us a starting-point from which to carry out some detailed logical analyses of the 'anatomy' of the planning proposals concerned.

The two reports which we will consider in this chapter, that on Shopping in Coventry and that on the Coventry Road System, differed widely both in the nature of their recommendations and in the choice of analytical technique. However, both were recognized to have strategic implications for the future evolution of the city, and both were extensively debated in Coventry during the period of our research. The report on shopping was the first in the series of review documents to be issued after our arrival in Coventry, and so we were able to observe the various initial reactions to it at first hand; the report on the road system, although it had already been issued some months before our arrival, continued to have repercussions within and beyond the City Council throughout the duration of our research.

THE PROBLEMS OF SHOPPING IN THE CITY CENTRE

The report 'Shopping in Coventry', issued in 1964 by the Department of Architecture and Planning [13], arrived at over twenty different recommendations, many of which concerned design and layout standards for future shopping facilities both within and beyond the central area of the city. However, the recommendation which attracted most attention, both within the Council and in the columns of the local press, concerned the additional reservation of land to be made for future shopping development in the city centre, over and above that allocated in the original Development Plan approved in 1957. It was proposed that an additional four acres should be reserved for shopping within the central area, whose confines were at that time clearly demarcated by the line already agreed for the city's inner ring road. This figure was based on an estimated requirement for an additional 100,000 square feet of retail floor space by 1981, the year chosen as the planning horizon for the Development Plan Review.

This particular proposal was supported in the document by a good deal of quantitative analysis, as opposed to the more qualitative assessments on which many of the recommendations for more detailed design standards were based. We will therefore concentrate our attention in the following pages on this one recommendation which, as we shall see, raised some important questions for the future of Coventry as a centre of attraction for the surrounding region.

The recommendation to allow for an additional 100,000 square feet of retail floor space in the city centre was arrived at by the planners in a way which we can outline as follows (*Figure 14*).

In this diagram, we introduce some conventions which we will develop further as this chapter proceeds. Each block represents a particular body of information which was taken into account at some stage in the derivation of the final proposal, and each of the linkages shown between blocks represents an operation of combining two different bodies of information to produce a third. In this example, the operations are simple arithmetical ones of division and subtraction which can be traced through without any difficulty; as we shall see later, this may not always be the case, particularly where the information within a block is of a qualitative rather than a quantitative nature, or where it consists of a more complex array of numerical estimates whose manipulation requires recourse to more sophisticated methods than those of simple arithmetic.

Figure 14

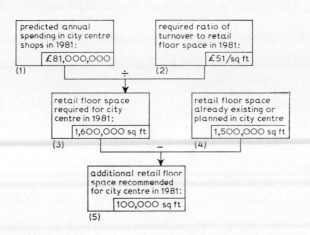

Figure 14 shows that the final estimate of additional floor space required rested on a combination of the three separate estimates shown in blocks 1, 2, and 4. The last of these (block 4, relating to the retail floor space already existing or planned in the central area) was relatively easy to arrive at, given a clear-cut demarcation of the extent of the central area by the proposed line of the inner ring road. However, the other two estimates (block 1, relating to the future volume of spending in the city centre, and block 2, relating to the appropriate ratio of turnover to retail floor space) are clearly much more open to question, so we will now consider each of them rather more closely.

THE PREDICTION OF FUTURE SPENDING

The prediction of the level of future spending was, as the Coventry shopping report made clear, in itself an exercise which involved the combination of many different kinds of information drawn from many different sources. In Figure 15 we use the same kind of block diagram as in Figure 14 in order to trace through the chain of argument used by the planners in this earlier stage of their analysis.

The final block in this diagram (block G) corresponds to the first block (block 1) in Figure 14, so the two diagrams can in fact be merged to give a representation of the whole procedure from initial prediction of future expenditure per head to final prescription of additional floor-space requirements.

The data and assumptions used in blocks (A) and (B) below were derived mainly from national rather than local sources, although certain adjustments were made by the planners to allow for the higher levels of earnings in Coventry than in the country as a whole. The prediction of future growth in the level of personal spending of course required some very basic assumptions about the future of the national and local economies. The local population estimates in block (D) were derived from the earlier review document on the Coventry City Region, in which the planners set out to define the approximate bounds of Coventry's wider sphere of

Figure 15

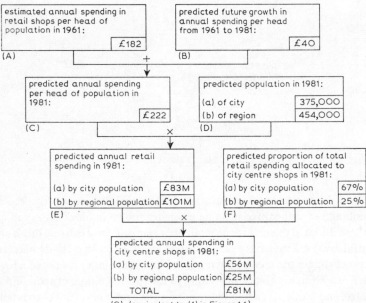

(G) (equivalent to (1) in Figure 14)

influence, and to make a general assessment of the potential for growth within this area. It is important to note that these population estimates required not only the choice of certain assumptions as to local and national population trends, but also the choice of certain assumptions as to the actions that might be taken by central and local government in response to those trends: in particular, the decisions of central government in relation to the location of industry, and the decisions of local planning authorities in relation to the release of land for housing development. This meant in effect that the City Council itself, through its plans for housing and possibly for other forms of development, could expect to exercise some degree of control over the realization of the population estimates appearing in block (D). This raises in specific form the important general problem of interdependence between one planning activity and another; we will have more to say on this topic later in this chapter.

Figure 16

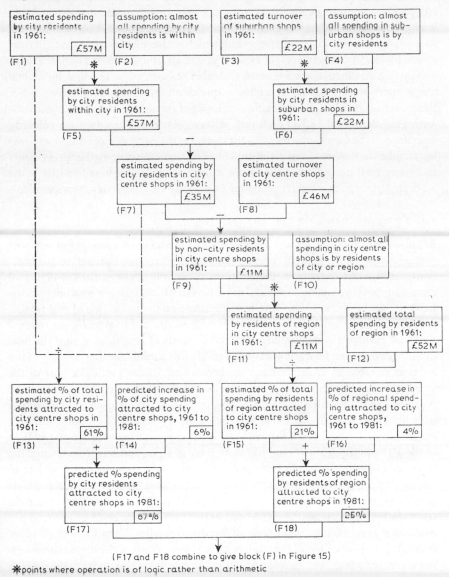

(F17 and F18 combine to give block (F) in Figure 15)
*points where operation is of logic rather than arithmetic

The information appearing in block (F) of *Figure 15* was derived by the planners through a particularly devious series of calculations, because of a lack of direct information as to the existing spending habits of the residents of the city and of the surrounding region, and in particular the factors which might be expected to induce them to spend within the central area. The indirect argument used by the planners is traced in *Figure 16*.

This diagram indicates that the prediction of future tendencies to shop in the city centre was quite a complex exercise not only of arithmetic but also of logic. The information used in this exercise came from three distinct sources: first, the data on population and personal spending which we have already discussed in relation to blocks (A), (B), and (D) of *Figure 15*; second, the results of a survey held in Coventry with the co-operation of the Chamber of Commerce, in which individual shopkeepers were asked to complete a questionnaire requesting, among other things, some confidential information on levels of turnover; and, third, some subjective estimates of the effect on future patterns of trade of certain other planning intentions of the City Council itself – for instance, the provision of additional parking facilities in the central area, the implementation of the proposed improvements to the city road network, and the future scaling down of shopping facilities in the inner suburbs which was envisaged in the Council's existing redevelopment plans.

THE COMPOUNDING OF UNCERTAINTIES

Because the estimates shown in *Figure 16* were derived from a number of different sources, their validity must of course be subject to several separate sets of qualifications, relating for instance to the accuracy of sample surveys, the credibility of certain simplifying assumptions, and the extent to which it may or may not be justifiable to base predictions for the long-term future on the projection of past trends. Any progression through a series of steps such as those shown in *Figure 16* must therefore involve a compounding of different kinds of uncertainty until the final estimates can be put forward with considerably less confidence than can any of the intermediate blocks of information in themselves. In the particular part of the analysis covered by *Figure 16*, it might be expected that some of the most sensitive points would be those where estimates of demand based on household expenditure were linked directly to other estimates based on the results of the local turnover survey, as at (F7) and (F9): for instance, if the expenditure estimate of £57M in block (F1) was thought to be subject to an error of 5 per cent either way, while the turnover estimates in blocks (F3) and (F8) were each thought to be subject to errors of 10 per cent either way, then the application of standard statistical methods would suggest that the resulting estimate of £11M in block (F11) might, on certain conservative assumptions,* be expected to be subject to an error of up to 66 per cent either way. Following the train of argument further down to block (F15) of *Figure 16*, the proportion of the total spending by residents of the region surrounding Coventry which was actually drawn to the city centre in 1961 might then be

* Technical footnote: assuming that the limits quoted represent 2σ points of independent normal distributions, that any errors in the two turnover estimates are fully correlated but are independent of the error in the expenditure estimates, and that the possibility of errors in the assumptions (F2), (F4), and (F10) can be ignored.

impossible to pinpoint with reasonable confidence anywhere between limits of 7 and 35 per cent, even assuming that the effects of further uncertainties in block (F12) can be ignored.

The predictions of future changes in the proportions of city and regional spending which will be attracted to the city centre shops, appearing in blocks (F14) and (F16) of *Figure 16*, are subject to uncertainties of a rather different kind. Not only do they assume that the Council will adhere firmly to its intentions of improving access to the city centre by provision of new roads and generous car-parking facilities, but also they rest on some implicit assumptions as to how far the local authorities of the other towns and cities which compete for shopping custom within the region will take parallel actions to increase the attraction and accessibility of their own central areas. This raises an even more fundamental question: how justifiable is it likely to be, in this or any similar exercise, to treat the prediction of future shopping demand in the city centre as an operation which should logically precede the prescription of an appropriate level of shopping supply? If there is any reason for suspecting that the level of supply will of itself be a major factor in stimulating future demand, then some modification to the logic of the planning procedure may be called for. This brings us back to a consideration of the later steps of the planners' analysis, whereby the prediction of total shopping demand was converted into a recommendation to provide for an additional 100,000 square feet of retail floor space within the central area.

THE PRESCRIPTION OF FUTURE SHOPPING CAPACITY

Returning to the original diagram of *Figure 14* (p. 71), we see that the crucial transition from a prediction of future shopping demand in block (1) to a prescription of future shopping supply in block (3) was effected by introducing an assessment of the most satisfactory relationship of annual turnover to retail floor space in the 'horizon' year of 1981. The suggested ratio of £51 per square foot represents an estimated increase of about 40 per cent since 1961, assuming a continuation into the future of an upward trend observed over the preceding five years.

The use of this ratio provides an illustration of the 'requirements' approach to planning which, as is argued in the book by McKean [19], is prevalent in many fields of governmental activity; in this approach, the appropriate level of supply for some facility is assessed by first making an estimate of demand, and then applying some generally acceptable numerical standard for converting demand to supply. Despite its attractions of simplicity, McKean points out that this approach inevitably carries with it the drawback of suppressing any direct consideration of the effects of alternative courses of action.

In considering the effect of applying the standard of £51 per square foot to the assessment of shopping provision, it is important to note from the original block diagram of *Figure 14* that the additional floor space finally recommended represents only a 7 per cent increase over that already existing or planned. This means that the use of a slightly higher ratio of turnover to retail floor space would have led to the conclusion that existing plans were adequate, while a slightly lower ratio could easily have doubled or trebled the estimate of additional floor space to be allowed for. This indicates a need to examine closely the justification for selecting a ratio of £51 as opposed to an alternative of (say) £41 or £61. How far does the chosen ratio represent some expected point of equilibrium in the provision of shopping facilities, which market forces will tend inevitably to seek irrespective of any interventions which may be made by the City Council? Is it justifiable, in other words, to regard the chosen ratio as a purely predictive assumption, or should it rather be regarded as setting a prescriptive standard?

THE PRACTICAL IMPLICATIONS OF THE SHOPPING RECOMMENDATION

The true significance of the chosen ratio of floor space to turnover might in reality be expected to lie somewhere between these two extremes of prediction and prescription. To explore its significance more fully, it is necessary to speculate as to what the practical effects might be on the future of the city if a marginal change were made in the amount of retail floor space proposed in the planners' report on city centre shopping.

Inevitably, any speculation of this kind requires an ability to trace through a complex pattern of possible future consequences. Supposing, for instance, that a marginal increase had been made (say 10 per cent) in the estimated requirement for retail floor space in the city centre, the first consequence would have been a change in the brief of those other members of the Planning Department who were responsible for preparing designs for the future development of the city centre as a balanced whole, for submission within the context of the Development Plan Review. This modified brief would have required them to reserve marginally more land for shopping development, and possibly for associated facilities such as car parks, at the expense of other forms of central area development. How quickly the additional floor space provided for in this modified design could in fact be expected to materialize (if at all) would depend on the expected assessments of property developers as to the investment opportunities thus created, on expected levels of growth in the national economy, and possibly on the readiness of the City Council to undertake shopping development of its own at certain strategic points in the central area. In turn, the expected consequences of actually achieving a marginal increase in the rate of shopping development might include a marginal tendency for rents to be reduced in order to attract new traders, a marginal reduction in levels of turnover and profit for existing traders, a marginal increase in employment opportunities (particularly for women), a marginal increase in the range of choice for consumers – possibly accompanied by a marginal reduction in price levels – and a marginal rise in the rateable value of the city. Of course, one would not necessarily expect these various marginal adjustments in the commercial activity of the city to be governed by any simple relationships of proportionality, either to each other or to the assumed 10 per cent change in the planners' estimate of retail floor space requirement.

It is probable, in particular, that the consequences of any planned increase in the retail floor space within the central area would be dependent to a large extent on the character of the retailers who could be attracted. If, as the planners in fact suggested in their report, any increase in the total floor-space provision could be exploited in such a way as to make good a generally recognized deficiency of large 'quality' shops within the city, then this might be expected to be particularly influential in attracting new trade from the region beyond the city boundary; in which case, the additional benefit to the city might be more than proportional to any marginal increase in the aggregate provision of retail floor space within the central area.

These considerations suggest that the question of whether or not more trade is ultimately drawn into the city centre may in practice be influenced by a whole complex of forces over which no local authority can ever expect to have more than a limited degree of control. The extent to which the various decision-makers involved in such a situation are dependent on assumptions as to each others' future intentions is explored more fully in Part II of the previously mentioned project paper by Paul Spencer [6], where the question of shopping in Coventry is discussed in relation to the concepts of the self-fulfilling and self-defeating prophecy.

The limited influence of the local authority on future shopping development within its area suggests that the achievement of accuracy in predicting future demand may in fact be a good deal less important than it might at first sight appear. Although the unambiguous determination of future land uses was officially demanded by the development plan procedures with which Coventry was required to conform at the time of the shopping study, the trend since then has been in the direction of greater flexibility and of more continuous review, with recognition of the possibility for adaptation to changing circumstances through conversion of land and property from one type of use to another.

However, it would be unrealistic to suppose that the case for flexibility absolves the local authority from all responsibility for decisions related to future shopping development. However limited its control may be, the local authority still has certain real powers of intervention in the developing situation within its area. Within the limits of these powers, it is indisputable that some freedom of choice exists, and that the use made of this freedom of choice will have certain real consequences, implying some redistribution of costs and benefits among different sectors of the population. Clearly, there is a danger that the policy implications of this redistribution will tend to be masked by the adoption of a 'requirements' approach based on an assumption of a prescribed numerical standard for conversion of turnover estimates into retail floor-space requirements.

These implications emerged clearly during our observation of the progress of the report on shopping through the successive stages of discussion in the Planning and Redevelopment Committee, of submission for comment to representative bodies, of debate in the Council Chamber, and of discussion in the columns of the local and specialist press. We found that a number of the elected members were concerned to question the assumptions underlying the planners' predictions of future demand, to offer suggestions as to what the future effects of providing 'too much' or 'too little' shopping capacity might be, and to speculate about ways and means of attracting more 'quality' traders into the city.

Since the period when the Coventry shopping study was carried out (during 1963) research workers have made a good deal of progress in the development of more sophisticated models for the planning of shopping development, taking more explicit account of factors such as competition between rival centres of attraction. The Coventry planners were of course aware of the deficiencies of existing techniques and were concerned to keep abreast of these subsequent improvements; and, in fact, in 1967 the City Architect and Planning Officer was appointed as a member of a working group set up under the auspices of the National Economic Development Office to carry out a systematic evaluation of the various models available, and their potential value as aids to those concerned in the actual decision process.

The main inference which we drew from our analysis of the Coventry shopping report, and our observation of reactions to its publication, was that it was necessary to regard the problem of planning the future shopping provision within a city centre as a problem of decision-making under many different kinds of uncertainty, including not only uncertainties of a purely predictive nature, but also uncertainties relating to the choice of appropriate value judgements, and uncertainties as to the future actions of the City Council and other agencies in certain related fields of planning activity.

We will return to consider these various classes of uncertainty in more general terms later in this chapter. Meanwhile, we will turn our attention to another of the survey documents prepared by the Coventry planners as a contribution to the Development Plan Review: the report on the Coventry Road System. This, as we shall see, differed from the shopping report in at least two important respects: in the much more elaborate models it made use of for the prediction of future demand, and in the substitution for the 'requirements' approach of a much more explicit comparison of alternative courses of action.

THE PREDICTION OF FUTURE TRAFFIC FLOWS

The object of the two-part report on the Coventry Road System [11] was to present the results of a substantial programme of research carried out over the period from 1961 to 1963 by a study team drawn jointly from the Department of Architecture and Planning and the City Engineer's Department. This research was initiated after it had become clear that the volume of traffic in the city was increasing at a rate well in excess of that predicted at the time the city's first Development Plan was formulated, and that the road pattern then proposed, which was formally approved in 1957, might well have to be modified drastically within the context of the forth-coming Development Plan Review.

The methods used by the joint roads team for obtaining new predictions of the demand for road travel were much more sophisticated than those used in the pre-diction of shopping demand in the city centre. These methods are described fully in the first volume of the report itself, and in the following diagram we confine our-selves to a bare outline of what was involved:

Figure 17

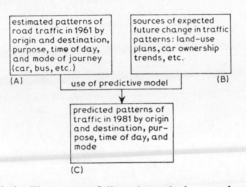

It is not possible in *Figure 17* to follow through the actual numerical steps in-volved in the prediction process, as in the equivalent diagram for the shopping prediction (*Figure 15*). This is because, for the purposes of road design, it was not sufficient for the planners to calculate a single aggregate estimate of 'demand'; rather, they required a large number of separate estimates of future traffic demands between different origins and destinations at different times of day and using different forms of transport.

The collection of detailed information of this kind, even for existing patterns of movement, was a major undertaking in itself and involved the use of a roadside traffic survey, a home interview survey, and a journey-to-work survey, the last of which required the co-operation of employers and employees at the major work centres within the city. By cross-checks between these different surveys, the study team was able to obtain some encouraging evidence as to the reliability of the estimates obtained. In assessing the potential sources of future change, however, the study team found it necessary to make a wide range of assumptions about car-ownership trends and about the future population and employment potentials of each of a set of 57 'generation zones', within the city boundary. Predictions had also to be made as to the future tendencies of people living in one zone of the city to make journeys to other zones, and for this purpose a particular algebraic formula was chosen, whose validity rested on the assumption that the volume of traffic between any pair of zones in 1981 would change in a way determined solely by the expected changes in the total number of journeys originating or terminating at either end.

In the choice of their predictive techniques, the study team was able to draw extensively on the experience of the large-scale transportation studies which were then under development in several urban areas in the United States (though not yet at that time in the United Kingdom). They were also able to arrange access to a

Map 2. Desire lines 1981 – journey to work trips
        Source: The Coventry Road System (*Coventry City Council, 1963*)

Employment zones

1. Central Area	11. Radford
2. Chapelfields	12. Foleshill
3. Holyhead Road	13. Courthouse Green
4. Canley/Torrington Avenue	14. Aldermans Green
5. Allesley	15. Whitley
6. Banner Lane	16. Humber Road
7. Browns Lane	17. Copsewood
8. Rowley Green	18. Binley
9. Holbrooks	19. Ryton/Baginton
10. Little Heath	20. Hillfields

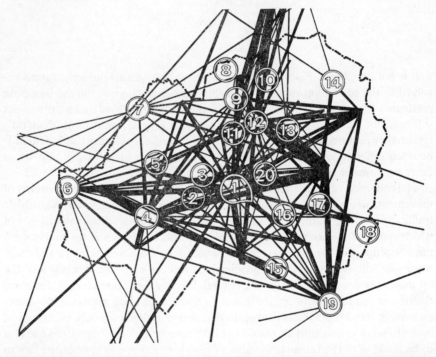

large electronic computer for the processing of the extensive arrays of information collected during their field surveys. The basic steps in the process of predicting demand for roads were in fact not dissimilar to those in the process of predicting shopping demand, even though the large volumes of information to be handled inevitably had the consequences of making the prediction process much more difficult for the layman to follow. One particularly difficult challenge for the study team concerned the presentation of the final sets of traffic predictions in such a form that their implications could be readily understood: in their report, the team in fact chose to use the device of a 'desire-line' diagram, consisting of an outline map of the city showing the traffic volumes between different origins and destinations by means of straight lines of proportionate thickness. Map 2 reproduces from the report on the Coventry Roads System a network of predicted desire lines for journeys to work in Coventry in 1981. This diagram is itself selective in that it shows only peak-hour journeys into and out of the principal employment zones (numbered from 1 to 20). Clearly, any attempt to superimpose further desire lines for other forms of traffic would make the diagram even more difficult to interpret as a guide to the requirements for a future road network.

THE COMPARISON OF ALTERNATIVE ROAD PATTERNS

With the help of the desire-line diagram reproduced above, and of their background knowledge of the physical characteristics of the city, the study team was in a position to start developing possible designs for the future city road network. The possibilities considered included in particular one based primarily on the construction of two new urban motor roads, linking the main industrial zones but avoiding the central area and linking up with each other to form an inverted 'Y' pattern. This new design differed considerably from that approved in the 1957 development plan (but still at that time only partially realized): the contrast is brought out in the two outline maps reproduced as *Maps 3* and *4* overleaf. In this case the thicknesses of lines represent varying standards of road construction rather than variations of predicted traffic flow as was the case in *Map 2*. The very thick lines indicate the approximate lines of the national M6 motorway and the two proposed urban motor roads; while the medium and thin lines indicate dual carriageway and other main roads respectively.

A number of other alternatives were also examined by the study team in varying degrees of detail, including at one extreme a 'minimum change' plan based on the option of retaining the existing pattern of roads virtually unchanged, and at the other extreme a more ambitious version of the inverted 'Y' pattern, in which the number of urban motor roads was increased so as to cope more completely with all anticipated flows of peak-hour commuter traffic; it was argued that this alternative might form the basis for a possible further stage of development should the basic 'Y' pattern prove inadequate.

Figure 18 attempts to show, in block diagram form, the processes which were used by the study team to arrive at a statement of preference between the two alternative designs illustrated in *Maps 3* and *4*. This diagram represents a downward extension of *Figure 17*. It can be seen that the information introduced in block (E) brings a new factor into the prediction process: the ability to predict how a road-user wishing to travel from point A to point B would select a route when

Map 3. 1957 Development Plan pattern – outline plan
Source: The Coventry Road System (*Coventry City Council, 1963*)

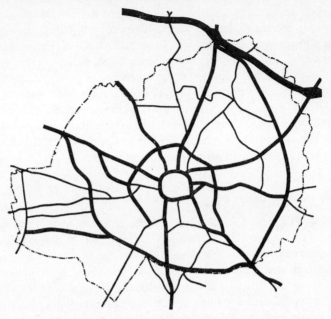

Map 4. Modified Development Plan pattern (inverted 'Y') – outline plan
Source: The Coventry Road System (*Coventry City Council, 1963*)

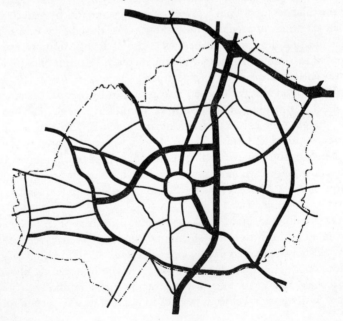

confronted with any particular configuration of the total road network. The study team describe in their report how they were unable to formulate sufficiently realistic decision rules to allow this assignment process to be carried out by computer, and so decided to rely on their own judgement and local knowledge to insert a whole series of assumptions as to the route which a particular type of road-user might select to travel from each possible origin to each possible destination, given a particular configuration of roads between them.

Figure 18

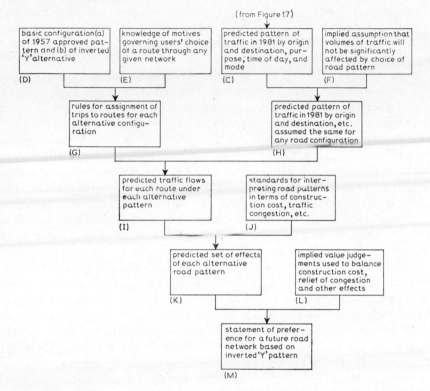

Block (F) of *Figure 18* brings out the implicit assumption that it is reasonable to ignore the effects that an improved road network might itself have in inducing fresh traffic, or that a more constrained network might have in reducing the effective level of demand: had this assumption not been considered acceptable, then block (H) would have had to include a reassessment of the predictive information in block (C) to take account of each of the alternative road networks proposed in block (D).

Blocks (I) to (M) of *Figure 18* attempt to reproduce in outline form the final stages through which the two alternative road patterns were assessed and compared in terms of construction cost, relief of traffic congestion, and other more intangible factors. The comparative levels of construction cost were set out in the report in the form of bar charts; these included an estimate of £11M for the 1957 approved pattern as compared with one of £23M for the higher capacity network of the inverted 'Y' alternative. The principal alternatives were also compared in terms of relief of traffic congestion by means of outline maps showing lengths of saturated road. We reproduce the maps presented for the 1957 approved pattern and the inverted 'Y' alternative as *Maps 5* and *6*.

Although the definition of a 'saturated road' inevitably assumes a prescriptive standard whose significance can only be fully appreciated by the expert, the visual comparison of these two maps does give the layman at any rate some indication that there is a significant difference in levels of congestion between the two alternatives. There is perhaps in these maps some scope for making some rough and ready numerical comparisons between total levels of congestion – for instance through measuring the respective mileages of saturated roads on the two maps, or through counting the respective numbers of congested junctions – but it is doubtful whether the basis of decision could thereby be significantly improved, because every part of the map is likely to require its own localized interpretation.

The study team were in the end content to rest their case for recommending the new 'Y' pattern in preference to the approved 1957 design on the visual evidence of the two maps reproduced above, together with the associated estimates of construction cost and certain supporting arguments of a more qualitative nature. The reader was in effect being asked to confirm the judgement of the experts concerning the most desirable social balance between the cost of public works, the benefit of relief to traffic congestion, and other less tangible factors relating in particular to the quality of the environment.

Value judgements relating to these different social implications were, of course, not demanded only at this comparatively late stage in the selection of a preferred road pattern. The earlier processes through which the team had selected a shortlist of patterns for final evaluation had themselves involved judgements as to what was 'good' or 'bad', acceptable or unacceptable, in the way of cost, traffic congestion, and disruption of the physical and social environment. This would still have been so even if it had been technically possible (as it was not) to replace the processes of inference from a desire-line map by more systematic procedures of search through all the possible variations of road network which could conceivably have been imagined by the planners.

Although they felt confident in discarding the design of the 1957 plan, the study team found some difficulty in the final analysis in expressing a preference between the basic 'Y' pattern and the more ambitious version in which further urban motor roads were added. Because the latter was in effect an extension of the former, these two patterns were referred to as Stage One and Stage Two respectively. It was argued that the Stage One pattern would be inadequate to deal with peak-hour traffic loads without the support of other measures such as improvements in the public transport service and restrictions of car-parking development. The final ·

Map 5. Saturated roads 1981, under 1957 Development Plan pattern
Source: The Coventry Road System (*Coventry City Council, 1963*)

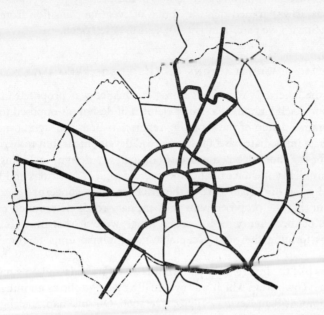

Map 6. Saturated roads 1981, under modified Development Plan pattern (inverted 'Y')
Source: The Coventry Road System (*Coventry City Council, 1963*)

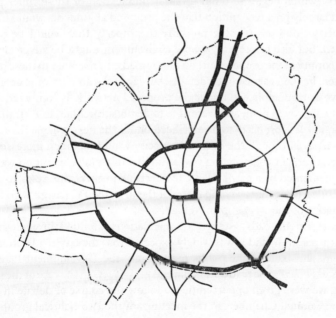

recommendation for acceptance of the Stage One design was therefore linked with further recommendations as to actions in these related fields; in the absence of such actions, it was argued that the option of eventual transition from the Stage One to the Stage Two pattern might still have to be left open.

THE PRACTICAL IMPLICATIONS OF THE ROADS RECOMMENDATION

Although the inverted 'Y' pattern whose acceptance was proposed in the study team's report itself embodied a strong element of design (as opposed to the floor-space recommendation of the shopping report), its practical significance was not so much as an immediate basis for future road development, but rather as a working brief for the more detailed processes of highway design, including the more localized problems of choice of alignment and design of junctions and bridges. It also served as an important part of the brief for those concerned with land-use planning, in that the proposed pattern of primary roads determined most of the boundaries of the 'environmental areas' which were at that time coming to be accepted as forming the most acceptable geographical units for local land-use planning.

The choice of the inverted 'Y' pattern was therefore reflected, in a multitude of ways, in the Town Map which was eventually made public as an integral part of the Development Plan Review proposals in 1966. On this map, the alignments of roads and the locations of access points were of course more closely defined than at the time of initial acceptance of the inverted 'Y' pattern, and the public and political controversy which began to build up after publication of these fuller proposals was based largely on a recognition that the proposed alignments would injure certain property interests, relating not only to property that would be physically demolished, but also to property whose environment might be adversely affected by the proximity of the proposed urban motor roads. In response to these pressures, the planners in 1966 carried out a detailed survey of the amount of property which might have to be demolished under the proposed network as compared with that of the 1957 approved plan, and were able to demonstrate that, in fact, they would expect slightly less property to be sacrificed under the new scheme than under its predecessor, even though the network capacity would be much increased. Thus, the earlier criteria of construction cost and relief of traffic congestion were at this stage supplemented by a new measure of effects on property interests, to provide a more extended basis for the comparison of the inverted 'Y' design with the *status quo* alternative of the 1957 approved plan.

The debate on the roads system recommendations extended throughout the four years of our research, and it was widely expected that the city road pattern would be the dominant issue in the public inquiry into the Development Plan Review which was expected to be held before the end of 1968. As in the case of the shopping proposals, we were given opportunities to follow the course of debate in committees, in the Council Chamber, in the meetings of the two political groups, and in the columns of the local press. Although it was clear that some of the elected members had difficulty in coming to grips with the full implications of the proposals, particularly in the earlier stages of discussion before public anxieties had been aroused, it was also clear that many of them had a shrewd awareness of the persistence of the many uncertainties which the study team had had to resolve through assumption in order to produce a sufficient set of data for processing on the computer. On the one hand, there was an implicit awareness of uncertainties in the purely predictive field, relating to such factors as the increasing levels of car-ownership and the self-defeating effects of new road construction in generating new traffic; on the other hand, there was also an awareness of the difficulty of attempting to select a preferred road design without being able to consider fully at the same time the options for public transport development, for car-parking policy, for traffic management, and for the location of future growth within the surrounding region. Furthermore, there was a continuing awareness of the difficulty of agreeing an appropriate balance between the competing objectives of improving traffic flows, of minimizing disturbance to the existing social fabric of the city, and of keeping public investment within politically acceptable limits.

UNCERTAINTY AND DISCRETION

We have now pursued our analysis of these two selected planning proposals, on city centre shopping and on the city road pattern, sufficiently far to indicate the wide range of different types of information which in each case required to be assembled in order to provide an acceptable basis for strategic choice. We have seen in particular that few of the contributory elements of information could be regarded as 'data', in the literal sense of information which is 'given' to the planners from an external source and can therefore be made use of immediately without the need for discretionary interpretation.

A particularly relevant concept at this stage is that of the 'discretion content of information', which has been discussed in relation to urban planning in a paper by Levin to the 1967 Conference of the Operational Research Society [20]. Levin argues that every piece of information used in the planning process can be regarded as having associated with it a certain 'level' of discretion, and that the character of the information fed into the planning process influences not only the decisions reached but also the planner's area of discretion and thus his decision-making behaviour.

Our analysis of the shopping and road proposals has allowed us to identify some of the many areas of uncertainty – and therefore the many areas of discretion for the planners – which arise at different stages both in the predictive process and in the process of selection of a preferred solution. Although it was clear in both instances that the officers responsible for producing recommendations to committees were not themselves insensitive to the existence of these uncertainties, their role in the decision-making process influenced them to exercise their own

8

discretion in reducing the overall level of uncertainty, through the acceptance of certain explicit or implicit assumptions, to a point where they could put forward either a single recommendation, or at most a limited set of alternatives with some clear guidance as to the factors which they believed should determine the committee's choice between them.

Thus our analysis of the shopping and road proposals has lent some specific confirmation to the general point which emerged in the previous chapter, that the reality of the decision-making process (in so far as it concerns the exercise of discretion or choice at whatever stage in the formulation of preferred courses of action) was tending to become largely concentrated within the departmental offices, at any rate so far as the more strategic planning decisions were concerned. It was not surprising that, when both the shopping and the road proposals were debated in committee, some signs of frustration were apparent on the part of the elected members at their inability to make any significant contribution to the formulation of the policies of the Council in these two important strategic fields. The problem of imbalance between the areas of discretion of the officer and of the elected members is not, we suggest, a simple one to solve; but we will have some suggestions to make as to ways in which solutions can be sought in Part IV, where we discuss the general problem of organization for strategic choice in local government.

Before concluding Part I, however, we shall first attempt to crystallize further the concepts relating to the analysis of uncertainties which have so far emerged, in order to provide a foundation for the more generalized discussion of the next few chapters. Although these concepts were suggested in particular by our analyses of the shopping and road recommendations, they were also substantially borne out by our opportunities to study the information structure of a number of other planning proposals, both at the strategic and at the more tactical levels, and by our observation of the continuing processes of policy discussion within the various group settings which we described in Chapter 3.

THE COMPONENTS OF UNCERTAINTY

In our analysis of the city centre shopping proposal, and again in our analysis of the road system proposal, we found it was possible to classify the various uncertainties which contributed to the difficulty of making a clear statement of preference into three broad categories. While the first of these categories concerned what might be thought of as the external planning environment, a second category concerned assumptions about the future intentions of the local authority itself in related areas of choice, and a third class concerned the appropriate value judgements to be applied in the selection of a preferred solution. These three broad classes of uncertainty can be defined rather more formally as follows:

Class UE : uncertainties in knowledge of the external planning *environment* including all uncertainties relating to the structure of the world external to the decision-making system – in the local government context this can be seen as including the entire physical, social, and economic environment of the local authority concerned – and also all uncertainties relating to expected patterns of future change in this environment, and to its expected responses to any possible future interventions by the decision-making system.

Class UR: uncertainties as to future intentions in *related fields of choice* including all uncertainties relating to the choices which might in future be taken, within the decision-making system itself, in respect of other fields of discretion beyond the limited problem which is currently under consideration.

Class UV: uncertainties as to appropriate *value judgements* including all uncertainties relating to the relative degrees of importance the decision-makers ought to attach to any expected consequences of their choice which cannot be related to each other through an unambiguous common scale – either because the consequences are of a fundamentally different nature, or because they affect different sections of the community, or because they concern different periods of future time.

These definitions may themselves require some interpretation according to context. In our case, we will for the time being consider 'the decision-makers' to include all officers and members of the local authority, and the 'decision-making system' to stand for the local authority as a whole; in other circumstances, however, one might wish to extend the concept of the 'decision-makers' to embrace certain other agencies with whom the local authority could expect some degree of working collaboration.

Our basic classification of uncertainties can perhaps be made more clear by means of a practical illustration, and so in *Figure 19* we give an indication of those points in the information structure of the shopping recommendation where uncertainties belonging to each of these three classes can be identified. Basically, *Figure 19* merely represents a combination of the information from two of the earlier block diagrams (*Figure 14*, p. 71, and *Figure 15*, p. 72), allowing the derivation of the shopping recommendation to be traced through the whole sequence of stages from the initial prediction of future expenditure per head to the final prescription of a preferred level of shopping provision for the city centre. However, for most of the blocks in *Figure 19*, we have also added references to the components UE, UR, and UV, to bring out the point that each of the three classes of uncertainty is encountered at some stage of the logical argument leading to the derivation of the final recommendation. Uncertainties in the category UE appear in the initial estimates of spending per head in 1961 (block A), in the predictions of future change in spending levels (blocks B, D, and F), and in the specification of a required turnover/floor-space ratio (block H) – at any rate in so far as this last element of information can be interpreted as a prediction of an equilibrium level for market forces. However, in so far as the turnover/floor-space ratio can be given a prescriptive rather than a predictive interpretation, a further element of uncertainty within the UV category can be identified at this same point. Uncertainties in the class UR can be identified in at least two positions in *Figure 19*, in that both the future growth of the population (block D) and the future allocation of spending

Figure 19

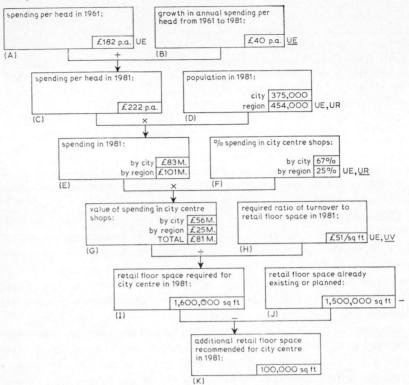

between the city centre and other shopping areas (block F) will in part be determined by the future decisions of the City Council in certain related fields of choice (including, among others, the field of choice relating to the design of the city road system).

MEASURING THE EFFECTS OF UNCERTAINTY

The three components UE, UR, and UV can therefore be identified at a number of different points in the block diagram of *Figure 19*. It will be noticed that some of the references to these components have been underlined; this is to emphasize that there may be some particular sources of uncertainty to which the final recommendation might be expected to show an especially high degree of sensitivity. For instance, the element of uncertainty in class UE shown against block (B) has been underlined because the future growth in personal spending power between 1961 and 1981 is a figure which might be considered particularly difficult to estimate with any degree of confidence. The effect of this particular element of uncertainty can be followed through by substituting some alternative prediction of growth which does not appear to fall outside the bounds of reasonable expectation – say a predicted increase between 1961 and 1981 of £60 instead of £40 in real annual expenditure per head – and then tracing the consequential effects through the whole structural diagram. Such an exercise turns out to produce a required increase in floor space of something over 300,000 square feet, instead of the 100,000 square feet which was actually estimated. There are other points in the diagram where a similar or even greater degree of sensitivity to assumptions might be expected to arise; for instance, as we suggested earlier in this chapter, the proportion of total regional spending-power attracted to the city centre in 1961 might, even under some fairly optimistic assumptions as to the accuracy of the contributory survey information, be expected to fall anywhere within the region from 7 to 35 per cent, even before any element of uncertainty in predicting future change in this proportion is taken into account. This would mean that, within the bounds of reasonable expectation, the planners' prediction that 25 per cent of regional trade would in future be attracted to the city centre might reasonably be replaced by any other figure in the range from 11 to 39 per cent. By tracing through the remaining steps of the calculation, it can be seen that the upper figure would lead to a required increase in floor space of almost 400,000 square feet instead of 100,000, while the lower would lead to a conclusion that the floor space already existing or planned was already in excess of future requirements by some 200,000 square feet. The choice of a future target for shopping development in the city centre is therefore shown to be highly sensitive to the possibility of error in this one estimate alone.

This technique of tracing through the effects of certain 'reasonable' variations in assumptions is known to statisticians and operational research workers by the name of sensitivity analysis. A more demanding but potentially more powerful technique is that known as risk analysis [21], in which limits of reasonable expectation are first assessed (subjectively if need be) for every contributory assumption, and statistical methods are then used to estimate limits of reasonable expectation for the final result of the calculation: in other words, the effects of uncertainties in the various contributory assumptions are tested in combination rather than one at a time. For practical application, this method requires certain simplifying assumptions as to the forms of probability distributions and the independence of estimates, and these may not always be easy to justify in the context of a long-range planning activity; however, even when the strict validity of the method is dubious, it can still provide a useful approximate guide as to the overall range of uncertainty associated with the final recommendation, and the contributions to this overall uncertainty of the various individual elements.

A RISK ANALYSIS OF THE SHOPPING PROPOSAL

Figure 20 provides a numerical example of the risk analysis technique, based on the actual data of the shopping report with the addition of what appear (in the subjective judgement of the research team) to be some approximate bounds of reasonable expectation for each estimate; comparison of *Figure 20* with *Figure 19* will show that the mid-point of each pair of limits quoted corresponds, at least approximately, to the single estimate which was in fact selected by the planners in Coventry. For those particular blocks of *Figure 19* where two or more different classes of uncertainty were identified, *Figure 20* includes an estimate as to the relative degree of importance of each element: for instance, in estimating the growth of the city population the classes UE and UR have been assessed as equally important and given a weighting of 50 per cent each, while in estimating the growth of the regional

Figure 20

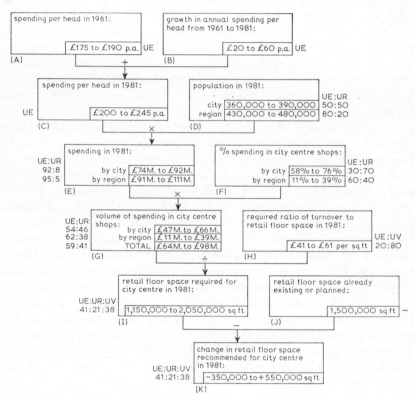

population the future actions of the City Council are judged to be much less influential than external factors, and so the component UR is given a rating of only 20 per cent as against 80 per cent for UE.

Because in this example the procedure for combining the various blocks of information consisted of a straightforward sequence of relatively simple arithmetical operations, it is possible to apply accepted statistical techniques in a stepwise manner to calculate a measure of the uncertainty which has so far accumulated at each successive stage of the structural block diagram; it is also possible at each stage to derive an estimate of the proportion of this cumulative measure of uncertainty which is attributable to each of the three components UE, UR, and UV. By the end of the calculation, the total measure of uncertainty is in fact found to be such that the estimated requirement for change in the total floor space within the central area might reasonably vary anywhere within the limits of a 23 per cent reduction (350,000 less than allowed for by the existing plans for 1,500,000 square feet) and a 37 per cent increase (550,000 square feet more than the existing area). Of this total uncertainty, the analysis shows only about 41 per cent to be associated with estimation of external factors, while an almost equally high proportion (38 per cent) is estimated to be associated with questions of value judgement. The inference is that, provided the subjective assessments of uncertainty entered in each block of *Figure 20* are accepted as reasonable, calculation of a target for shopping development in the city centre must depend as much on policy considerations as on technical predictions of future 'requirements'.

In considering the implications of any risk analysis of this kind, it is important to bear in mind the point that the quality of any information which emerges can only be as good or as bad as the quality of the subjective estimates of uncertainty that are fed in: it is only to be expected that the range of 'reasonable expectation' for each contributory estimate will tend to be a subject of disagreement between different experts (and non-experts) and, although in any particular case the area of disagreement might be narrowed either through further analysis of the sources of information or through processes of mutual adjustment, there can never be any practical hope of eliminating all elements of subjectivity (or discretion) at every stage in the chain of reasoning leading to the final expression of a preference between alternative courses of action.

Another general point to be emphasized is that, even though the range of uncertainty associated with a particular calculation may appear to be disconcertingly wide, as was the case with Coventry's estimation of required retail floor space, the practical effects of error may not be as serious as they might at first appear – particularly if the calculation is to be used not as a basis for some single grand commitment to immediate and irrevocable action, but rather as a first foundation for a series of future decisions, allowing some adaptation to future changes of circumstances. These are conditions which certainly apply to the growth of an existing shopping centre; although had a similar calculation of floor-space requirements been made for the planning of an out-of-town shopping centre, where for early impact a large initial commitment would have been essential, the consequences of error could have been a good deal more costly.

RISK ANALYSIS AND THE CHOICE BETWEEN ALTERNATIVES

The question of the 'cost of error' in a calculation of future requirements leads us on to consider the related question of how important the practical consequences of uncertainty may be in situations where an explicit choice is being considered between two or more alternative courses of action, as in the case of the Coventry roads pattern.

Because we were able to analyse the logical structure of the Coventry roads recommendation by the same block diagram technique that we applied to the shopping recommendation, there is no reason in theory why the same principle of risk analysis should not be applied to the exploration of different sources of uncertainty.

However, in this case the comparative sophistication of the predictive model makes the computational problems of risk analysis very much more daunting than in the case of the shopping proposal, and impossible even to contemplate without the use of an electronic computer and of approximate methods – such as that of the 'Monte Carlo' technique [22] – for calculating the cumulative effects of the many different sources of uncertainty involved. The full application of risk analysis to the Coventry roads proposal is also made difficult by the fact that the final step of the argument, in which a statement of preference between alternatives was reached on the basis of an overall appraisal of construction costs, traffic flows, and certain other consequences, required assumptions of relative value which it was not found possible to present in quantitative terms.

Despite these practical obstacles to the application of risk analysis, the fact that the calculations of the study team led in this case to an explicit comparison of alternative schemes rather than a single specification of 'requirements' means that the example of the roads proposal affords a much clearer basis than that of the shopping proposal for appreciating the real significance of the risk-analysis concept in relation to the general problem of decision-making under uncertainty. For instance, it becomes possible in theory not simply to estimate the margins of uncertainty attaching to the assessments of each alternative road pattern in terms of cost and traffic flow, but also to examine whether or not these uncertainties are of such a magnitude as to cast doubt on the final statement of preference for the inverted 'Y' pattern over the alternative of the 1957 approved plan; and, if any doubt exists, it becomes possible (again in theory) to examine which of the three classes of uncertainty UE, UR, and UV make the most prominent contributions to the overall range of uncertainty, and therefore what courses of action might be contemplated to reduce this uncertainty to a more acceptable level.

Again, as in the case of the shopping study, the problem of uncertainty must be judged in relation to the degree of commitment or irrevocability associated with a particular choice. In the case of the road pattern decision, the execution of the required construction works will again be a sequential process, possibly spanning two or more decades, and so opportunities for adaptation to new circumstances will never be entirely absent. The practical argument for a particular choice of road pattern is above all that it provides a framework for a comprehensive approach to problems of urban structure, and that it allows possible route alignments to be safeguarded against compromising development in the intervening years.

Although it will not be profitable for us to attempt to extend our analysis any

further in the historical context of the road system proposal, the concepts of uncertainty which we have introduced in this chapter have, we believe, a much more
general relevance to the problems of decision-making in local government. It is
this more general aspect of the uncertainty problem that we will develop further in
the next few pages, and subsequently in a more dynamic context in Part II.

THE PRESSURES FOR REDUCTION OF UNCERTAINTY

Our role as observers in departmental, committee, and political meetings at
Coventry gave us many opportunities to see the ways in which the decision-makers
reacted to difficulties in arriving at a clear choice between alternatives. Among the
themes which we saw to recur most frequently were demands for more 'research'
(in the sense of investigations designed to improve the technical basis for decision),
demands for more co-ordination with other participants in the decision-making
system, and demands for more clear-cut guidance on policy. These reactions we

Figure 21

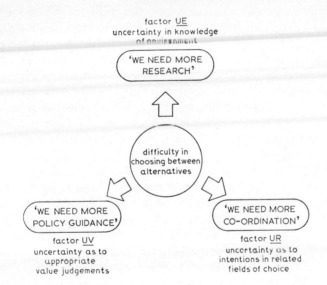

were able to link to our basic concept of the three classes of uncertainty, in the way
shown in *Figure 21* above.

In this diagram we suggest that each of the three types of observed reaction to
difficulty in making a clear choice between alternatives can in fact be related directly
to one of the three classes of uncertainty which we identified earlier in this chapter.
Although there is no basic reason why any attempt to reduce the total level of uncertainty should be confined to action in only one of the three directions shown, it
was our experience as observers that the particular perspectives of those participants who happened to be present at a meeting could often exercise an important

influence on the course of action recommended. For instance, in considering alternative traffic management schemes for a district, a traffic engineer, with a particular awareness of the need to reduce UE, might typically advocate an emphasis on more sensitive measurements or predictions of traffic flows; meanwhile a town planner, with a particular awareness of the need to reduce UR, might advocate collaborative working on the wider problem of environmental management, of which he might see the traffic management problem as only one component; and a chief officer or committee chairman, with a particular awareness of the need to reduce UV, might advocate a reference to his committee or his political party for more clear-cut guidance on policy.

It gradually came to be apparent to us that many of the stresses which arose from time to time between the different parts of the decision-making system in Coventry could be attributed to a failure to bring about some reconciliation between such variations of perspective at a formative stage of the decision process. Extreme emphasis on the need for research (in our somewhat limited sense of resolving uncertainties in the external environment) could be seen to lead to an attenuation in time of the whole decision process, and often to an undue preoccupation with some of the more measurable variables; extreme emphasis on the need for co-ordination could often lead to the drawing together of more and more decisions under the umbrella of a single grand design or master plan, making it very difficult in the later stages for those concerned to review any alternative courses of action without calling the whole balance of the plan into question; and extreme emphasis on the need for policy guidance could lead to resentment in some quarters – particularly among the less senior officers – because of a feeling that too many issues were being taken out of the hands of experts and resolved at a political rather than an analytical level.

There was, of course, general agreement that 'research', 'co-ordination', and 'policy' were all good things to have – and good things to have more of. What seemed to be less widely appreciated was that there might be certain tendencies within the decision-making system which operated in such a way that, the more emphasis was placed on any one of the three dimensions, the more difficult it might become to give sufficient weight to the other two. In terms of the decision-flow model of *Figure 12*, demands for more research would tend to drive an issue upwards into the departmental processes, while demands for more policy guidance would tend to drive it downwards into the political processes, where very different perspectives and pressures might be brought into play. Demands for more co-ordination, although they would sometimes tend at a formal level to drive an issue outwards to the setting of the 'senior committee' as shown in *Figure 12*, would serve above all to widen the range of interests involved on both the official and the elected sides, and so make it even more difficult to promote a meaningful dialogue across the interface between them. We will return to consider some possible ways of resolving these organizational conflicts in Part IV, after we have had the opportunity of introducing some relevant technological aids in Part III.

PLANNING AS A PROCESS OF STRATEGIC CHOICE

In Chapter 2, we attempted to identify some of the many different streams of planning activity which are liable to impinge on the affairs of a major local authority. Without attempting to define too closely what we meant by 'planning', we were able to build up a picture of an intricate fabric of interdependence between these various activities, as well as an underlying continuity capable of adapting to many kinds of change in the external environment. In the present chapter, we have attempted a more systematic exploration of the structure of two selected planning proposals, both having important strategic implications, and this has brought out the many different classes of uncertainty with which those involved in the total planning activity must in some way contend. Among these categories of uncertainty, we were able to identify not only the element of uncertainty in the more familiar sense relating to imperfect knowledge of the environment, and the more 'political' element of uncertainty relating to appropriate value judgements, but also a third element appertaining to future intentions in other related areas of choice. In effect, this third element can simply be regarded as a rather more explicit way of taking into account the effects on any one planning activity of the various strands of interdependence which link it to the other parallel streams of activity which we reviewed in Chapter 2.

The view of planning which emerges through the analysis of the present chapter is that of a process of decision-making under uncertainty, in that choices are repeatedly made between alternative courses of action with only an inadequate picture of their future implications. However, in putting forward such a definition, it is clear that the concept of uncertainty needs to be interpreted in a rather unconventional way, to embrace the factors UR and UV as well as the more commonly envisaged UE; and the fact that the element of discretion enters so pervasively into the selection of the various contributory assumptions suggests also that the interpretation of the word 'decision' must be an equally broad one, embracing all choices of assumptions or prescriptive standards which contribute in any way to the continuing processes of selection between alternative courses of action.

Because the definition of planning as a process of decision-making under uncertainty requires such unconventional interpretations of the two words 'decision' and 'uncertainty', we suggest, as a working definition for the chapters that follow, the somewhat more concise alternative of planning as a *process of strategic choice*. The word 'choice' is here used to embrace all areas of discretion whether or not they imply the formal commitment of a decision; the word "process' is used to suggest the property of continuity over time; and the word 'strategic' is inserted to give at least a hint that we are dealing with a level of choice where difficult challenges are likely to arise from the various classes of uncertainty we have now identified, and where corresponding stresses are likely to develop within the decision-making system. In Part II, we will be concerned to develop further this concept of planning as a process of strategic choice, and so to lay the basis for the guidelines for innovation and change which we offer in Parts III and IV.

References for Part I

[1] Fox, Levi: Coventry's Heritage. *Coventry Evening Telegraph*, 1947.
[2] Prest, John: *The Industrial Revolution in Coventry*. London: Oxford University Press, 1960.
[3] Geographical Association, Coventry Branch: Coventry, A Geographical Study. Geographical Association, 1964.
[4] City Treasurer, Coventry: Estimates for the General Rate for the Year Ending 31st March, 1968. Coventry City Council, 1967.
[5] City Treasurer, Coventry: Long Term Capital Programme for the Years 1966–67 to 1971–72. Coventry City Council, 1967.
[6] Spencer, P.: The Nature of the Planning Process in Coventry. Institute for Operational Research internal document T.930, 1967.
[7] City Architect & Planning Officer, Coventry: City of Coventry Review Plan, 1966, Analysis and Written Statement. Coventry City Council, 1967.
[8] Planning Advisory Group: *The Future of Development Plans*. London: HMSO, 1965.
[9] City Architect & Planning Officer, Coventry: Coventry 66, the Making of a Development Plan. Coventry City Council, 1966.
[10] City Architect & Planning Officer, Coventry: Coventry City Region. Coventry City Council, 1963.
[11] City Architect & Planning Officer and City Engineer, Coventry: *The Coventry Road System* (Part 1 Survey Methods and Analysis; Part 2, Principles of Design). Coventry City Council, 1963.
[12] City Architect & Planning Officer, Coventry: Work in Coventry. Coventry City Council, 1963.
[13] City Architect & Planning Officer, Coventry: Shopping in Coventry. Coventry City Council, 1964.
[14] City Architect & Planning Officer, Coventry: People and Housing. Coventry City Council, 1966.
[15] Griffith, J. A. G.: *Central Departments and Local Authorities*. London: Allen & Unwin, 1966.
[16] Friend, J. K.: Transport Planning and City Government. Institute for Operational Research internal document T.931, 1967.
[17] Department of Economic Affairs: *The West Midlands: A Regional Study*. London: HMSO, 1965.
[18] West Midlands Economic Planning Council: *The West Midlands: Patterns of Growth*. London: HMSO, 1967.
[19] McKean, R. N.: *Efficiency in Government through Systems Analysis*. New York: Wiley, 1958.
[20] Levin, P. H.: Decision Making Rules for Urban Planners. *Journal of the Town Planning Institute*, December 1967.
[21] Hertz, D. B.: Risk Analysis in Capital Investment. *Harvard Business Review*, Jan-Feb. 1964.
[22] Jessop, W. N.: Monte Carlo Methods and Industrial Problems. *Applied Statistics*, Vol. V, No. 3, November 1956.

PART II

Planning: a process of strategic choice

5. The nature of planning

MODELS OF THE PLANNING PROCESS

In Part 2 we shall be concerned to use our experience in Coventry as a starting-point from which to explore, at a more generalized level, the *dynamics* of planning regarded as a process of strategic choice, and to isolate certain characteristic classes of problem which it presents to those in positions of responsibility, not only in local authorities but in other agencies of government as well. Our object will be to gain insights into the kinds of capability which public authorities must develop if they are to cope effectively yet democratically with the challenges of strategic choice.

In exploring the dynamics of the planning process, our first objective will be to look more closely into the distinction between planning and other activities of government. This we shall seek to do, in the present chapter, by building up a series of diagrammatic models of the processes of interaction between government and community. The word 'model' is here used to mean a generalized representation of the relationships of a process, which serves to throw light on how these relationships might be expected to respond to different forms of change.

A SYSTEMS APPROACH

In relation to the community it serves, a local authority is both a regulator and a provider. On the one hand, it regulates certain aspects of behaviour and development within the community; on the other hand, it procures and uses resources, powers, and information in order to provide a variety of services for the members of that community. This description is, of course, equally applicable to the activities of central government and indeed to the whole network of governmental agencies at international, national, regional, and local levels.

Because we believe that our analysis of the public planning process has some validity at each of these levels, we will develop it in the most general possible terms, and will take as our basic framework the idea of a continuing dialogue between a *governmental system* and a *community system*. The former may include several distinct public authorities which jointly provide for and regulate the latter. The precise boundary between the two systems may not always be easy to define; but this need not deter us provided the basic concept of two interacting systems provides an adequate framework for our analysis. Perhaps one of the most satisfactory ways of differentiating the two systems is that suggested by Sir Geoffrey Vickers [1],

101

when he draws a distinction between the realm of 'market choice' (in which people make choices on their own behalf) and the realm of 'political choice' (in which people make choices on behalf of others). Such a distinction may, if anything, lead to an unduly broad definition of what should be included within the 'governmental system'; however, it does relate to the popular view of 'us' (the people) and 'them' (the 'authorities'). Also, a distinction based on contrasting fields of *choice* is highly relevant to our own view of planning as a process of strategic choice.

In using the word 'system' our intention is to embrace all the many perspectives from which government and community can be viewed. In writing about the governmental system, we have in mind that its reality extends beyond its formal and legal aspects, and can only be described adequately through a combination of social, political, economic, functional, and many other frames of references; likewise, in writing about the community system we will have in mind a rich network of relationships between people and the environment in which they live. Families, individuals, and organizations may participate in the community system in many different capacities; for instance Mr Smith may participate as a local resident, as a shopper, as a car-driver, and as an employee of a local industrial firm. Perhaps, of course, his employers may be the local authority itself, or he may be an elected member of the local council; in which case he participates both in the realm of 'market choice' and in that of 'political choice', and may therefore be said to 'belong' both to the governmental and to the community systems at the same time.

THE 'DIALOGUE' MODEL

The first of our diagrammatic models, which appears as *Figure 22*, concerns a 'dialogue' between these two systems consisting of a continuing interchange of information and influence across the interface between them. Each 'round' of the dialogue is shown as beginning with a *situation* arising within the community system; this may be in the nature of a clear-cut demand, such as a request by Mrs Brown for provision of home help because of a physical disability, or an application from a local sports club for development of land under current town-planning legislation. On the other hand, it may be something a good deal less explicit, such as a persistent state of congestion at some road junction, or a progressive deterioration of housing in some neighbourhood, which might lead somebody to perceive, perhaps gradually over time, that 'something ought to be done'. Situations requiring action within the governmental system may therefore be detected not only through the receipt of specific demands, but also through a sensitivity to more diffuse and continuous forms of pressure.

In *Figure 22*, we show the appraisal of situations as leading to a choice of actions within the governmental system, each resulting in some form of change within the community system (unless of course the 'action' selected is one of doing nothing for the time being). The original situation then becomes modified, so completing what we may call an 'action circuit'. The continuing dialogue between government and community can be visualized in terms of a rich variety of such 'action circuits', cutting across the interface between the two systems in many different ways.

The existence of many different channels of communication inevitably leads to

Figure 22. Model 1: the basic dialogue

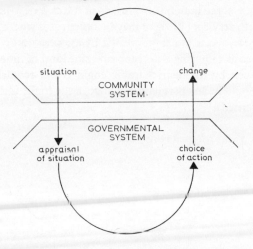

the growth of many different perspectives of the governmental system within the community system, and many different perspectives of the community system within the governmental system; it is only through a bringing together of several such perspectives that the richness and complexity of interaction between the two systems can be appreciated in any degree of depth.

THE SELECTION OF RESPONSE

We will now take that part of the 'action circuit' which lies within the boundaries of the governmental system and examine it more closely from the point of view of the *operations* required. Here we are using the word 'operation' in the sense defined by Ackoff when he says:

An operation is a *set* of acts *required* for the accomplishment of a desired outcome; that is, it is not a single act but a complex of interrelated acts performed simultaneously or in sequence, which leads to the accomplishment of some desired outcome [2].

The operation with which we are here concerned is that of the *selection of response* by the governmental system to a situation which is seen to arise within the community; the desired outcome in this case is the achievement of an *intervention* in the community system which is believed to be in some way 'right' or 'appropriate' to the situation in hand.

9

In *Figure 23*, we extend our original picture by identifying three successive stages in the operation of selecting an appropriate response. The first stage involves a 'perception of the decision field', by which we mean the initial understanding of what kind of problem it is that the situation creates for the governmental system. The question at this stage is one of appreciating what *kind* of response is called for, rather than what particular courses of action might be feasible. Perception of the decision field may sometimes be obvious, as in the case of Mrs Brown's application for home help service, but there may be other cases where it is open to some doubt; for instance, a local situation created by a severe traffic hold-up might be seen by the police as requiring a decision on some kind of immediate emergency action, but be seen by the district traffic engineers as requiring a decision on whether there should be any permanent change in the traffic control arrangements for the area concerned.

Figure 23. Model 2: the selection of response

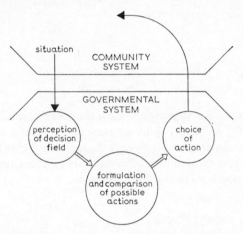

The initial perception of the decision field is depicted in *Figure 23* as leading to a process of formulation and comparison of alternative actions within that decision field. No clear separation has been shown between the activities of formulation and of comparison, because they may not always take place in strict sequence; perhaps, after certain initial possibilities for action have been compared and some of them discarded, a need to formulate further possibilities will be diagnosed before the final step of selecting a preferred course of action is taken. Sometimes, the process of formulating and comparing alternative solutions will cause the original perception of the decision field to be modified; this is a possibility we will explore more fully later in this chapter.

Sooner or later, the formulation and comparison of possible actions leads to choice of one particular course of action; a formal commitment is then generated through an assignment of resources or a public statement of intent, and the stage of intervention in the community system begins. This is the stage of decision-*taking* as opposed to the wider process of decision-*making* which can be said to embrace all three stages of the total operation shown in *Figure 23*.

THE CONTEXT OF OPERATIONS

The model of *Figure 23* is sufficiently general to apply to all situations from the most trivial to the most complex. At a complex level – for instance, in the choice of response to a situation created by the closure of a major industrial enterprise on which much of the life of a town depends – there may be few guidelines or precedents to be followed. The level of discretion is high and selection of a preferred set of responses may require a good deal of thought and discussion. At the other extreme, a clerk dealing with applications for renewal of vehicle licences may require little discretion and his response may be virtually instantaneous.

Operations which allow little discretion of response tend to arise in any setting where situations arise with high frequency in the form of explicit demands, so that classes of similar situations can be recognized and responses can be determined by rules of procedure or conventions based on whatever classifying features are agreed to be most relevant. This means that the decision-making process of *Figure 23* follows a course which is essentially determined by a *generic* viewpoint, whether this is made explicit through the laying-down of formal regulations, or is implied in the growth of conventions which reflect the perspectives and experience of those concerned. We will use the term *operational policies* to refer to any such generically determined forms of response, whether or not they are embodied in any formal rules of procedure.

Whenever a situation cannot easily be related to existing operational policies, then the choice of a response may be shaped partly by the personal and group objectives of those concerned, and partly by their appreciation of the constraints which may inhibit the attainment of those objectives: such constraints may apply in particular to their ability to mobilize the resources for certain desired courses of action. All these factors – the operational policies themselves, the local objectives, and the appreciation of external constraints – contribute towards the general view of the way in which appropriate actions should be selected. We will refer to this general view as the *context of operations*, and *Figure 24* attempts to show its influence on the continuing decision process.

Here, we represent the current context of operations by use of broken lines, so as to distinguish the idea of *context* from the idea of *process* as represented by the 'action circuit' with its origins in a given situation. The context is shown as influencing all three stages of the ongoing decision process; and also as itself continually undergoing modification as situations arise within the community which cannot easily be dealt with within the existing context. The extent to which the context of operations changes will depend on the governmental system's capacity to *learn* about the changing pressures and relationships of the community system.

Through such a learning process, the appreciation of factors relevant to decision-making may gradually change, so that the range of situations covered by operational policies will either extend or diminish over time; meanwhile, objectives may

Figure 24. Model 3: the context of operations

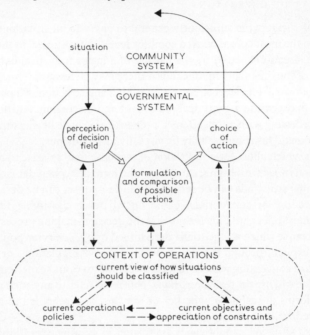

gradually become modified and the ability to mobilize resources become either more or less constrained.

In the remainder of this chapter, we will be concerned to explore further the implications of situations where it is found difficult to select a response within the current context of operations.

THE PERCEPTION OF UNCERTAINTIES

At this point, it becomes possible to link the concept of the changing context of operations to the concepts of *uncertainty* which we introduced in Chapter 4. Towards the end of that chapter, we identified three fundamental causes of difficulty in making a selection between alternative courses of action, which we defined as uncertainties in knowledge of the external environment (abbreviated to UE), uncertainties as to future intentions in related fields of choice (UR), and uncertainties as to appropriate value judgements (UV). A perception of uncertainties of the first kind can, as we then argued, lead to demands for further gathering and interpreting of information about the present and future state of the community or its physical setting (sometimes expressed in the form of demands for 'more re-search'); while a perception of uncertainties of the second kind can lead to demands for a widening of the field of decision (often expressed as a demand for 'more co ordination'), and a perception of uncertainties of the third kind can lead to demands for 'more policy guidance'. These all represent demands for a change of some kind in the context of decision for the situation now being considered. We can express these different opportunities for modifying the context of decision by super-imposing our basic model of three kinds of uncertainty, which we introduced in Chapter 4 (*Figure 21*), onto the 'process' model of *Figure 23*. The result is shown in *Figure 25*.

A perception of significant uncertainties in any one of the three directions UE, UR, and UV is here shown as creating a pressure for a particular kind of change in

Figure 25. Model 4: responses to uncertainty

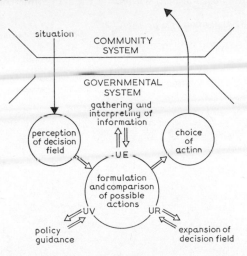

the context of operations. However, whether or not such pressures affect the choice of action in this particular situation will depend on an appreciation of the pressures for early decision which arise from within the community. To adopt a physical analogy, it is possible to think of a driving force which operates through-out the action circuit and has its origin in the community system, pressing all the time for commitment: this has to contend with three kinds of frictional force associated with the UE, UR, and UV components of uncertainty respectively, all coming into operation at the stage labelled 'formulation and comparison of possible actions' so as to create a resistance which the driving force may or may not immedi-ately be able to overcome.

As was demonstrated by our analysis of the Coventry shopping and road pro-posals in Chapter 4, the nature of the uncertainties which may exist in any of the three directions is unlikely to be fully perceived by any one individual or specialist group within the governmental system; and it is only to be expected that any local variations in perceptions of uncertainty may influence both the speed with which a decision is reached and also the particular course of action which is ultimately chosen. We will call any element of uncertainty which is relevant to a particular choice, but which is not perceived by those responsible, a *latent uncertainty* in relation to the choice concerned. The concept of latent uncertainty has some important operational and organizational implications which we will explore in later chapters.

THE NEED TO PLAN

It is through a perception of our second kind of uncertainty – uncertainty as to intentions in related fields of choice – that the process of decision first begins to become one of planning or *strategic* choice. If there is a belief that it is difficult to select actions in one decision field without at the same time considering possible

Figure 26. Model 5: expansion of a decision field

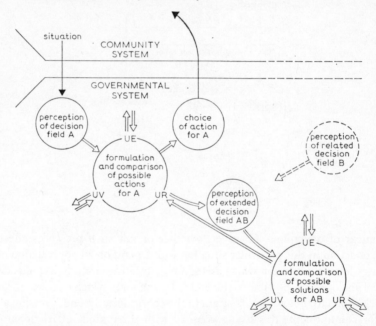

actions (now or later) in other fields, then this creates a pressure for all the fields concerned to be brought together to form a single wider field of choice. This process is illustrated in *Figure 26* for the case of one original decision field A and a single related decision field B; this model can, however, easily be extended to the more general case where there are several separate decision fields B, C, D, . . ., each of which is seen to be related in some way to the original decision field A.

In this extended model, the choice of action for A is shown as being deferred until possible solutions have been formulated and compared over a wider decision field AB; the action circuit is in effect diverted into a subsidiary loop in order to reduce some of the uncertainties (of class UR) arising in the consideration of A alone. An example might be the situation where a decision on road design (decision field A) is deferred until it has been considered in relation to various possibilities for the future development of the public transport system (decision field D).

As *Figure 26* shows, however, there may still be uncertainties of all three kinds in formulating and comparing possible solutions over the wider field AB; (indeed in some organizational contexts the level of perceived uncertainty in the class UV may even be increased, because the bringing-together of the groups responsible for decision fields A and B may expose conflicts between their assumptions of value which hitherto had remained latent). Any awareness of uncertainties which may remain in the new context of the extended decision field may lead to a new set of pressures for gathering and interpreting of information, for policy guidance, or for still further extensions to the decision field; eventually, therefore, the decision-makers may be led to formulate and compare possible actions over a still wider field of choice embracing many other situations which seem to be related either to A or to B or perhaps to both.

In *Figure 26*, we have not shown a full action circuit for B to correspond to that for A, because the situation from which decision field B is seen to arise may be an *anticipated* one rather than one which has actually developed within the community. In this case, no immediate commitment to a specific course of action for B may be required; the concern may simply be to select a preferred *action* for A through a comparison of joint *solutions* for A and B together. In our example, the joint consideration of alternative road designs and public transport systems might lead to a clear choice in respect of the former but to the leaving open of a range of different options in respect of the latter; however, the road design selected might well be *different* from that which would have been selected if the decision field had not been extended by the consideration of possible future solutions to the public transport problem.

This state of affairs, in which A has a higher degree of urgency than B, is more typical than that in which A and B both require simultaneous commitment, because the process by which the community presents situations requiring intervention by government is essentially a continuous one: it is not like the presentation of a brief to an architect or engineer as a result of which some set of related choices must be made in order to produce a 'finished' design by some particular point in time. In a process of continuous choice in a changing environment, it may be purely accidental if any two related situations requiring decision both arise at the same time; a capacity for anticipation of future situations therefore becomes inevitable. This means that the governmental system must, whether consciously or otherwise, develop *predictive models* of the community system and the way its internal relationships can be expected to change and develop over future time. Of course, every decision-maker has to develop some capability to make predictions even if only so that he may assess the more long-term consequences of his *current* actions; but it is only when he also applies this predictive ability to appraise the consequences of certain possible *future* actions that he can be said to have become a planner.

Sometimes, of course, it may be only through the anticipation of future situations that the governmental system comes to recognize other current situations where more immediate initiatives might be taken. For instance, it may be only because of an anticipated future situation in which population growth will have outstripped the supply of dwellings that a local authority recognizes a need to consider immediate initiatives to reserve or acquire land, to recruit extra architectural staff, or to approach neighbouring authorities with proposals to form a regional housing consortium. The anticipated decision field – relating to alternative ways in which a future housing shortage might be tackled – has in this case what Sir Geoffrey Vickers [1] calls a 'latent urgency' which induces the governmental system to consider carefully the choice of a response to certain current situations which would otherwise probably have been ignored. Certain fields of current choice in effect remain *latent* until another future decision field has been anticipated.

There may be many such fields of current choice, which only emerge through the existence of a forward planning activity; and not all of these may relate to choice of action across the interface between government and community. Some may concern choice of action within the boundaries of the governmental system itself: the allocation of existing staff to particular tasks, the initiation of different stages of design activity, and other such acts of internal mobilization. Clearly, the basic theme of *Figure 26*, showing the relationship of a current decision field A to an anticipated decision field B, is capable of many variations. There may in fact be many A's and many B's, some of the A's remaining latent until certain of the B's have been identified; while some of the A's may relate to purely internal actions within the governmental system, rather than interventions by government in the affairs of the community system.

We have now developed our basic model of the selection of response to a stage where it can provide some further insights into the nature of the governmental planning process. In particular, it enables us to appraise more clearly the operational definition of planning as a *process of strategic choice*, which we offered at the end of Chapter 4. We can now put forward the proposition that *any process of choice will become a process of planning* (or *strategic* choice) *if the selection of current actions is made only after a formulation and comparison of possible solutions over a wider field of decision relating to certain anticipated as well as current situations.*

PROGRAMMES, POLICIES, AND PLANS

According to the above proposition, the significance of any planning activity – no matter how far into the future it may set out to look – will depend on the guidance that it can give in the selection of appropriate courses of action to deal with current circumstances. Sometimes, of course, it is possible to lose sight of the connection between a long-range planning activity and the more immediate operations of the governmental system; the process of visualizing possible designs for the long-term future of a community can easily acquire its own internal momentum, and the danger may then arise that it ceases to exert due influence on the solution of current problems.

In making this point, however, it is necessary to make a careful distinction between the 'planning process', in the sense of the activity of formulating and comparing possible solutions over a wide decision field, and the making public of 'plans' or statements of future intent. Whenever a plan is made public, this means that knowledge of its content is seen as having a value not only to the governmental system but also to the community system, in providing a more firm basis for the selection of current actions by private individuals, families, or institutions; in effect, it then becomes a framework not only for the processes of 'political choice' but also for those of 'market choice' on the opposite side of the government/community interface. In a sense, publication of any plan or policy can be seen as a form of response to direct or indirect pressures within the community for access to the future intentions of government; the act of publication must then itself be considered an intervention by government in the affairs of the community.

At this point, it is appropriate for us to put forward some operational definitions of words such as 'programme', 'policy', and 'plan', which are liable to arise frequently in practice and are sometimes regarded as interchangeable. We will find it useful to distinguish a *programme* as a set of related future intentions in respect of certain *specific* situations which are anticipated in the future, and a *policy* as a set of future intentions in relation to certain *classes* of situation; this is consistent with our earlier definition of an *operational* policy, but allows a somewhat wider interpretation. The distinction can be expressed another way; a programme relates to intentions for future action *when* certain expected situations arise, while a policy relates to intentions for action *whenever* situations arise which are seen as belonging to certain defined classes. In putting forward these definitions, it is however necessary to note that 'policy' used as an adjective does not always carry the same generic connotations as 'policy' used as a noun. Sometimes, where a situation arises which does not appear to fit into any existing classification, it will be said that a 'policy decision' or 'policy guidance' is required. In this case, the generic implications are indirect; a precedent is set which may help to determine how similar situations should be classified in future, and the context of future operations is modified accordingly. There is a close parallel with the process by which the context of legal judgements may develop from a succession of case decisions over time.

The word 'plan' we will use to describe any co-ordinated set of future intentions which includes elements of both a specific and a generic character, as in a development plan which may include a statement both of intended development projects and of policies for development control. Occasionally, a plan may have aspects of a *contingency plan* in that it specifies certain alternative sets of intentions depending on whether certain specific future situations do or do not arise. The statements of intent may now include not only 'when' and 'whenever' clauses but also 'if' clauses.

The concept of a contingency plan has much in common with the concept of a *strategy* as it is commonly used, for instance in relation to an armed conflict or a game of chess. This idea of a strategy has been given more formal definition in the theory of games [3], which relates to situations in which a decision-maker wishes to anticipate a range of alternative actions either by some readily identifiable 'opponent' or by other less clear-cut groups of forces operating within his environment, and to select his present and future responses accordingly.

ADAPTIVE PLANNING

In public planning, however, it is exceptionally difficult to formulate strategies in advance which are sufficient to cope with all conceivable contingencies; the complexity of the community system, and the imperfect understanding of it in the governmental system, combine to prevent any complete enumeration of the situations which the former might be expected to present. In these circumstances, planning must become in some degree an *adaptive* process. Although firm commitments may from time to time be required in particular sectors of a complex decision field, it may also become particularly important to retain an element of *flexibility* in other sectors in the expectation that, by the time commitment in these sectors becomes inevitable, the state of knowledge of the environment may be very different and the whole context of decision may have changed.

This does not necessarily mean that the process has reverted from one of planning to one of unco-ordinated short-term response: by adopting a *strategic approach*, involving formulation and comparison of possible solutions over a wide decision field embracing anticipated as well as current situations, the governmental system may find that it is led to select a very different set of immediate actions than would otherwise have been the case. For instance, the most immediately attractive solution to a problem of coping with increasing local demand for technical college or hospital facilities might be to extend an existing group of buildings; but this might limit the scope for further extensions in the future, and a strategic approach might reveal that a move to a new site would allow greater flexibility of future choice in response to changes in circumstances which cannot yet be clearly foreseen.

In the United Kingdom, a significant step towards a more adaptive philosophy of planning was taken by the Planning Advisory Group which was set up to produce recommendations on the future of Development Plans [4]. As already mentioned in Chapter 2, the Group's report paved the way for legislation whereby the traditional idea of the 'Town Map', incorporating specific commitments over a wide decision field relating to future land uses, was superseded by a system of 'urban structure maps' and 'district plans' allowing more flexible interpretation, to be augmented by more detailed 'action area' plans wherever pressures for action and statements of intent were currently seen to be strongest. It was significant perhaps that publication of the new proposals gave rise to a good deal of public discussion as to how a proper balance between flexibility and commitment should be drawn; and concern was expressed in some quarters [5] that the new proposals might in fact have moved too far in the direction of flexibility, at the expense of those members of the community whose interests might be most affected by the decisions of the local planning authority.

IMPROVEMENT IN THE PLANNING PROCESS

The formation of the Planning Advisory Group, and the legislative changes which followed, provide only one instance of a more widespread search for improvement in the mechanisms of public planning. In Part I, we were able to see the course which this search for improvement followed within one particular local authority; members and officers alike were much concerned with the problems of reconciling planning with democracy, of forming adequate bridges between the mechanisms of departmental and political choice, and of striking a balance between commitment and adaptiveness.

During the four years of our research, dissatisfaction with existing mechanisms for public planning was equally evident at many other levels of the governmental system, and also within the community at large. In the United Kingdom, perhaps the outstanding example within this period concerned the siting of London's third airport. The main implication of the criticisms which eventually led to the re-examination of the Stansted decision was that too many uncertainties of value judgement, and of future intentions in related areas of choice, had been allowed to remain latent in the process by which the original decision was taken. Through basing many other decisions on the assumption that Stansted was the only acceptable site, the planners in effect found themselves caught in what might be called a 'policy trap'. Escape (or resolution) was then seen to lie in only one direction; and it was argued that, right or wrong, the Stansted decision would have to remain. By the time the case for a full inquiry into possible alternatives had been conceded, a great deal of time had been lost, with far-reaching consequences for many sectors of the community and of government itself.

Many other examples could be quoted of this kind of breakdown in the credibility of established methods of strategic choice, at local, regional, and national levels. However, it is of course much easier to agree that improvement is necessary than to agree how 'improvement' should be defined, particularly in relation to a continually changing environment where 'before' and 'after' comparisons may be misleading and where many competing interests may be involved. Perhaps the only yardstick of a 'better' planning process can be the degree to which it becomes generally accepted as increasing the capacity of government to make *intelligent* decisions on behalf of the community; in other words to choose what actions to take with a fuller awareness of what the consequences are likely to be.

This does not itself resolve all the practical problems of defining improvement, for in any governmental system there are many different groups whose aims may not always coincide, and an increase in the power of one group to make intelligent choices may sometimes only be achieved at the cost of a reduction in the power of another group. Neither can an absolute definition of 'improvement' be constructed by relating it to some such abstraction as the 'common interest' or the 'general good of the community', whose interpretation is likely to differ from individual to individual and from group to group. In the last resort, the test of 'improvement' can only be an empirical and to some extent a political one; whatever change is proposed in existing mechanisms of choice, it must be such as to gain acceptance in practice, by convincing a sufficient number of people that it offers them a better instrument for achieving the things they want to achieve.

6. The operational problems of the planning process

So far, our series of models of the interaction of government and community has ignored the complications arising from the existence of organizational boundaries within the governmental system. However, these models do provide a foundation from which we can isolate certain basic types of *problem* which are characteristic of any public planning process whatever its organizational setting. We will refer to these as *operational* problems to distinguish them from the further *organizational* problems which arise as soon as the planning process begins to cut across internal boundaries within the governmental system, and which we will consider in the next chapter.

In this chapter we will attempt to define the operational problems of public planning according to five broad headings. Taking *Figure 26* (p. 108) as our main frame of reference, we will start at the point where the process of decision first moves into the context of *strategic* choice; where the case for an extension to the original decision field has been established, and the need arises to formulate and compare possible solutions for the joint decision field AB.

The range of feasible solutions for AB will of course depend partly on the range of feasible alternatives for A on its own. This may not in itself be difficult to envisage; perhaps only a few alternatives are conceivable, as in the choice between outright acceptance, qualified acceptance, or rejection of a planning proposal, or the choice as to the financial year in which an approved development project should be programmed to start. If, on the other hand, the set of possible solutions to A cannot easily be enumerated, as in the design of a building, then the problem will arise as to how wide a range of solutions should be formulated, and whether the process by which they are generated should be purely intuitive or should attempt to embody elements of more systematic search procedure.

Of course, once the original decision field A becomes extended to embrace other related areas of present or future choice, the problem of formulating a sufficient range of alternatives may take on a new order of difficulty, in that it may be necessary to envisage very many different *combinations* of choices, not all of which may be mutually compatible. At the level of strategic choice, it may therefore become particularly difficult to achieve any clear comprehension of the range of possible solutions, or the configuration of what Britton Harris and Ackoff have described as the 'policy space' [6].

This difficulty leads us to formulate the first of our five types of operational problem as follows:

OPERATIONAL PROBLEM I

The problem of finding solutions

in circumstances where the range of possible solutions is not easily enumerated, and where it may be difficult either to discover any feasible solution at all, or to be sure that certain significant alternatives will not remain undiscovered.

Assuming that by some means a sufficient set of alternative solutions has been discovered, then some means of comparing their effects is required if there is to be any discrimination between them as a basis for present or future action. Before any statements of preference can be made, it is necessary first to have some appreciation of the *range* of possible effects within the community system (and also within the governmental system itself), both in the immediate and in the more long-term future: then some appreciation is required as to the *scale* of each type of effect, and finally judgements must be made as to their relative *values*.

Provided these appreciations can be expressed in specific terms, then it may be possible to express preferences in terms of a single numerical measure; perhaps each solution can be evaluated according to some kind of 'social benefit criterion' equivalent to the profit criterion of the private entrepreneur. At the other extreme, it may be difficult to do more than make certain statements as to the *order* of preference of alternative solutions (e.g. 'we definitely prefer solution x to solution y, and solution z to solution y, but we cannot express a clear preference between x and z'). In this case, all assumptions about the range, scale and value of effects remain implicit, and only limited inferences about them can be made.

In public planning, it is rarely practicable to attempt a complete enumeration, measurement, and valuation of all future social effects, so some compromise must be sought between the extremes of comparing solutions according to a single numerical criterion on the one hand, and according to unsubstantiated preference statements on the other. The search for ways of assisting the expression of preferences is central to the growing methodology of cost-benefit analysis [7]. We can express the problem formally as follows:

OPERATIONAL PROBLEM 2

The problem of expressing preferences

between alternative solutions given only imperfect information as to the range, scale, and value of their anticipated effects.

THE CHALLENGES OF UNCERTAINTY

Any expression of preference between alternative solutions is liable to be subject in some degree to uncertainties relating to the environment (UE), to intentions in related fields of choice (UR), and to appropriate value judgements (UV). However, some of these uncertainties may be 'latent' in that those concerned are not immediately aware of their existence; and if there is any possibility of deferring a commitment until it can be made with more confidence, it may be important to try to discover which classes of uncertainty are dominant. Then it will become possible to judge how much might be gained through action to modify the context of choice in any of the three directions shown in *Figure 25*.

The possible existence of latent uncertainties therefore poses an important problem which is not often faced explicitly in practice. As we argued in Chapter 4, an unbalanced emphasis on particular classes of uncertainty may affect the whole course of the decision-making process, often by diverting it into either a more 'technical' or a more 'political' context than would otherwise be the case. We will define the basic problem as follows:

OPERATIONAL PROBLEM 3

The problem of exposing latent uncertainties
in order to establish the relative dominance of uncertainties in the three classes UE, UR, and UV as inhibiting factors in the clear expression of preferences.

The exposure of uncertainties is, however, not in itself sufficient to enable a decision to be reached as to what *actions* should be taken to improve the basis of choice. Any such exploratory action will require to be appraised not only according to its *effectiveness* in increasing the capacity to express preferences, but also according to its *cost* in terms of time, money, or other appropriate yardsticks. For instance, the level of UE might be reduced either by carrying out social surveys to improve knowledge of the existing structure of the community, or by developing more sensitive predictive models (each bearing a cost in research time not necessarily proportional to its value); the level of UR might be reduced by joint working with others on an extended decision field, with a cost to be measured in terms of the time (and possibly stress) expended in inter-group consultations; while the level of UV might be reduced by a series of meetings to clarify policy issues, with a cost to be measured primarily in terms of the time of politicians and their senior advisers, which might be in particularly short supply. In some circumstances, there might be opportunities to pursue two or more of these exploratory actions either simultaneously or in sequence: more generally, the decision-makers are faced with a problem of 'value for money' in choosing between alternative ways of improving the basis of decision. This problem, like the previous one, is not often explicitly recognized in practice; we can phrase it more formally as follows:

OPERATIONAL PROBLEM 4

The problem of selecting exploratory actions
which can be expected to improve the confidence of choice in as economical a way as possible.

COMMITMENT AND FLEXIBILITY

In this analysis of the basic problems presented by the planning process, it is important to draw a distinction between the problem of expressing preferences within an extended decision field, including some sectors where full commitment may be at present unnecessary, and the problem of selecting a set of immediate actions to be undertaken in the more urgent of these sectors. This may involve not only selecting between certain particular alternatives, but also judging what is the appropriate balance between commitment and flexibility at that particular time; judgements must be made as to whether the pressures for commitment in particular parts of the decision field are such as to outweigh the benefits of delay while further exploratory actions are taken to improve the basis of decision.

Of course, there may be circumstances in which the passage of time will itself operate so as to improve the basis of decision: with every week, month, or year that passes, new information about certain facets of the community system may materialize, and more credible predictions about its future may become possible. There is, of course, always a danger that such an argument can be used merely in order to make a virtue of procrastination; and the acid test must be whether the social cost of resisting the pressures for commitment a little longer can be expected to outweigh the expected gains from 'keeping the options open' until preferences can be more clearly established.

The basic point to be borne in mind is that flexibility may have a value of its own and, as we shall demonstrate in Part III, circumstances may arise where certain courses of immediate action will provide a greater margin of flexibility for future choice than other alternative actions even within the same decision field. This leads to the proposition that, in making a choice of immediate *actions*, as opposed to stating a preference between ultimate *solutions*, *it may be important to take into account in some way an assessment of the value of retained flexibility for the future.* This brings us to our fifth and last operational problem which we can now define as follows:

OPERATIONAL PROBLEM 5
The problem of selecting immediate commitments
at any particular point in time, taking into account the balance of advantage between the pressures for commitment, on the one hand, and the retention of future flexibility, on the other.

A BRIEF FOR A TECHNOLOGY OF STRATEGIC CHOICE

The five basic operational problems which we have now identified are summarized below.

Summary of operational problems of strategic choice
1. The problem of finding solutions
2. The problem of expressing preferences
3. The problem of exposing latent uncertainties
4. The problem of selecting exploratory actions
5. The problem of selecting immediate commitments.

Each of these problems is, we suggest, implicit in any process of public planning, and it is inevitable that any governmental body will tend to develop certain methods for dealing with them, even if these are never made explicit. Improvement in the planning process, however this may be defined, is much more likely to take place if these problems can be formally recognized and solutions sought at a more conscious level; and for this reason, we suggest that they can collectively be regarded as forming a brief for the development of a more purposive 'technology of strategic choice' in any governmental setting. This is the brief to which we shall address ourselves in Part III.

7. Planning in its organizational context

The responses of the governmental system to situations presented by the community system are almost always effected by specialist groups which we will call 'agencies'. Depending on the level of the governmental system with which we may be currently concerned, an 'agency' may be a local authority as a whole, a particular department within a local authority, a specialist section within a department, or even a particular individual who has certain defined powers to take action in particular classes of situation. In the course of our discussion, we will sometimes wish to consider 'agencies' which fall outside the local sector of the total governmental system: for example, departments of central government, area offices of regional gas or electricity authorities, or even branches of certain public corporations which are of only a quasi-governmental character. The term 'agency' thus allows for considerable flexibility of interpretation.

The basic feature of an 'agency', in the sense in which we shall use the word, is the existence of formal terms of reference which define, in greater or lesser detail, the classes of situations with which it has authority to deal, the powers it has to mobilize resources for dealing with these situations, and the general goals which it should strive for. Within an agency, discretion as to alternative actions rests with some set of people – managers, administrators, or operators – who will usually be hierarchically organized but all of whom are in a sense 'controllers'. Individually or collectively, these controllers will tend to develop their own operational policies and working procedures and may succeed over the course of time in gaining extensions to their resources and powers to deal more effectively with the situations which confront them.

Figure 27 shows a situation in which operations of response are taking place continuously in several different agencies (for simplicity, we show only two of them). The context of operations differs of course from agency to agency, in respect of operational policies, internal goals, and powers to mobilize resources. Such differences may be a reflection not only of functional distinctions, but also of the personal attributes and experience of the controllers concerned and the social relationships between them. Each agency in effect has its own identity as what may be called a 'socio-technical system' [8].

In this model, each agency is shown as being concerned with a different facet of the community system. The distinction between one facet and another may be partly geographical, but also partly related to the different roles which people may play within the community – as taxpayers, tenants, employees, bus passengers, and so forth. However clearly defined may be the divisions between agencies

Figure 27. Model 6: operations by several agencies

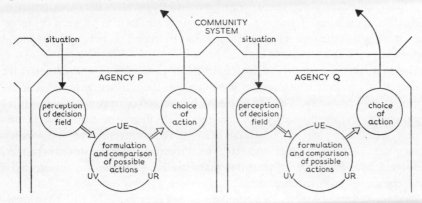

within the governmental system, the community system can never be divided neatly into self-contained parts, and there are many strands of interconnection behind the various different facets that it presents. Inevitably, corresponding relationships come to be recognized between agencies, so that various forms of organizational connection develop between them.

ORGANIZATION AND MULTI-ORGANIZATION

There are many ways, formal and informal, in which agencies such as those shown in *Figure 27* may be connected to each other. At one extreme is the situation where two or more agencies are connected through allegiance to a common *authority* as in the case of the departments of a local authority. Even here, however, authority may not be absolute, since some of the departments may also be directly accountable for certain purposes to departments of central government. In other cases, two or more agencies may be connected through the nature of their operations even though no common authority exists. A distinction has been drawn between these two cases in a paper on 'Operational Research for "Multi-Organisations"' by Stringer [9]. This distinction reads as follows:

'An organisation (an industrial firm, a hospital board or a partnership of architects, for example) has unifying characteristics, e.g.:

(i) It has imposed upon it, or is capable of defining for itself, a set of goals ultimately applicable to all its parts.

(ii) It has established means for pursuing these goals.

(iii) There is some ultimate expression of the organisation's authority as an entity. (Its internal structure is usually hierarchical, and there is a "boss" or a "board of directors").

(iv) It has a permanence which transcends particular tasks.
A multi-organisation, on the other hand, is the union of parts of several organisations, each part being a subset of the interests of its own organisation. It is defined by the performance of a particular task (which may be a continuing one) through the interaction between individuals.'

A 'multi-organization', as here defined, necessarily involves the participation of more than one agency. There are, of course, many similarities between organizations and multi-organizations, including the fact that conflicts between groups and individuals are liable to arise in both.

However, an organization is distinguished in particular by the potential for resolution of conflicts which resides in whatever is the ultimate expression of the organization's authority. This is reinforced by the power to commit and control resources which this authority gives, even though the degree of authority may ultimately be limited by various constraints of a legal and social character and possibly also by the sanctions of other organizations. Provided these constraints are met, the organization has power to act and to shape itself in whatever way appears to be most consonant with its objectives.

As we shall argue later, all the advantages do not necessarily lie with the organizational as opposed to the multi-organizational form of connection between agencies; in particular, the multi-organizational form has an innovative capacity which has its own special value in relation to the governmental planning process. However, before we can explore this question more fully, it is necessary for us to develop a little further our model of decision-making within a single agency.

AN AGENCY-CENTRED VIEW

Figure 28 gives an impression of how each agency, once it becomes aware of uncertainties in selecting appropriate courses of action, will begin to develop its own internal mechanisms for resolution of these uncertainties. These mechanisms contribute substantially to the context of that agency's operations. In *Figure 28* they are represented by the symbols m(UE), m(UR) and m(UV), as a natural extension of the shorthand used in earlier diagrams. Each of these symbols may stand for a variety of human activity by individuals or groups whether at the level of the formal or the informal, the professional or the political.

Where an agency recognizes not only that there exist deficiencies in its knowledge of the community system (uncertainty of the class UE), but also that it is important to overcome these deficiencies, then it will tend to develop *mechanisms for reducing uncertainties in the environment*, (m(UE)). These mechanisms will supplement the normal flow of information through operational channels, and may take various different forms; the carrying-out of sample surveys, the study of experience elsewhere, or simply a more general attitude of 'keeping one's eyes open'. The mechanisms m(UE) may also include the use of more systematic interpretative procedures, from the simple collation of operating statistics to the manipulation of complex predictive models which attempt to reproduce the dynamic relationships of an entire urban system [10]. Either in a deliberate or an *ad hoc* manner, each agency tends to build its own internal system for gathering and interpreting of information; and it is a common experience for this tendency to operate in such a way that any potential value of the information to other agencies becomes very difficult to realize.

Similarly, a recognition of uncertainties as to appropriate value judgements (UV) will lead each agency to develop over time certain internal procedures for seeking policy guidance, in a way which reflects, albeit often imperfectly, the range

Figure 28. Model 7: mechanisms for reducing uncertainties within an agency

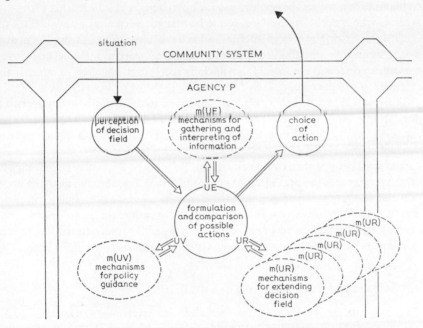

of community interests with which that agency comes into contact. Any such procedures can be regarded as *mechanisms for reducing uncertainties as to appropriate value judgements* (m(UV)).

In the case of a local authority department, the mechanisms m(UV) may include both the formal procedures of submitting matters to committee and also any informal arrangements for testing the acceptability of proposals to the committee chairman or to particular interest groups within the community. If the agency is a section within a department, the mechanisms m(UV) may include any conventions as to matters on which the section head should seek the guidance of his departmental head, because of uncertainty about any political implications or about the 'right' system of values to apply in putting forward a reccommendation. All such mechanisms will generally be responsive in some degree to the changing pressures of the community; and in so far as they involve consultations with representatives of the community, they can be regarded as introducing further channels of communication across the interface between governmental and community systems.

An agency's *mechanisms for reducing uncertainties as to intentions in related fields of choice* (m(UR)) will include all processes by which a decision field may be extended because of a perceived relationship to other decision fields. Included within m(UR) would be any processes by which individual controllers within the agency come to view their current problems as requiring consideration as part of a wider process of strategic choice. This might embrace arrangements both for internal communication within the agency, and for interchanges of information with other agencies whose decision fields are seen to be related. Such arrangements form the agency's mechanisms for both internal and external *connection*. In using the neutral word 'connection' our aim is to cover the whole network of informal and formal communication, and not merely the officially recognized channels of internal and external 'co-ordination'.

There will clearly be some practical limitations to the capacity of any agency to develop mechanisms for external connection. One hypothesis suggested by our experience is that any agency will tend to adjust the number and capacities of its external channels of communication only to such a level as does not result in any serious instability within the agency itself. Too 'open' a set of connections with other agencies may have the effect of raising all kinds of doubts and anxieties about personal and group responsibilities; these may be expressed through a complaint that 'We don't know where we stand'. In effect, some kind of 'law of conservation of stress' may come into play to ensure that many of the uncertainties due to relationships between the decision fields of different agencies will remain latent.

THE STRATEGIC VIEW: MANY AGENCIES

To the extent that such protective forces can be overcome, networks of *ad hoc* arrangements for consultation between agencies can be expected to develop. Our review of planning in Coventry brought to light several instances where a limited field of decision arising within one department tended to become enlarged because of perceived relationships with other areas of choice, not only within the department's own field of responsibility but within those of other departments and sometimes other authorities. This is why, in *Figure 28*, we have deliberately tried to give the impression that there may exist a number of different mechanisms of the type m(UR), some but not all of which may cause problems to 'spill over' beyond the organizational boundaries of the agency concerned.

Our eighth model, appearing in *Figure 29*, takes up the implications of this crossing of boundaries from a many-agency point of view. Here we take an instance in which certain perceived relationships between decision fields have led to the development of a set of connective arrangements between five different agencies which we label P, Q, R, S, and T.

We have supposed here that the growth of mechanisms m(IJR) within agencies has been such that some kind of 'planning framework' – at the very least, an informal acceptance of the need for consultation in respect of certain limited classes of situation – has developed between agencies P and Q, and also between agencies Q and R. At a multilateral level, we suppose that another planning framework has also developed to link agencies R, S, and T; this might be either a formally established 'planning team', or perhaps some less formal convention of holding occasional tripartite meetings to deal with certain agreed classes of situation. We have also in *Figure 29* included another still wider planning framework linking P, Q, S, and T to demonstrate the point that certain pairs of agencies (such as P and Q) may

Figure 29. Model 8: planning activities involving several agencies

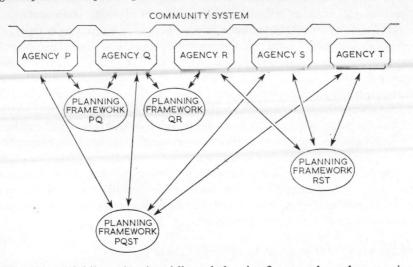

be linked in both bilateral and multilateral planning frameworks at the same time. There may of course be many options as to the pattern of linkages through which any given set of agencies are connected; for instance, in the case of the five agencies in *Figure 29*, the four planning frameworks shown form only a minority of the total of twenty-six combinations which could conceivably be formed, ranging from the ten possible forms of bilateral linkage to the one ultimate possibility of an all-embracing planning framework PQRST. In practice, any particular subset of these 26 possible combinations might be in existence at any particular time, although it is most unlikely that the agencies concerned would be able to cope with more than a limited number of them. For one thing, time for consultations between agencies is itself a scarce resource; for another thing, those in control of agencies may, as we have already suggested, be motivated by the need to restrict external connections so as to protect their own internal stability.

The set of connections between agencies is always likely to be a changing one; connections will always tend to form in an *ad hoc* way to deal with particular current problems, and these may tend to fade away when these problems have been resolved in an acceptable way. Sometimes, one planning framework (for instance PQ) will tend to grow into a wider framework (say PQS) because of a perception of a need for further extensions to a particular field of decision.

Our model of inter-agency planning frameworks is essentially a non-hierarchical one; it implies that each agency may 'belong' to more than one planning framework and is therefore not necessarily 'subordinate' to any one such framework at a 'higher level' of the governmental system. Herein lies the fundamental difference between what we have called a 'planning framework' and what we have called an 'authority', although in practice we must be prepared to recognize instances in which the same group of people acts in both capacities.

The point about the non-hierarchical pattern of planning frameworks is an important one, since in practice formal systems of planning often seem to be designed with a hierarchical image in mind. There is an interesting parallel here between the design of formal planning frameworks and the design of urban settlements. In his paper entitled 'A City is not a Tree' [11], Christopher Alexander argues persuasively that the design of a town or city for a community to live in is too often distorted by the tendency of the human mind to simplify the problem by imposing hierarchical patterns of thought, whereas in fact social relationships tend to follow much more intricate patterns of interaction cutting across the boundaries of neighbourhoods, environmental areas, 'communities', or whatever hierarchical units the designer may attempt to impose.

A similar tendency to distort reality through imposing hierarchical patterns of thought is, we suggest, prevalent in much of the thinking about the design of governmental planning systems, as well as in the understanding of the community systems with which they are required to interact.

THE MOBILIZATION OF PLANNING ACTIVITIES

We have now developed a picture of inter-agency planning activities which suggests the desirability of a flexible pattern of organization for planning, in which planning frameworks are not necessarily constrained either by hierarchical relationships or by continued existence over time. Such a flexible pattern may however itself introduce problems as to how the planning process is to be mobilized and regulated.

Because of the limited perspectives of agencies, and the protective forces within them, it is by no means certain that local initiatives alone will be sufficient to generate a relevant pattern of connections, and to adapt it to changing circumstances within the community. Even if, for instance, agency P perceives the need for a connection with agency Q, it is by no means certain that the desire for a connection will be reciprocated, particularly if the problems faced by Q are less pressing than those faced by P. It may perhaps only be some third party who can see with clarity the need for a connection between P and Q, or can appreciate the urgency of connection at a particular time; perhaps, for instance, the members of the planning framework RST require a crystallization of possible joint actions by P and Q before they can begin to clarify possible courses of action within their own decision field.

Such problems of mobilization, regulation, and scheduling of planning activities involving several different combinations of agencies call for another kind of activity which we will call *strategic control*, to distinguish it from the activity of *strategic choice* which is the preserve of those working within the planning frameworks themselves. The problems of strategic control do not concern which *specific* lines of action should be selected within the governmental system in response to situations which develop within the community system; they concern how the planning process should itself be organized where questions of joint working between agencies are seen to arise.

We are now in a position to define formally the first of six classes of problem which we believe to be basic to the planning process in any organizational context where more than one agency is concerned.

ORGANIZATIONAL PROBLEM I

The problem of mechanisms for strategic control
including the development of processes for connecting, and sometimes disconnecting, different agencies which are seen to have related fields of decision, and for regulating the activities of the various planning frameworks so formed wherever these are seen to be interdependent.

STRATEGIC CONTROL WITHIN AN AUTHORITY

The setting up of mechanisms for strategic control can be expected to become particularly difficult where the agencies concerned belong to different authorities, and where there is no obvious arbiter between agencies whose representatives do not see eye to eye. Before we consider this case, however, we will first consider the rather more straightforward case in which all agencies are formally subordinate to the same authority. For this purpose, we extend *Figure 29*, with its example of five agencies P, Q, R, S, and T linked through the activities of four planning teams, as shown in *Figure 30*.

Here, we have added a new element to the picture of *Figure 29*, in the form of a strategic control function spanning all five agencies. This function is concerned with regulating, in some undefined way which we represent by broken lines, the activities which take place in each of the four planning frameworks PQ, QR, RST, and PQST : it is also concerned with the mobilization of such other planning frameworks as subsequent events may seem to call for. It is at this level that any stresses must be borne which arise from the differing views of individual agencies as to what connections should be formed between them, or what urgency should be attached to the resulting joint activities.

Stresses may also result because those working within different planning frameworks may have developed their sets of mechanisms m(UE), m(UR), and m(UV), along very different lines. They may therefore tend to generate planning proposals which are either inconsistent or inadequately related in some other way: for instance, perhaps there is inadequate sharing of information on relevant aspects of the community, or a discrepancy in the extent to which policy guidance is sought from public representatives.

If the strategic control machinery is to embody any capacity to ensure consistency between the actions proposed within the various planning groups which fall within its span, then questions arise of *authority* at an inter-agency level.

Figure 30. Model 9: the function of strategic control

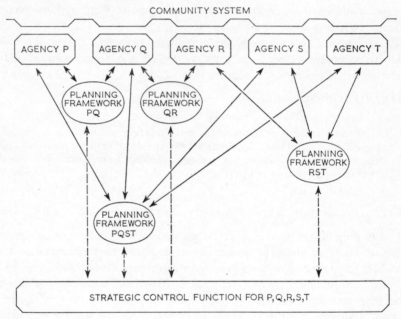

Where all the agencies concerned owe formal allegiance to a single organization, there already exists some group or individual in a position of ultimate authority, having the power to withhold sanction from certain types of action which may be proposed by individual agencies. Such a group or individual is clearly in a position to fulfil a similar function in respect to the actions which may be proposed within inter-agency planning frameworks; in other words, to extend its authority to cover *strategic* as well as *operational* control over the affairs of the organization.

It is not, of course, inevitable that the function of strategic control should be entirely associated with the central source of authority within the organization concerned. An alternative possibility is that the function might be divided so that separate mechanisms of strategic control would apply to different groupings of agencies within the same authority. However, as soon as it is discovered that any of these agencies need to develop connections across these group boundaries, the case for another level of strategic control begins to emerge. Unless the various activities within an authority are so clearly sub-divided as to bring the very need for a common authority into question, we can postulate that there must exist a need for a centralized strategic control function spanning all the component agencies of the organization.

THE MULTI-ORGANIZATIONAL CASE

In any planning activity involving agencies drawn from different authorities, the question of authority in strategic control becomes much more difficult to resolve. Processes of mutual adjustment, reinforced by indirect pressures from the community or from other parts of the governmental system, may not always be sufficient to achieve and maintain the level of connection which some parties believe to be necessary; and proposals may then be heard for the setting-up of some degree of formal accountability where none previously existed. Under such conditions, the original multi-organizational grouping of agencies may begin to assume more and more of the characteristics of a single organization. Alternatively, the planners may become subject to an intensification of indirect control through the implied threat of being placed in a publicly untenable position; in a sense, the only authority for strategic control now becomes of a moral rather than an organizational character.

There are, of course, many possible solutions to the problem of how far, and in what ways, ultimate authority is to be exercised in the multi-agency planning process, both in the organizational and in the multi-organizational case, though it is in the latter case that the challenge is liable to become particularly acute. We therefore now introduce the second of our set of organizational problems which are characteristic of the public planning process, defining it as follows:

ORGANIZATIONAL PROBLEM 2
The problem of authority for strategic control
including the question of where, within an organization, responsibility for the function of strategic control is to be located; and, in the multi-organizational case, the question of how to develop a nucleus for strategic control which is both effective and acceptable to all the agencies concerned.

LEARNING AND THE NEED FOR SUFFICIENT INFORMATION

We have seen the function of strategic control as one of maintaining a relevant set of connections between agencies and ensuring consistency between the inter-agency activities so generated. The ability to select appropriate connections must however depend on a capacity to *learn* about the continually changing patterns of interdependence between the operations of the various agencies concerned.

Capacity to learn in turn depends on a flow of relevant information, and the question then arises as to the volume of information that is required, the basis on which it should be selected, and the way in which its flow should be stimulated and maintained.*

At one extreme, those responsible for strategic control can rely entirely on local initiatives for the supply of information as to areas where new connections between agencies are required; however, this places absolute reliance on the perceptions of people whose view of the community system may often derive from a somewhat limited field of operations. Alternatively, members of the strategic control group may themselves take on the responsibility of keeping informed on the actual or proposed actions of individual agencies. In the case where all agencies are subordinate to a common authority, channels for obtaining such information will normally already exist; established procedures of *operational* control will typically require that certain classes of action must be reported by the agencies, either before or after the event, to a central group (or individual) with the power to withhold resources, or to apply other indirect pressures in respect of any action of which it disapproves.

If it can form some kind of association with existing procedures of this kind, a strategic control group can expect to enhance its ability to learn about the changing needs for connection between individual agencies. In effect, the mechanisms for central control over operations – including any existing procedures of budgetary control – will then provide the strategic control function with a set of sensory mechanisms which are distinct from, and complementary to, the 'eyes and ears' through which individual agencies perceive needs for connection between their own operations.

In this way, a strategic control group may find itself in a position to delay certain commitments to action by agencies, while the context is modified through mobilization of inter-agency planning groups. However, an intervention at this late stage in the 'action circuit' of *Figure 27*, after the agency has completed its own internal processes of formulating and comparing possible courses of action, may be much less efficient, and more frustrating to the agency concerned, than an intervention at an earlier stage when the decision field is still comparatively open. The question arises of whether the strategic control group can develop ways of supplementing its flow of 'hard' information on specific proposals for action by a flow of 'soft' information on decision fields where possible courses of action are still at a comparatively early stage of formulation. To do this, the strategic control function must find some means of *scanning* the activities of agencies, in a sufficiently flexible way to provide an early warning of areas where new connections between agencies ought to be made. It may then be able to take initiatives to mobilize certain inter-

---

* The fundamental relationship between control and information has been explored by cyberneticians, including Ross Ashby [12] who has formulated what he calls the *law of requisite variety*: briefly, this states that any control system can only be effective to the extent that it succeeds in developing a similar level of complexity (or variety) to the system it sets out to control.

agency planning activities at a stage before the agencies themselves have developed firm commitments to particular lines of solution.

The extent to which a strategic control group may decide to develop scanning mechanisms of its own, rather than relying on the initiatives of the agencies themselves or on 'hard' information received through the mechanisms of resource control, will depend on the level of connection which the central authority (if any exists) believes to be necessary between the activities of the agencies concerned. An awareness of insufficient connection at the planning level may itself provide an argument for the establishment of some form of common authority on an *ad hoc* basis even where none existed before. The general problem of developing a set of sensory mechanisms for the strategic control function can be defined formally as follows:

ORGANIZATIONAL PROBLEM 3

The problem of sufficient information
embracing the questions of how much information is necessary to provide the requisite level of strategic control, how far for these purposes it is necessary to supplement 'hard' information by 'soft', and how the requisite level of information flow may be stimulated and maintained

PLANNING AND DEMOCRACY

It is a fundamental requirement of government in a democracy that all parts of the governmental system should be responsive to the changing values and pressures which operate within the community system, even though there may be many different interpretations as to what is or is not 'in the public interest'. The most basic (but not the only) mechanisms for providing this element of responsiveness are the procedures of local and national election, through which the community periodically elects *representatives* who in turn make a contribution to the various mechanisms for policy guidance m(UV) which operate within the governmental system. Of course, any formal mechanisms of democratic control are liable to become modified in practice through the conventions of party politics; however it may be argued, from experience in Britain and elsewhere, that the influence of party politics is on balance beneficial, in so far as it allows a set of formal mechanisms which is difficult to operate in a connected way to be transformed into a more workable instrument for control of government by the community.

In the case of some agencies and authorities, the representatives of the community system may be nominated rather than elected, but their purpose is still to be reflective of current values and pressures in particular sectors of the community system.

If these representatives, elected or nominated, are to influence the processes of *strategic* choice and control within the governmental system, then their influence cannot be confined to the mechanisms m(UV) for guiding operations within individual agencies; means must be found of making their influence effective at the level of the inter-agency planning framework and of the strategic control function itself. The challenges at these levels are, of course, much more difficult ones because a different level of comprehension is required; and the argument is sometimes heard that the representative can play little useful part at this level, with the implication that other kinds of mechanism for responding to community values and pressures must be developed. However, instances of public disaffection arising from bureaucratic as opposed to democratic forms of planning are sufficiently pervasive as to suggest that a good deal of attention requires to be given to exploring ways in which the role of the representative in the planning process might be increased rather than diminished. We can pose the basic problem as follows:

ORGANIZATIONAL PROBLEM 4

The problem of democratic guidance
including the questions of developing mechanisms for participation by representatives of the community system in the governmental planning process, and of exploring how far their participation can be supplemented by other forms of public involvement.

One particular question arising under this heading is that of how far the elected or nominated representatives of the community can contribute to whatever scanning function, or early warning system, may be developed to assist the function of strategic control. The law of requisite variety [12] suggests that a system of strategic control will only succeed to the extent to which it can develop a similar level of complexity to the system it sets out to influence; it can never, however, be expected to achieve this if it is forced to rely entirely on the scanning abilities of one individual or even a single small group of individuals who occupy a central position in relation to the agencies concerned. It is here, if anywhere, that potential may exist for drawing on the diversity of perspectives which may be provided by a larger body of representatives, particularly where these are directly elected on a ward or constituency basis, and therefore have a direct motivation to keep in touch with events and pressures within defined sectors of the total community system. If the strategic control group can find effective ways of drawing on the existing scanning functions of all elected representatives, it may thereby considerably enhance its own internal capacity to identify areas of relevant connection between agencies.

THE NETWORK OF COMMUNICATIONS

All the organizational problems we have identified so far imply problems of communication between groups or between individuals. Agencies must be able to communicate with each other through what we have called 'planning frameworks'; both agencies and inter-agency planning groups require to communicate effectively with those who are responsible for strategic control; and at all three levels, those who formulate and compare different courses of action can only be responsive to the pressures of the community system in so far as they can develop effective channels of communication with lay representatives. All these problems of communication involve problems of language, since any set of specialist agencies (for instance, the set of departments within a local authority) may include many different professions each with its own mode of thought and its own forms of expression. Differences in forms of expression may extend beyond questions of professional jargon to other non-verbal forms of communication; for instance, members of a town-planning department might tend to present information on a given situation in terms of maps, whereas a finance department might tend to describe the same situation in terms of tables of figures, an engineer in terms of graphs, and a legal adviser in terms of a purely verbal appreciation.

The problems of communication are, of course, aggravated by any increase in the complexity of the subject-matter to be communicated. The level of complexity encountered in the planning process is liable to be very much higher than in the normal operations of agencies, because of its connective nature; as we shall see in Part III, the operational problems which we posed in the last chapter may suggest new forms of language, but these will only be effective in so far as they can serve as a link between professions and between disciplines, rather than simply a new form of jargon for a new type of specialist. In so far as some parts of this language may be abstract and symbolic in form, there will require to be means for interpreting it into lay terms so that any power which it creates for more effective processes of strategic choice does not become inaccessible to the representatives of the community system. We will now define the basic problem of communication in planning as follows:

ORGANIZATIONAL PROBLEM 5

The problem of common language
including the question of developing languages for communication between different professions, and between professional and lay participants in the governmental system, which will provide a basis for clearer expression and wider comprehension of the implications of complex planning problems.

THE HUMAN RELATIONS ASPECT

However skilfully an organizational setting for a planning process may be designed, it will be successful only to the extent that it takes into account the personal and group motivations of all the parties concerned. The withholding of information from a central authority until a particular course of action has been worked out is one way in which individual or group interests may be protected and overall control of planning frustrated. Matters of professional status and career progression may be involved, as well as personal preferences and antipathies and a host of other factors. In local government in particular, the most outstanding organizational rift is that between the officials on the one hand and the elected members on the other. Whatever may be the divisive forces within either group, communication across the interface between them is always liable to be attended by a measure of anxiety, which frustrates the recognition of common interests. Thus any increase which elected members may seek in facilities for access to 'soft' information may be seen by the officials as creating new risks of misinterpretation or misapplication. Whatever justification such fears may have, they require in the final analysis to be balanced against the dangers of allowing planning to drift out of the hands of the representatives of the community because it is considered 'too difficult' for them.

It would of course be unrealistic to expect that the level of misunderstanding and stress between the participants in the governmental planning process can ever be reduced except by a process of gradual evolutionary change. Professional attitudes and rivalries do not change overnight, and barriers to a free interchange of information are not readily dismantled unless those concerned can be convinced that they will stand to gain more than they will lose. Such adjustments of attitude or behaviour cannot be brought about solely by the introduction of formal changes in organizational structure or procedure.

Any changes in established processes of strategic choice are likely to gain acceptance only if they recognize the motivations of all participants and do not so frustrate their various personal objectives as to lead to the taking of counter-measures which prevent the intentions of the would-be agents of change being realized. However, in the long term, personal and group motivations are never completely immutable, and the prospect for improvement in the planning process – whatever definition of 'improvement' we choose to adopt – must depend on an ability to guide this potential for motivational change along channels which are seen to be in keeping with the ideal requirements of a democratic planning process.

We suggest that the process of developing a planning process in any specific organizational setting must itself be an adaptive one, with a capacity to learn from whatever difficulties of human relations are seen to arise in practice. This leads us to state the last of our six organizational problems as follows:

ORGANIZATIONAL PROBLEM 6

The problem of sufficient motivation
or the question of how the processes of strategic choice and control can be made to evolve in the direction of a more effective approach to the fundamental problems of public planning, while retaining a sufficient level of acceptability to all concerned in their operation.

A BRIEF FOR ORGANIZATIONAL CHOICE

Just as at the end of the last chapter we were able to conclude with a brief for developing a technology of strategic choice, so we conclude this chapter with a brief for the development of an appropriate organizational setting. The interpretation of such a brief as a basis for organizational change must, of course, depend on the particular circumstances of whatever authority or multi-organizational system may be concerned. We will give an illustration of how such a brief might be applied in a given organizational context in Chapter 14.

The brief we propose consists of a reiteration of the six basic organizational problems we have identified during the course of this chapter, as follows:

Summary of organizational problems of strategic choice
1. The problem of mechanisms for strategic control
2. The problem of authority for strategic control
3. The problem of sufficient information
4. The problem of democratic guidance
5. The problem of common language
6. The problem of sufficient motivation.

References for Part II

[1] Vickers, Sir Geoffrey: *The Art of Judgement: A Study of Policy Making.* London: Chapman & Hall, 1965.
[2] Ackoff, R. L. (Ed.): *Progress in Operations Research*, Vol. I, Chapter I. New York: Wiley, 1961.
[3] Luce, R. D. and Raiffa, H.: *Games and Decisions.* New York: Wiley, 1957.
[4] Planning Advisory Group: *The Future of Development Plans.* London: HMSO, 1965.
[5] Sharp, T.: Planning Planning. *Journal of the Town Planning Institute*, June 1966.
[6] Harris, B. and Ackoff, R. L.: Strategies for Operations Research in Urban Metropolitan Planning. Proceedings of Fourth Conference of International Federation of Operational Research Societies, Boston, 1966.
[7] Feldstein, M. S.: Cost-Benefit Analysis and Investment in the Public Sector. *Public Administration*, Vol. 42, Winter 1964.
[8] Trist, E. L., Higgin, G. W., Murray, H., and Pollock, A. B.: *Organizational Choice.* London: Tavistock, 1963.
[9] Stringer, J.: Operational Research for 'Multi-Organisations'. *Operational Research Quarterly*, Vol. 18, No. 2, June 1967.
[10] Harris, B. (Ed.): Urban Development Models: New Tools for Planning. *Journal of the American Institute of Planners*, May 1965.
[11] Alexander, C.: A City is Not a Tree: *Design*, February 1966.
[12] Ashby, W. Ross: *An Introduction to Cybernetics.* London: Chapman and Hall, 1956.

PART III

Towards a technology for strategic choice

8. An approach through case examples

Our object in Part III is to introduce and develop a body of technique which we believe will be helpful to all those who are concerned with the processes of planning and policy-making in local government, and may also have some wider relevance to other levels of the public planning process. Our aim is not so much to suggest methods for deriving clear-cut 'best solutions' to problems of strategic choice on paper, but rather to indicate ways in which it may be possible to open up and enrich the continuing dialogue between those who are responsible for the formulation of planning proposals (the officials) and those who are publicly accountable for the resulting decisions (the elected representatives).

For this reason, we decided it would be most appropriate for us to introduce the various aspects of our 'technology of choice' gradually through the discussion of a series of extended case examples, so designed as to reflect the continuing nature of the planning process, and more especially the ways in which perceptions of problems may change over time as new influences are brought to bear and new information comes to light.

Throughout these case examples, we shall try to maintain an emphasis on the idea of a body of technique (in the singular) rather than a set of techniques (in the plural). This is because, in approaching any particular problem of strategic choice, we believe it is important that those concerned should be able to draw freely on the technology as a whole, rather than feel bound to classify the problem at the outset as one that is most suited to the application of any one particular technique. Among the different approaches which we will attempt to draw together through discussion of our case examples are the approach of AIDA (Analysis of Interconnected Decision Areas) to the finding of solutions where there are many combinations of choices to be considered; the approach of cost-benefit analysis to the evaluation of alternatives with a wide range of different social implications; the approach of sensitivity and risk analysis to the exploration of sources of uncertainty; and the use of 'robustness' criteria to help in striking a balance between current commitment and flexibility of future choice. We will make more limited reference to other techniques, such as that of critical path analysis, whose application is now well established in relation to more specialized classes of decision problem; and we will also introduce certain broad concepts which derive from more general theories of decision and value. We shall not assume that the reader has any

139

prior acquaintance with any of these concepts or techniques, although in the case of risk analysis we shall be able to refer back to Chapter 4, where we introduced the basic approach in relation to the analysis of particular planning proposals in Coventry.

Most of the approaches upon which we shall draw are of quite recent origin. Our aim is not only to demonstrate the application of methods whose value is already proven, but also to indicate the directions in which we believe these methods must be extended, if they are to realize their full value to those concerned in the governmental planning process. In the case of cost-benefit analysis, for example, a good deal of interest has been shown lately in its application to local government but – because of our desire to integrate the basic concept into a coherent 'technology of choice' taking explicit account of such factors as uncertainty, variety of alternatives, and flexibility – our own treatment differs a good deal from that of other writers.

At the end of Part III, we shall try to summarize the salient points which have emerged through discussion of the case examples, by referring back to the brief which we set out at the end of Chapter 6 for the development of a technology of strategic choice. We shall also give a number of references to books and journals in which fuller discussion and exposition of particular techniques may be found.

THE CASE EXAMPLES

The case studies in planning which we develop in the following three chapters all relate to the same fictitious local setting. Obviously, in constructing these case examples we have been considerably influenced by certain real planning problems which arose during the course of our research in Coventry; however, we have also drawn at some points on what we have been able to see of planning in other towns and cities. Our object is to focus as far as possible on certain general types of problem which are likely to be relevant in a wide range of different urban and regional settings.

Our first case concerns what is initially seen as a problem of land allocation in a fairly well-defined redevelopment area close to the centre of an existing town. We introduce the AIDA formulation of this problem and consider the implications of leaving certain options open until a later stage in the decision process; we also consider the problems of uncertainty associated with a proposal for a new central bypass road passing through the area concerned. We then reconsider the problems of this redevelopment area in relation to its wider surroundings, and show how a local planning problem of this kind may relate to other wider issues concerning the needs and resources of the town as a whole.

From this first case example, in which the options at all times remain fairly limited, we move to a second case relating to another sector of the same town. In this sector, stretching from the town centre to the rural fringe, there are assumed to be few pressing problems of land allocation, but many interconnected choices of timing and of design, relating on the one hand to redevelopment and improvement in the inner and older neighbourhoods, and on the other hand to new development in the outer areas. The initial analysis focuses on the problem of priorities within these outer areas, and the AIDA approach is used as a means of identifying the many possible development programmes which might be considered. A more explicit approach to costs and benefits is introduced than in the earlier example, and methods are developed for assisting the expression of social and political preferences between alternative programmes. The example is used to demonstrate how ways can be found of maintaining a meaningful dialogue between officers and elected representatives, even when a problem is so complex as to justify recourse to a computer for the drudgery of generating and sifting alternative solutions.

As in the previous case example, the immediate problem is seen as one of selecting a set of short-term actions which will go some way towards satisfying the more immediate pressures for commitment, and yet leave a sufficient range of options open for future choice when conditions may have undergone substantial change. After a full discussion of the problem of priorities in this area of new development, a review is made of the possibilities for extending the analysis to relate to the sector as a whole. Altogether, this case study is treated at considerable length, because we believe it is at this level of the planning process that the emergent technology of choice is most likely to be immediately useful to decision-makers in local government.

The third case example relates to the wider sub-region within which this town is set. The problem considered here is a more open one of choosing a long-term strategy for transportation and for the disposition of housing and industry, under conditions where the options are not initially clear and where it is believed that a considerable outlay in terms of survey, experiment, and consultation will be necessary before the range of feasible solutions can be fully appreciated. The initial task is therefore seen as one of designing a co-ordinated programme of exploratory activities, which can be expected to lead as effectively as possible towards a reduction of the uncertainties which initially cloud the judgement of the policy-makers.

Our three case studies should not be read as attempts to describe planning as it is *now* done, or necessarily as prescriptions of ways in which planning *should* be done; they are offered simply as illustrations of ways in which we think planning *could* be done. A good deal of experiment in practical implementation may be required, in a variety of different organizational settings, before their potential value to local government can be regarded as fully evaluated. In our discussion of the case examples, we will (so far as possible) avoid making any assumptions as to the particular type of organizational structure within which the planners and policy-makers may be working; this will leave us free, in Part IV, to consider the further problem of how the organizational structure of local government can be helped to evolve in such a way as to increase its capacity to cope effectively, yet democratically, with the challenges of strategic choice.

9. Case one: land allocation in a redevelopment area

Area A adjoins the central business area of our fictitious town and is bounded by two radial roads and a railway, as shown in *Map 7*. It contains a disused gasworks and some residential property whose present condition is considered by the local policy-makers to provide a clear case for comprehensive redevelopment.

By 'the local policy-makers' we mean the group of people who are publicly accountable for the land-use decisions made in respect of area A: under the existing system of urban government in Great Britain, this is likely to mean first and foremost the members of the majority party group on the Council of the local planning authority. We do not intend in these case examples to give explicit consideration to questions of organization and procedure within the local government system (we shall come to these questions in Part IV); we shall, however, find it necessary for the purposes of Part III to distinguish between *the policy-makers* in the above sense and *the local planners*, by which we mean the group of individuals whose judgement contributes towards the formulation and pre-selection of land-use proposals for area A for submission to the policy-makers. The group of local planners, as so defined, might be expected to include a number of specialist local government officers, drawn not only from the department directly responsible for land-use planning, but also from certain other departments which have responsibilities in relation to area A; it might also perhaps include one or two elected members who have particular interests in the problem of land use within this area. We therefore consider 'the local planners' and 'the policy-makers' as being in effect two separately identifiable but possibly overlapping groups within the total local government system.

In order to consider the possible options for allocation of the land in area A between different categories of land use, we will assume in the first place that the local planners have been able to make a fairly natural sub-division of the whole area into three smaller areas of approximately similar size, as is shown in *Map 8*.

We will suppose initially that only two categories of land use are being considered: commercial (i.e. shops and offices), because of demands for expansion arising from the central business district, and residential, because of a deficiency of satisfactory housing over the town as a whole. Assuming that it is difficult to combine both uses within the same area, the problem may therefore appear to the local planners as one of deciding whether each of the three areas should be zoned as predominantly commercial or predominantly residential: however they may consider A3 unsuitable for commercial development because of its comparative remoteness both from the central business district and from the railway station,

Map 7. Boundaries of area A

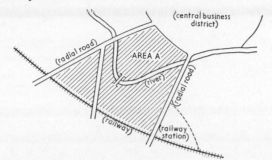

Map 8. Sub-divisions of area A

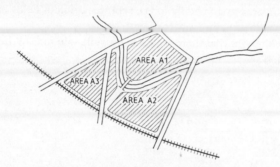

The only other factor which they may decide to take into account at this stage is the assumption that the foreseeable future demand for expansion of the central business area would make it wasteful to zone more than one of the two remaining areas for commercial use.

THE AIDA REPRESENTATION

The problem which we have now defined can be represented symbolically as shown in *Figure 31*.

This diagram simply indicates that there is a choice of commercial or residential use in each of areas A1 and A2, but that the option of commercial use in area A1 is considered incompatible with the option of commercial use in area A2. In the language of the technique known as Analysis of Interconnected Decision Areas (AIDA for short) [1], we call the complete diagram an *option graph* and the line linking areas A1 and A2 an *option bar*, in that it bars the specific combination of the commercial option in A1 with the commercial option in A2. Each of the oval areas in the diagram will be termed a *decision area*, in that it represents a particular field of choice for the planners – although in area A3 it will clearly be a case of Hobson's choice if no alternative possibility is envisaged to the residential zoning shown in the diagram. In this initial example, each decision area corresponds directly to a

Figure 31

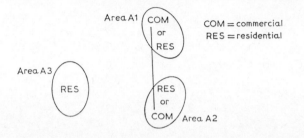

particular area of land – but as our analysis develops we shall wish to apply the idea of a decision area more widely to the representation of fields of choice other than those which are directly concerned with land use.

It is not difficult to see that there are three possible solutions to the overall problem as formulated above. These are:

Table 6

	Area A1	*Area A2*	*Area A3*
Solution *a*	RES	RES	RES
Solution *b*	RES	COM	RES
Solution *c*	COM	RES	RES

We note in passing that, were it not for the 'bar' ruling out the combination of the commercial option in area A1 with the commercial option in area A2, it would have been necessary to add a fourth solution (COM, COM, RES) to this list.

THE ORDERING OF PREFERENCES

Those who are directly concerned in the formulation of proposals for the redevelopment of area A may or may not be able at this stage to express some preference between the alternative solutions, based on their own perception of the most appropriate system of values to be applied. It is convenient at this stage to introduce a form of shorthand to express the various kinds of preference statement which might be made.

We will write

$$S_a) \ S_b) \ S_c$$

to indicate the statement that solution a is preferred to solution b, which in turn is preferred to solution c; if the order of preference is the other way round, we could write it either as

$$S_c) \, S_b) \, S_a \quad \text{or} \quad S_a(\, S_b(\, S_c.$$

If those concerned are not able to express a clear preference between the alternative solutions, we will write

$$S_a / \, S_b / \, S_c.$$

One possibility in practice is that the local planners might feel justified in discarding one of the three solutions (say S_c) but be unable to state a clear preference between the other two. This could be expressed as

$S_a / S_b) \, S_c$ or, more explicitly, S_a / S_b with $S_b) \, S_c$ and $S_a) \, S_c.$

We will assume in this instance that – looking at the problem of area A in isolation – the planners have a clear preference for solution a, mainly because it goes furthest towards a solution of the local authority's housing problem; and that their next preference is for solution b, mainly because this brings housing closer to the city centre than solution c and therefore helps fulfil the planning objective of keeping the central area alive outside normal working and shopping hours. However, the order of preference expressed by local commercial interests might be in direct contradiction to that of the local planners: they might argue that solution c, by providing for a direct extension of the existing commercial area, would provide the most profitable opportunities for commercial investment, while solution a, by allowing for no commercial development in any part of area A, would tend to stifle the commercial life of the town. We might therefore have a direct conflict between

Planners' preference $\quad S_a) \, S_b) \, S_c$

and *Commercial preference* $\quad S_c) \, S_b) \, S_a.$

In this situation, the policy-makers might well be subject to pressures of various kinds from the local commercial interests, and so the local planners might not be able to feel confident that their own preferences would ultimately be endorsed by the Council (i.e. by the full membership of the majority party). In other words, the local planners, despite their own preferences as a group within the local government system, might feel some uncertainty as to the value system with which they ought to conform in putting forward proposals for the future of area A; in the language of Chapter 4, they become particularly aware of the importance of uncertainties within the third main category UV.

At this point, the planners might well decide to try to resolve most of this uncertainty by taking soundings among elected members. As a result of these soundings, we will suppose that the planners' preference $S_a) \, S_b) S_c$ appears to carry the clear endorsement of the policy-makers, and so the planners decide to accept it as a basis for more detailed design work in relation to the redevelopment of area A.

THE COMPLICATION OF THE BYPASS ALIGNMENT

However, other contingencies may subsequently arise which cast doubt upon this initial judgement. We will suppose that, because of an increasing volume of traffic through the city centre, the possibility of an inner bypass road has been raised, and alternative alignments for this road are under discussion between the local planners and the relevant department of central government. One possible alignment passes through area A, on the line of the existing road which *Map 8* shows as cutting across area A3. It is still uncertain what the outcome of these discussions will be: the government department is advocating the route through area A, while the local planners (with a measure of support from the policy-makers) are pressing the claims of an alternative route passing to the other side of the central area. The current betting among the local planners is that their own proposal has a 75 per cent chance of clearing the double hurdles of acceptance by the local council and authorization by the government department concerned.

This new complication to the problem of area A can be considered as an instance of uncertainty which falls into the second of the three categories which we introduced in Chapter 4 – UR, defined as uncertainty of future intention in related areas of choice. This assumes, however, that the government department concerned can be treated as part of the total system of public planning, within which some degree of collaboration is possible. Another view would be that the government department should be regarded by the local planners as a wholly external influence, so that some of the uncertainty falls into the category which we labelled UE, relating to imperfect knowledge of the external environment. Whichever attitude the planners subscribe to, they are now confronted by a new cause of uncertainty which is external to the problem of area A as so far defined.

We will now suppose that the prospect of having to agree to a major road across area A opens up, in the eyes of the planners, the need to consider the further options of industrial zonings for areas A2 and A3. Before the proposal to route the bypass through area A had been mooted, no part of this area had appeared to have adequate communications to support industrial development, but now the possibility of ready access to a major through road (as well as to an existing railway) makes industrial development of either A2 or A3 appear a viable proposition.

The option graph might now be redrawn as follows:

Figure 32

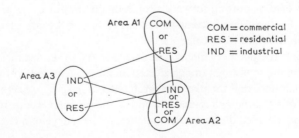

COM = commercial
RES = residential
IND = industrial

We have supposed here that the local planners are working to a brief which imposes severe restraints on the adjacency of housing and industry; the new diagram therefore incorporates four new option bars ruling out the combination of industrial development in any one area with residential development in any adjoining area. By a process of logical elimination it is possible to show that, of the twelve possible combinations of commercial, residential, and industrial zonings in the three areas, no less than eight must be excluded because of the various restrictions that have now been imposed. Of the remaining four solutions, three are identical to those which were considered before the possibility of industrial development arose, but a fourth solution is now added as follows:

Table 7

	Area A1	Area A2	Area A3
Solution a	RES	RES	RES
Solution b	RES	COM	RES
Solution c	COM	RES	RES
Solution d	COM	IND	IND

In other words, if the planners wish to consider industrial development at all in area A, they must permit it in both areas A2 and A3 in combination with commercial development in A1. This raises the question of whether the planners' initial brief was in fact unnecessarily restrictive: whether for instance it might have been possible to relax the rules of adjacency so as to permit the development of light industry next door to a housing area, or whether a mixed residential and commercial zoning might have been possible in one or more of the three areas. We will pass over the possibility of relaxing the brief for the time being, but return to it later in this chapter.

Solution d is in a somewhat different category from solutions a, b, and c, in that it will only come up for consideration if the planners' proposal for routeing the bypass road on the other side of the town is eventually overruled. Because the planners have assessed the probability of this contingency at only about 1 in 4, we can say that, under present circumstances, the prospect of actually being in a position to achieve solution d in practice appears to be more remote than that of achieving one of the other solutions. The relative prospects of achievement may of course change with time if the likelihood that the planners' suggested alignment will be rejected appears to increase or diminish during subsequent discussions or negotiations.

Despite the likelihood that the conditions for achieving solution d will not arise, we will suppose that, in the event of their being forced to route the bypass road through A3, the policy-makers will have reasons for preferring solution d to all others – perhaps because a previous intention to develop new industry alongside the proposed bypass route on the other side of town then becomes unattractive from the point of view of poor communications, and a large-scale switch between housing and industrial zonings therefore appears to be desirable. The planners' overall order of preference would then become a conditional one:

$$S_d) \; S_a) \; S_b) \; S_c \quad \textit{if conditions permitting } S_d \textit{ arise.}$$

$$S_a) \; S_b) \; S_c \quad \textit{if these conditions do not arise.}$$

THE OPPORTUNITIES FOR FLEXIBILITY

Under the conditions of uncertainty created by the bypass negotiations, it now looks as if it might be unwise for the local planners to become committed at this point in time to a solution which completely determines the future pattern of land uses in area A, unless of course they are obliged to do so by whatever statutory procedures of land-use planning apply at the time.

If we admit the possibility of leaving certain options open until a later time, then we can transform the problem of area A from one of making a final choice between three or possibly four full solutions into one of making an initial choice between sixteen different 'action sets' as follows:

Table 8

| Action set | Commitments now | | | Solutions remaining open |
	Area A1	Area A2	Area A3	
1	RES	RES	RES	(= full commitment to S_a)
2	RES	COM	RES	(= full commitment to S_b)
3	COM	RES	RES	(= full commitment to S_c)
4	RES	RES	–	S_a only
5	RES	–	RES	S_a or S_b
6	–	RES	RES	S_a or S_c
7	RES	COM	–	S_b only
8	–	COM	RES	S_b only
9	COM	RES	–	S_c only
10	COM	–	RES	S_c only
11	RES	–	–	S_a or S_b
12	–	RES	–	S_a or S_c
13	–	–	RES	S_a or S_b or S_c
14	COM	–	–	S_c or $S_d\star$
15	–	COM	–	S_b only
16	–	–	–	S_a or S_b or S_c or $S_d\star$

$\star$ solution S_d available only if planners' proposal to route the bypass road away from area A is rejected.

It will be seen that the first three action sets in this list correspond to the options of full commitment to solutions S_a, S_b, and S_c respectively. On the other hand, the option of full commitment to solution S_d cannot be available before a decision on the bypass line is obtained, so there is no corresponding action set to be considered at this particular point in time. Action sets 4 to 10 differ from the first three action sets in that they each involve specific land-use commitments in two of the three areas only, while action sets 11 to 15 each involve commitment in one area only. Under action set 16, all options are left open and no commitments at all are made for the time being.

THE PRESSURES FOR COMMITMENT

The choice of an action set from a list of this kind must depend to a large extent on the intensity of the various pressures which may be pushing the planners to commit themselves to immediate action: for instance, if they were being pressed particularly strongly by local commercial interests for a clear policy on the zoning of land for commercial expansion, they might be more inclined than otherwise to select one of the seven action sets 2, 3, 7, 8, 9, 10, 14, or 15, each of which includes a firm commitment to allocate land for commercial development somewhere within area A. If they were subject to particularly strong local authority pressures for an opportunity to start work on design and land-acquisition procedures for new local authority housing schemes, they would clearly be less inclined to select any of the last three action sets on the list; while, if it was considered possible and desirable to start these procedures immediately in more than one area at a time, this would create a further bias towards the choice of an action set from among the first six of those listed in *Table 8*.

We will suppose in this case that, because of their awareness of the various pressures for commitment, the planners see some advantage (which they might not find easy to quantify) in making an immediate selection of one area for commercial development, and also an immediate selection of one area, or perhaps two areas at most, for housing development; however, we will suppose that no further advantage is seen in immediately zoning all three areas for housing development (as under action set 1), since there might be insufficient resources available to allow preliminary work to start in more than two areas at a time. In order to see more clearly how far each of the various action sets succeeds in accommodating these pressures for commitment, we will rearrange *Table 8* as shown in *Table 9* overleaf.

SOME CRITERIA FOR CHOICE

Now that we have set out the full list of possible action sets in this way, we can begin to consider in what ways it might be possible to reduce it to a shorter list, from which a final selection of a preferred action set might be made. Our discussion of the problem so far suggests that it might be appropriate to attempt this by applying a combination of three different criteria:

(i) *The response-to-pressure criterion.* If any action set A permits exactly the same choice of full solutions as another action set B, but satisfies the pressures for commitment less fully, then A should be rejected (i.e. other things being equal, response to pressures for commitment is a good thing).

(ii) *The preferred-full-solution criterion.* If any action set A satisfies the pressures for commitment to exactly the same degree as another action set B, and permits the same choice of full solutions except that one or more solutions permitted by B are replaced in A by other solutions lower in the order of preference, then A should be rejected (i.e. other things being equal, it is a good thing to go for full solutions higher up the order of preference).

(iii) *The flexibility criterion.* If any action set A satisfies the pressures for commitment to exactly the same degree as another action set B, and permits the same choice of full solutions except that it *omits* one or more full solutions allowed by B, then A should be rejected (i.e. other things being equal, flexibility is a good thing, even to the extent of retaining extra options which at present do not appear very desirable).

Table 9

Degree of response to pressures for commitment		Firm allocations of land	Action set	Full solutions available
commercial	housing			
full	full	one area for COM and two for RES	2 or 3	S_b only S_c only
full	partial	one area for COM and one for RES	7 or 8 or 9 or 10	S_b only S_b only S_c only S_c only
full	none	one area for COM but none for RES	14 or 15	S_c or $S_d\star$ S_b only
none	full	two (or more) areas for RES but none for COM	1 or 4 or 5 or 6	S_a only S_a only S_a or S_b S_a or S_c
none	partial	one area for RES but none for COM	11 or 12 or 13	S_a or S_b S_a or S_c S_a or S_b or S_c
none	none	no areas either for RES or for COM	16	S_a or S_b or S_c or $S_d\star$

$\star$ meaning of asterisk as in *Table 8*.

Referring back to the information in *Table 9*, application of these three criteria in turn allows the total of sixteen possible action sets to be reduced as follows:

(i) by the response-to-pressure criterion:

reject action sets 7, 8, 15   (prefer action set 2)
reject action sets 9, 10   (prefer action set 3)
reject action set 11   (prefer action set 5)
reject action set 12   (prefer action set 6)
(leaving action sets 1, 2, 3, 4, 5, 6, 13, 14, 16).

(ii) by the preferred-solution criterion (accepting the order of preference between solutions as S_a) S_b) S_c, together with S_d) S_a if the planners' preference for the bypass route is rejected):

reject action set 3   (prefer action set 2)
reject action set 6   (prefer action set 5)
*reject action sets 9, 10   (prefer action set 7 or 8)
*reject action set 12   (prefer action set 11)
(leaving action sets 1, 2, 4, 5, 13, 14, 16).
(iii) by the flexibility criterion:

reject action sets 1, 4   (prefer action set 5)
*reject action sets 11, 12   (prefer action set 13)
(leaving action sets 2, 5, 13, 14, 16).

* but these action sets are also rejected according to earlier criteria.

The application of these three criteria in turn has resulted in what we may call a *partial preference ordering* of the sixteen action sets, in that some but not all of them have been sorted into a relative order of merit. The various relationships of preference so far established can conveniently be shown in the form of what is sometimes called a 'directed graph' as follows:

Figure 33

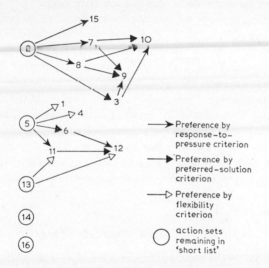

This graph represents an extension into two dimensions of the shorthand which we used at an earlier stage of the analysis to express preferences between pairs of full solutions. It will be noticed that the five short-listed action sets (2, 5, 13, 14, and 16) are the only ones without any arrows leading inwards; in other words, the only action sets which cannot be rejected by comparison with others according to the three criteria laid down so far.

To eliminate any of the five action sets which remain, the three criteria of response to pressure, preferred full solution, and flexibility are no longer enough in themselves. It is necessary to make some further assumptions as to the balance to be drawn between the three criteria, and this involves problems which may have far-reaching political implications. What is it worth to the policy-makers to satisfy

12

immediate pressures for commitment, and how strong are the advantages of keeping options open ? What, in comparison with these considerations, are their relative strengths of preference between the four possible full solutions ? These are questions which will have to be answered, bearing in mind various other external judgements such as the latest betting odds on the outcome of the bypass negotiations, before the short-list can be reduced to a single preferred action set for early implementation.

Our definition of the flexibility criterion implicitly recognized that there may be underlying uncertainties as to the appropriate order of preference for the four possible full solutions; there is no point in retaining the flexibility to choose an apparently bad solution, unless there is a belief that ultimately circumstances might conceivably change in such a way as to make it become a good solution. Perhaps in this case the policy-makers are particularly conscious of doubt in relation to their preference for S_b over S_c: they find it quite conceivable either that circumstances might cause them to revise their order of preference in the long term, or that a deeper analysis of the implications of each alternative might lead them to a revision in the shorter term. Perhaps the policy-makers' uncertainty about their present order of preference reflects partly a state of doubt about the future effects of each solution on different sectors of the local community (i.e. uncertainty of the type UE) and partly a state of doubt as to their own future planning intentions in the other areas which surround area A (i.e. uncertainty of the type UR). In these circumstances, the planners and policy-makers might agree that they should attach a high value to the flexibility criterion in the short term, and select action set 16 for the time being, while taking a closer look at the problem of A in relation to its wider environment. In other words, the immediate decision is in a sense a non-decision; to keep all options open and carry out some further analyses while fending off for a little longer the pressures for commitment to specific actions within area A.

AREA A IN RELATION TO THE SURROUNDING DISTRICT

In order to consider area A in relation to its immediate surroundings, we will first extend our map of the district as shown in *Map 9* opposite.

We will assume that, over this wider area, the options for future land use are initially seen by the local planners as in *Map 10* below. For the sake of simplicity we will not for the time being include the options of industrial zoning within area AI, which are only available if the planners' preference for the bypass line is rejected. We will however come back later in this chapter to discuss briefly how these options might affect the problem of area A in its more extended form.

The new choices of land use which are revealed by *Map 10*, in certain parts of the wider district surrounding area A, are all associated with the internal problems of area A in one way or another. The need to replace the sub-standard secondary school which at present serves area A and adjoining areas will arise at, if not before, the time of comprehensive redevelopment of area A2: the only reasonable sites available are at B1 (which would only be easy to acquire if – as rumour has it – the cricket club intends to move out to the periphery of the town) and at B2 (which the

Map 9. Area A in relation to its surroundings

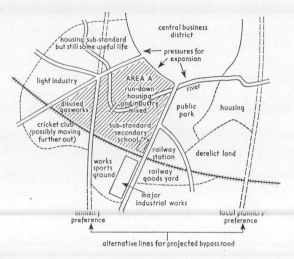

Map 10. Area A and surroundings: options for future land use

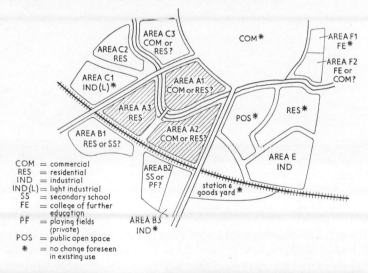

industrial employer may be unwilling to sell because he is believed to be holding it in reserve in the hope of gaining permission for future works expansions and car-parking extensions). Doubts therefore exist at present about the relative prospects of achievement of either proposed location for the new school: if there is ultimately a need to consider resorting to compulsory purchase procedures, it is not clear which proposal would be easier to defend at a public inquiry.

The commercial options in C3 and F2 arise because the planners foresee a need to provide for future commercial expansion in some other location near to the city centre, in the event of a decision not to allocate any land within area A, or to allocate insufficient land to allow for ultimate requirements. We will suppose that area F2 is the only location outside area A which might be available for early commercial development, but that this site is also in demand by the adjoining college of further education, which has expansion plans that would otherwise have to be provided for by acquiring a second site on the edge of the town. In the longer term, there is a possibility that commercial expansion might be considered in area C3, which the planners believe may ultimately become ripe for comprehensive redevelopment.

AIDA REPRESENTATION OF THE EXTENDED PROBLEM

These new considerations allow us to extend the original graph of *Figure 31* as follows:

Figure 34

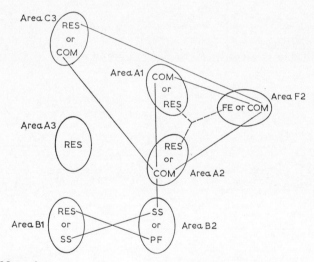

(Key as in *Map 10*)

We have in this diagram added a number of new option bars relating to the various decision areas for land use outside area A. The bar between option SS in B1 and option SS in B2 states that there is no need to build secondary schools on both sites; the bar between option RES in B1 and option PF in B2 states that the planners consider that the school must inevitably go in one or other of these two locations. The bar between option SS in B2 and option COM in A2 states the planners' belief that the school will be badly located in B2 if the adjoining area A2 is developed commercially, and this solution is therefore ruled out, at any rate for the time being.

This diagram introduces one *multiple option bar* in the form of a triple link between A1, A2, and F2, to indicate that the combined solution of RES in A1, RES in A2, and FE in F2 is unacceptable because this provides no location for short-term commercial development; we use broken lines for this multiple bar to make the point that it does not necessarily rule out any combination which involves only two out of the three options concerned: for instance RES in A1 together with RES in A2 is acceptable provided COM rather than FE is chosen in F2. The triangle of ordinary option bars linking the COM options in areas A1, A2, and F2 indicate that only one of these three areas is required for commercial development in the shorter term; there is, however, a bar between COM in F2 and RES in C3 because area F2 is smaller than either A1 and A2, and it is considered that its use for early commercial development would require ultimately to be supplemented by further commercial development in C3. Of the three possible locations for shorter-term commercial development, we will suppose that only A2 contains sufficient land to satisfy expected long-term requirements as well, so that the COM option in A2 renders unnecessary (and therefore rules out) the COM option in C3.

The complexity of the option graph has now increased considerably in comparison with the original graph of *Figure 31*. However, we can express the extended problem rather more simply by translating it into another form, in which decision areas no longer correspond directly to particular areas of land. The crucial choices can now be seen as:

    1 to choose a site for the new secondary school

and 2 to choose an area for short-term commercial development.

These two choices between them will determine the site for extension of the college of further education, and also the future development of each of the various areas of land represented in *Map 10*, apart possibly from C3. We can therefore draw a new option graph as follows:

Figure 35

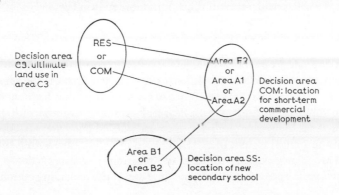

VARIATIONS OF PLANNING PERSPECTIVE

By drawing this alternative option graph, we have in effect altered our perspective from one of local land-use planning to one of the planning of particular operational systems: namely the planning of the education authority's school system (reflected in decision area SS) and the planning of the community's town centre system of commercial transactions (decision area COM). This case example therefore illustrates, among other things, the existence of an overlap at the local level between certain different perspectives of the governmental planning process. We can illustrate this symbolically by means of the following diagram:

Figure 36

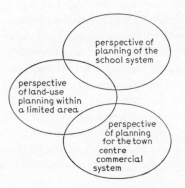

In translating the option graph of *Figure 34* into that of *Figure 35*, we were in effect shifting our perspective from that of the left-hand area of *Figure 36* to that of the two right-hand areas. This kind of diagram could, of course, be extended to show the interaction with other perspectives such as that associated with the planning of the further educational system. Clearly, each such perspective is likely to correspond to that of a different group of participants in the public planning process, and so the overlapping of perspectives may have some important implications for the pattern of organization and of communication within the local government system. We will consider these implications more fully in Part IV.

SOLUTIONS TO THE EXTENDED PROBLEM

It is not difficult, by a process of logical elimination, to arrive at the set of all possible solutions to the extended problem of area A. The result is the same whether the process is carried out with reference to the simplified option graph of *Figure 35* or to the original graph of *Figure 34*. A useful technique is to start with the decision area which has the greatest number of connections to other areas (COM in *Figure 35*, or A2 in *Figure 34*) and then, taking each option in turn within this decision area, to work methodically through the remaining decision areas to find what combinations are possible without violating any of the remaining option bars.

This kind of process of systematic elimination leads to the discovery that there are seven feasible solutions to the problem as a whole. In terms of the designated uses of different areas of land, these solutions can be listed as follows:

Table 10

Area:	A_1	A_2	A_3	B_1	B_2	C_3	F_2	X
Solution a_1	RES	RES	RES	SS	PF	COM	COM	FE
Solution a_2	RES	RES	RES	RES	SS	COM	COM	FE
Solution b_1	RES	COM	RES	SS	PF	RES	FE	Ag
Solution c_1	COM	RES	RES	SS	PF	COM	FE	Ag
Solution c_2	COM	RES	RES	SS	PF	RES	FE	Ag
Solution c_3	COM	RES	RES	RES	SS	COM	FE	Ag
Solution c_4	COM	RES	RES	RES	SS	RES	FE	Ag
Assumed no. of units of area	14	18	13	13	10	12	7	10

This table has been set out in such a way as to permit ready comparison with the original table of solutions to the restricted problem of area A (*Table 6*): each of the three groups of solutions in the new list derives from one of the three solutions *a*, *b*, or *c* of this earlier list. For completeness, the table includes one piece of land which was too remote to have appeared in *Map 10*: this is the alternative site (which we have called area X) for the extension of the college of further education, which is assumed to be on the edge of the town and at present in agricultural use (Ag).

One way in which these seven solutions can be compared is by working out how much land will be allocated to each of the various possible uses for each alternative. Assuming that the relative areas are as shown in the table above (in terms of units which might or might not be acres: for purposes of this example the question of scale is not important), then the total of 97 units of area would be divided under each solution as follows:

Table 11

Area:	RES	COM	SS	PF	FE	Ag.	Total
Solution a_1	45	19	13	10	10	0	97
Solution a_2	58	19	10	0	10	0	97
Solution b_1	39	18	13	10	7	10	97
Solution c_1	31	26	13	10	7	10	97
Solution c_2	43	14	13	10	7	10	97
Solution c_3	44	26	10	0	7	10	97
Solution c_4	56	14	10	0	7	10	97

On considerations of area alone, certain solutions might now appear unattractive to the planners – for instance, solution c_1, which appears to make the least contribution to the town's overall housing problem (to bring yet another new perspective into the argument). However, if they are going to take considerations of area into account more explicitly at this stage, the planners might also feel bound to consider more explicitly certain other factors such as the relative costs of redevelopment in different areas, and the implications of alternative solutions in terms of environment and accessibility. For instance, the college of further education might be much happier with a smaller site adjoining its existing buildings than with a larger but more remote site, whose detachment might cause all kinds of administrative complications within the further education system; while the planners' earlier argument that it was desirable to encourage housing rather than commerce in areas adjacent to the town centre would have to be looked at more closely according to a range of different economic and social implications.

We will assume that, because of an awareness of complications of this kind, neither the planners nor the policy-makers now find it easy to express any obvious preferences between any of the seven full solutions to the extended problem (perhaps an initial objection to solution c_1, which permits only 31 units of residential land, might be overcome if sufficient land could be released in other parts of town, or in adjoining rural districts). Although a more explicit evaluation of environmental and accessibility factors might help them to clarify their preferences to some degree, we will suppose in this case that time for further analysis is running out; by this time, the pressures for early decision on locations for commercial expansion and for local authority housing may have intensified, while new pressures may also have arisen for housing development by private builders. As a result, the policy-makers may find themselves faced with no alternative but to make an immediate commitment to one or other of the alternative full solutions within area A. Also, there may be strong pressures from the college of further education for a firm decision on location for future expansion, which is itself determined by the choice of full solution for area A. This means that it is now necessary to make a choice between three alternative action sets which correspond to action sets 1, 2, and 3 of *Table 8* in that they imply full commitment within area A to solutions S_a, S_b, and S_c respectively; however, in terms of the extended problem they also imply a specific choice of land use in area F2. The three available action sets can now be listed as follows:

Table 12

| Action set | Commitments now | | | | |
	Area A1	Area A2	Area A3	Site for FE	Solutions remaining open
1'	RES	RES	RES	X	a_1 or a_2
2'	RES	COM	RES	F2	b_1
3'	COM	RES	RES	F2	$c_1, c_2, c_3,$ or c_4

The action sets corresponding to the original 1, 2, and 3 of *Table 8* have been renumbered 1', 2', and 3' so as to emphasize the point that time has passed since the original comparison, and the context of choice has by now become very different. Perhaps solution *a* may still be seen as a particularly good solution within area A, and this will lead now to a certain bias towards action set 1'; however, it can now be seen to lead to a less desirable location for the college extension than would 2' or 3', and also to leave less flexibility for future choice than does 3' (with its four possible full solutions, leaving open not only the choice of location for the secondary school but also the choice of ultimate use for area C3).

To introduce some more new terminology which will be useful later on, we say that action set 3' is more *robust* than the alternatives of 1' and 2', in that it leaves a wider range of full solutions available. The question of whether or not the robustness of action set 3', together with its ability to satisfy the demands of the college, is sufficient to justify its acceptance despite its disadvantages within area A is one which is likely to raise some difficult problems of value judgement; this will be so however detailed the picture which has by now been built up of the various social and economic consequences of each alternative.

A RECONSIDERATION OF THE EFFECTS OF THE BYPASS PROPOSAL

So far, the planners have limited their appraisal of the extended problem by ignoring the further complications which would arise from a realization of the threat (as they see it) to route the bypass road through area A. However, this contingency may still have to be considered – it may even by now have grown more likely – and so the possibility of industrial development in certain parts of area A may still have to be examined. However, the planners may now be able to see that the only industrial solution permitted by their original brief – solution *d*, which zoned areas A2 and A3 for industrial use and A1 for commercial – might throw many more choices out of balance in the surrounding areas. For instance, because housing would now be excluded altogether from area A, the case for a new secondary school in either B1 or B2 might well disappear. Referring to *Map 10*, the remaining option of residential development in B1 might now be considered incompatible with the decision to develop industry across the railway in A3, in which case no solution based on S_d is possible, and the whole idea of industrial development in area A might have to be abandoned. Alternatively, the planners' brief might be modified so as to permit the adjacency of housing and industry when separated by a railway track, or to allow the consideration of some third option for the future use of the land in area B1.

We will not go on to consider in detail the complete reformulation of the problem which might then take place in these circumstances. Rather, we will suppose that, even under a modified brief, the planners are unable to find any solution which allows eventual industrial development within area A while satisfying the short-term demands for the release of land for housing development in the town as a whole. Perhaps they may investigate a possible transfer of proposed industrial development from area E (see *Map 10*) into area A, thus releasing area E for housing development, but this may lead them to discover physical restrictions which prevent the land becoming available in time to satisfy short-term pressures for development.

The immediate choice therefore still rests between action sets $1'$, $2'$, and $3'$ with their implied commitments to solutions a, b, and c respectively within area A. We will suppose that, after a meeting in which the implications of all three alternatives are given a thorough airing, the policy-makers decide that the balance of advantage lies with action set $3'$ and proceed to undertake commitments accordingly: to authorize commercial development in area A1, to start preliminary work on housing in areas A2 and A3, and to allow the college of further education to develop alongside its existing site. This solution is, as we have already seen, a satisfactory one from the point of view of the college, a less satisfactory one from the point of view of the planners' preferences in area A, and a fully satisfactory one from the point of view of retaining flexibility in the siting of the secondary school and the future zoning of area C. Through their more extended analysis, the planners and policy-makers have at any rate avoided making a commitment to a course of action for area A which might have appeared more satisfactory from the point of view of the area considered in isolation, while having hidden disadvantages from the point of view of the town as a whole.

SUMMARY OF GENERAL POINTS FROM THIS CASE EXAMPLE

In this case example, we started with a limited problem of land-use choices within a redevelopment area and then demonstrated how, through the recognition of various kinds of uncertainty, such a problem might come gradually to be seen as part of a more complex problem concerned with the large-scale disposition of housing, industry, commerce, and other land uses over the town as a whole.

Through discussion of this particular example, we have attempted not only to lay some of the foundations for a 'technology of strategic choice', but also to simulate as realistically as possible the kind of environment in which such a technology will have to be applied. In particular, we have tried to simulate the constantly changing pattern of events and influences which may make it desirable not always to look for complete solutions to well-defined problems, but rather to concentrate on the search for an acceptable partial solution which may go some way towards meeting the pressures for early commitment in respect of certain key choices, while leaving other options open until a later stage when more information may be available. Our particular concern is with a technology for the continuous process of public planning, as opposed to the more finite kind of decision process such as might arise in the design of a particular building or machine.

We have introduced, as contributions to our technology, the AIDA representation as a means of clarifying the relationships between different areas of choice; the idea of a distinction between full solutions and more limited 'action sets' which may leave the planner with a degree of flexibility in the face of uncertainty; a method of reducing the list of alternative action sets through the use of separate criteria of response to pressures, of preferred full solution, and of flexibility (or robustness); and a demonstration of the way in which the context of choice may be changed by the enlargement of the initial planning perspective.

Our methodology in this case example has been based largely on logic and hardly at all on measurement. A good deal of what we have said may, we believe, only represent a more formal expression of the kind of reasoning processes which the experienced planner may already be applying in practice at a more intuitive level. However, the mere act of making these processes more explicit may, in our opinion, be of real value if it thereby becomes possible to bring to the surface – and allow wider discussion of – some of the arguments and assumptions which would otherwise remain buried in the mind of the individual.

This first case example was so devised that there was at no time a need to consider more than a limited number of alternative options, solutions, or action sets. This, together with the avoidance of any explicit measurements of cost and benefit, meant that it raised no serious computational problems. In the next chapter, we will develop our technology further by considering another case example in which the number of possible combinations is very large; and we will this time show how, in order to facilitate judgement in such circumstances, it may be desirable to attempt a more explicit evaluation of those kinds of social cost and benefit which the planners and policy-makers consider to be most important. This will lead us to consider, more fully than in the present chapter, the problems of resolving the conflicting value judgements which may underlie any discrepancies in stated orders of preference.

In Chapter 9, we focused on the problem of area A, an inner area of our fictitious town which we supposed to be ripe for comprehensive redevelopment. We now turn our attention to sector Z, which we suppose to be a larger and much more heterogeneous area on the opposite side of the same town, extending outwards from the central area to the rural fringe, and posing immediate problems of improvement and new development rather than of total renewal. We will at this point give the town a name – Fluxton – which is intended to be suggestive of any urban community in a state of continuing physical and social change. As in the previous chapter, we will maintain a distinction between 'the local planners' (who formulate proposals) and 'the policy-makers' (who are publicly accountable for planning decisions), although there is a possibility that these may not represent exactly the same groups of people as for area A, since we are now dealing with a different part of town and perhaps therefore with a different set of problems and of planning perspectives.

The relationship of area A and sector Z to the map of Fluxton we will suppose to be as shown in *Map 11*.

We will suppose that the local planners are able to divide sector Z into a number of smaller areas, each of which has its own particular characteristics and its own particular problems, as shown in *Map 12*.

To review the various problems within sector Z, we will start with the older and more central areas and work outwards.

In area P1, the housing is old and well below current standards, but is still considered to have some useful life before redevelopment. It is becoming increasingly overcrowded, since it serves as a reception area for new immigrants brought to Fluxton by the search for work opportunities. These immigrants may find it difficult to find accommodation in other parts of town, though a combination of several factors – the existing ownership and rent structures, the method of assessing priorities for municipal housing, and possibly a certain amount of discrimination by landlords or others against particular social or ethnic groups. There may be the seeds of many long-term problems in this area, but we will assume that the planners are particularly aware of two particular problems in the shorter term: first, how to provide better play facilities for the residents' children, and, second, whether or not to spend public money on the provision of grants for improvements in standard

162

housing amenities, in the face of uncertainty about how soon the area will be scheduled for comprehensive redevelopment.

Meanwhile, the noisy industrial site at P2 creates a nuisance for the residents of
both P1 and S1, and the planners are exerting pressure on the owners to move out
to a new industrial estate (whose location is, however, uncertain until a firm line is

Map 11. Outline map of Fluxton

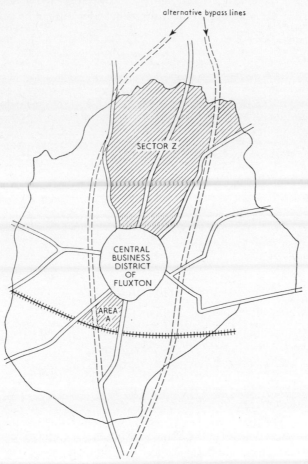

agreed for the proposed bypass road). Assuming that the site at P2 can be made
available for another use in advance of the comprehensive redevelopment of P1, it
could provide either a playground for the children of P1 (which is considered by the
planners to be socially desirable) or a set of lock-up garages for the residents of S1
(which would be commercially attractive to private developers). There is some
possibility that, as a compromise, the site might be divided between these two uses.

The housing in area Q is again sub-standard, though it is not thought to justify wholesale redevelopment within the foreseeable future. The problem here is seen as one of selecting particular sub-areas whose life might be prolonged by the application of more comprehensive improvement policies, both in relation to the houses themselves and also in relation to their immediate environment.

The shopping area at R has a serious environmental problem: it straddles a main through traffic route and there is constant interference between through traffic, local traffic, stationary vehicles, and pedestrians. Present regulations permit loading and short-term waiting in the main road, and it will not be easy to justify

Map 12. Fluxton: sector Z

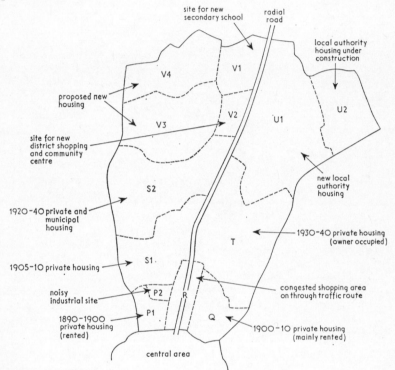

any more restrictive policies in the immediate future. One way of relieving traffic congestion would be for the local authority to promote, at its own expense, a scheme for rear servicing and off-street parking facilities, but even this would involve difficult land-acquisition problems. In the long term, hopes are centred on the elimination of through traffic when the bypass is built, together with the creation of a second shopping centre for sector Z at V2, farther out from the town centre.

We will suppose that there are few immediate problems in areas S and T, apart from the difficulty we have already referred to of finding garage space for the car-owners of S1. The only difficulty in area U is the remoteness of the existing shopping facilities at R and of the nearest secondary school. It is planned that these deficiencies will be met through the building of a new local authority secondary school at V1, and of the new district shopping centre at V2, with an adjoining community centre including library, youth, clinic, and old peoples' facilities. It is considered that the shopping centre might be developed either by the local authority itself or through a private agency, although the latter option might carry with it a less immediate prospect of implementation and hence an unnecessary prolongation of the current congestion problem in area R.

Areas V3 and V4 we suppose to be earmarked for housing development, although it is still uncertain whether the housing should be municipal or private. There are no serious problems of land acquisition, but there is a problem of inadequate main drainage capacity for the residential development of this area. The ability to proceed with a main drainage extension scheme in the immediate future is, however, dependent on the ability of the local authority engineer's department to marshal sufficient resources of skilled survey and design staff: this is limited both by difficulty in recruiting engineers of the necessary calibre and by the many competing claims on the services of private design consultants.

The case of sector Z differs from that of area A in that there are at this point of time few unresolved choices of land allocation, the principal exception relating to area P2. There may, however, be many options of priority and of design for specific development projects. We will now consider the more important of these options, and the relationships between them, in a rather more systematic way.

THE OPTIONS OF TIMING AND DESIGN

As a first basis for the more systematic study of the problems of sector Z, *Table 13* itemizes the various possibilities for future development within the sector, each with a separate project reference number. The table then goes on to discuss other possible fields of action in sector Z which are not directly concerned with development of land, and concludes with a listing of certain activities beyond the sector boundary which are seen to have a close bearing on decisions within the sector itself.

Under the existing system of local government in Great Britain, it may be noted that responsibility for the various public development projects listed in this table might in practice be divided between different tiers of the local government system, depending on whether or not the population of Fluxton is sufficiently large for the town to have been designated as a County Borough. For the purposes of this case example, we will suppose that, even if a two-tier structure of local government applies in Fluxton, there is a sufficient degree of co-ordination between tiers for our identification of a single group of 'local planners' and a corresponding group of 'policy-makers' to be as meaningful as in the earlier case example.

For each possible action listed in *Table 13* – whether it concerns physical development, or the procurement of additional resources, or the application of certain

Table 13

Public development projects in sector Z	Nature of principal design choices	Timing options, by year of programme measured from current year as year 0											
		0	1	2	3	4	5	6	7	8	9	10	later
Z1 Housing in U2	None at this stage	·	×	×	×	×	×	×	×	×	×	×	×
Z2 Main drainage for V	Engineering	×	×	·	·	·	·	×	×	×	×	×	×
Z3 Secondary school in V1	Architectural	×	×	×	·	·	·	·	×	×	×	×	×
Z4 Community Centre in V2	Architectural	×	×	×	×	×	·	·	·	·	×	×	×
Z5 Playground in P2	Land allocation Z5/Z11	×	×	×	×	×	×	·	·	·	·	·	×
Z6 Parking/service area in R	Layout	×	×	×	·	·	×	×	×				
Z7 Redevelopment of P1	Layout, density, etc.*	×	×	×	×	×	×	×	×	·	·	·	·
Development projects in Z with public/private options													
Z8 Housing in V3	Type, density, layout*	×	×	:	:	:	:	:	×	×	×	×	×
Z9 Housing in V4	Type, density, layout*	×	×	×	:	:	:	:	:	:	×	×	×
Z10 Shopping centre in V2	Floor space, layout	×	×	×	×	×	×	:	:	×	:	×	×
Z11 Garages in P2	Land allocation, layout	×	×	×	×	×	×	:	:	:	:	×	×

166

Other intended actions in sector Z

Code	Action	Design option	0	1	2	3	4	5	6	7	8	9	10	later
Z12	Waiting restrictions in R	Legal*	×	×	×	×	·	·	·	·	·	×	×	×
Z13	Works relocation from P2	Contractual	×	×	×	·	·	·	·	·	×	×	×	×
Z14	Improvements in P1	Areas for allocation of standard improvement grants*	×	·	·	·	·	·	·	·	·	·	·	·
Z15	Improvements in Q	Areas for discretionary grants and environmental improvement*	×	·	·	·	·	·	·	·	·	·	·	·

Related actions beyond sector Z: developmental

Code	Action	Design option	0	1	2	3	4	5	6	7	8	9	10	later
Y1	Various housing projects	Type and density*	×	×	·	·	·	·	·	·	·	·	×	·
Y2	Other secondary schools	Location, catchments*	×	×	×	·	·	·	·	·	×	×	×	×
Y3	Industrial estate project	Location*	×	×	×	×	·	·	·	·	·	×	×	×
Y4	Bypass road	Route*	×	×	×	×	·	·	·	·	·	×	×	×

Related actions beyond sector Z: non-developmental

Code	Action	Design option
Y5	Housing allocation system	Priority rules for allocation of municipal tenancies*
Y6	Housing rent structure	General rent levels and system of differentiation*
Y7	Resource procurement – money	Level of local taxation for next financial year*
Y8	Resource procurement – staff	Reinforcement of engineering design resources by recruitment or contracting out*

Key: × = not conceivable that implementation by local authority could start during year shown.
: = implementation could under certain circumstances start during year shown.
: = implementation could start during year shown *if* public development option is chosen.
* = highly significant design options.

13

167

inducements or constraints to the actions of others – we have attempted to specify the nature of the principal design choices which face the local planners. Here we use the word 'design' in the broad sense to include not only the design of buildings and engineering works but also, for instance, the design of coherent systems of local waiting restrictions or rules for allocation of municipal tenancies. Those design choices which are at this point in time considered particularly crucial for the future of sector Z are marked with an asterisk.

Map 13. Sector Z: location of decision problems

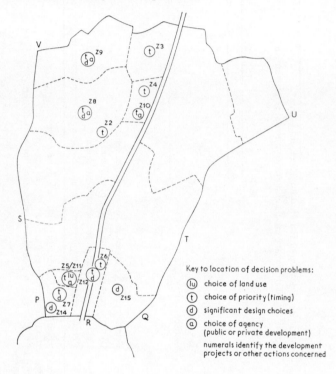

Key to location of decision problems:

(lu) choice of land use
(t) choice of priority (timing)
(d) significant design choices
(a) choice of agency
(public or private development)

numerals identify the development projects or other actions concerned

For those actions, developmental and other, where important questions of timing arise, *Table 13* also indicates the range of alternative years in which implementation might reasonably be programmed to start, subject perhaps to certain qualifying conditions in each case (we will consider these later). For instance, the entry for project Z3, relating to the building of a secondary school in V1, indicates a belief that its physical implementation must be programmed to start in some year between year 3 and year 6; any year earlier than year 3 is excluded because it is considered that it would be technically impossible to complete the preliminary site acquisition, design, and tendering procedures in less than three years under any conceivable conditions, and any year later than year 6 is excluded because it is considered politically inconceivable – in view of the social pressures for more secondary school places – that the project could in any circumstances be deferred beyond that date. The implementation of project Z1, on the other hand, is due to begin at any time and no option needs to be considered other than year 0, because the project is so far advanced that it is impossible to imagine that a start on construction work might under any conditions be deferred beyond the current financial year.

We have not attempted in *Table 13* to suggest what *specific* design options might be available, even for the more significant design problems marked with an asterisk. Clearly, in some of these cases a good deal of preliminary work might be necessary before a sufficient range of feasible alternatives can be formulated.

In *Map 13*, we use an outline map of sector Z to pick out the approximate locations where some kind of localized discretion is now seen to arise. Different types of symbol are used to indicate projects and other intended actions for which significant choices of priority and of design have been identified, accompanied in some cases by choices of agency and of land use. As is typical in urban planning situations, there is a marked clustering of problems in the inner 'twilight' zones, on the one hand, and in the peripheral areas of new development, on the other.

A CLOSER LOOK AT THE CHOICES IN AREA V

Even assuming that a sufficient range of design options can at this stage be formulated for each scheme in *Table 13*, it is not likely to be easy to enumerate all the relationships between the various different choices of priority and design over sector Z as a whole. The planners might therefore decide to focus initially on those choices which particularly concern area V, which is the part of sector Z where most of the early development will take place and where most of the more immediate timing options arise. Later in this chapter, we shall return to take another look at the problems of area V within the wider perspective of sector Z as a whole, with particular reference to the longer-term problem of the future of the 'twilight' areas P, Q, and R.

In looking at area V, we will suppose that the planners decide not to spend any time exploring different design options for the two housing projects (they may have a strong conviction that one particular type of layout should be adopted), nor do they wish to consider development of these estates through a private agency, except in certain exceptional circumstances (because there is a strong unfulfilled demand for municipal housing). For the time being, they may consider that their most crucial choices concern the relative *priorities* of the various development projects which are being considered within area V.

Map 13 shows that there are in all six projects within area V where choices of priority are seen to arise: these are the mains drainage project (Z2), the secondary school project (Z3), the community centre project (Z4), the two housing projects (Z8 and Z9), and the shopping centre project (Z10). We will suppose that the drainage project (which is a necessary preliminary to housing development in area V) happens to be a very expensive one because of the nature of the terrain, and that its timing is believed to be critically dependent on a reinforcement of the Council's resources of skilled engineering design staff. Also, we will suppose that the accounting structure of municipal housing is such that any public investment in new housing development must be supported mainly through income from the rents of existing tenants. Accordingly, in considering the six choices of project priority within area V, it is believed essential at the same time to consider the range of choices available in the two related fields of housing rent structure and design staff procurement (identified in *Table 13* as Y6 and Y8 respectively).

We have therefore now identified a total of eight decision areas relating directly or indirectly to the problem of priorities within area V, and we can proceed to explore the relationships between them in rather more detail. The task of drawing up a complete option graph will be more difficult than in the earlier case study of area A, in that there are more options to consider in each decision area and potentially many more 'option bars' between them. As a first step, we will draw up an outline option graph in which the various decision areas and options are all specified in full, but the relationships between decision areas are only shown in outline form: the parts of the graph where such relationships are believed to exist are indicated by the drawing of dotted lines or *links* between particular pairs of decision areas. Each link implies a belief that certain particular combinations of options from the decision areas concerned may either be incompatible or have certain joint effects over and above the effects of either option considered independently.

The outline option graph for the eight decision areas we have now picked out is shown in *Figure 37*.

The reference number inside each decision area relates to the corresponding reference in *Table 13*, with the suffixes t and d standing for choices of timing and design respectively. Decision area Z10t/a embraces a joint choice of timing and of development agency for the shopping centre, since both public and private development are being considered and it is believed that the range of possible starting years will differ in each case; the development is not likely to be attractive commercially for at least five years, although the local authority might possibly be prepared to develop it early and let it initially at subsidized rentals in order to achieve the social benefit of relieving congestion in the existing shopping area at R.

Within each of the six decision areas which relate to a specific project, *Figure 37* indicates the range of possible years in which physical work might reasonably be programmed to start. In the decision area relating to housing rents, it is supposed that only three options are currently under consideration: no increase at all in rents in the current year, a moderate increase, and a large increase. These options may correspond simply to alternative flat-rate increases in the general level of rents, say 0 per cent, 20 per cent, and 40 per cent. Alternatively, their specification might be more complex; for instance, the larger increase might be accompanied by special measures to provide relief for tenants in lower income groups. For the procurement of extra design resources, the planners might again be able to identify three alternatives which we call the nil, expansion, and crash strategies respectively. The

Figure 37

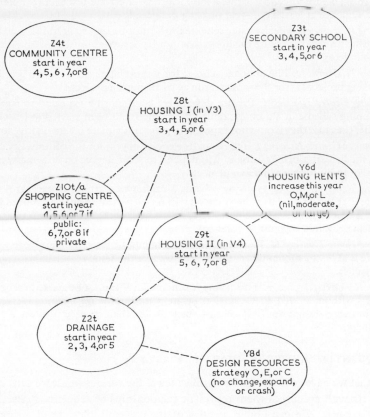

expansion strategy might consist of a new recruiting drive for engineers within the local authority itself, while the crash strategy might require extensive contracting out of design work to outside consultants.

THE MEANING OF THE LINKS

In order to translate the outline option graph into a full option graph, it is necessary to look more closely into the practical significance of each of the nine links shown in *Figure 37*. We will suppose that a close scrutiny of the problem brings out the following specific interpretations:

Secondary School/Housing I. The secondary school project cannot be started more than a year before housing project I is started (because the national education authority is giving priority to 'roofs over heads' and is not expected to include the school in its school building programme without some evidence that new housing is on the way).

Housing I/Housing II. Housing project II cannot be started earlier than two years after the start of housing project I (because there are physical reasons for developing in V3 before V4, and because a local shortage of certain resources for construction demands at least a two-year phasing between them).

Housing I/Drainage. The drainage scheme for V must be started at least a year before housing project I (because the houses cannot be occupied until the main drainage is complete).

Housing II/Drainage. The drainage scheme for V must be started at least a year before housing project II (for the same reason as with housing project I).

Shopping Centre/Housing I. Private developers could not be expected to start on a shopping scheme in V2 unless housing scheme I had been started at least a year earlier (because they would not expect it to give an adequate return on investment).

Community Centre/Housing I. There is a free choice of year for the community centre, but the benefit it brings initially will depend to some degree on how many houses have been built under housing project I.

Housing Rents/Housing I. Housing scheme I cannot be started before year 6 unless there is at least a moderate increase now in rent levels; it cannot be started before year 4 unless there is a large rent increase (because of the requirement to keep the housing revenue account in balance).

Housing Rents/Housing II. Housing project II cannot be started before year 7 unless there is at least a moderate rent increase now (for the same reason as with housing project I).

Design Resources/Drainage. The drainage scheme for V cannot be started earlier than year 5 without at least an 'expansion' strategy for reinforcing existing resources of engineering design staff; it cannot start earlier than year 3 without a 'crash' strategy.

A SEQUENTIAL NETWORK CHART FOR AREA V

Now that we have considered the significance of the various links, we can see that many (though not all) of them represent relationships of sequence between different projects. We can obtain an idea of their overall effect by drawing up a sequential network diagram for area V, of the type now often used for critical path analysis of individual projects [2]. Without going into too much detail on the individual projects in this case, the necessary sequence of activities might be seen broadly as shown in *Figure 38*.

In this diagram, the figures in brackets for each main activity represent expected (and very approximate) activity times measured in years. The initial 'activity' marked by a broken horizontal line for each project represents a possible delay before a decision to proceed with preliminary work is taken.

Figure 38, while drawn according to the conventions of critical path analysis, indicates that the problem is not one which can be tackled through the search for a single 'critical path' to represent the fastest possible way of achieving the programme as a whole. Each project (except the drainage scheme for the new housing developments) can function independently as soon as it is completed, and can bring corresponding social benefits from that point on; there is no single end-point in the programme to which it is clear that all effort should be directed. The picture presented by the sequential network diagram is also limited by the fact that it does

Figure 38

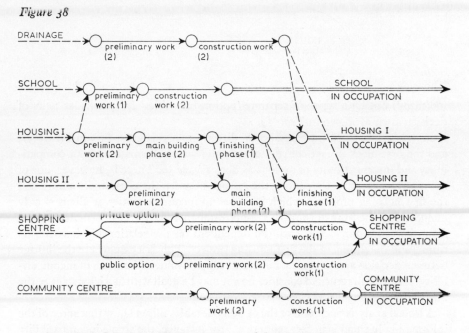

not show the influence on the programme of the external choices concerned with housing rents and design resources. Despite these limitations, it gives a useful view of the pattern of sequential relationships linking one project to another in this particular area.

THE COMPATIBILITY OF OPTIONS

The planners have by now carried out sufficient investigation of the relationships within area V to allow many of the links between decision areas to be defined more specifically in terms of 'option bars', such as were used in our earlier case example to represent incompatibilities between particular pairs of options. For instance, the proviso that a physical start on the school project cannot be realistically programmed more than one year ahead of a start on the first housing project can be represented as in *Figure 39* overleaf.

It is possible in the same way to replace every other dotted line in the outline option graph of *Figure 37* by a set of specific option bars, so that eventually a complete option graph can be built up. However, we will find it more convenient in this example to express the various option bars not by lines on a graph (there would be

Figure 39

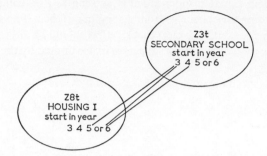

too many) but by a series of separate 'option bar tables' for particular pairs of decision areas as shown in *Table 14*.

Each block of *Table 14* corresponds directly to a particular link in *Figure 37*, and the first block in fact conveys exactly the same information about compatibility and incompatibility of options as does *Figure 39*. There is, however, one of the nine blocks – that concerning the linkage between the community centre and the first housing project – which includes no incompatibilities at all; it is only included here because of the earlier supposition that the degree of benefit obtained from the community centre will be dependent on the relationship between its timing and the timing of the first housing project. This is a case where the linkage between decision areas stands for a relationship of value rather than of incompatibility: and we will return to consider how it may be dealt with at a later stage of the analysis.

A logical analysis of certain of the option bar tables might show that some of the information in them is in fact redundant: for instance, the single incompatibility shown in table (d) (housing II/drainage) is already implicit in tables (b) and (c) (housing I/drainage and housing I/housing II) considered together: if the drainage is deferred to year 5, the first housing scheme must then be deferred to year 6, which means that the second housing scheme cannot be started until year 8 whatever happens.

It is interesting to detect this kind of redundancy in the option bar tables, but not essential so far as the analysis is concerned. What is more important is to detect whether the combined effect of all the option bars is in fact so restrictive as to leave no feasible solutions to the problem as a whole, necessitating a reformulation of the original brief. But, as we shall see, the number of feasible solutions in fact turns out to be very large, even when all the constraints have been taken into account, and the problem in this case example lies not so much in the paucity of choice as in its variety.

SOLUTIONS TO THE PROBLEM OF AREA V

If there had been no restrictions to the freedom to combine options from different decision areas, then we could have worked out the number of possible solutions to

Table 14

(a) **Secondary school** year:

Housing I year:	3	4	5	6
3	.	.	.	.
4	.	.	.	.
5	×	.	.	.
6	×	×	.	.

(b) **Housing II** year:

Housing I year:	5	6	7	8
3	.	.	.	.
4	×	.	.	.
5	×	×	.	.
6	×	×	×	.

(c) **Drainage** year:

Housing I year:	2	3	4	5
3	.	×	×	×
4	.	.	×	×
5	.	.	.	×
6	.	.	.	.

(d) **Drainage** year:

Housing II year:	2	3	4	5
5	.	.	.	×
6	.	.	.	.
7	.	.	.	.
8	.	.	.	.

(e) **Shopping centre** year:

Housing I year:	Public 4	5	6	7	Private 6′	7′	8′
3	.	.	.	.	.	.	.
4	.	.	.	.	.	.	.
5	.	.	.	.	×	.	.
6	.	.	.	.	×	×	.

(f) **Community centre** year:

Housing I year:	4	5	6	7	8
3	.	.	.	.	.
4	.	.	.	.	.
5	.	.	.	.	.
6	.	.	.	.	.

(g) **Housing I** year:

Housing rents increase:	3	4	5	6
O	×	×	×	.
M	×	.	.	.
L	.	.	.	.

(h) **Housing II** year:

Housing rents increase:	5	6	7	8
O	×	×	.	.
M	.	.	.	.
L	.	.	.	.

(i) **Drainage** year:

Design resources strategy:	2	3	4	5
O	×	×	×	.
E	×	.	.	.
C	.	.	.	.

Key: × = option bar
   . = feasible combination
  O = nil (no change)
  M = moderate
  L = large
  E = expansion
  C = crash

the problem of area V by multiplying together the number of options in each decision area, as shown in *Table 15* overleaf.

Of these 80,640 possible solutions, only 6,080 in fact remain when the various option bars shown in *Table 14* are taken into account. The derivation of this latter figure requires logic and tenacity rather than any acquired mathematical skill: one way of obtaining it is to start with any one of the decision areas in *Figure 37* – preferably Z8t, relating to the timing of Housing I, because it has more connecting links than any of the others – and to fix for the time being the initial option of year 3.

Table 15

	Decision area	No. of options
Z2t	Drainage priority	4
Z3t	Secondary school priority	×4
Z4t	Community centre priority	×5
Z8t	Housing I priority	×4
Z9t	Housing II priority	×4
Z10t/a	Shopping centre priority/agency	×7
Y6d	Housing rent increase	×3
Y8d	Design resources strategy	×3
		= 80,640 solutions

Then, by working methodically through the various links of the diagram, it is possible to eliminate certain options in other decision areas as being ruled out by the option bars of *Table 14*, and to arrive at a total of 560 solutions involving the particular option of year 3 for the first housing project. The solutions permitted by this initial option are as set out in *Figure 40*.

In the same way, it is possible to show that the particular options of years 4, 5, and 6 for the first housing project allow 2,520, 1,800, and 1,200 solutions respectively, giving a total of 6,080 solutions altogether.

Because we have assumed that there are no incompatibilities between any option for the timing of the community centre (Z4t) and any option in any of the other decision areas, we can simplify the problem to some extent by dividing the total of 6,080 solutions into five sets of 1,216 each, each set being identical apart from its association with one particular option in Z4t. In other words, the list of 'basic' solutions can be cut down to 1,216 by excluding consideration of the community centre problem at all for the time being.

In the case example of the previous chapter, it was found that the number of feasible solutions at no time exceeded seven, so that it was not difficult to proceed on the basis of statements of preference or indifference between them. However, in the present case example, the number of feasible solutions is clearly a good deal too large for the planners to handle in this way, and they will have to look for some means of reducing the problem to more tractable proportions. Perhaps the most obvious way of sifting out the more promising of the 1,216 possible solutions is through a more explicit *measurement* of what the various consequences of each solution are expected to be, and so the question now arises: what yardsticks should the planners choose as a means of selecting the more promising solutions for closer scrutiny and discussion with the policy-makers?

Figure 40

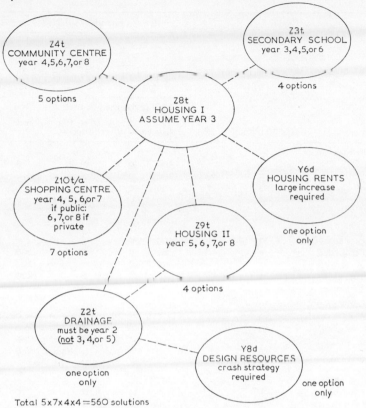

Total 5x7x4x4 =560 solutions

THE MEASUREMENT OF EFFECTS

The effects of any particular choice of solution for the problem of area V will be felt by many different kinds of people – by local residents, by schoolchildren, by families now on the waiting-list for municipal housing, by tenants in all parts of town whose rents may be increased, and by payers of local or national taxes. Initially, the planners may decide to estimate only certain direct effects associated with the particular decision areas being considered; for instance, the direct effect of alternative priorities for the secondary school project on schoolchildren and on local taxpayers, and the direct effect of alternative levels of rent increase on the existing tenants of existing municipal dwellings. Later, we will introduce the possibility that the planners might also wish to estimate certain joint effects associated with particular combinations of decision areas; for instance, they might feel that the benefit to be derived from early completion of the shopping centre would depend on how much progress had by then been made on the adjacent housing developments.

Table 16

Decision area	Options	Sector of community affected					
		local taxpayers	national taxpayers	existing tenants	prospective tenants	school-children	local shoppers
		Unit (explained in text)					
		eu_r	eu_n	eu_t	eu_p	eu_c	eu_s
		Estimated effect (direct)					
Priority of drainage scheme ($Z2t$) (to serve area V) year of start on construction:	2	300	0	0	0	0	0
	3	200	0	0	0	0	0
	4	100	0	0	0	0	0
	5	0	0	0	0	0	0
Priority of new secondary school ($Z3t$) (for 600 children) year of start on construction:	3	90	0	0	0	0	0
	4	60	0	0	0	600	0
	5	30	0	0	0	1200	0
	6	0	0	0	0	1800	0
Priority of housing scheme I ($Z8t$) (for 500 families) year of start on construction:	3	0	75	0	0	0	0
	4	0	50	0	500	0	0
	5	0	25	0	1000	0	0
	6	0	0	0	1500	0	0
Priority of housing scheme II ($Z9t$) (for 300 families) year of start on construction:	5	0	45	0	0	0	0
	6	0	30	0	300	0	0
	7	0	15	0	600	0	0
	8	0	0	0	900	0	0
Priority and agency of shopping development ($Z10t/a$) (to serve 2,000 families) year of start on construction:	4 (public)	90	0	0	0	0	0
	5 (public)	75	0	0	0	0	2000
	6 (public)	60	0	0	0	0	4000
	7 (public)	45	0	0	0	0	6000
	6' (private)	0	0	0	0	0	4000
	7' (private)	0	0	0	0	0	6000
	8' (private)	0	0	0	0	0	8000
Housing rents ($Y6d$) (for 300 existing tenants) size of increase this year:	O (nil)	0	0	0	0	0	0
	M (moderate)	0	0	3000	0	0	0
	L (large)	0	0	6000	0	0	0
Design resources ($Y8d$) strategy for expanding engineering design resources:	O (no change)	0	0	0	0	0	0
	E (expansion)	40	0	0	0	0	0
	C (crash)	120	0	0	0	0	0

At this stage, however, our first step will be to draw up a table of expected effects (beneficial or otherwise) associated with choice of particular options within individual decision areas. This we do in *Table 16*.

Table 16 sets out, in separate columns, a set of estimates of the direct effects of selecting particular options for six different classes of people; local taxpayers (known as ratepayers in the United Kingdom), national taxpayers, existing municipal tenants, prospective tenants of new houses, local schoolchildren, and local shoppers. Each column in *Table 16* therefore requires its own specific unit of measurement, whose definition must be given careful consideration.

For each of these units, what matters is not so much the ability to estimate future effects in any absolute sense, as the ability to estimate the relative effects of choosing different options within the same decision area. In order to be consistent, we have in *Table 16* adopted the same convention for each of the six scales of measurement: the most beneficial option in each relevant decision area is taken as a reference point and given the value zero, so that any non-zero entry represents a measure of the *penalty*, if any, of choosing some other option in the particular decision area concerned. In other words, the larger the numbers appearing in any column for a given option, the less beneficial that option will be from the point of view of that sector of the community. The specific units of measurement used in each of the six columns we will define as follows:

1 *Effect on local taxpayers (ratepayers).* One ratepayer effect unit (eu$_r$ for short) represents the total effect on local taxpayers of applying a unit increment to the existing rate of local taxation for the duration of one year. For instance, under the rating system which at present applies in Great Britain, this unit increment might be taken as the equivalent of one-tenth of a 'penny rate'. In practical terms, such an increment would mean that the occupier of a house of rateable value £50 would pay an extra 5d. a year, while the occupier of a house of rateable value £100 would pay an extra 10d. a year.

In this exercise we assume that, as is normal practice in British local government, the financing of each public development project is effected through a capital loan over some period which is fixed by statute, so that each year by which a project is brought forward in the programme penalizes the local taxpayers by a number of ratepayer effect units equivalent to the annual servicing cost of this loan, together perhaps with certain associated running costs for the development concerned. Not all of these costs would begin to come into operation in the same year, but it is a reasonable assumption that the bringing forward of a project by a whole year would make a marginal impact on the local taxpayer equivalent to the loan and running costs over a complete year after the development becomes operative. The corresponding reduction of the burden on future local taxpayers after the completion of the loan period is likely to be given much less weight by the planners and policy-makers, and we will ignore it at this stage of the analysis.

In *Table 16*, we have supposed the annual loan and running costs to be equivalent to 100 eu$_r$ a year in the case of the drainage scheme, and 30 eu$_r$ a year in the case of the school scheme; this means that, on our earlier assumption that one eu$_r$ corresponds to an annual rate charge of one-tenth of a penny per pound, the ratepayer with the house of rateable value £50 would in effect be paying an extra £2 approximately for every year the drainage scheme is brought forward in relation to its latest possible starting-time (assumed to be year 7), and an extra 12s. 6d. for every year the school project is brought forward in relation to year 6. Also, *Table 16* shows that he is affected in some degree by the choice of strategy for engineering design resources, and the choice of year for the shopping project if it is to be developed publicly. He is not affected directly by the choice of year for either housing project, on the assumption that the allocation from the rate fund to the housing account is fixed at an agreed annual sum irrespective of the state of either account.

2 *Effect on national taxpayers.* One national taxpayer effect unit (eu_n for short) represents the effect of applying some notional increment to the existing level of national taxation for the duration of one year. We suppose in *Table 16* that the only choices which carry direct implications for the national taxpayer are those concerned with the two housing projects, since each of them carries a direct subsidy from the national housing budget at a fixed annual rate per house built. We have supposed in *Table 16* that the two projects include 500 and 300 houses respectively, each house attracting an annual subsidy of ·05 eu_n. Whatever the 'national taxpayer effect unit' represents in money terms, its effect on any individual taxpayer in the country at large will clearly be extremely marginal, although the cumulative impact of all local authority housing schemes may be quite large.

3 *Effect on existing municipal tenants in Fluxton.* One existing tenant effect unit (eu_t for short) represents a given percentage increment (say 20 per cent) in the rents of municipal housing, assumed to apply to all existing local authority tenants as from the beginning of the next financial year, and to remain in force for some agreed period of years under a cyclic review procedure. In *Table 16*, we have supposed that there are 3,000 such tenants in Fluxton, that the 'moderate' increase represents a 20 per cent rise and the 'large' increment a 40 per cent one, and that all tenants are affected equally. Of course, at some stage the local council might wish to consider a scheme which involved discrimination between tenants according to income; it might then be necessary to adopt two or more different units to differentiate between one category of tenant and another. We will not however consider this complication for the time being.

4 *Effect on prospective municipal tenants in Fluxton.* One prospective tenant effect unit (eu_p for short) represents a delay of one year in providing a new home for one family at present on the waiting-list for municipal housing: the assumption is, of course, that the new house will be in some way more beneficial to the family than their present accommodation, whatever this may be. It is important to note that this measure makes the simplifying assumption that the benefit of moving to a new home is of equal magnitude for each family likely to be affected, whatever their present circumstances.

5 *Effect on schoolchildren in sector Z.* One schoolchildren's effect unit (eu_c for short) represents a delay of one year in improving the school environment of one child of secondary school age residing within the proposed catchment area of the new school, which might cover most of the outer zones of sector Z. For every year by which the new school is delayed, it is assumed that these children will then have to continue for one more year to attend an existing school which is less beneficial in some way; perhaps because it is more distant, or because it is overcrowded, or because it has inferior facilities.

6 *Effect on shoppers in sector Z.* One shoppers' effect unit (eu_s for short) represents a delay of one year in improving the shopping opportunities of one family residing

within reasonable reach of the proposed new shopping centre in area V2, i.e. anywhere in the outer zones of sector Z. In *Table 16*, it is assumed that there are 2000 such families; at this stage of the analysis we will ignore the complication that the number of such families will grow as the two new housing estates in area V become occupied.

Each of these measures has required careful definition, since the choices to be considered in area V affect a large number of different people in their many different roles as local and national taxpayers, actual and would-be tenants, schoolchildren (and their parents), and shoppers. The underlying problem is not simply to estimate total costs or to count up total numbers of houses or school places, but rather to develop working measures to represent, however crudely, a reality compounded of large numbers of different types of disturbance to the affairs of particular people who interact within a complex social system. The estimates given in *Table 16* represent only a first step in this direction, but they will suffice for the time being.

MINIMUM TAX SOLUTIONS FOR THE PROBLEM OF AREA V

For each option in each of the seven decision areas which the planners are at present considering, they now have an estimate of impact on each of six different (but overlapping) sectors of the community. They have also discovered that the options concerned can be combined in various different ways to give a choice between 1,216 feasible solutions to the problem of priorities in area V as a whole.

The next step is to explore how the range of alternative solutions might be narrowed down by reference to the six effect measures established so far. An obvious starting-point might be to look at those solutions which impose as small a burden as possible on the local taxpayer. This would involve some tedious calculations if done by hand; given access to an electronic computer, however, it is not difficult to obtain a list of the first ten, or fifty, or hundred solutions selected according to the single criterion of minimizing the local tax burden. Such a list would start as shown in *Table 17* overleaf.

In this list, the computer has worked out the total value of each effect measure for each of the top twelve solutions by simply adding together the corresponding measures for each option included within that solution. For instance, the entry in the eu_p column (effect on prospective tenants) depends on the pair of options selected for the priority of the two housing schemes. Solution 1 involves a three-year deferment from the earliest possible year both for scheme I, involving 500 prospective tenants, and for scheme II, involving 300 further prospective tenants, giving a total penalty of $3 \times 500 + 3 \times 300 = 2400$ eu_p. The entry in the eu_r column (effect on local taxpayers) may be affected, as *Table 16* shows, by the options selected for four different decision areas, concerning the priorities of the drainage, school, and shopping schemes and the strategy for design resources. It will be noticed that each of the first three solutions in the list has a zero entry in the column for eu_r, because each selects the most favourable set of options in the four decision areas which directly concern the local taxpayer. Of course, this does not mean the local taxpayer will pay nothing at all towards the drainage and school projects or towards the cost of engineering design work: it simply means the burden on local taxpayers is at a minimum level within the range of options allowed in the initial formulation of the problem.

Table 17

	Decision areas							Sectors of community affected					
Solution no.	drainage	school	housing I	housing II	shopping	rents	designers	local taxpayers	national taxpayers	existing tenants	prospective tenants	school-children	local shoppers
	Options*							Effect measures†					
								eu_r	eu_n	eu_t	eu_p	eu_c	eu_s
1	5	6	6	8	8′	O	O	0	0	0	2400	1800	8000
2	5	6	6	8	8′	M	O	0	0	3000	2400	1800	8000
3	5	6	6	8	8′	L	O	0	0	6000	2400	1800	8000
4	5	5	6	8	8′	O	O	30	0	0	2400	1200	8000
5	5	5	6	8	8′	M	O	30	0	3000	2400	1200	8000
6	5	5	6	8	8′	L	O	30	0	6000	2400	1200	8000
7	5	6	6	8	8′	O	E	40	0	0	2400	1800	8000
8	5	6	6	8	8′	M	E	40	0	3000	2400	1800	8000
9	5	6	6	8	8′	L	E	40	0	6000	2400	1800	8000
10	5	6	6	8	7	O	O	45	0	0	2400	1800	6000
11	5	6	6	8	7	M	O	45	0	3000	2400	1800	6000
12	5	6	6	8	7	L	O	45	0	6000	2400	1800	6000
–	–	–	–	–	–	–	–	–	–	–	–	–	–
–	–	–	–	–	–	–	–	–	–	–	–	–	–

* as defined in Table 16
† units defined pp. 179–81

THE IDENTIFICATION OF LEADING SOLUTIONS

Looking down the 'local taxpayer' column of Table 17, it will be noticed that the solutions tend to fall into groups of three in ascending order of their effect on the local taxpayers. It will also be seen that each successive group of three solutions is in fact identical apart from its association with a different option for the level of the rent increase (nil, moderate, or large), a choice which has been assumed to have no direct impact other than on the 3,000 existing municipal tenants within the town. It appears that, at any rate among these first few solutions in the full list of 1,216, the choice of a rent level for existing tenants in the town as a whole is not relevant to the problem of priorities in area V. For our present purposes, we need therefore to make comparisons only between certain 'clusters' of related solutions such as (1, 2, 3), (4, 5, 6) and (7, 8, 9); and in order to do this, we will represent each such group of solutions by a *leading solution* which is at first sight preferable to the others because it imposes a minimum burden on existing tenants. The leading solutions in the first three groups mentioned above can be seen to be solutions 1, 4, and 7 respectively. It is important to note that the remaining solutions in each group will not necessarily be ruled out in the final analysis; it is simply that, if a case is to be made out for the rent increases which they imply, it will have to rest on other considerations which are external to our present limited problem of priorities within area V.

The picking-out of leading solutions enables the full list of solutions to be set out in a rather more compact form. This is shown in *Table 18*, where the list of all solutions with an effect on local taxpayers of 150 eu_r or below (numbering 74 in all)

Table 18

Leading solution	Options*							Effect measures†					
	drainage	school	housing I	housing II	shopping	rents	designers	local taxpayers eu_r	national taxpayers eu_n	existing tenants eu_t	prospective tenants eu_p	school-children eu_c	local shoppers eu_s
1(2,3)	5	6	6	8	8′	O	O	0	0	0	2400	1800	8000
4(5,6)	5	5	6	8	8′	O	O	30	0	0	2400	1200	8000
7(8,9)	5	6	6	8	8′	O	E	40	0	0	2400	1800	8000
10(11,12)	5	6	6	8	7	O	O	45	0	0	2400	1800	6000
13(14,15)	5	6	6	8	6	O	O	60	0	0	2400	1800	4000
16(17,18)	5	5	6	8	8′	O	E	70	0	0	2400	1200	8000
19(20,21)	5	5	6	8	7	O	O	75	0	0	2400	1200	6000
22(23,24)	5	6	6	8	5	O	O	75	0	0	2400	1800	2000
25(26,27)	5	6	6	8	7	O	E	85	0	0	2400	1800	6000
28(29,30)	5	5	6	8	6	O	O	90	0	0	2400	1200	4000
31(32,33)	5	6	6	8	4	O	O	90	0	0	2400	1800	0
34(35,36)	5	6	6	8	6	O	E	100	0	0	2400	1800	4000
37(38,39)	5	5	6	8	5	O	O	105	0	0	2400	1200	2000
40(41,42)	5	5	6	8	7	O	E	115	0	0	2400	1200	6000
43(44,45)	5	6	6	8	5	O	E	115	0	0	2400	1800	2000
46(47,48)	5	5	6	8	4	O	O	120	0	0	2400	1200	0
49(50,51)	5	6	6	8	8′	O	C	120	0	0	2400	1800	8000
52(53,54)	5	5	6	8	6	O	E	130	0	0	2400	1200	4000
55(56,57)	5	6	6	8	4	O	E	130	0	0	2400	1800	0
58(59)	4	6	5	7	7′	M	E	140	40	3000	1600	1800	6000
60(61)	4	6	5	7	8′	M	E	140	40	3000	1600	1800	8000
62(63)	4	6	5	8	7′	M	E	140	25	3000	1900	1800	6000
64(65)	4	6	5	8	8′	M	E	140	25	3000	1900	1800	8000
66(67,68)	4	6	6	8	8′	O	E	140	0	0	2400	1800	8000
69(70,71)	5	5	6	8	5	O	E	145	0	0	2400	1200	2000
72(73,74)	5	5	6	8	8′	O	C	150	0	0	2400	1200	8000

* as defined in *Table 16*
† units defined pp. 179–81
14

has been compressed into a list of 26 leading solutions, with associated non-leading solutions in parenthesis.

It will be noticed that the solutions do not continue to group themselves in threes indefinitely; there are four groups of solutions from 58 onwards where the possibility of a nil rent increase does not arise, the computer having detected that it would violate one of the option bars set out in *Table 14*. Another point which emerges from *Table 18* is that those leading solutions which include an E or a C in the final option column require an allocation of local tax revenue to the extension of existing design resources, without any corresponding benefit in speeding up the development of area V, at any rate until solution 58 is reached. Again, there is no reason to select such a solution unless it is justified by considerations outside area V, so the list of leading solutions with a local tax penalty of 150 eu_r or below can be compressed still further from 26 to 14, as shown in *Table 19*.

Table 19

Leading solution	Decision areas							Sectors of community affected					
	drainage	*school*	*housing I*	*housing II*	*shopping*	*rents*	*designers*	*local taxpayers*	*national taxpayers*	*existing tenants*	*prospective tenants*	*school-children*	*local shoppers*
	Options*							Effect measures†					
								eu_r	eu_n	eu_t	eu_p	eu_c	eu_s
1	5	6	6	8	8′	O	O	0	0	0	2400	1800	8000
4	5	5	6	8	8′	O	O	30	0	0	2400	1200	8000
10	5	6	6	8	7	O	O	45	0	0	2400	1800	6000
13	5	6	6	8	6	O	O	60	0	0	2400	1800	4000
19	5	5	6	8	7	O	O	75	0	0	2400	1200	6000
22	5	6	6	8	5	O	O	75	0	0	2400	1800	2000
28	5	5	6	8	6	O	O	90	0	0	2400	1200	4000
31	5	6	6	8	4	O	O	90	0	0	2400	1800	0
37	5	5	6	8	5	O	O	105	0	0	2400	1200	2000
46	5	5	6	8	4	O	O	120	0	0	2400	1200	0
58	4	6	5	7	7′	M	E	140	40	3000	1600	1800	6000
60	4	6	5	7	8′	M	E	140	40	3000	1600	1800	8000
62	4	6	5	8	7′	M	E	140	25	3000	1900	1800	6000
64	4	6	5	8	8′	M	E	140	25	3000	1900	1800	8000
—	—	—	—	—	—	—	—	—	—	—	—	—	—
—	—	—	—	—	—	—	—	—	—	—	—	—	—

* as defined in *Table 16*
† units defined pp. 179–81

For the leading solutions which now remain, it will be seen that each increase in the impact on local taxpayers carries with it real benefits for one or more sectors of the community, as indicated by reducing figures in one or more of the last four effect columns. For instance, leading solution 4 brings the school project forward from year 6 to year 5 and reduces the schoolchildren's effect measure from 1,800 to 1,200 eu_c, representing the benefit of one year's improved schooling for each of the 600 schoolchildren affected: on the other hand, leading solutions 10, 13, 22, and 31 progressively reduce the shopping effect measure from 8,000 eu_s to zero, representing up to four years' bringing forward of access to improved shopping facilities for the 2,000 families affected. Other solutions can be seen to produce various degrees of benefit to schoolchildren, shoppers, and prospective municipal tenants in a number of different combinations.

THE BALANCING OF COSTS AND BENEFITS

Unless the local policy-makers are dedicated to a policy of minimizing the local tax burden at any cost, their preferred solution to the problem of priorities in area V will not necessarily be that appearing on the first line of *Table 19*. For an extra expenditure of 30 eu_r (in practical terms, say, an extra 3d. on the local rate levy for one year), they might note that it would be possible – subject, perhaps to central government approval – to obtain an extra year of use of the new secondary school, to the direct benefit of the 600 children who would expect to be transferred to it. On the other hand, it would involve a sacrifice of 45 eu_r to 'buy' an extra year of improved access to shopping facilities for 2,000 families; while for 75 eu_r they would have a choice of one year's benefit for the 600 schoolchildren and also for the 2,000 shoppers, or no benefit for the former and three years' benefit for the latter. They might be surprised to see that no benefit to those on the waiting-list for new homes could be obtained without at least a sacrifice of 140 eu_r (in this case required to pay not for the building of the houses themselves, but for the construction of the necessary drainage system and the mobilization of sufficient resources to allow design work to begin).

If we pick out from *Table 19* only those solutions which provide progressive increases in benefit to local shoppers, then we have a list as follows:

Table 20

Solution	Options							Effect on local taxpayers in eu_r	Effect on shoppers in eu_s
I	5	6	6	8	8'	O	O	0	8000
10	5	6	6	8	7	O	O	45	6000
13	5	6	6	8	6	O	O	60	4000
22	5	6	6	8	5	O	O	75	2000
31	5	6	6	8	4	O	O	90	0

It will be noticed that, while the impact on local shoppers reduces from 8,000 eu_s to zero in a series of equal steps, the impact on local taxpayers rises first by an increment of 45 eu_r and then by a series of smaller steps of 15 eu_r each. This stems from the initial assumption that the shopping scheme can only be started before the housing development is under way provided it is undertaken publicly rather than privately. The policy-makers will have to consider whether they are prepared to spend money from the local taxation account in order to advance the shopping development before year 8, and their assessment will inevitably reflect the conflicting pressures to which they may be exposed as elected representatives.

We will suppose in this case that a certain amount of information can be obtained, in one way or another, as to the 'appropriate' balance between the conflicting objectives of improving shopping facilities and minimizing the level of local taxes. One form in which this might be expressed is that of a 'trade-off rate' between local taxpayer effect units (eu_r) and local shoppers' effect units (eu_s). We will suppose that in this case the appropriate rate is agreed to be:

$$100 \; eu_s : 1 \; eu_r$$

which implies that the policy-makers would be prepared to sacrifice 1 eu_r (in practical terms, we suggested that this might translate as an increase of one-tenth of a penny on the local rates for one year) if by so doing they could advance by one year the provision of improved shopping facilities for 100 families at present served by the overcrowded shopping centre in area R. By application of this trade-off rate to the figures of *Table 20*, it is possible to convert the effect of each solution on local shoppers from units of eu_s to units of eu_r, and combine it with the figures in the previous column to give an equivalent measure of the combined effect of each solution on these two sectors of the community, providing a basis for the expression of preferences between solutions. The order of preference between solutions may however be quite sensitive to the choice of trade-off rate, as we illustrate in *Table 21* by showing the combined effect measure under alternative trade-off rates of 80:1, 100:1 and 120:1 respectively.

Table 21

Solution	Combined effect measure (in units of eu_r) for alternative assumptions of trade-off rate between eu_s and eu_r		
	(a) 80 eu_s: 1 eu_r	(b) 100 eu_s: 1 eu_r	(c) 120 eu_s: 1 eu_r
1	100	<u>80</u>	67
10	120	125	95
13	110	100	93
22	100	95	100
31	<u>90</u>	90	90

In this table, we have underlined the solution which gives the minimum (or most beneficial) combined effect measure according to each of the three alternative trade-off rates. Solution 1, which is marginally to be preferred at a trade-off rate of 100:1, has a much clearer advantage at a trade-off rate of 120:1 but is inferior to solution 31 at a trade-off rate of 80:1.

Trade-off rates of this kind represent assumptions of value which can in practice be arrived at by a number of different methods. One possibility is that assumptions can be made by the local planners themselves on the basis of their past experience of the value judgements of the policy-makers; another is that the policy-makers can be asked to state explicitly how much they would be prepared to ask the local taxpayers to pay for any given gain in shopping opportunities in area V. Yet again, the policy-makers can be presented with selected lists of alternative solutions and asked to place them in order of preference, so that the relative values they give to different effects can be inferred by the planners. For instance, faced with a choice between the five solutions in *Table 21*, the policy-makers might express a strong preference for solution 1 and little preference over the remaining solutions (a pattern according approximately with the results of a 120:1 trade-off was shown in *Table 21*); on the other hand, they might show indecision between solutions 1 and 31 (suggesting, by interpolation in *Table 21*, a trade-off rate of the order of 90:1). Another type of exercise might require them to express a preference between solutions which incur the same local tax penalty but provide benefits to different sectors of the community. For instance, knowledge of the policy-makers' preference between solutions 19 and 22 in *Table 19* would allow the planners to make some further inferences as to the relative values which they attach to educational and shopping improvements respectively.

Whatever the procedure by which trade-off rates are estimated, they can of course represent no more than very rough indicators of the values which should be given to certain broad classes of social effect. The effect measures themselves can do no more than present a highly simplified picture of a complex social reality; and when assessing rates of trade-off between them, it may be necessary to give a good deal of consideration to the particular local circumstances of those affected – in what ways the present opportunities of these particular shoppers or this particular group of schoolchildren may be deficient, and whether in each case certain particular sub-groups may stand to gain or lose more than others.

Having stated these qualifications, we will suppose that an initial set of trade-off rates has been arrived at, by direct or indirect methods, linking all six effect measures through the common 'currency' of the unit eu_r used to measure the effect on local taxpayers. This is shown in *Table 22* overleaf.

Embodied in this table are a variety of important assumptions about social and political values: for instance, the fact that the eu_n unit has been given ten times the value of the eu_s unit implies an assessment that the policy-makers are prepared to pay ten times as much to provide a home one year earlier for a family on the housing waiting-list, as they are prepared to pay to bring forward by one year the provision of improved shopping facilities for one family which already has a home in this area.

By giving no weight at all to the effect on national taxpayers, *Table 22* reflects the viewpoint that a local authority cannot be held responsible for protecting the interests of the national taxpayer. From the local authority's point of view, the

Table 22

Effect on existing tenants	40 eu$_t$: 1 eu$_r$	i.e. 1 eu$_t$: 0.025 eu$_r$
Effect on prospective tenants	10 eu$_p$: 1 eu$_r$	i.e. 1 eu$_p$: 0·1 eu$_r$
Effect on schoolchildren in sector Z	15 eu$_c$: 1 eu$_r$	i.e. 1 eu$_c$: 0·0667 eu$_r$
Effect on shoppers in sector Z	100 eu$_s$: 1 eu$_r$	i.e. 1 eu$_s$: 0·01 eu$_r$
Effect on national taxpayers	to be ignored	i.e. 1 eu$_n$: 0 eu$_r$

national taxpayer can be regarded as fair game provided the central government has provided the mechanisms for the provision of grants or subsidies at his expense. It is up to central government to construct a framework which will ensure that money provided from the central exchequer will be used in effective pursuit of the policies which the government of the day wishes to promote.

THE RANKING OF SOLUTIONS USING ASSUMED TRADE-OFF RATES

Now that a set of initial assumptions has been made as to the relative values of the various effect measures, it is possible to attach a *combined effect measure* to each of the 1,216 possible solutions for the problem which has been defined for area V. Because each of the trade-off rates in *Table 22* is linked to the 'common currency' of eu$_r$ (the local taxpayers effect unit), this particular unit provides perhaps the most convenient base for expression of the combined effect. However, it is important to avoid confusion between quantities which represent combinations of effects and those which express effects on local taxpayers alone, and so for the former purpose we will define a new *aggregate effect unit* eu(A) at the 'exchange rate' of 1 eu$_r$ = 1 eu(A). Using the trade-off rates assumed in *Table 22*, the combined effect measure for any solution can then be expressed in units of eu(A) as follows:

Table 23

Contributions to combined effect measure	Illustration for solution 1 of Table 19		
Effect on local taxpayers, measured in eu$_r$, 1 eu$_r$ = 1 eu(A)	0 eu$_r$	=	0 eu(A)
Effect on existing tenants, measured in eu$_t$, ×0·025	0 × 0·025	=	0 eu(A)
Effect on prospective tenants, measured in eu$_p$, ×0·1	2400 × 0·1	=	240 eu(A)
Effect on local schoolchildren, measured in eu$_c$, ×0·667	1800 × 0·667	=	120 eu(A)
Effect on local shoppers, measured in eu$_s$, ×0·01	8000 × 0·01	=	80 eu(A)
Combined effect measure			440 eu(A)

Because we adopted the convention of defining each of the original effect measures in a negative sense – to express the degree of penalty or disadvantage associated with deviations from the most favourable set of options for the sector of the community concerned – the combined effect measure will also now have a negative interpretation; the higher the combined effect measure for a given solution, the less beneficial will it be from the point of view of 'the public interest' as defined by the assumed set of trade-off rates. As we shall see later, this first set of assumptions about trade-off rates must be regarded as open to question at all stages of the analysis; and it is especially important that the 'combined effect measure' should not come to be regarded as a final criterion for the expression of preferences between solutions. Rather, it should be used solely as a means to the end of creating a more meaningful dialogue between planners and policy-makers in the context of a continuing planning process.

Just as a computer can be programmed to sort the 1,216 possible solutions according to the criterion of minimizing impact on local taxpayers, so it can be made to re-sort them according to a new criterion of minimum 'combined effect measure', adopting the assumed conversion rates given in *Table 23*. This time, the solutions may appear in a very different order, as shown in *Table 24*, which lists the first twelve solutions in order of minimum (i.e. most favourable) combined effect measure. The numbers in parentheses refer to the corresponding positions of these same solutions in the earlier order of preference based on impact on local taxpayers alone (see *Tables 17* and *18*).

Table 24

Solution rank	Decision areas							Sectors of community affected						Combined effect measure‡
	drainage	school	housing I	housing II	shopping	rents	designers	local taxpayers	national taxpayers	existing tenants	prospective tenants	school-children	local shoppers	
	Options*							Effect measures†						eu(A)
								eu_r	eu_n	eu_t	eu_p	eu_c	eu_s	
1 (4)	5	5	6	8	8′	O	O	30	0	0	2400	1200	8000	430
2 (46)	5	5	6	8	4	O	O	120	0	0	2400	1200	0	440
3 (1)	5	6	6	8	8′	O	O	0	0	0	2400	1800	8000	440
4 (37)	5	5	6	8	5	O	O	105	0	0	2400	1200	4000	445
5 (28)	5	5	6	8	6	O	O	90	0	0	2400	1200	4000	450
6 (31)	5	6	6	8	4	O	O	90	0	0	2400	1800	0	450
7 (19)	5	5	6	8	7	O	O	75	0	0	2400	1200	6000	455
8 (22)	5	6	6	8	5	O	O	75	0	0	2400	1800	0	455
9 (13)	5	6	6	8	6	O	O	60	0	0	2400	1800	4000	460
10 (10)	5	6	6	8	7	O	O	45	0	0	2400	1800	6000	465
11 (16)	5	5	6	8	8′	O	E	70	0	0	2400	1200	8000	470
12 (75)	5	5	6	8	4	O	E	150	0	0	2400	1200	0	480
– –	–	–	–	–	–	–	–	–	–	–	–	–	–	–
– –	–	–	–	–	–	–	–	–	–	–	–	–	–	–

* as defined in *Table 16*   † units defined pp. 179–81   ‡ defined *Table 23*

A REVISION OF TRADE-OFF RATES

Presented with a list of solutions in the order of preference given by *Table 24*, the policy-makers might note that the first dozen solutions give some choice of schooling or shopping benefits, but none of them hold out any benefits to prospective housing tenants through acceleration of the two housing projects; the first solution which produces some benefit to this sector of the community in fact turns out to come twenty-fifth in the new listing, and to carry a combined effects measure of 525 eu(A).

Faced with this evidence, the policy-makers might perhaps begin to wonder whether, in the original estimates of trade-off rates, sufficient weight had been attached to the social urgency, as they see it, of rehousing families at present on the waiting-list: their new awareness of the difficulty of overcoming the drainage problem may lead them to a more extensive discussion of the social and political aspects of the housing shortage, in the course of which a clearer picture of relative values may begin to emerge. Perhaps they may also feel that the order of preference given by *Table 24* does not adequately reflect the importance they attach to early completion of the secondary school, and that it tends to overstress the social benefits arising from the early completion of the shopping centre. The policy-makers might therefore decide that the original set of trade-off rates should be modified to give a closer approximation to their own system of value judgements, as follows:

Effect on prospective tenants : value to be increased by 50 per cent
Effect on local schoolchildren : value to be increased by 50 per cent
Effect on local shoppers   : value to be decreased by 40 per cent

The definition of the combined effect measure, as originally given in *Table 23*, would now be modified as follows:

Table 25

Contributions to combined effect measure (modified)	Illustration for solution 1 of Table 19
Effect on local taxpayers, measured in eu_r ($1 \ eu_r = 1 \ eu(A')$)	$0 \ eu_r$ $= 0 \ eu(A')$
Effect on existing tenants, measured in eu_t, ×0·025	$0 × 0·025 = 0 \ eu(A')$
Effect on prospective tenants, measured in eu_p, ×0·15	$2400 × 0·15 = 360 \ eu(A')$
Effect on local schoolchildren, measured in eu_c, ×0·1	$1800 × 0·10 = 180 \ eu(A')$
Effect on local shoppers, measured in eu_s, ×0·006	$8000 × 0·006 = 48 \ eu(A')$
Combined effect measure (modified)	$588 \ eu(A')$

The unit for this modified version of the combined effect measure is now referred to as eu(A′), to distinguish it from the aggregate effect unit eu(A) originally defined in *Table 23*. With this modification, the computer can be made to repeat the calculations and come up with a revised order of preference. The first twelve solutions in the new order of preference are shown in *Table 26*.

The solutions which are now thrown to the top of the list include some which have not appeared in any of our previous tables: in particular, six of the first twelve involve an impact on local taxpayers of 300 eu_r or more, making use of the extra local revenue to bring the drainage and housing programmes forward by up to two

Table 26

	Decision areas							Sectors of community affected							
	drainage	*school*	*housing I*	*housing II*	*shopping*	*rents*	*designers*	*local taxpayers*	*national taxpayers*	*existing tenants*	*prospective tenants*	*school-children*	*local shoppers*		*Combined effect measure‡*
Solution rank	Options*							Effect measures†							*eu(A′)*
								eu_r	*eu_n*	*eu_t*	*eu_p*	*eu_c*	*eu_s*		
1	3	3	4	6	6′	M	E	330	80	3000	800	0	4000		549
2	5	5	6	8	8′	O	O	30	0	0	2400	1200	8000		558
3	3	3	4	6	7′	M	E	330	80	3000	800	0	6000		561
4	3	3	4	6	8′	M	E	330	80	3000	800	0	8000		573
5	3	4	4	6	6′	M	E	330	80	3000	800	600	4000		579
6	5	6	6	8	8′	O	O	0	0	0	2400	1800	8000		588
7	5	5	6	8	7	O	O	75	0	0	2400	1200	6000		591
8	3	4	4	6	7′	M	E	300	80	3000	800	600	6000		591
9	5	5	6	8	6	O	O	90	0	0	2400	1200	4000		594
10	3	3	4	7	6′	M	E	330	65	3000	1100	0	4000		594
11	5	5	6	8	5	O	O	105	0	0	2400	1200	2000		597
12	5	5	6	8	8′	O	O	70	0	0	2400	1200	8000		598
–	–	–	–	–	–	–	–	–	–	–	–	–	–		–
–	–	–	–	–	–	–	–	–	–	–	–	–	–		–

* as defined in *Table 16*   † units defined pp. 179–81   ‡ defined *Table 25*

years. Nevertheless, some of the earlier low tax solutions still appear near the top of the list; for instance, the sixth solution in the new list corresponds to the original minimum tax solution and to the third solution in the ranking of *Table 24*. If the trade-off rates are now correctly adjusted to reflect the relative values of the policy-makers, then one would expect them to agree that the revised listing gave a reasonable indication of their true order of preference. This could be tested by picking pairs of solutions with the same or similar combined effect measures (e.g. 7 and 8, 9 and 10, 11 and 12) and asking the policy-makers whether they still felt any strong preference between them; if so, then some further adjustments to assumed rates of trade-off could be made.

CHOICE OF ACTION IN THE FACE OF UNCERTAINTY

Assuming for the time being that the policy-makers are satisfied that the new list accords reasonably well with their political preferences, then at last an acceptable basis for choice exists in relation to the problem of priorities in area V.

If they were to ignore the existence of uncertainties in the estimation of combined effects, then there would be no reason why the policy-makers should not select solution 1 in *Table 26*, whose overall penalty is lower than that of the 'second-best' solution by a differential of 9 eu(A′). However, it is extremely unlikely in practice that the various assumptions required for the estimation of a combined effects measure (including the value assumptions implicit in the selected trade-off rates) would be sufficiently clear cut for a differential of 9 eu(A') – or even perhaps a differential of 50 or 100 eu(A') – to be regarded as a clear-cut index of preference between alternatives. In fact, as a result of the way the problem was initially defined, one important source of uncertainty is clearly exposed in the first few solutions of *Table 26*: solutions 1, 3, and 4 will be seen to differ only in the choice of year 6, 7, or 8 for the priority of the shopping development, assuming in each case that this is to be achieved through a private agency. However, the planners may have only a very limited amount of control over the choice of years in which private developers might start; the difference between these three solutions might not therefore be a question of planners' choice so much as of uncertainty (of category UE) in this aspect of their environment. If the conscious choice of solution 1 is likely to result in achievement of solution 3 or 4 in practice, then a case may exist for selecting solution 2 in preference to it, even though its combined effects appear to be slightly less beneficial.

As in our earlier case example, the presence of uncertainties suggests that it might be advisable for the policy-makers at this stage to become committed not to any particular full solution but only to a more restricted 'action set' in which a clear choice is made in respect of some of the more urgent decision areas, while as many options as possible are left open within the remaining ones. We will suppose that in this case the most urgent decision areas are thought to be those covered by the second, sixth, and seventh of the option columns in *Table 26*. The reasons for urgency might be as follows:

Secondary school (Z3t). Decision on whether or not to start in year 3 is considered urgent because, if so, then an application must be submitted shortly to the department of central government responsible for the national school building programme.

Housing rents (Y6d). Decision between nil, moderate, and large rent increase (O, M, or L) must be made shortly in respect of the coming financial year.

Design resources (Y8d). Decision between no change, expansion, and crash strategy (O, E, or C) for reinforcement of existing engineering design resources must be decided shortly to allow staff recruitment or consultant contract arrangements to be made.

There are therefore eighteen distinct action sets from which a choice might be made, as follows:

Table 27

		Start school in year 3 Rent increase			Start school later (year X = 4, 5, or 6) Rent increase		
		O	M	L	O	M	L
Design	O	(3,O,O)	(3,M,O)	(3,L,O)	(X,O,O)	(X,M,O)	(X,L,O)
resources	E	(3,O,E)	(3,M,E)	(3,L,E)	(X,O,E)	(X,M,E)	(X,L,E)
	C	(3,O,C)	(3,M,C)	(3,L,C)	(X,O,C)	(X,M,C)	(X,L,C)

Here, the first symbol in each group of three refers to the option selected for secondary school priority, the second to the option selected for housing rents, and the third to the option selected for engineering design resources. We have used the symbol X to represent the action of not submitting an immediate application for the school to be built in year 3: in other words, inclusion of X as an element within the action set leaves open the future options of starting work on the school in any of years 4, 5, or 6.

Taking the first twelve solutions as shown in *Table 26*, the corresponding action sets can be picked out from the second, sixth, and seventh option columns as shown in *Table 28*.

Table 28

Solution rank	Options							Action set	Combined effect measure
1	3	3̲	4	6	6′	M̲	E̲	(3,M,E)	549
2	5	5̲	6	8	8′	O̲	O̲	(X,O,O)	558
3	3	3̲	4	6	7′	M̲	E̲	(3,M,E)	561
4	3	3̲	4	6	8′	M̲	E̲	(3,M,E)	573
5	3	4̲	4	6	6′	M̲	E̲	(X,M,E)	579
6	5	6̲	6	8	8′	O̲	O̲	(X,O,O)	588
7	5	5̲	6	8	7	O̲	O̲	(X,O,O)	591
8	3	4̲	4	6	7′	M̲	E̲	(X,M,E)	591
9	5	5̲	6	8	6	O̲	O̲	(X,O,O)	594
10	3	3̲	4	7	6′	M̲	E̲	(3,M,E)	594
11	5	5̲	6	8	5	O̲	O̲	(X,O,O)	597
12	5	5̲	6	8	8′	O̲	O̲	(X,O,O)	598
–	–	–	–	–	–	–	–	–	–
–	–	–	–	–	–	–	–	–	–

Of the twelve solutions, we can see that four require the action set (3,M,E) while two require the action set (X,M,E), with X in this case standing for the option of year 4 for the school building project. The other six solutions all involve the action set (X,O,O), with X representing either year 5 or year 6.

THE ROBUSTNESS OF ALTERNATIVE ACTION SETS

If the pattern of occurrence of the various action sets is followed further down the list, the frequencies gradually change and further action sets begin to make an appearance as shown in *Table 29* overleaf.

Although we have here worked considerably further down the order of preference than in any of the earlier tables, the 138 solutions which are shown as having a combined effect measure of 700 units or less can still all be regarded as reasonably 'good' solutions, in that they comprise the top 12 per cent or so of the complete list of 1,216 feasible solutions. One point that emerges strongly from this table is the high frequency with which the action set (X,M,E) appears: although

Table 29

Cumulative number of solutions with aggregate effect at or below given level of eu(A')

Combined effect measure (eu(A'))	Total	Breakdown of total by action set								
		(3,M,E)	(X,O,O)	(X,M,E)	(X,O,E)	(3,L,E)	(3,M,C)	(X,M,O)	(X,L,E)	Other
560	2	1	1	–	–	–	–	–	–	–
580	5	3	1	1	–	–	–	–	–	–
600	13	4	6	2	1	–	–	–	–	–
620	22	10	6	5	1	–	–	–	–	–
640	44	11	10	13	6	2	1	1	–	–
660	64	16	10	23	6	3	3	1	1	1
680	93	17	10	36	10	4	4	6	3	3
700	138	19	10	54	11	10	10	8	8	8

choice of this particular action set only permits one solution with a combined effect measure of 580 units or less, it does leave open a future choice from a large variety of alternative solutions whose combined effect measure is at present estimated to lie somewhere in the region between 580 and 700 units. Action set (X,M,E) is therefore particularly 'robust' in the sense in which we used the word in our previous case example; and again the problem arises of whether it is worth while to 'buy' this degree of robustness (or flexibility in future choice) at the expense of ruling out those few solutions which at present appear at the very top of the order of preference. In our first case example, we regarded this kind of question as largely a matter for the judgement of the policy-makers; however, in the present case example, we have built up a good deal of quantitative information on the considerations which determine the order of preference, and so a certain amount of further analysis is possible before the final judgement is made.

A CLOSER APPRAISAL OF SOME ALTERNATIVE ACTION SETS

Of the action sets appearing in *Table 29*, it is only the first three – (3,M,E), (X,O,O) and (X,M,E) – which seem at first sight to provide clear advantages either of low overall penalty or of robustness. The planners might therefore decide to take a closer look at the particular implications of these three alternatives, without yet dismissing any of the remaining action sets out of hand.

The attraction of (3,M,E) – a compromise policy on rents and on design resources, combined with an early priority for the school project – is in that it permits the best solution of all according to the combined effect measure (solution 1 at 549 units), while also scoring reasonably well on 'robustness', if this is measured by the frequency with which this action set appears in any selected row in the lower part of *Table 29*. The attraction of (X,O,O) – a *laissez-faire* policy, with no increase in rents or design resources, and a lower priority for the school project – is that it permits a next-best solution (solution 2 at 558 units), while being slightly more robust than (3,M,E) at one limited stage in the build-up of *Table 29*. The attraction of (X,M,E) – a lower priority for school building combined with a compromise policy on rents and design resources – is that it also permits a few reasonably high-ranking solutions, such as solutions 5 and 8 at 579 and 591 units respectively, while preserving an exceptionally high degree of robustness in any of the lower rows of *Table 29*.

It would, however, be a wise precaution for the planners to examine the relative robustness of these three action sets not simply according to the number of reasonably good alternative solutions which each leaves open for future choice, but also according to whether the options which remain available do in fact extend the policy-makers' freedom of choice in directions which may be of some real value to them.

For instance, it is revealing to discover, from a more detailed analysis of those ten solutions of *Table 29* which are permitted by action set (X,O,O), that they leave open no future options on the drainage or housing schemes, which must each be deferred until their latest possible starting times. The only choices which do remain open under choice of this action set in fact turn out to relate to the school project – a choice of year 5 or 6 – and the shopping project – a choice of year 4, 5, 6, or 7 (public) or year 8 (private). Under the choice of action set (3,M,E), the options remaining open turn out to relate only to the year of the second housing project and to the year and agency for the shopping project. However, in this case, the available options for shopping all relate to the year in which it might be undertaken as a private venture, and therefore do very little to extend the freedom of choice of the local authority. As already suggested, any inducements to develop in a particular year would in all probability be strictly limited, and so the planners might be reduced to making predictions as to which solutions stood the best chances of achievement, instead of attempting to make a deliberate choice between them.

The third action set in our short-list, (X,M,E), occurs with exceptionally high frequency – 54 times in the first 138 solutions – and it is not surprising that, on further analysis, it turns out to leave a substantial range of options open on most of the remaining variables. As in the case of (3,M,E), the more detailed analysis – which we do not reproduce here – shows that some of the flexibility apparently allowed by this action set relates to the choice of year for private development of the shopping centre, so does not signify real extension to the freedom of action of the local authority. Also, several of the solutions remaining open can be grouped under 'leading solutions' as in *Tables 18* and *19*, in that they incur additional penalties that could never be justified in terms of the limited problem of area V alone. Nevertheless, a detailed analysis of the solutions permitted by action set (X,M,E) does indicate that, even after all these factors have been taken into account, there still remains a genuine freedom of action for the local authority which is superior to that allowed by any other action set.

As a result of this kind of analysis, extended over all alternative action sets, a much clearer case can be established for restricting the final choice of action set to either (3,M,E) or (X,M,E). Neither (X,O,O) nor any other alternative turns out to carry any specific advantages in terms of leaving open particular choices which would otherwise be closed. The choice between (3,M,E), which permits the best solution of all according to current estimates, and (X,M,E), which leaves a somewhat wider margin of flexibility, might perhaps be clarified further through a statistical analysis of the degree of confidence attached to each element of information used in estimating the combined effect measure. However, the application of statistical method is by no means straightforward, because of the subjectivity and interdependence of the estimates concerned.

Another consideration which may affect the final choice is that action set (3,M,E) will not necessarily be successful, because there may be a possibility that the application to start building the school in year 3 will be turned down by the national education authority. This consideration might well influence the local policy-makers towards a strategy of acting first on the basis of (3,M,E) – in other words raising the rents, recruiting further design staff, and going ahead with the school building application – with the assurance that, if this application failed, the resultant transformation of (3,M,E) into (X,M,E) would still leave them set on a course of action which conformed both with their current assessments of relative value and with their desire to retain flexibility of future choice.

Although pressures of time might at this stage preclude any further analysis in depth, the planners might be well advised to carry out some quick checks to test whether the policy-makers' emerging preference for a course of action based on (3,M,E) – with the option of (X,M,E) if this fails – might in fact be sensitive to variations in any of the many simplifying assumptions they have made in their analysis of the limited problem of area V. In the remainder of this chapter, we will take a second look at some of these simplifying assumptions, relating them to the three basic categories of uncertainty which we introduced in Chapter 4; uncertainties in knowledge of the environment (UE), uncertainties as to future intention in related fields of choice (UR), and uncertainties as to appropriate value judgements (UV).

THE QUESTIONING OF ASSUMPTIONS ON OPTIONS AND EFFECTS

Some of the most basic assumptions which underlie the analysis so far relate to the range of alternative options defined within each decision area (first set out in *Figure 37*), and the set of option bars which define the compatibility of pairs of options from different decision areas (as first set down in *Table 14*). The planners might, however, have doubts whether some of the options included would be feasible in practice, or whether perhaps certain new options could be added; they might also have some doubts in assessing the compatibility or incompatibility of particular option pairs. For instance, it might be just possible (though technically very difficult) to start the two housing projects simultaneously, or it might be quite feasible (though socially very undesirable) to consider deferring the school project until beyond year 6.

If the planners feel particularly doubtful about the validity of some of their initial assumptions in defining options and their interrelationships, and if computer facilities are freely available to them, then they will have little difficulty in repeating their evaluation of solutions under alternative sets of assumptions, to test whether these would lead to any modification of the policy-makers' emerging preference for a course of immediate action based on (3,M,E).

Some further basic assumptions were introduced in *Table 16*, where the effects of each option were estimated according to six different measures, whose significance was explained more fully in the text. It was assumed in each case that the number of people who stood to gain or lose by the choices of the policy-makers could be estimated with some precision: that there were known to be 3,000 existing council tenants, that the two housing projects would accommodate 500 and 300 families respectively, that the school would accommodate 600 pupils, and that the shopping centre would create improved facilities for 2,000 families living in the surrounding areas. In the case of this last estimate, no allowance was made for the expected growth in the number of families from 2,000 to 2,800 as the two housing estates came into occupation, the assumption being that this factor could reasonably be ignored. If, however, it is considered that the validity of this particular simplifying assumption should not be left untested, then it becomes necessary to introduce a new type of refinement into the analytical approach: the idea of attaching an effect measure not only to the choice of any particular option within a decision area, but also, where appropriate, to the choice of a particular *combination* of options from different decision areas. This complication raises no insuperable difficulties in the analysis, and we will consider it briefly below with particular reference to the interaction of the shopping centre project with the first of the two housing projects.

THE CONSTRUCTION OF A JOINT EFFECT TABLE FOR HOUSING AND SHOPPING

We will suppose that the expected rate of progress on the first housing project is such that the number of new residents on the estate will increase as follows:

Number of new families in area V3:

1 year after start of housing scheme I	100
2 years after start of housing scheme I	300
3 years after start of housing scheme I	500
thereafter	500

The 2,000 existing families that would stand to benefit from the provision of shops in V2 are all assumed to be resident in the surrounding areas which in *Map 12* were labelled S, T, and U. The total number of families within the sphere of influence of V2 can therefore be expected to grow as follows, according to the year in which work on housing scheme I is started:

Table 30

Year of start of housing scheme I	Total no. of families resident in areas S, T, U, and V3 who would benefit from shopping centre in V2						
	Year: 3	4	5	6	7	8	9 & after
Year 3	2000	2100	2300	2500	2500	2500	2500
4	2000	2000	2100	2300	2500	2500	2500
5	2000	2000	2000	2100	2300	2500	2500
6	2000	2000	2000	2000	2100	2300	2500

Assuming that the shops will be in full occupation during the second year after work on the shopping centre is started, then the effect of each solution on local shoppers will now depend not only on the timing of the shopping development but also on the timing of the first housing scheme. The new set of estimates, derived by adding certain sets of neighbouring columns in *Table 30*, are given in *Table 31*.

Table 31

Year of start of housing scheme I	Shopping project started in year				
	4	5	6	7	8
	First year of occupation				
	6	7	8	9	10
	Effect on shoppers measured in eu_s				
Year 3	0	2500	5000	7500	10000
4	0	2300	4800	7300	9800
5	0	2100	4400	6900	9400
6	0	2000	4100	6400	8900

Compare with original estimates of shoppers' effect units ignoring residents of housing scheme I:

0	2000	4000	6000	8000

As in the earlier analysis, the effect on local shoppers is measured according to a relative scale taking the earliest possible starting year for the shopping project (year 4) as zero. If the start is delayed from year 4 to year 5, the penalty in effect corresponds to the loss of a full year's trading in year 6, so that the second column in *Table 31* corresponds directly to the fourth column in *Table 30*. If the start is delayed a further year to year 6, the penalty corresponds to the loss of two full year's trading in years 6 and 7, so that the third column in *Table 31* corresponds to the sum of the fourth and fifth columns in *Table 30*, and so on. We can now see what difference the new assumptions have made to the original estimates of shopping penalties, which we reproduce for purposes of comparison at the foot of *Table 31*. For instance, the effect on shoppers associated with deferring a start on the shopping project until year 7 now exceeds the original estimate of 6,000 eu_s by a margin of 400, 900, 1,300, or 1,500 eu_s, depending on whether the housing project is started in year 6, 5, 4, or 3. In order to allow these adjustments to be incorporated in the main analysis, we will set them out in the form of what we will call a 'joint effect table' for the two decision areas, as follows:

Table 32

Housing I year	Shopping centre (agency/year)						
	Public				Private		
	4	5	6	7	6'	7'	8'
3	0	500	1000	1500	1000	1500	2000
4	0	500	800	1300	800	1300	1800
5	0	100	400	900	×	900	1400
6	0	0	100	400	×	×	900

All entries in shoppers' effect units (eu_s)

In this table, the crosses merely reflect those combinations which have already been ruled out by the option bar assumptions of *Table 14* (e). In fact, *Table 32*

15

differs from this earlier option-bar table in that each spot, representing a pair of compatible options, is replaced by a numerical entry, representing the joint effect of choosing that particular option pair in units of eu_s, over and above any effects these options may have when each is applied independently. Each entry in the new table can if required be converted to an equivalent in terms of the combined effect measure, by applying the appropriate trade-off rate. In this case, the conversion can be carried out by multiplying by a factor of 0·006, as was indicated in *Table 25*.

THE SIGNIFICANCE OF THE JOINT EFFECT TABLES

The significance of this particular joint effect table can be judged by making the appropriate modifications to the first few solutions in the order of preference shown in *Table 26*. For instance, the top solution in *Table 26* involves options of year 4 and year 6' (private) in the two decision areas with which we are now concerned; reading off from *Table 32*, this combination is seen to incur an additional effect on shoppers of 800 eu_s, which converts to 4·8 units in the aggregate effect measure: the combined effect estimate of this solution therefore rises from 549 eu(A') to 553·8 eu(A') when the joint effect of the housing I and shopping choices is taken into account. When similar adjustments are made to other solutions, certain marginal adjustments appear in the order of preference; within the top twelve solutions as shown in *Table 26*, solution 8 drops by two places and solution 10 by one. The crucial test, however, will be whether any significant variations arise in the frequencies of occurrence of the various action sets within the more extensive tabulation of *Table 29*. In fact, the variations turn out to be fairly marginal, and so the local planners can feel reassured that they were not introducing any serious distortions in their analysis when they initially made the simplifying assumption of ignoring this particular joint effect. They have in effect used the principle of sensitivity analysis (which we first discussed in Chapter 4) to satisfy themselves that their choice of action set is not very sensitive to the additional benefit which the new shopping centre will bring to the new families in area V3. A similar joint effect table could, of course, be constructed to link the shopping project with the second of the two housing schemes in the adjoining area V4.

The device of the joint effect table makes it possible to extend the AIDA method to deal with further types of relationship between options, other than those of total compatibility or incompatibility. In fact, the original spots and crosses in *Table 14* can be interpreted as assumptions that the joint effects associated with particular pairs of options can be treated as either infinitely low or infinitely high. The point at which the magnitude of a joint effect becomes so high as to be treated as an absolute prohibition is of necessity a matter for judgement; here again, the planners might be wise to carry out some quick sensitivity analyses, to test whether the replacement of particular incompatibilities by finite penalty measures would make any significant difference to the final choice of action set.

The device of the joint effect table also makes it possible for the planners, if they so desire, to reintroduce into the analysis at this stage the problem of priority for the new community centre in area V2. While it was assumed in *Figure 3* that the timing of this project would be related in some way to that of the first housing project, it was also assumed (in *Table 14*(f)) that this relationship could not be expressed in terms of statements of compatibility or incompatibility between particular option pairs. At this later stage, however, the planners might decide to replace *Table 14*(f) by a numerical table giving the estimated joint effect of particular combinations upon the prospective tenants of the new housing scheme in V3. There is in fact a strong case to be made that the early development of a community centre to serve a new housing estate (perhaps even before the first houses are occupied) can create all the difference between disaffection and delinquency on the one hand and a stable and secure social environment on the other. Measurement of such an effect may in practice be particularly difficult; but this does not necessarily preclude the making of *assumptions* about its scale and value in order to test the sensitivity to such assumptions of the emerging preference for particular courses of immediate action.

THE RANGE OF EFFECT MEASURES

In introducing this new consideration of the social value of the community centre, we have in effect been questioning whether the range of effect measures taken into account in the earlier evaluation was sufficiently wide to form a reasonable basis for choice by the policy makers. Clearly, the range of six effect measures which the planners chose to take into account in the main analysis is by no means exhaustive, and it is conceivable that the policy-makers might wish to extend this range further by consideration of costs and benefits incurred by various other sectors of the community.

For example, if there was a high level of unemployment in the town, the policy-makers might wish to evaluate alternative solutions according to the extra employment they could be expected to provide for the workers in the local construction trades. They might also wish perhaps to make an explicit evaluation of the traffic and environmental benefits in area R which could be expected to result indirectly from the early completion of the new shopping centre in V2, or the potential loss of trade which might be inflicted on existing traders. Even if these other effects had not originally been considered sufficiently relevant to the problem of area V to have been included in the main analysis, there is no reason why some rough estimates of their magnitude should not be attempted at this later stage, so as to test whether there is in fact any likelihood that they are sufficiently critical to influence the final judgement of the policy-makers.

Another possibility is that the policy-makers might wish to extend the range of effects measures not only by the inclusion of certain effects impinging on other sectors of the community, but also by a further division of some of the six original sectors into sub-groups to whose interests they might wish to give differential treatment. For instance, they might wish to consider separately the interests of those existing council tenants with particularly low incomes, or those would-be tenants now living in particularly overcrowded conditions, or those schoolchildren with particularly difficult travelling problems. They might consider that the benefit of the new shopping centre to the new residents of V3 should be rated higher than its benefit to existing residents of areas S and T, because the former are much more remote from existing shopping facilities than the latter. Perhaps, in the definition of a 'shoppers' effect unit', it might be considered appropriate to give, say, double weighting to each new family in area V3 or area U as opposed to each existing family in area S or T. Perhaps in the same way the policy-makers might feel that the definition of a 'prospective tenants' effect unit' ought to be adjusted so as to attach extra value to certain particularly deserving categories of would-be tenants.

It is by now becoming apparent that the original choice of a fairly limited set of effects measures rested in fact on a whole range of assumptions about the need to give equity of consideration to many different individuals within the community, each with his or her own special needs or circumstances but each treated for convenience of analysis as a member of some wider group. It is only to be expected that the members of the policy-making group, as politicians and as public representatives, may wish to single out certain sub-groups for preferential treatment; and whatever set of effect measures is chosen must incorporate sufficient diversity to allow legitimate discrimination of this kind.

The search for a satisfactory range of effect measures in fact represents an attempt to achieve a reasonable working balance between two opposing considerations: the need to keep the variety of costs and benefits under consideration sufficiently limited for the analysis as a whole to be widely comprehensible, and the need to include within the analysis a sufficient element of 'political richness', defined as the capacity to discriminate between different sectors of the community in pursuit of legitimate social objectives. The search for a sufficient set of effect measures for the evaluation of alternative planning solutions may not be an easy one, and must of itself form an important aspect of the continuing dialogue between officers and elected members.

THE INCIDENCE OF COSTS AND BENEFITS OVER TIME

We have now seen how the definition of any set of effect measures may in fact mask a variety of uncertainties of appropriate value judgement (i.e. uncertainties of the category UV). However, such uncertainties may not be limited entirely to the problem of setting values to effects which impinge on different sectors of the community; they may also extend to the problem of allocating differential values to similar kinds of effect which impinge over different periods of future time.

The idea that a given expenditure arising in five years' time may be preferable to the same expenditure arising today (because the money can be invested with profit in the meantime) is a familiar one in economic analysis, and has led to the development of techniques such as that of discounted cash flow for the appraisal of capital investment projects [3]. In a rather different way, the idea that a given social benefit today may be preferable to the same benefit in five years' time is accepted intuitively by all politicians – particularly if they have to stand for re-election in the intervening period.

In terms of our particular problem of priorities in area V, these considerations suggest that there may be a case for modifying the definition of some or all of the original effect measures in order to give more weight to costs or benefits incurred during the first year or two than to those incurred in later years. In the absence of any specific reasons to the contrary, it is reasonable to assume that the weighting given to future effects should decline at a steady rate from year to year, the rate of reduction (or discounting) depending to some extent on the judgement of the policy-makers.

To take a specific example, in *Table 16* it was assumed that the first year by which the school project was postponed beyond year 3 would bring a benefit to local taxpayers of 30 eu_r, while also costing a penalty to local schoolchildren of 600 eu_s. Without the application of a discount rate, a further postponement from year 4 to year 5 would have exactly similar effects; however, the assumption of an annual discount rate of (say) 10 per cent would mean that, in the case of the second year's postponement, the additional benefit to local taxpayers would become 27 instead of 30 eu_r, while the additional penalty to local schoolchildren would become 540 instead of 600 eu_c. For the third year's postponement, from year 5 to year 6, the corresponding figures would again fall by 10 per cent, to 24·3 eu_r and 486 eu_c respectively.

However, it is arguable that the discount rates applied to these very different types of social effect, on local taxpayers and on schoolchildren, should not necessarily be the same, but should reflect both the political horizons of the policy-makers (with or without the inevitable distortions attributable to the local electoral cycle) and also the wider variety of planning horizons which exist within the community itself. It is a basic characteristic of local government (and for that matter of national government as well) that the policy-makers can never afford to be either very much more forward-looking, or on the other hand very much more immersed in the present, than are the members of the community they represent. Within these limitations, there will always be some scope for the policy-makers to induce the public by persuasion to accept a higher level of current investment for the creation of long-term benefits than they would otherwise have been prepared to stand. In practice, an acceptable balance between short-term sacrifices and long-term gains can only be arrived at through the continuing dialogue between the local planners and the representatives of the wider community; and the use of methods such as time-discounting can only be seen as part of the process of clarifying uncertainties as to relevant value judgements in so far as these judgements relate to effects arising at different periods of future time.

LONG-TERM EFFECTS OF THE CHOICE OF PRIORITIES IN AREA V

The main analysis of the problem of priorities in area V ignored the time-discounting problem; in other words, it assumed a zero discount rate. The sensitivity of the analysis to this assumption can however be tested by repeating it under a range of alternative 'reasonable' discount rates, such as 5, 10, and 15 per cent. However, the choice of action set in fact turns out to be fairly insensitive to modifications of this order, because the *differential* effects of any change in project priority tend to be concentrated within a comparatively narrow band of years. For instance, the total impact on the local taxpayers of the new secondary school in VI may be distributed over time according to the kind of profile shown in *Figure 41*, with the amount of displacement to the left depending on the choice of starting year.

In so far as the total cost of the school to local taxpayers represents the effect of loan charges over a fixed repayment period, then it can of course be argued that each year by which the school project is brought forward not only increases the

Figure 41

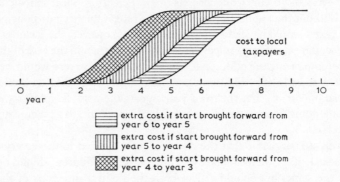

year

cost to local
taxpayers

extra cost if start brought forward from
year 6 to year 5

extra cost if start brought forward from
year 5 to year 4

extra cost if start brought forward from
year 4 to year 3

short-term burden on existing local taxpayers, but implies an equivalent easing in the burden on their successors a generation or more hence. In disregarding this balancing factor in their main analysis, the planners were in effect making the assumption that, at this period of future time, the weight to be attached to anticipated effects would be so small that it could safely be neglected.

However, a somewhat different situation arises in the case of the shopping centre project, where the decision to develop publicly rather than privately means that the local taxpayers must pay additional loan charges not only during the initial years but also over the whole period of the loan. This cost will, of course, have to be assessed against an ultimate financial return from rentals which might, under favourable future trading conditions, provide a steady inflow of cash into the local tax account. The chart of expected cash flow over time might in this case appear somewhat as shown in *Figure 42*, assuming a physical start in year 4.

The original estimates of the effect of this project on local taxpayers assumed that, taking the option of public development starting in year 4, they would suffer a net penalty of 90 eu, compared with the alternative of private development (which would require no direct contribution from local taxes). In effect, the assumption was made that the appropriate rate of discounting should be such as to make the area of *Figure 42* above the line outweigh the area below the line by an overall margin of 90 eu,.

One would expect this particular estimate to be a good deal more sensitive to the choice of discount rate than most of the other estimates presented in *Table 16*, because the differential effects of public and private development are not confined to a narrow band of future time as are the differential effects of alternative project start dates. Also, the estimate of a net local tax burden of 90 eu, may be very sensitive to predictions of future market potential for traders in that part of town, and

Figure 42

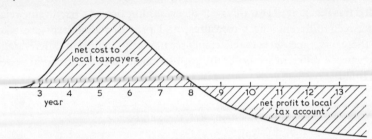

to assumptions about future planning intentions – for instance, the planners' intentions in relation to the future of the existing shopping street in area R. Thus, the estimated effect on local taxpayers of choosing public rather than private development for the shopping centre in area V may turn out to be highly sensitive to uncertainties in each of the three main categories: uncertainties in knowledge of the environment (UE), uncertainties of future intention in related areas of choice (UR), and uncertainties of appropriate value judgement (UV).

Within the last category, uncertainty relates in particular to determination of the political balance between the losses of present ratepayers and the potential gains of their successors. We therefore have, in the question of agency for the shopping centre project, one particular area of choice which is likely to repay a very full exploration both by the local planners and by the public representatives.

THE ASSUMPTION OF FIXED TRADE-OFF RATES

In the preceding pages, we have come across uncertainties of value judgement in several different contexts – in the problem of evaluating similar effects over different time periods, in the problem of adjusting effects measures in order to give preferential treatment to particular groups of people, and in the earlier problem of choosing a 'trade-off rate' for comparison of different types of cost and benefit. The very idea of a trade-off 'rate' itself embodies an assumption that the willingness of the policy-makers to provide, for instance, new school places at the cost of additional local tax expenditure does not vary in any way as the tax burden rises and as the demand for school places becomes progressively more fully satisfied. If this assumption is not accepted, then the concept of a trade-off rate must be replaced by the wider concept of a 'trade-off curve' for any pair of effects, or a 'trade-off function' relating to any number of effects, acknowledging that the appropriate levels of trade-off for any given situation may be dependent on the particular levels of demand – and of satisfaction of demand – which apply at the time. The idea of the trade-off curve is very much akin to the idea of the indifference curve in economic analysis.

To take explicit account of this further complication would be to make the whole analysis very much more cumbersome from a computational point of view. In practice, the idea of a 'trade-off rate' is often likely to be a justifiable simplification, provided it is recognized that this rests on an assumption of a fixed value relationship between different effect measures, and provided that steps are taken to adjust these effect measures to reflect any particularly significant differentiation of values between different sectors of the population, or between different periods of future time.

A RETURN TO THE WIDER PROBLEM OF SECTOR Z

Having now reviewed some of the environmental uncertainties (UE) and the value uncertainties (UV) which underlie their analysis of priorities in area V, it remains for the planners to review those uncertainties in the final category (UR) concerned with future planning intentions in related fields of choice. In particular, it may be asked whether the planners' choice of action set within area V might have been unduly influenced by their initial decision to concentrate their attention on one particular set of eight decision areas selected from the wider field of choice identified in sector Z as a whole.

Returning to the original list of choices set out in *Table 13*, the planners might now decide to pick out the following additional decision areas as being related in some degree to the eight decision areas they selected for the original analysis of area V:

Table 33

Z6t	Parking/service area in R (choice of timing)
Z7t	Redevelopment of P1 (choice of timing)
Z8d	Housing scheme I in V3 (choice of design)
Z8a	Housing scheme I in V3 (choice of agency: public/private)
Z9d	Housing scheme II in V4 (choice of design)
Z9a	Housing scheme II in V4 (choice of agency: public/private)
Y1t	Other housing schemes outside Z (choice of timing)
Y2t	Secondary school schemes outside Z (choice of timing)
Y2d	Secondary school schemes outside Z (location and catchments)
Y7d	Level of local taxation for next financial year (or years)

We will not go into detail as to all the various ways in which these further choices might impinge on the problem of priorities in area V: but, to give selected examples, the early provision of a parking and service area in R might reduce somewhat the potential advantage of the new shopping centre at V2, at least so far as existing residents of areas S and T were concerned; the choice of a higher density layout than previously envisaged for the housing scheme in V3 might increase the number of families which could be housed, but on the other hand might set back the earliest feasible starting date; the options (hitherto put to one side) of private development for either of the two housing schemes might now be seen to afford an attractive way of meeting overall demand for new accommodation without putting an excessive strain on the local authority's housing account; the claim for a secondary school in area V might have to be judged on its merits against certain other claims for new secondary schools (or perhaps primary schools) in different parts of the town; and, last but not least, an unwillingness by the policy-makers to raise the level of local taxation by more than some limited annual increment might restrict the availability of some of the more expensive solutions so far considered to the problem of priorities in area V.

In theory, the original analysis of the eight decision areas could now be extended to a wider problem of eighteen decision areas. However, some of the new decision areas might involve a range of options which could be particularly difficult to define; this would certainly be so in the case of 'omnibus' decision areas such as Y1t which have been so defined as to include more than one development project. There is therefore a danger that, by extending their field of analysis at this stage, the local planners might find themselves embarking on an exercise which could quickly get out of hand. A less ambitious alternative would be to carry out a series of trials to test how far their proposed choice of action set $(3,M,E)$ is sensitive to the choice of certain selected options in each of the additional decision areas which appear to be relevant. For instance, the number of prospective tenants who are assumed to benefit from the first housing scheme might be varied from the original 500, first downwards to 400 and then upwards to 600, to test the effects of alternative housing densities on the main analysis of area V.

A STRATEGY GRAPH FOR SECTOR Z

In order to provide a framework for a still wider view of the problems of sector Z as a whole, we have drawn up, in *Figure 43*, an outline option graph in which all the various choices of timing, agency, and design which were originally listed in *Table 13* have been included (with the exception only of those design choices which were not regarded as sufficiently significant to be marked with an asterisk). In *Figure 43*, the eight decision areas which were originally selected for the analysis of priorities within area V have all been grouped in the top left-hand corner, and are identified by means of a double outline. The links between decision areas in *Figure 43* include all those which have been specified at earlier stages of the analysis, together with certain others which are now seen to interconnect the choices arising beyond area V among themselves. Although each of these new links may have its own intuitive interpretation, a good deal of further analysis may be necessary before they can all be interpreted more precisely in terms of option-bar or joint effect tables.

Figure 43

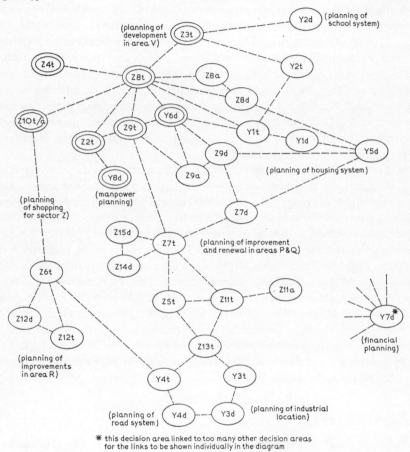

✳ this decision area linked to too many other decision areas
   for the links to be shown individually in the diagram

The kind of outline option graph presented in *Figure 43* is even less specific than the outline option graph of *Figure 37* in that it does not attempt to specify particular options within decision areas; this is what is known as a 'strategy graph' in the terminology of the AIDA method. Its usefulness lies in the extent to which it can clarify the structure of a complex problem at a stage before the options have been clearly identified, and suggest in what ways, if any, the problem might be broken down into smaller components.

PLANNING PERSPECTIVES RELATING TO SECTOR Z

The complexity of *Figure 43* makes it impossible to include a full verbal description of each decision area, but a key is given to the parts of the graph where certain broad planning perspectives are involved. The interplay of these various perspectives is brought out more clearly in *Figure 44*; here, the various decision areas have been grouped within a number of overlapping 'zones' of the overall strategy graph, each representing the planning perspective of a particular geographical area, operational system, or system of resources (just as, during the discussion of our first case example, we at one point used this kind of diagram to draw attention to

Figure 44

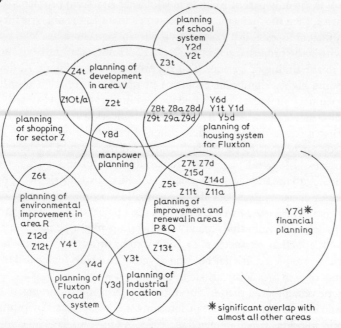

the overlapping perspectives of land-use planning in area A, of planning for the school system, and of planning for the town centre commercial system).

Figure 44 shows that a high proportion of the decision areas in the overall strategy graph can be viewed according to more than one planning perspective. The diagram can, of course, give only a broad overall impression of the more significant zones of overlap and can make no claims to completeness. For instance, decision area Z5t (relating to the children's playground in P2) might be included within a further overlapping oval relating to the planning of Fluxton's total system of recreational facilities; or, again, the diagram might be extended to distinguish separate planning perspectives for certain other districts of new residential development outside sector Z – and so perhaps to bring out the linkage between the problems of sector Z and the earlier problem of area A.

Despite its incompleteness, a broad picture such as that of *Figure 44* can serve as a means of provoking some important questions about the original choice of eight decision areas for detailed consideration in relation to the development of area V. The eight decision areas originally selected do not in fact correspond exactly to those shown within the oval for area V in *Figure 44*: in the initial analysis, certain decisions of design and agency for housing schemes were excluded (Z8a, Z8d, Z9a, Z9d) on the understanding that they might be re-introduced later, while the decision as to rent levels for council tenants in the town as a whole (Y6d) was added into the analysis because it was supposed to be of critical importance in relation to the choice of priorities within area V.

If area V is the only part of Fluxton in which shorter-term problems of housing priority arise, then the inclusion of Y6d as an element in the analysis for that area may be sufficient to establish a case for a moderate rent increase (M as opposed to O or L) within the proposed action set (X,M,E). However, if the decision area Y1t (relating to the timing of 'various housing projects' beyond zone Z) does in fact include some highly significant problems of priority in relation to other areas, then the planners might be well advised to re-examine action set (3,M,E) – with its implied alternative of (X,M,E) if the school application is rejected – in order to test whether it leaves open a sufficient range of promising solutions to Fluxton's overall problem of housing priorities. In other words, it might be desirable to test the 'robustness' of (3,M,E) according to two different planning frameworks: not only according to the framework of area V, as defined by the original option graph with its eight decision areas, but also according to a second framework developed from that part of *Figure 43* which describes the interrelationships of the Fluxton housing problem. Within this second framework, it might be necessary to take a second look at action sets such as (3,L,E) which, through a further increase in rents, could provide additional housing revenue to bring forward development projects not only in area V but also in other parts of town.

It may be remembered that, in our initial comparison of solutions to the problem of priorities in area V, the list of solutions was compressed by putting to one side certain solutions which involved increases in rents but gave no compensating benefits compared to equivalent 'leading' solutions in which rents were kept as low as possible. At that time, we made the proviso that the non-leading solutions should not necessarily be discarded out of hand, because they might incur certain benefits not considered in the limited problem of area V. It is this kind of possibility which might now be tested through an analysis of the robustness of (3,M,E) within a new planning framework relating to housing priorities over Fluxton as a whole. Of course, there might also be a case for testing the robustness of this same action set according to a third or even a fourth planning framework. For instance, it might be examined within a framework relating to the Fluxton school system, so as to bring out the implications of any competition for priorities between school projects in different parts of town.

By focusing in their main analysis on area V, rather than on the housing system or on the school system, the planners were in effect working to an initial hypothesis that the overall strategy graph for priorities in sector Z (and for that matter in Fluxton as a whole) was likely to be more strongly connected in the region concerned with area V as a locality than in that concerned with the housing or school systems for the town as a whole. This hypothesis might well have been a reasonable one if there were seen to be few significant shorter-term problems of priority for housing and school projects in other parts of town. We may note in passing that, in the case example of the previous chapter, we did in fact come across some short-term pressures for local authority housing development in area A; but we supposed that the priority problem was settled at that time by allowing preliminary work to begin in areas A2 and A3, and we will now assume that allowance was duly made for this commitment in the municipal housing account, so that the options for future rent increases in Case Two are not affected. We may also note that we came across a secondary school project in the discussion of the earlier case example, but that the site could not yet be determined; it is therefore a reasonable assumption that this particular school project will not be competing against that in area V for any shorter-term allocation of priorities. At this point in time, though not necessarily at other future times, the planners may therefore be justified in treating the problems of area A and area V as if they are completely independent of each other.

We will suppose in this case that the policy-makers' preference for action set (3,M,E) is confirmed by these further tests of its sensitivity to variations in the assumptions of the main analysis; but in practice the local planners will always have to be prepared for the possibility that the processes of sensitivity analysis might lead them to a complete rejection of these initial assumptions. Then the problem might arise as to what forms of exploratory action, if any, they should propose as a means of clarifying the basis for decision by the policy-makers. This is a problem which will arise more directly in our third case example, so we will not pursue it further for the time being.

THE FINANCIAL IMPLICATIONS OF PROJECT PRIORITIES IN SECTOR Z

As we indicated in *Figure 43*, the choice of a local tax level for the next few years is likely to be linked to some extent with very many other decision areas, both in sector Z and beyond. We will suppose at this stage that – as is often the case in British local government – the policy-makers are becoming alarmed about the political implications of the rising burden of local taxation, and decide to impose some overall constraint on the annual rate of increase. It might be decided that the amount of finance available for development projects should be rationed as between different areas of the city, and that it would be unreasonable to allow sector Z (or area V within sector Z) to take up more than some given percentage of the total increase that could be permitted over the next five or ten years. If such a constraint could be interpreted as imposing an upper limit of (say) 200 eu$_r$ on the admissible local tax impact of any solution to the problem of area V, then a large proportion of the 1,216 solutions would become liable to automatic rejection, with the result that, in the final analysis of action sets, the *laissez-faire* alternative of (X,O,O) might be found to come strongly back into favour.

The imposition of a maximum allocation of local finance to each area of the town would, of course, represent a rather blunt weapon for keeping the overall level of local taxation under control, and it can be argued that a more discriminating method would be to carry out some kind of marginal analysis of the various social benefits which could be obtained by channelling investment into different sectors within the city, before deciding where economies might be made. However, if the overall level of local taxation was known to be a subject of concern, much could be learnt by repeating the analysis of priorities in area V under various alternative upper limits on the local tax burden, as part of a systematic programme to test the sensitivity of the result to a range of possible variations in the underlying assumptions.

THE CHALLENGES OF THE INNER ZONE

In our discussion of this case example, we have not dealt in any detail with the inner 'twilight' areas of sector Z – those marked P and Q on *Map 12* – although we suggested that these areas might well contain a number of social problems which were likely to be particularly difficult to solve in the long term. By concentrating on the shorter-term problems of priorities in area V, we were able to illustrate many aspects of our 'technology of choice' with reference to a situation which could be defined in reasonably clear-cut terms. Whatever qualifications might have to be made about the validity of certain assumptions, it was at least possible to identify a distinct set of options for each decision area, and to put forward a reasonably restricted set of effect measures for the comparison of total solutions. In the case of areas P and Q, however, the problems of improving the general environment, of providing adequate community facilities, and of planning the long-term assimilation of an immigrant population, may well present challenges of a different order, and a good deal of survey, analysis, and consultation may be necessary before any attempt can be made even to identify options or to put forward a sufficient set of effect measures. In the short term, the main question may there-fore be not one of making an early commitment to future policies in area P and Q (although certain immediate actions on a more limited scale might be unavoidable), but rather one of drawing up a co-ordinated programme of survey work and con-sultation designed to improve the quality of the information available for longer-term decisions. This is the kind of problem which we will consider more fully in our next case example.

A SUMMING-UP OF CASE TWO

In our extensive discussion of this case example, we have touched on many dif-ferent types of analytical approach which we believe can make a contribution to a balanced 'technology for strategic choice' in a local planning context. While we will defer a final appraisal of these approaches until the final chapter of Part III, there is one general comment which it is perhaps appropriate for us to make at the close of this chapter. This is that, although our analysis of the problems of sector Z and area V may have appeared protracted at times, it does not necessarily follow that any exercises in practical application to local planning problems are liable to be correspondingly time-consuming for those concerned.

This chapter has been a long one because we have considered it particularly important, during the discussion of this case example, to explore in some depth the validity of every type of working assumption on which such an analysis must rest. In practice, of course, any particular group of local planners would expect to become progressively more familiar with the implications of the decision technology they use – whether it is of the kind we suggest or of some more intuitive nature – and will acquire a 'nose' for the types of assumption with which special care may be required. In particular, their continuing dialogue with the policy-makers will give them an appreciation of those types of assumption which may be particularly sensitive to the value judgements of the policy-makers; in time, one might expect mutually acceptable arrangements to develop as to those points where it is most essential for the policy-makers to be involved.

Once the value of any decision technology has successfully been established within any particular problem area, what is required may be not so much a periodic grand review of the whole problem area taking every consideration into account at an explicit level, as a series of continuing marginal adjustments to reflect the influence of new information about the environment, new pressures for commitment from different sectors of the community, new expressions of value judgement by the policy-makers, and new insights into interactions with other areas of choice.

11. Case three: strategy for a sub-region

In Case One, the alignment of the Fluxton bypass emerged as a major source of uncertainty in relation to the choice of a land-use pattern for area A. In Case Two, the timing of this same bypass project was seen to have certain implications for the relocation of the noisy industry in area P, and for the question of improving the environment of the shopping centre in area R.

We will suppose now that some further time has elapsed, and that the problem of the bypass has by now risen to a new and more public level of controversy. Previously, the question of its alignment had been a source of disagreement only between the local planners and the government department whose sanction they would ultimately require, and we supposed that the local planners had been prepared to bet 3 to 1 on the eventual acceptance of their own preferred route. By now, however, we will suppose that the alternative proposals have become public knowledge and that a hostile reaction has built up from owner-occupiers whose property would either require demolition or would be adversely affected in other ways. This reaction is most vocal in the case of the planners' preferred eastern route, but is also sufficiently strong in the case of the western alternative to make the planners wonder whether they might not eventually have to settle for some third option which they have not yet seriously considered.

There are a number of alternative proposals which are now being brought up for discussion in public meetings and in letters to the local press. Why not route the bypass around the outskirts of the town, so avoiding the demolition of existing property and the disturbance of residential environments? Why not at the same time look to a public transport solution for the problem of commuter traffic into and out of the town centre? Could not the railway line – now only used for occasional through trains – also provide a local 'bus stop' service at peak hours? What might be done to make the existing bus services more attractive, either by injecting further public funds or by providing special traffic privileges? Are there any more novel systems of public transport which could make a contribution? Could a more restrictive policy for car-parking in the town centre and possibly also in the industrial areas, help to discourage the use of private cars – or would this be politically unacceptable? Could employers and trade unions be expected to co-operate by staggering working hours to a greater extent than they do already?

Even though the uncertainty over the Fluxton bypass is now making it difficult to consider alternatives for the future pattern of land use in Fluxton as a whole, it is by now becoming apparent to the local planners that it will not be politically feasible for any early action to be taken to resolve this uncertainty. Both the government department and the local political leadership are finding it increasingly difficult to ignore public criticism that the planners' predictions of future traffic volumes rest on assumptions which are open to doubt, and that too few options for solution to the traffic problem have yet been explored. Against this background, the buying of further time to improve the basis for decision is seen to be virtually unavoidable, and the main problem for the planners and the policy-makers becomes one, first, of judging how much time they can afford to buy, and, second, of deciding what steps they might take to ensure that this time is used to good effect.

Meanwhile, however, other changes of planning perspective may be taking place both in Fluxton itself and in other neighbouring towns. We will suppose in particular that not far from Fluxton there is a larger city, which forms a natural commercial and administrative centre for a number of surrounding towns and rural areas. We will call this city Adminster, and we will suppose that the growing recognition of a need for a sub-regional planning activity covering Adminster and its surrounding sphere of influence has led to the formation of a special planning team, whose brief is to consider a wider range of alternatives for transportation and physical and economic development within this area. From the viewpoint of this planning team, the problem of the Fluxton transport system may appear as only one of many interacting components in the search for an imaginative and acceptable sub-regional strategy.

Where we refer to 'the planners' in the present chapter, it will be this team in particular that we have in mind. We will suppose as before that this group of planners is primarily accountable to a clearly defined group of 'policy-makers' – which in this case will be so constituted as to include explicit representation of the local interests of Adminster, Fluxton, and other communities within the sub-region.

THE PLANNING PROBLEMS OF THE SUB-REGION

We will suppose that the map of Adminster and its sub-region appears as shown in *Map 14*.

The broken line indicates the administrative boundary which has been drawn to define the sub-region for the purposes of the joint planning activity. This boundary includes not only Adminster itself, but also Fluxton, together with two other towns of comparable size whose planning problems are of a rather more specialized kind. The town of Grumwich is characterized by declining industries and by a poor environment which suggests that any future increase in population would be undesirable. Brawley, on the other hand, is a new town set up to divert some of the pressure for growth from Adminster itself. So far, the strategy of diverting growth to Brawley has been only partially successful; industries have been slow to move out to the new town, and the population pressures in Adminster have continued to increase, so that the future rate of expansion of Brawley is still uncertain. There is a possibility that, if the Fluxton bypass is routed sufficiently far to the west, it could also provide improved communications for Brawley, and so help to make its future expansion a more viable proposition.

Map 14. Adminster and its sub-region

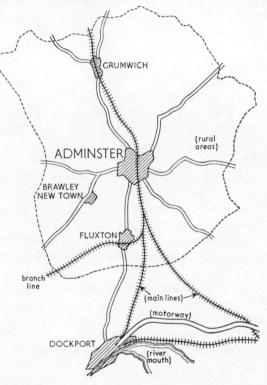

Communications with the large modern docks at Dockport, a major seaport situated beyond the boundaries of the sub-region, are seen as particularly important to local industries. There have been indications that the authorities of Dockport may themselves have a strong interest in the choice of a route for the Fluxton bypass because, if it could be fed into the city from the eastern side, then it could be made to link up with a new stretch of urban motorway which Dockport has just constructed, at considerable expense, to prevent traffic to and from the docks from destroying the environment of residential areas.

IDENTIFICATION OF DECISION AREAS AND PLANNING PERSPECTIVES

A first attempt by the planners to identify the principal problems with which they will be concerned might lead them to identify a provisional set of decision areas as follows:

Adminster

A1   Choice of locations for residential development on periphery.
A2   Choice of rate of peripheral expansion to be permitted.
A3   Choice of rate of public investment in urban renewal.
A4   Choice of primary road pattern within city.
A5   Choice of system for constraining flow of traffic through central area.
A6   Choice of system of parking facilities for central area.
A7   Choice of degree of constraint on parking in industrial areas.
A8   Choice of provision to be made in central area for development of regional facilities (e.g. polytechnic, concert hall, swimming pool, department stores, bus station).

Brawley

B1   Choice of rate of public investment in residential development.
B2   Choice of rate of expenditure on incentives to industrial development.
B3   Choice of area of land to be reserved for central shopping development.

Fluxton

F1   Choice of rate of public investment in residential development.
F2   Choice of rate of investment in urban renewal and rehabilitation.
F3   Choice of whether to proceed with proposed industrial estate on east side.
F4   Choice of system of parking facilities for central area.

Grumwich

G1   Choice of rate of investment in environmental improvements.
G2   Choice of severity of measures to remove noxious industries.

Sub-region

S1   Choice of areas (if any) for linear development of housing and industry.
S2   Choice of measures to achieve a balanced social structure within the sub-region (policies for allocation of tenancies, etc.).

Transportation System for Sub-region

T1   Choice of route for Fluxton bypass (Adminster-Dockport trunk road).
T2   Choice of level of investment in development of public transport.
T3   Choice of forms of public transport to be developed (rail, bus, new forms).
T4   Choice of measures for giving support to public transport operations from public funds.
T5   Choice of axes for development of rapid transit system.

At this stage, there may be little point in attempting to define an exhaustive list of decision areas, and the above list is only intended as a broad indication of the scope of the sub-regional planning activity. At a later stage, the planners would probably wish both to introduce further areas of choice and also to formulate some of their original choices in a rather different way; for instance, if a strong case began to emerge for a development of local rail services, they might wish to regroup certain aspects of decision areas T2, T3, T4, and A6 within a single decision area relating to the choice of a general strategy for rail system development.

For the time being, we will suppose that the planners see their initial set of decision areas as grouping themselves into certain broad planning perspectives which overlap with each other as shown in *Figure 45*:

Figure 45

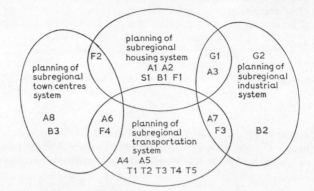

There may also be a limited degree of multiple overlapping which it is difficult to show clearly in a diagram of this kind; for instance, problems of town centre, residential, and industrial planning may all become closely interconnected in the inner areas of certain towns (as was seen to be the case in area A of Fluxton).

THE DEFINITION OF SETS OF FEASIBLE OPTIONS

Before the planners can begin to make any comparisons of alternative planning solutions, either for the whole field of choice shown in *Figure 45* or for selected parts of it, they may find that there are many preliminary problems of definition to be solved: first, there may be a number of decision areas within which they find it difficult to define a sufficient set of feasible options and, second, they may have some difficulty at the outset in defining a sufficient set of effect measures for the subsequent comparison of alternatives.

Considering first the problem of defining sets of feasible options within particular decision areas, there are many reasons why this may prove to be difficult. In the case of a decision area such as A4 – concerning the choice of a future road pattern for Adminster – a very large number of different patterns might be conceivable and it might not be clear to the planners on what principles a short-list of feasible alternatives should be drawn up: the formulation of such a short-list might of itself require a good deal of design work, in the course of which the application of systematic design methods might prove to be well justified. On the other hand, in the case of a decision area such as T3 – concerning the choice between alternative types of public transport system for future development – it might not be clear whether or not certain novel systems currently under development elsewhere might be considered as possible 'starters' in the particular local setting of Adminster and its surrounding area. A good deal of preliminary research and development work might be necessary for each such system to establish whether or not it was worth carrying it forward into the wider comparison of planning solutions; this preliminary work might include reviews of published information on each system, consultations with manufacturers, and visits to sites where the system could be seen in operation. In the case of certain other decision areas, such as T4 or A5, it might not be possible to formulate a sufficient range of feasible options until the ability to overcome certain legal or administrative difficulties had been explored.

The amount of effort which the planners might usefully expend on preliminary explorations of the feasibility of particular options can itself be regarded as a matter for strategic choice, in which many factors must be taken into account: the resources of time, skill, and money available to the planners, the risk of devoting too high a proportion of these resources to the exploration of what might subsequently turn out to be blind alleys, and the opposite risk of rejecting out of hand certain options which might in the end have opened up prospects of significantly better planning solutions. All these factors may require to be weighed not only against each other, but against the constant pressures for early decision in particular areas of choice. In such circumstances the selection of a preliminary programme of research and development work for the deeper exploration of particular decision areas becomes by no means a simple matter, and may in some circumstances be regarded as itself a fruitful area for the application of analytical techniques; however, we will suppose in this case that, to get the planning activity under way, the planners feel they have no alternative but to rely on their own intuitive judgement as to the selection of options whose feasibility should be explored more fully during the course of their programme of preliminary studies. Of course, there is no reason why their initial attempts to define sets of feasible alternatives for each decision area should prevent them at a later stage from exploring new options – or even redefining the decision areas themselves – in accordance with any new information that might meanwhile come to light.

THE CHOICE OF EFFECT MEASURES

The choice of a sufficient set of effect measures for the comparison of alternative options, and subsequently of alternative planning solutions, is itself a matter to which the planners might wish to give a good deal of attention during the preliminary phase of their planning activity. The definition of such measures might well be a much more difficult matter than in our second case example, in which it was possible to make some reasonably confident estimates of the numbers of people who would stand to incur certain well defined types of personal loss or gain, such as the payment of additional taxes or rents, or the earlier availability of new housing, educational, or shopping opportunities.

The social implications of, for example, an improved road network for Adminster or a faster rate of expansion for Brawley New Town might be much more difficult to assess even in approximate terms. To pursue the example of the Adminster road network, each alternative design under consideration might affect many different kinds of road-user in many different ways, depending in particular on their points of origin and destination and on the purpose of their journeys – whether this is travel to and from work, the paying of social visits, the carriage of industrial goods, or the provision of emergency services. It would clearly be misleading simply to make broad numerical estimates of the total numbers of road-users affected by the Adminster road network, and then to assume that each incurred the same level of benefit or penalty from each proposed scheme irrespective of the length and nature of his or her journey; in other words, the type of effect measure which proved adequate in Case Two would not be meaningful for the evaluation of alternative road patterns without an extensive classification of road-users according to many different categories.

Above and beyond the direct effects of any given road pattern on the road-users themselves, there will be a number of other important effects for the planners to evaluate: the effects on pedestrians and on people living or working near existing main roads whose environments might be improved by the channelling of through traffic into a few purpose-built arterial highways; the effects on owners and occupiers of property which would have to be demolished, perhaps without adequate compensation for the personal hardships and losses they might suffer; the effects, beneficial or otherwise, on other owners and occupiers of property in districts adjoining the proposed new roads; the effects on any local communities which might find themselves severed and their stable patterns of social relationships disrupted; and of course, last but not least, the financial effects of the construction and compensation payments on local and national taxpayers.

As in Case Two, the choice of a set of effect measures for comparison of alternative solutions requires the striking of a careful balance between convenience of analysis and 'political richness', in the sense of capacity to discriminate between the interests of many different sectors of the community. In this case, we will suppose that informal discussion between the planners and the policy-makers reveals that, so far as the effects on traffic flow are concerned, the policy-makers would like to be able to make separate evaluations of the effects of each alternative road pattern not only according to certain basic categories of road-user – commuters, shoppers, commercial road-users, and emergency services – but also according to different geographical sectors of the city. For example, one of the assessments required might concern the expected effect of each scheme on those commuters who travel daily from the suburban areas on the east side of Adminster to places of employment in the city centre or in the nearby industrial areas; each alternative might therefore have to be assessed on a scale of 'eastern commuter effect units' (which we will abbreviate to eu_{ec}) together with perhaps half a dozen similar effect measures relating to commuters from other sectors of the city.

Even with this level of disaggregation, the estimation of effects can be expected to raise some very difficult problems for the planners. There is the question of developing predictive models which will allow some estimation not only of how existing commuter journeys might be changed, but also of what new commuter journeys might be generated; and there is the question of finding some meaningful way of combining estimates of effects on all journeys, long or short, radial or inter-suburban, by those who fall within the broad category of 'eastern commuters'.

One possible approach is through the development of what is sometimes called a 'bounded interval scale' for the subjective assessment of the effect of each alternative road pattern on the eastern commuters, and on any other category of road-user that may be affected. Assuming that any of the alternative road patterns under consideration will allow at any rate some marginal improvement in traffic flow compared with the option of doing nothing at all, the planners might be able to visualize two extreme situations that could be regarded as defining upper and lower bounds for the required scale of measurement. First, they might postulate an ideal road pattern of such capacity as to give all the residents of Adminster unimpeded access to their places of employment in their own vehicles, with no restrictions other than those imposed by the accepted speed limitations for urban traffic; they might give this hypothetical pattern a rating of zero on their scale of 'eastern commuter effect units' (eu_{ec}). Then, they might postulate at the other extreme a 'do nothing' solution which offered no prospect at all of bringing any relief to the increasing level of congestion at peak hours, and they might decide to give this *laissez-faire* strategy a maximum rating of 100 eu_{ec}. Given any set of alternative road patterns whose effects might be expected to lie somewhere between these two extremes, and given some set of maps, tabulations, or graphs summarizing whatever information is available as to the traffic implications of each alternative, the planners – perhaps in consultation with the policy-makers – might find it possible to apply their expert judgement, together with any special local knowledge, to give an estimate of the rating of each scheme on the scale between 0 and 100 as shown in *Table 34*:

Table 34

Alternative	Estimated effect in 'eastern commuter effect units' (eu_{ec})
Hypothetical solution giving maximum conceivable benefit to eastern commuters:	
'Ideal' road pattern	0
Practical alternatives:	
Proposed road pattern A	between 20 and 45
Proposed road pattern B	between 50 and 80
Proposed road pattern C	between 30 and 65
Hypothetical solution giving minimum conceivable benefit to eastern commuters:	
Existing road pattern preserved indefinitely	100

As in Case Two, the convention is here adopted that the 'best' solution from the point of view of this particular sector of the community is treated as the zero point of the scale, so that the larger the effect measure, the less satisfactory the solution from the eastern commuters' point of view. The conditions assumed for the two extreme cases will require to be defined with some care. For instance, the assessment of the 'do nothing' alternative must be related to a changing environment in which the volume of traffic can be expected to increase and congestion to become steadily worse; while the 'ideal' pattern may have to take into account an assumption that the implementation of such a scheme could not take less than some minimum period of years even if it should be given maximum priority in the development programme. It will be seen that the estimated ratings on this scale for schemes A, B, and C (which we will suppose for the time being represent as full a range of options as the planners believe it is necessary to carry forward into their wider analysis of planning solutions) have all been expressed in terms of ranges, rather than of single estimates. This allows for some expression (albeit at a subjective level) of the degree of uncertainty which the planners believe to attach to each of their assessments in relation to the two end-points of the scale. The particular ranges of figures quoted in *Table 34* indicate, for instance, that the planners believe at this point in time that option A is likely to be the most effective of the three options in improving peak-hour traffic conditions on the east side of Adminster, and option B the least effective on this particular criterion; however, the degree of overlapping between the respective estimates shows that they still feel a certain amount of doubt whether, given further information, option A would turn out to be more favourable than option C from the eastern commuters' point of view.

In exactly the same way, the planners might be able to develop bounded interval scales for estimating the effects of these same alternative road patterns on other sectors of the road-using community. It might also be possible (though much more difficult) to develop crude working measures of this kind for other less tangible types of effect such as the deterioration or improvement in the environments of residents in particular areas, or the degree of disruption to existing social networks. A possible approach to the measurement of this latter type of effect has been discussed elsewhere by Spencer [4].

AN EXPLORATION OF THE CAUSES OF UNCERTAINTY

At this preliminary stage of their exploratory programme, it can be accepted that any assessments by the planners of the effect of alternative road patterns on the commuters living on the east side of Adminster (or any other broadly defined sector of the community) will be open to the criticism that they embody a substantial element of subjective judgement. This does not necessarily mean that their assessments are to be rejected; it does, however, suggest that the planners will be well advised to make at least a rough appraisal of the uncertainties underlying the various different assumptions on which their judgement must depend. Using the device of the structural block diagram which we introduced in Chapter 4, it becomes possible to build up a general picture of the chain of assumptions that are implicit in any assessments by the planners of the effect of alternative road schemes on the commuters of the east side of Adminster. The result might be as shown in *Figure 46*.

No structural block diagram of this kind can ever be regarded as complete, nor

Figure 46

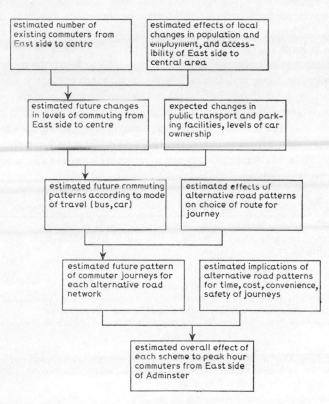

can its structure be regarded as in any way inviolate. In practice, discussion of its implications by officers and elected representatives with different planning perspectives might lead to the identification of further significant areas of doubt, such as, perhaps, the questionable assumption that there will be no appreciable change over time in the degree to which commuter traffic will concentrate itself within the morning and evening peak periods. The value of a diagram of this kind is that, even without the inclusion of any quantitative estimates, it can help the planners to form an overall view of the various underlying types of uncertainty that contribute in some degree to their difficulties in assessing the merits of alternative solutions.

Perhaps the planners might feel sufficiently confident at this stage to attempt to quantify, in terms of upper and lower limits, the relative degrees of uncertainty they believe they should attach to each of the blocks of information in *Figure 46*; if this is so, then they have a basis for the application of techniques such as sensitivity analysis or risk analysis [5] as a means of exploring more fully the causes of their difficulty in making a selection between alternative road patterns. The conduct of this kind of analysis may, however, require a considerable degree of care and expertise, particularly if the various contributory assumptions are not believed to be independent of each other: for instance, if the same economic forces are believed to determine future trends in local employment opportunities, future trends in car-ownership, and future availability of funds for road construction. For reasons of this kind, any formal applications of risk or sensitivity analysis may have to await the development of comprehensive predictive models in which the interactions of transportation, land use, and economic activity are taken explicitly into account; however, before committing themselves to the development of such models, the planners may be well advised to attempt some assessment at a more qualitative level of those stages in the build-up of their structural block diagrams where they expect the points of greatest uncertainty to lie. We will suppose in this case that the planners do in fact decide to carry out a quick assessment of this kind, with the following result:

Table 35

Difficulty in evaluating alternative road patterns in terms of eu_{ec} (i.e. implications for commuters from east side of city) is believed to be particularly attributable to uncertainties in the following types of assumption:

Extremely critical assumptions

(1) Assumptions as to future residential growth on this side of city.
(2) Assumptions as to locations of future industrial development in Adminster.
(3) Assumptions as to future development of public transport facilities.
(4) Assumptions as to factors determining commuters' choice of bus or private car.

Very critical assumptions

(5) Assumptions as to future car-parking facilities in centre of Adminster.
(6) Assumptions as to how time, cost, convenience, and safety factors should be combined in the definition of an effect measure.

Fairly critical assumptions

(7) Assumptions as to the choice of timing for implementation of each alternative.
(8) Assumptions as to what the current levels of commuter traffic are from the eastern sector of the city.
(9) Assumptions as to the relative importance to be attached to shorter-term and longer-term traffic improvements.

Some of these assumptions – in particular those numbered (4) and (8) – concern the structure of the planners' environment (uncertainty category UE), and any attempt to reduce the level of uncertainty in this direction would require activities normally classified under the heading of research and development; in the case of

(4), the requirement would be for development of behavioural models to indicate how the commuters' choice of mode of travel might respond to various forms of intervention or inducement by the planners, while in the case of (8), it would be for the planning and execution of traffic surveys with a view to obtaining fuller information about existing movement patterns.

Other types of assumption – in particular those numbered (6) and (9) – may concern value judgements (uncertainty category UV), and one obvious means of reducing the level of uncertainty in this direction is through an early discussion of preferences between alternative patterns with members of the policy-making group. The remaining types of assumption – those which we numbered (1), (2), (3), (5), and (7) respectively – all concern related areas of choice which come to some extent within the field of discretion of the planners and the policy-making group (uncertainty category UR). In order to reduce the level of uncertainty in this direction, the planners would have to begin making broader evaluations of the effects of alternative road patterns in conjunction with other contingent choices; they would then find themselves inexorably drawn into a wider context of choice, in which they are considering not merely alternative road patterns for Adminster, but alternative land-use and transportation solutions for the city and the whole surrounding area.

THE CHOICE OF ACTIONS TO REDUCE UNCERTAINTY

It does not necessarily follow from *Table 35* that, in their attempts to reduce the total level of uncertainty, the planners should concentrate most of their attention initially on the further exploration of those types of assumption which they have placed in the 'extremely critical' category. Any course of action to reduce uncertainty will inevitably incur its own particular type of cost – whether this is the cost of allocating skilled manpower to research activities, or the cost of time spent in the exploration of preferences and values with the policy-makers, or the cost of time spent in making comparisons between planning solutions embracing large numbers of related variables. Even assuming that these various costs can all be measured on some common scale, a given level of investment in one particular type of exploratory activity will not necessarily produce the same rate of pay-off (in the form of a reduction in the total level of uncertainty) as a similar investment in some other alternative line of exploration. For instance, the planners might judge that an early joint evaluation of alternative road and public transport solutions to the Adminster traffic problem – relying perhaps on very crude estimates of the proportions of commuters choosing to travel by bus and by private car – might be expected to cost less in terms of both time and money than a research programme designed to provide a clearer picture of the factors governing choice of mode of transport. If the planners also judged that the former course of action could be expected to yield at least as high a dividend as the latter in terms of improvement in their ability to choose between alternative planning solutions, then they would clearly be well advised to concentrate their resources initially on a reduction of the uncertainty level for assumption (3) in preference to a reduction in the level for assumption (4). Of course, another group of planners with a different organizational perspective might disagree with this assessment, and a certain amount of discussion between groups might be advisable before the final shape of the planners' exploratory programme was approved.

Through our discussion of the problem of the Adminster road pattern, we have attempted to illustrate the general point that the choice of a programme of exploratory actions requires a balancing between their expected costs and their expected effectiveness as means of improving the basis of strategic choice. Even though these factors may be impossible to quantify in any satisfactory way, much useful clarification may be obtained merely by stating clearly the problem of cost versus effectiveness before any commitments to exploratory action are undertaken.

Although we have been focusing, for illustrative purposes, on one decision area and on one effect measure (the effect on commuters in one sector of Adminster), the selection of a co-ordinated programme of exploratory activities will, of course, in practice have to be considered in the light of many different decision areas and many different effect measures; it is only to be expected that some of the most worth-while areas of exploratory activity will be those which simultaneously reduce the levels of uncertainty in several different effect measures entering into the assessment of different decision areas. Such activities might include, for instance, a survey of the existing family structure of households throughout the sub-region, or a series of exploratory discussions with the policy-makers to determine their preferences between shorter-term and longer-term benefits, or a programme of initial comparisons between alternative planning solutions over some particularly closely connected set of decision areas.

In practice, there may not of course be time for any very extensive analysis to determine the initial working priorities for the planning team, and it is likely that such assessments as are possible will have to be essentially at a qualitative rather than a quantitative level: their later task of measuring the effectiveness of alternative planning solutions for the sub-region is likely to be sufficiently daunting in itself, and it may be quite impracticable for those concerned to spend much time in advance attempting to measure the expected effectiveness of alternative programmes of exploratory activity. Nevertheless, the planners may find that there is a great deal to be gained through a conscious attempt merely to expose the various types of uncertainty that initially cloud their problems of strategic choice, through discussion both among themselves and with representatives of the policy-making group. This kind of discussion – aided where possible by logical aids such as the structural block diagram – may at least help the planners to avoid the kind of situation in which they become committed at an early stage to time-consuming lines of research, whose expected results might on closer inspection be seen to have only a marginal value in improving the ability to decide between alternative courses of action.

A PROGRAMME FOR IMPROVING THE BASIS OF DECISION

We will suppose that, through a series of discussions of this kind, the planners have been able to draw up an initial programme for a set of exploratory activities, one sector of which relates to the planning of the sub-regional transportation system – in other words to those decision areas which fall within the lower central area of *Figure 45*. Within this sector of the programme, the set of activities which are likely to be most rewarding, as contributions to an improvement in the basis for strategic choice, may be seen as follows:

Table 36

Activity 1	Exploration of the feasibility of various novel systems of public transport for the region (i.e. developing a set of feasible options for decision area T3).
Activity 2	Exploration of the feasibility of various possible lines for the Fluxton bypass (i.e. development of a set of feasible options for decision area T1).
Activity 3	Discussions with the representatives of Dockport to explore the strength of their case for linking the Fluxton bypass to the Dockport urban motorway (possibly influencing the range of options brought forward from activity 2, or causing significant modifications to preferences between them).
Activity 4	Discussions with representatives of the regional rail authority to explore different possibilities for developing an integrated road and rail solution to the commuter traffic problem on the Administer-Fluxton axis (directly affecting decision areas T4 and T5; indirectly affecting areas T1, T2, T3, S1, and A6).
Activity 5	Exploration of the pattern of incompatibilities between options in decision areas T1, T3, T4, and T5.
Activity 6	Discussion with policy-makers of the requirements for a set of effect measures which will allow them to exercise a sufficient level of discretion in the choice between alternative transportation systems for the sub-region.
Activity 7	Exploration of patterns of joint effects between options in decision areas T1, T3, T4, and T5.

After some further discussion, it may be agreed that these various activities can best be carried out in the sequence shown in *Figure 47* overleaf:

In this diagram, the convention is used that ovals represent processes of selection between alternatives, while rectangular blocks represent activities designed to improve the basis of selection. Some of these activities may, of course, be particularly demanding in terms of resources, and the allocation of effort between parallel activities may have to take such considerations into account. The processes of choice indicated within the ovals may not of themselves be time-consuming, but they do of course represent an integral part of the total pattern of planning activity. The conventions used in *Figure 47* inevitably involve some degree of over-simplification, in that in reality the activities of choice may not be clearly separated in time from the exploratory activities which link them; nevertheless, the drawing up of a sequential network diagram of this kind may be of considerable value to the

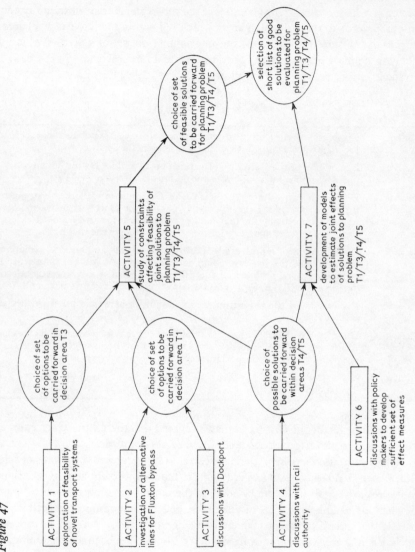

Figure 47

planners in clarifying the directions in which their planning activity should evolve in the more immediate future. The diagram could, of course, be further extended into the more long-term future when it can be expected that the stream of exploratory activities associated with transportation planning will begin to merge with other streams relating to the planning perspectives of housing, industrial, and town centre development. However, the value of extending the diagram in this way at the outset would probably be very marginal; by the time the later stages of the planning activity are reached, the planners might expect to have some very different perceptions of the nature of their problems and it is doubtful how far they would still wish to conform to guidelines which they laid down at a stage when very little relevant information was available.

THE REALIZATION OF THE SUB-REGIONAL STRATEGY

The successive activities of analysis and of choice which are indicated in *Figure 47* may, on closer inspection, turn out to be susceptible to some of the methods which we discussed in some detail in relation to the previous case example: the identification of 'option bars' between particular decision areas, the drawing-up of joint effect tables, the search for leading solutions, and – if there are certain choices of a particularly pressing nature to be made at this stage – the selection of preferred action sets. As in Case Two, the presence of significant uncertainties may mean that the policy-makers will not necessarily be wise simply to select that set of immediate actions which permits the best planning solution according to some agreed set of trade-off rates between the various effect measures chosen; it may first be necessary for the planners to consider whether that action set also has a reasonable degree of 'robustness', in terms of the wider planning of the transportation system and also perhaps in terms of certain other overlapping planning perspectives.

For instance, if the policy-makers are under pressure from the residents of Fluxton to resolve as soon as possible the uncertainty (and the public anxiety) that now surrounds the question of route for the Fluxton bypass, they may decide that they will have to make an early commitment to a particular line for at least the central section of this route, while perhaps leaving the lines of the northern and southern sections open until a later stage of their planning activity. They may find that, by selecting a line for the central section which skirts the south western fringes of Fluxton, they can avoid extensive demolition of property while at the same time leaving several alternatives open for the line of the northern section leading into Adminster (to be decided in relation to the problem of the city's internal road pattern) and also for the line of the southern section (to be decided in relation to the consultations with Dockport, which we suppose to be proceeding unexpectedly slowly). This particular choice of line for the central section may also be found to be a reasonably robust one in relation to the future of Brawley, in that it leaves open an option of taking the northern section of the Adminster-Dockport trunk road within striking distance of the new town; this in turn would open up a number of options for more rapid residential and industrial development either in Brawley itself or along an Adminster/Brawley axis. The policy-makers' emerging preference for the south-western line of the new Fluxton bypass may not, of course, be completely without snags. It may run insufficiently close to the centre of the town to attract any of the commuter traffic which now uses the direct Fluxton-Adminster road (which, it will be remembered from Case Two, passes through a congested shopping centre in area R), and so the planners might have to accept the need for a high level of investment in some form of public transport alternative, based either on the existing road through area R or on the development of commuter services on the branch railway line.

Even the limited and pressing choice of line for the central section of the bypass may therefore carry a wide range of different social implications. The formal publication of a proposal for a south-westerly alignment, even though it may have been preceded by full opportunities for public debate, can still be expected to give rise to some degree of public controversy; it is not necessarily the final stage of commitment to action, in that the proposal may still require central government approval, but so far as the sub-regional planners and policy-makers are concerned, it is a key point of decision in the ongoing planning process.

Decisions of this kind on a sub-regional scale will never be other than difficult because of the range of public interests that can never be completely reconciled and the range of uncertainties that can never be completely resolved. The ultimate test of any analytical aids to the processes of strategic choice will be the extent to which they help the policy-makers to gain confidence that they are discharging their responsibilities for strategic choice with a fuller awareness of their implications for the future welfare (in all its many aspects) of the communities they represent.

The practical results of the ongoing planning activity within the sub-region are more likely to be realized through a series of successive commitments to particular interventions in the evolution of the community at different points in time, than through a single grand decision to implement a carefully balanced master-plan covering the entire future development of the sub-region. For this reason this case study, to an even greater degree than the two more limited case studies that preceded it, must end on an inconclusive note.

12. A general appraisal of the technology

OPERATIONAL REQUIREMENTS FOR A PLANNING PROCESS

The case examples of the last three chapters have all related to governmental planning activities at a local or sub-regional level, in which a spatial element was prominent. However, the methodology which we have introduced has, we believe, a more general relevance to other levels of governmental activity, in so far as these may also involve problems of choosing a series of interventions over time in a complex and continually changing social environment, within which there are many conflicting systems of values to be reconciled.

During our discussion of the case examples, we have drawn on a number of different analytical methods. These vary both in the amount of attention they have so far received from research workers, and in their record of successful application to practical decision situations. Through the case-example approach, we have tried to give emphasis not only to the methods themselves, but also to the political nature of the decision process to which they must adjust if they are to make a significant contribution to the solution of public planning problems.

We have deliberately introduced a certain amount of variation in methodology from one case example to another. It is, of course, difficult to make firm predictions as to which lines of approach have the greatest potential for future development; this will depend on experience of application to a variety of decision situations in different social and political environments. However, it is only appropriate before closing Part III to take stock of the various lines of approach which we have introduced in one or other of the case examples, together with certain alternative approaches which have been adopted by other research workers. This we will do with reference to the brief for a 'technology of strategic choice' which we developed in Chapter 6. This brief took the form of a statement of five main classes of operational (as opposed to organizational) problem which are characteristic of the public planning process. These were defined as follows:

OPERATIONAL PROBLEM I
The problem of finding solutions
in circumstances where the range of possible solutions is not easily enumerated, and where it may be difficult either to discover any feasible solution at all, or to be sure that certain significant alternatives will not remain undiscovered.

OPERATIONAL PROBLEM 2

The problem of expressing preferences

between alternative solutions given only imperfect information as to the range, scale, and value of their anticipated effects.

OPERATIONAL PROBLEM 3

The problem of exposing latent uncertainties

in order to establish the relative dominance of uncertainties in the three classes UE, UR, and UV as inhibiting factors in the clear expression of preferences.

OPERATIONAL PROBLEM 4

The problem of selecting exploratory actions

which can be expected to improve the confidence of choice in as economical a way as possible.

OPERATIONAL PROBLEM 5

The problem of selecting immediate commitments

at any particular point in time, taking into account the balance of advantage between the pressures for commitment, on the one hand, and the retention of future flexibility, on the other.

Each of these problems has been encountered to some degree in each of the case examples we have considered – although the emphasis has varied somewhat from one case to another. The five headings above provide a convenient framework for our more general review of the methodology, so we will now consider each of them in turn.

METHODS OF FINDING SOLUTIONS

The problem of finding feasible solutions only becomes a difficult one in circumstances where the field of decision is so complex in its internal structure of choices and constraints that the opportunities for solution become difficult to visualize clearly except in piecemeal terms. These are circumstances which are often found to apply in public planning, and were reflected in all our three case examples. In our first case example, the identification of feasible solutions was initially quite simple, but became more difficult when we moved to the extended formulation of the land-use problem of area A; in our second case example, there were very many possible solutions, and it proved difficult to keep the whole field in view even when dealing with the restricted problem of priorities within area V. In the third case example, the planners were faced with two levels of difficulty in finding solutions; the difficulty of developing a range of feasible options for certain comparatively well-defined fields of decision (such as those concerned with road network design and with novel transport systems), and the difficulty of finding feasible combinations of options when many fields of decision are considered together.

There is an increasing recognition among planners [6] that the intuitive approach to the finding of solutions to complex planning problems may not always be sufficient in itself, and that much might be gained from an attempt to reduce some of the more hit-and-miss characteristics of the search for satisfactory solutions through the application of systematic design methods.

In our case examples, we have concentrated our attention on the AIDA approach [1], since we believe it offers the dual advantages of clear conceptualization of the problem and flexibility in the arrangement and presentation of solutions. For alternative approaches, reference may be made to the work of Christopher Alexander [7, 8] and to the literature on mathematical programming techniques [9]. The basic characteristic of the mathematical programming approach is that it is concerned not solely with exploration of the range of feasible solutions but with the search for an optimum solution according to some specified criterion of effectiveness; this may be of particular value when the number of feasible solutions is expected to be so large as to make it impracticable to carry out more extensive operations of comparison and rearrangement over the full range of alternatives.

However, the locating of a single 'best' solution may not always be sufficient to satisfy the needs of the planners and policy-makers for a fuller understanding of the opportunities that are available to them, and it is significant that workers in the field of mathematical programming are now giving increasing attention to ways of adapting their techniques to produce information on near-optimum as well as optimum solutions. Perhaps the most potentially useful variant of mathematical programming for local planners is that known as integer programming [10], which concerns itself with discrete choices rather than continuous variables. Any problem that can be expressed in terms of the AIDA formulation can also be expressed in the language of integer programming; the use of an integer programming procedure may in some circumstances bring about a reduction in computational difficulty, but only at the expense of a suppression of potentially valuable information on the pattern of alternative solutions.

METHODS OF EXPRESSING PREFERENCES

The problem of expressing preferences becomes difficult to tackle in circumstances where several alternative solutions are possible, where effects may be difficult to identify or to measure, or where there is no obvious single criterion for measuring their relative value. Such circumstances again arise in each of our three case examples; they are of course typical of problems of strategic choice in the public sector, where many different public services and many different sectors of the community may be involved.

There is a wide range of analytical methods that have relevance to the problem of expressing preferences in public planning. On the one hand, a great deal of effort has been expended on the development of models which simulate the behaviour of complex social and economic systems, to enable the policy makers to visualize more clearly the future effects of alternative strategies. Several such models have been developed at the urban and sub-regional level, particularly in the United States [11]. Although we did not refer to any elaborate predictive models of this kind in either of our first two case examples, we did discuss in the third case example the question of whether or not the planners should invest any resources in the development and application of mathematical models to predict the so-called 'modal split', or the proportion of commuters who would choose different forms of transport for the journey to work.

Although the use of predictive models can make for a better appreciation of the range and scale of the various effects that may result from the actions of the decision-makers, the expression of preferences between alternative solutions must depend also on an appreciation of their relative values. The problem of evaluation of alternatives where there are many different social effects to be considered has led to the development, by economists and others, of various analytical methods which are usually now grouped together under the heading of cost-benefit analysis [12, 13]. Of the applications which have recently been reported, some have concentrated on the attempt to subsume various different kinds of social effect within a single monetary criterion [14], while others have been content to present a 'balance sheet' of costs and benefits which are only partially quantified and leave considerable scope for political judgement [15].

Most of the published applications of cost-benefit analysis involve comparisons of only a limited number of alternative solutions; very often, the problem is regarded as one of choosing between two alternative 'plans', or between acceptance and rejection of a given scheme. In our second case example, however, we attempted to show how the philosophy of cost-benefit analysis can be applied to a more openly defined problem in which many solutions may have to be evaluated according to a set of criteria whose relative importance can only be established through a continuing dialogue between planners and policy-makers. In this and in the third case example, we discussed the problems of developing a set of effect measures which will not be so wide as to confuse the analysis, but will retain a sufficient degree of 'political richness' to satisfy the requirements of the policy-makers who are accountable to the public for the decisions in question.

In the first of the case examples, little attempt was made to measure the costs or benefits of alternative solutions, and the analysis was developed almost entirely from the basis of statements by the various parties concerned – planners, policy-makers, and commercial interests – as to their preference or indifference between particular pairs of solutions: such statements, assumed to be based on an intuitive though well-informed appreciation of the many probable implications of each alternative, may be all that can be hoped for in situations where the necessary time or resources cannot be made available for any more explicit evaluations.

Some of the methods of analysis which can be applied given only a simple ordering of preferences for alternative outcomes are discussed more fully in the treatise on decision and value theory by Fishburn [16]. These methods concern in particular the search for relationships of 'dominance' (or unconditional preference) between particular strategies whose outcomes may not be fully predictable. In our case examples, however, we have had to replace the concept of dominance by the somewhat weaker concept of the 'leading solution', because of the fact that in the planning process it is rarely possible to define hard-and-fast boundaries for the field of choice currently requiring to be considered: it may be dangerous to assume that a solution which is 'dominant' over another solution within some limited formulation of a current problem will still preserve its dominance once the boundaries of the problem have been further extended.

METHODS OF EXPOSING LATENT UNCERTAINTIES

The problem of exploring what kinds of uncertainty are present in cases where difficulty is experienced in choosing between alternative solutions was discussed in all three case examples; however, it was only in Cases Two and Three that we discussed how this process could be assisted by the use of analytical techniques. In Case Two, a number of possible causes of uncertainty were examined one at a time, and we demonstrated how the method of sensitivity analysis could be used to gauge whether any of these were sufficiently critical to cast doubt on the final expression of preference between solutions.

In Case Three, we referred to the more comprehensive approach of risk analysis, and used the device of a structural block diagram to identify all the various types of assumption on which a final statement of preference must depend. Because we could not assume the existence of any formal predictive model at that stage of analysis, the assessments of relative uncertainty had to be fairly rough and ready; for a more quantitative application of the risk analysis method, the reader is referred back to Chapter 4, where we examined the various types of uncertainty inherent in the derivation of certain proposals produced by the Coventry planners in connection with their Development Plan Review.

Much of the literature on risk analysis [5, 17] has been concerned in particular with applications to problems of capital investment in industry: to apply these concepts to the more generalized problem of choice between alternative planning proposals, we have found it necessary to widen the more limited definition of uncertainty (in the sense of lack of knowledge about the present and future environment) to embrace also any underlying uncertainties in value judgement, and any uncertainties as to intentions in related fields of choice that have been excluded from the definition of the problem currently in hand.

This wider definition of uncertainty does, however, create certain difficulties at an analytical level. Many of the contributory assumptions may be subject to uncertainties which cannot be estimated other than in a purely subjective way; and there may be little confidence in the validity of the standard statistical methods for the compounding of uncertainties, if several of the variables are thought to be interdependent. Where such interdependencies have been taken into account in a formal mathematical model, then this last difficulty can in theory be resolved by the use of random sampling procedures; however, this may be time-consuming and not always easy to justify in practice. Perhaps the greatest potential for the use of risk analysis lies in the exploration of uncertainties at a much less formal level, as suggested in Case Three; even if such exercises can only succeed in indicating the relative orders of magnitude of different kinds of obstacle to the clear statement of preferences, the benefit to the decision-makers may still be a substantial one.

METHODS OF SELECTING EXPLORATORY ACTIONS

In Chapter 6, we showed how uncertainties in the three classes UE, UR, and UV could be reduced respectively through the gathering and interpretation of further information about the environment, through the extension of the decision field, and through the seeking of policy guidance; and we argued that each of these three types of exploratory action could be seen as creating a modification of the original context of choice. In practice, as we saw in Part I, the balance that is selected between these three types of action tends to be influenced strongly by the personal and group biases of the decision-makers concerned.

Our third case example demonstrated how, once the pattern of latent uncertainties had been explored, the planners might go on to make a more conscious evaluation of any alternative courses of action designed to reduce these uncertainties. Conceptually, the problem can be seen as one of cost-effectiveness analysis, in that each alternative course of exploratory action will require to be judged both according to its effectiveness in reducing the total level of uncertainty, and also according to its 'cost' to the decision-makers. However, as we argued in the discussion of Case Three, the development of a convincing cost-effectiveness criterion may not be at all easy in practice; quite apart from problems of measuring 'effectiveness' in this context, the 'cost' element may itself have to embrace many different types of resource which are not themselves easily compared (for instance, time of officers may be difficult to balance against time of elected members). Again, the concept may be of value even where the formal technique is difficult to apply; although the derivation of clear-cut cost-effectiveness measures may not be feasible in any particular situation, there may still be substantial benefits to be gained simply by an attempt to pose the problem in cost-effectiveness terms.

This question of 'value for money' in the choice between different kinds of exploratory activity is not often explicitly formulated in practice. However, it is faced implicitly by every group of planners who have to decide whether, presented with some particularly difficult choice between alternatives, they should first devote their energies to further fact-gathering and predictive exercises, or to further analysis of the interactions with other related problems, or to further testing of the attitudes and values of their policy-making group. The planners' problem is, of course, not only a technical one but also an organizational one, particularly if any widening of the problem area involves a crossing of departmental or other boundaries. However, we will defer consideration of these organizational implications until Part IV.

METHODS OF SELECTING IMMEDIATE COMMITMENTS

Although such concepts as the theory of games and the decision tree [16, 18] may be of value in situations where a sequence of choices is to be made in the light of a limited range of alternative contingencies, there is little in the extensive literature of operational research and management science which provides practical guidance in the more loosely structured situation where complex commitments of a strategic nature must be developed continuously over time against a very imperfect appreciation of the possible future states of the environment. Perhaps the most substantial progress has been made in relation to the special case where the options for future decision are essentially similar in nature to the choices to be settled in the more immediate term. The method of dynamic programming [19] provides a useful conceptual approach (and sometimes but not always a satisfactory computational approach) to these multi-stage decision problems of a more repetitive nature, and may have some limited applications in the field of public planning.

However, in each of our three case examples we were concerned with a variety of different types of choice following no particular pattern of repetition over time: our concern was to strike an acceptable balance between the satisfaction of immediate pressures from the community and the retention of sufficient flexibility to adapt to unforeseen circumstances. In Case One, we made use of non-quantitative criteria of response to pressure and of flexibility in order to reduce the number of alternative 'action sets' being considered, but treated the final trade-off between commitment and flexibility as a matter for political judgement. Later in Case One, and again in Case Two, we introduced the possibility that the degree of flexibility of future choice could be quantified, using the concept of 'robustness' which was suggested in a recent paper by Gupta and Rosenhead [20]. In this sense, the robustness of an action set is measured by the number of 'good' full solutions which it leaves open, defining 'goodness' in relation to some agreed cut-off point in the order of preference; the hypothesis being that, although future conditions may bring some variations in the order of preference, the retention of a larger number of solutions which now appear near the top of the list increases the likelihood of being able to select a near-optimum solution at a later stage.

As we saw in Case Two, the definition of a satisfactory criterion of robustness may itself raise difficulties, and in any practical situation a good deal of judgement may be necessary in appraising which type of option it is most important to leave open, and how far it is worth holding out against pressures for early decision in order to preserve a greater degree of flexibility in future choice.

THE STATE OF PROGRESS

In this chapter, we have tried to gather together some threads of a technology of strategic choice, based on a range of analytical techniques some of which are themselves only in an embryonic state of development. The state of progress can be summarized as follows:

Methods of finding solutions
Analysis of Interconnected Decision Areas (AIDA)
Other systematic design methods (e.g. Alexander)
Mathematical Programming

Methods of expressing preferences
Various models for simulation of complex social systems
Cost-benefit analysis
Decision and value theory

Methods of exposing latent uncertainties
Sensitivity analysis
Risk analysis (with exploration of assumptions through structural block diagrams)

Methods of selecting exploratory actions
Cost-effectiveness concepts

Methods of selecting immediate commitments
Analysis of robustness of action sets.

It would be rash for us to attempt to predict too closely in what ways we should expect these and other methods to develop in future, but we believe it is important to emphasize clearly that their function can only be to aid, and not to replace, the exercise of human judgement. To use the language of cybernetics [21], the role of the technology must be that of an 'intelligence amplifier'; defining intelligence as the ability to make appropriate selections between alternatives, then any technology that gives the policy-makers an increased awareness of the implications of their choices in effect creates an amplification of intelligence within the total planning system.

In the long term, the usefulness of the technology must be measured not by any objective yardstick (in a continuous planning process, it is rarely possible to isolate the effects of particular decisions sufficiently clearly to enable 'improvements' to be measured), but by the extent to which it succeeds in winning the acceptance and the confidence of the policy-makers. The immediate need is for experimentation in relation to as wide a variety as possible of ongoing problem situations, recognizing that – as in our three case examples – pressures of time on the policy-makers may be so insistent that it becomes necessary to concentrate the use of analytical aids only at certain key points in the decision process, where the pay-off from a more systematic approach is likely to be particularly high. Experiment of this kind cannot be purely of a technical nature and will inevitably have important implications for planning organization; these implications we will explore more fully in Part IV.

References for Part III

[1] Luckman, J. *et al.*: An Approach to the Management of Design. *Operational Research Quarterly*, December 1967.

[2] Battersby, A.: *Network Analysis for Planning and Scheduling*. London: Macmillan, 1964.

[3] Merrett, A. J. and Sykes, A. M.: *The Finance and Analysis of Capital Projects*. London: Longmans Green, 1963.

[4] Spencer, P.: The Nature of the Planning Process in Coventry. I.O.R. research paper T.930, 1967.

[5] Hertz, D. B.: Risk Analysis in Capital Investment. *Harvard Business Review*, Jan.–Feb. 1964.

[6] Harris, Britton: The City of the Future — The Problem of Optimal Design. Papers of the Regional Science Association, 18, 1967.

[7] Alexander, Christopher: Notes on the Synthesis of Form, Harvard, 1964.

[8] Chermayeff, S. and Alexander, C.: *Community and Privacy*. Harmondsworth: Penguin, 1966; New York: Doubleday, 1963.

[9] Vajda, S.: *Mathematical Programming*. New York: Addison Wesley, 1961.

[10] Beale, E. M. L.: Survey of Integer Programming. *Operational Research Quarterly*, June 1965.

[11] Harris, B. (Ed.): Urban Development Models: New Tools for Planning. *Journal of the American Institute of Planners*, May 1965.

[12] Feldstein, M. S.: Cost-Benefit Analysis and Investment in the Public Sector. *Public Administration*, Vol. 42, Winter 1964.

[13] Prest, A. R. and Turvey, R.: Cost Benefit Analysis: A Survey. *The Economic Journal*, Vol. LXXV, No. 330, 1965.

[14] Foster, C. D. and Beesley, M.: Estimating the Social Benefit of Constructing an Underground Railway in London. *Journal of the Royal Statistical Society* Series A, Vol. 126, Part 1, 1963.

[15] Lichfield, N.: Cost Benefit Analysis in Town Planning – A Case Study. *Urban Studies*, November 1966.

[16] Fishburn, P. C.: *Decision and Value Theory*. New York: Wiley, 1964.

[17] Wagle, B.: A Statistical Analysis of Risk in Capital Investment Projects. *Operational Research Quarterly*, March, 1967.

[18] Luce, R. D. and Raiffa, H.: *Games and Decisions*. New York: Wiley, 1957.

[19] Bellman, R.: *Dynamic Programming*. Princeton University Press, 1957.

[20] Gupta, S. K. and Rosenhead, J.: Robustness in Sequential Decisions. *Management Science*, October 1968.

[21] Ashby, W. Ross: *An Introduction to Cybernetics*. London: Chapman & Hall, 1956.

PART IV

The organizational challenge

13. Organizational choice in local government

By means of the case examples of Part III, we have been able to suggest some ways in which the basic operational problems of the planning process (as we originally stated them in Chapter 6) might be more effectively tackled. Our objective in Part IV will be to offer some similar pointers to ways of dealing with the basic organizational problems that we posed in Chapter 7.

Inevitably, our discussion of ways in which the organizational problems of the planning process might be tackled will take us close to the heart of the current debate on the future of local government itself. Because our experience is intensive rather than broad, we do not regard ourselves as in a position to make any sweeping judgements concerning the future organizational structure of local government as a whole: we will not attempt to present any views as to how particular services should be administered, or what the ideal size of management unit might be, or how local government should be financed, or what particular range of services local authorities should set out to provide.

However, during the course of our research, these questions acquired a special topicality through the appointment of Royal Commissions on Local Government, one for England and one for Scotland, and the evidence subsequently submitted confirmed that there was a wide consensus of opinion that the time had arrived for a radical change in the whole structure of local government in the United Kingdom [1]. Whatever the proposals of the Royal Commissions themselves (and at the time of writing their reports are not yet published), they cannot be other than controversial, and can be expected to give rise to a prolonged period of intense public debate. Even though a reform so sweeping as the complete restructuring of local government may take several years to put into effect, the prospect of change will have been created and the constraints of law, tradition, and vested interest that at present limit the scope for organizational experiment in local government will be seen to have a much diminished significance.

In considering how local authorities can so organize themselves internally as to meet the special challenges of the planning process, we therefore face a choice between addressing ourselves to what might be done now within the present structure of local government, and what might be done in five or ten years' time when we can expect this structure to be in a process of transformation and the options for internal organization to become very much more open. In Chapter 14 we shall

243

adopt this more long-term perspective, and consider a fictitious case example in organizational choice set in this future period of change and opportunity. This case example will be presented as an extension of the series of linked case examples which we developed in Part III; we will assume that, following the report of the Royal Commission, a new local authority has been formed whose boundaries coincide largely with those of the sub-region considered in Chapter 11, and that its leaders face the task of structuring their internal organization in such a way as to make the best of the new opportunities that lie before them.

Our choice of this approach carries with it an element of risk, since we shall have to make a set of basic assumptions, some of which may be proved wrong by subsequent events, as to the general pattern of local government with which the new local authority will be expected to conform. However, we shall try to minimize this risk by making these assumptions as few as possible, and in Chapter 15, when our discussion of the case example is completed, we shall argue that much of what we propose in this fictitious setting can in fact form the basis of experiment in local authorities as at present constituted, so that its value can be put to the test before the period of radical change arrives.

Before embarking on the case example itself, we will, in the remainder of the present chapter, set the scene by reviewing briefly some of the options for change in the internal organization of local authorities that are opened up by some recent innovations in particular towns in the United Kingdom, by the proposals of the Maud Committee on Management in Local Government, and by some wider comparisons with local government overseas and with other fields of public administration.

EXPERIMENTS IN LOCAL GOVERNMENT ORGANIZATION

In Chapter 3, we described the continuing search for new forms of co-ordinating machinery that we saw in Coventry during the period of our research, and we interpreted these as responses to the inherent problems of strategic choice in local government. Coventry is, however, only one of a number of local authorities that has recently been attempting to find ways of adapting the traditional structure of British local government so as to produce more co-ordinated control over its various activities. Two other examples which it is particularly relevant for us to consider briefly at this stage are Newcastle upon Tyne – a city of comparable population to Coventry – and Basildon, one of the largest of the new towns which have been developed in order to absorb the post-war growth of population in the London area.

The recent innovations in both these places involved deliberate moves in the direction of centralized management, whereby fuller authority for co-ordination between the various parts of the local authority's organization would be vested in the hands of some form of City or Town Manager, who would not necessarily have the traditional legal qualifications of the Town Clerk in English local government.

Although precedents for the appointment of City Managers existed in other countries, notably in the United States and in Ireland, it was recognized that the City Manager system in its fullest sense was not compatible with the existing constitution of local government in Great Britain, under which all chief officers are primarily accountable to their various separate committees. For this reason, both the Newcastle and the Basildon experiments involved a good deal of compromise with more traditional forms.

Although, in Basildon, the Clerk of the Council was officially promoted to the position of Town Manager, he also retained his statutory title of Clerk and it was conceded that there was no possibility of giving him any executive powers over other chief officers which might have contravened existing statutes. The proposals submitted to Basildon Urban District Council in 1965 [2] did, however, include a number of other organizational changes of a more revolutionary nature, including the reconstitution of committees as much smaller three-member working groups meeting on an *ad hoc* basis, with members of the opposition party attending in a non-voting capacity. These working groups were to be accountable to the Council only through a nine-member 'executive committee' served by the Clerk; to compensate for the reduced involvement of rank-and-file Council members in committee work, it was suggested that a 'question time' procedure should be introduced in the monthly Council meeting.

In implementation, these proposals underwent a number of significant modifications [3], including the enlargement of the working groups, the restoration within them of voting rights for the opposition party, and the restoration to the Town Manager of direct responsibility for the administrative work of the Clerk's department. These measures all served to some extent to re-establish aspects of the former system, and to underline the practical difficulties of drawing a dividing line between matters of policy and matters of day-to-day administration.

In Basildon, the promotion of the Clerk to 'manager' was an integral part of the proposals for a new form of organization. In Newcastle, on the other hand, the proposal in 1964 to appoint a Principal City Officer to the vacant position of Town Clerk was taken prior to any other decisions concerning reorganization; Newcastle's principal aim was to attract a man of high calibre who could effectively co-ordinate the various activities involved in implementing the Council's ambitious development programme [4].

The candidate who was duly appointed as 'Principal City Officer with Town Clerk' came from a managerial post in industry. In February 1966, he presented to the Council his own proposals for reorganization, which included a substantial reduction in the number of committees, an increased emphasis on working through more specialized working groups, and the appointment of certain chief officers to more specialized co-ordinating roles for particular groups of services. As in Basildon and again in Coventry, the early reactions to these proposals for innovation suggested the existence of strong pressures for the preservation of certain aspects of the existing system. At the time of writing, it is still too early to judge the extent to which either Newcastle or Basildon will ultimately succeed in reconciling the principles of democratic control with the requirements of more effective co-ordination of departmental activities.

THE PROPOSALS OF THE MAUD COMMITTEE

In 1967, the committee on the Management of Local Government, which had been appointed some three years earlier by the Minister of Housing and Local Government under the chairmanship of Sir John Maud (now Lord Redcliffe-Maud), issued its final report [5]. This committee made a number of suggestions, some of them radical, as to how the internal organization of local authorities might be modified.

Some of the more significant proposals of the Maud Committee followed similar lines to the experiments in organization that had by that time already been initiated in Newcastle, Basildon, Coventry, and elsewhere. It was proposed that committees should be reduced in number and regarded as primarily 'deliberative and representative' in character rather than as directing or controlling bodies; that responsibility for co-ordination and control on behalf of the Council be concentrated in the hands of a 'Management Board' consisting of between five and nine elected members (which, it was argued, would preferably include some representation of the minority party); and that the Clerk should be recognized as head of the authority's paid service, reporting to the Management Board and having 'authority over the other principal officers so far as this is necessary for the efficient management and execution of the authority's functions'. It was recommended that the duties of Clerk should include, as well as general responsibilities for leadership and co-ordination in respect of all the Council's services, the more specific duties of providing secretarial services for committees and setting up an effective establishment organization to secure economy in the use of manpower. The Committee endorsed the view of the Mallaby Committee on Local Government Staffing [6] that Clerkships should be open to people of all professions and occupations. Emphasis was placed on the need to reduce the number of departments and to develop the use of management services, including in particular 'the rapidly developing tools of measurement and control including the use of computers'.

Initial reactions to the Maud Committee's report were on the whole favourable, although some concern was expressed over the invidious distinction between first-class and second-class councillors which the creation of a management board appeared to imply. Gradually, support began to build up for the note of dissent which Sir Andrew Wheatley appended to the report of the Maud Committee, in which he argued that unless committees were given some more direct say in the formulation of policy it would be difficult to attract people of the necessary calibre to serve as councillors. Sir Andrew therefore proposed that committees should retain the right to report directly to the Council on the discharge of their functions, although submitting any 'major issue of policy or new scheme involving capital expenditure' through the management board; in the event of disagreement, the committee and the management board would both have the right to submit their cases independently to the full Council.

SOME WIDER COMPARISONS

The report of the Maud Committee made a number of broad comparisons between patterns of local government organization in the United Kingdom and in other countries, following the studies carried out for the committee by Dr A. H. Marshall. These comparisons revealed that, although there were wide variations between the patterns of accountability that had developed in different countries, a number of sharp distinctions could be drawn between the United Kingdom, on the one hand, and the countries visited by Dr Marshall, on the other. In none of the countries studied (Canada, the Irish Republic, West Germany, the Netherlands, Sweden, and the United States) was the committee so prominent a feature of local government as in the United Kingdom, and where it existed its powers tended to be more advisory than administrative; in each case a considerable degree of authority tended to be concentrated in a small executive (sometimes a single individual) reporting to the full Council; delegation to officials tended to be more extensive than in the United Kingdom; and there was a less rigid departmental structure because of the virtual absence of any equivalent of the professional associations which had helped to mould and preserve departmental traditions in the United Kingdom.

Within the United Kingdom itself, the most direct comparisons that can be made are with the organization of those other public services which have become detached from the local government system during the course of the present century, notably gas, electricity, and hospitals. In each case, a pattern of regional organization has been introduced, providing greater scope for co-ordinated planning and operational control in meeting local demands, but only at the expense of a less direct representation of local interests. It is significant that similar moves towards the creation of special-purpose regional authorities are now taking place in other fields; for instance in the organization of the police and in the formation of Passenger Transport Authorities.

In the case of the hospital service, an organizational structure was chosen which attempted to combine the benefits of regional organization and of local control, by a division of responsibility between regional boards and local hospital management committees, both with a nominated rather than an elected membership. As in the case of local government, the internal processes of hospital management tend to be diffuse, in that there are many different decision-makers with few clear lines of authority; inevitably, the case for creating some kind of 'hospital general manager' tends to be quoted whenever the prospect of change is discussed. However, this is not necessarily the only option for organizational change; in a research project recently completed for the Ministry of Health, the Institute for Operational

18

Research carried out a study of the conditions for effective decision-making and adaptation to change by hospital management, and put forward in its final report the argument that the essential problem was to find ways of adjusting the existing set of pressures on a diffuse management system [7]. A high degree of diffusion of authority may indeed be seen as especially appropriate to a system that must respond rapidly to a variety of situations concerned with the immediacies of medical care.

Recent years have also seen an increased interest in the exploration of new forms of management structure in industrial organizations, particularly those where the emphasis must be on the capacity to adapt and to innovate rather than the capacity to operate efficiently under stable conditions [8, 9]. These approaches suggest an organic rather than a mechanistic view of the system of operations in an organization, in relation to the system of interpersonal relations with which it is invariably enmeshed.

EVOLUTION AND REVOLUTION IN ORGANIZATIONAL FORM

Having now considered some of the available options for organizational change in local government, we can now proceed to make some broad comparisons in the light of our analysis of the challenges presented by the public planning process – and to introduce certain further options that are suggested by our own experience. As already mentioned, we will approach this task through the medium of a fictitious case example, set in the period of fundamental restructuring of local government that can be expected to arise some time during the nineteen-seventies.

We thus now address ourself to a situation that is ostensibly one of revolutionary rather than evolutionary change. However, we believe it is important to avoid the pitfall of regarding the task as one of 'designing' a complete new organizational structure from scratch, and assuming it can be imposed willy-nilly on those who will have the responsibility of making it work. Inevitably, whatever formal system of decision-making and control is 'designed' for a particular local authority will in practice have to accommodate to political and personal relationships as well as administrative needs; furthermore it is only to be expected that any procedures initially laid down will be extended and adapted over time through the growth of new conventions, as those concerned learn how it can be made to respond more sensitively to the problems that arise in practice. This is not to dismiss as irrelevant the problem of designing an initial organizational 'skeleton'; the working system of communication and control that results from the growth of conventions around one formal structure may be very different in its characteristics and its effectiveness from the system that results from the growth of conventions around some alternative configuration.

In the following chapter, we will keep in mind the point that our apparently revolutionary situation, where an entirely new local authority is being created within an entirely new system of local government, will also have aspects of a more evolutionary nature. Many of the members and officers who are involved in the new challenge will themselves have been prominent in the various established authorities from which the new unit has been fashioned; they will bring with them certain views and predispositions based on their past experience, as well as certain deeply rooted professional and political loyalties; and the influence of these factors on the new situation will have to be taken into account.

Because of their anxiety that the new authority should get off to a smooth start, we can expect that the local leaders will initially be particularly preoccupied with the development of clear procedures of operational control over the running of the various services for which they are responsible; however much importance they themselves may attach to more strategic problems, their first concern must be to establish an adequate level of control over the taking of decisions and deployment of resources in the 'here-and-now' situations that will present themselves as soon as the new Council begins to operate. We will therefore not immediately approach our case example from our own particular perspective of the planning process; rather, we will work up gradually from the problem of building a basic management structure to the much more challenging task of developing the more exploratory and adaptive mechanisms that are required to tackle the challenges of strategic choice and strategic control. It is only at the end of Chapter 14 that we will pause to review how far the specific suggestions introduced through the medium of our case example can be seen as meeting the six basic organizational problems of the planning process that we originally formulated in Chapter 7.

14. A case example in organizational choice

At this stage, we will return to the setting of the fictitious region that provided the context for the three case examples of Part III. We will first make what we consider to be some essentially unrestrictive assumptions about the form of local government to which such a region might be expected to conform as a result of the fundamental changes that should ultimately follow the reports of the two Royal Commissions; and we will then consider how the skeleton of an appropriate control system might be fashioned within the region itself.

An initial assumption, which is in keeping with almost all the evidence submitted to the English Royal Commission [1], is that the basic units for the administration of most local services will tend to be larger than at present, and that to this end the traditional administrative separation of urban and rural areas, made more rigid with the formation of County Boroughs in the late nineteenth century, will tend to disappear. One might therefore expect that the sphere of influence of the city of Adminster, as indicated in *Map 14*, would coincide roughly with the boundary of a 'most-purpose' local authority, which we will refer to as Newbound. The administrative map of Newbound might appear as in *Map 15*.

In this map we have shown, in addition to those centres of population and lines of communication which were judged most important from the point of view of the planning problem considered in Chapter 11, a typical small market town (Market Sheeping), and a typical rural village (Smockley Parva) whose interests in rural conservation will require to be adequately represented in whatever control system is designed for the new local authority. There will, of course, be many such settlements in the area as a whole.

So far as electoral accountability is concerned, we will assume merely that Newbound is served by some form of directly elected Council, the members of which (all of whom we will call councillors) serve as representatives of the local interests of Adminster, of the surrounding towns, and of the rural areas. This elected Council will bear the primary responsibility for some range of public services which might well include most of the present services of local government. However, we will not exclude the possibility that, following the recommendations of the Royal Commission, certain new services will be added to the list, while certain of the existing services might no longer appear – accountability for them having been transferred either to other public authorities operating at a less localized level

250

of the total government system, or perhaps to District Councils operating at a more localized level. At the level of Newbound itself, although not necessarily at the level of any District Councils within its boundaries, we will assume that party

Map 15. Administrative map of Newbound

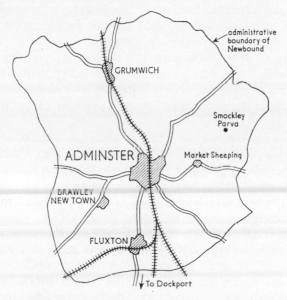

political organization will inevitably come to form an integral part of the overall system of democratic control. To quote the words of the Maud Committee (paragraph 389), 'Party politics are an inescapable part of public life and their influence is likely to grow in local government if reorganisation results in fewer and generally larger authorities'.

THE SCOPE FOR CHOICE IN INTERNAL ORGANIZATION

The first elections for Newbound's Council have, we will suppose, resulted in a clear but not overwhelming majority for one of the two or more political parties which fielded candidates. The group of councillors belonging to this party are therefore in a position to elect from within their number a leader and deputy leader of the new Council, and to fill any other key positions in whatever control structure they may decide to adopt.

For the purposes of this case example, we will assume that there are few external restrictions which limit the members' freedom to choose their own preferred pattern of internal organization for the new local authority. However, there are certain other factors which may have an important influence on the decisions which are eventually reached. First, there will be certain precedents which they might wish to take into account, including the example of the Maud Committee's proposals and the various local experiments such as those in Newcastle and Basildon referred to in the last chapter. Second, there is the likelihood that many of the leading members of the majority party group in Newbound will have had considerable experience of local government already, through past membership of one or other of the component authorities from which Newbound was fashioned. This background will, as we have already suggested, probably have given them certain predispositions towards the preservation of some features of the traditional system and towards the abandonment of others; for instance, it is probable that they will share a certain impatience with traditional procedures of decision by committee, balanced to some extent by a sensitivity to the political consequences of delegating too much power to the professional officers, or even to a select inner group of members.

Despite any misgivings they may have as to the concentration of power in the hands of a privileged few, the case for forming some kind of central group of members of the majority party is, we will suppose, agreed in Newbound to be unanswerable. Where scope for choice does exist is in deciding what role this central group is to play within the total machinery of decision: whether to work, for instance, on Coventry's original model of the 'Policy Advisory Committee' whose powers are non-executive and closely circumscribed by the majority party group, or the Maud Committee's model of the 'Management Board' exercising full control over all matters requiring the ultimate endorsement of the Council, or perhaps some intermediate pattern along the lines of those which have, at the time of writing, been introduced by a number of authorities including Coventry itself. Choice of title for the group is itself important, since the words 'management' and 'policy' are themselves suggestive of very different perspectives of the decision-making process.

Further options to be considered concern how many members the central group should have, how clearly individual roles should be identified within the group, and whether representatives of minority parties should be admitted; despite the Maud Committee's advocacy of opposition representation on the management board, it seems probable that the political experience of the controlling group will suggest to them that such a step should be rejected, since it would impose serious limitations on the central group's freedom of discussion and so on its practical effectiveness.

In choosing a pattern of internal organization for the Council as a whole, the one indisputable starting-point is that there will have to be some form of departmental structure related to the distinctive characteristics of the various services operated by the local authority, even though there will be scope for choice as to the size and number of departments and the extent of departmental autonomy. There will, of course, be a need for the setting-up of certain internal services that concern all departments and serve to provide a degree of internal co-ordination, although probably at the cost of some reduction in autonomy of operating departments; also, it will be difficult to dispute the case for appointing one senior officer to act as overall co-ordinator reporting to the central group of members. As in the case of the central group itself, however, there will be scope for choice as to what the precise role and status of this senior officer will be, and again the choice of title will itself be of some significance: the titles of 'manager', 'chief executive', 'chief administrative officer' and 'clerk' are by no means synonymous, and we will therefore here refer to the post concerned simply by the more neutral title of 'first officer of the Council'.

The bare skeleton of the internal organization of Newbound's local authority therefore consists so far of a central group or board of members, a set of departments controlling different public and internal services, and a 'first officer of the Council', all with powers which to some extent still remain to be defined. No assumptions have yet been made about the existence of committees, other than the central board itself. It is against this background that, in the remainder of this chapter, we will consider how Newbound might approach the challenge of developing an initial framework for the co-ordination of departmental activities, and for the evolution of effective processes of strategic choice.

THE ORGANIZATION OF INTERNAL SERVICES

Among the first priorities of the new Council we might expect to find the organization of a set of internal service functions to serve all operating departments. The members' previous experience in local government might be expected to suggest to them that their internal service organization would have to include at least the following main groupings:

Financial services

or services which relate to the activities of all departments as *spenders of money*. This grouping might cover management of funds and of payments; provision of accountancy and cost-control services; development of common financial procedures; scrutiny of departmental expenditures and estimates; and certain related aids to the more effective use of financial resources.

Manpower services

or services which relate to the activities of all departments as *employers of people*. This grouping might cover establishment and personnel work; negotiations concerning pay and conditions of service; co-ordination of recruitment and training procedures; provision of certain common administrative and secretarial services; and development of aids to better deployment of manpower such as work study and organization and methods.

Developmental services

or services which relate to the activities of all departments as *sponsors of physical development*. This grouping might cover design of all schemes involving change in the built environment, including both architectural and civil-engineering projects; the supervision of construction work; and the progressing of preliminary work concerned with securing the availability of sites.

Legal services

or services which relate to the activities of all departments as *agencies which must meet certain statutory obligations, and act generally within the framework of the law*. This grouping might cover advice on the legal aspects of contemplated action; ensuring the correct exercise of statutory powers; and representation of the Council in matters of dispute with other parties.

Although the above grouping of functions follows reasonably logical lines, and accords quite closely with most contemporary practice, the various groups of internal services are of course themselves interrelated in a number of ways, and there may therefore be some difficulties in drawing sharp distinctions between them; for instance, there may be areas of potential overlap between the financial and manpower services, or between the financial and developmental services, and it may not be easy to draw clear organizational boundaries between them.

Special difficulties are likely to arise in the internal organization of the developmental services, partly because of the professional demarcations between architects, engineers, town planners, and others, and partly because the inward-looking function of providing developmental services to departments of the local authority tends to become closely associated with other functions of a more outward-looking nature; in particular, an authority of the size of Newbound will almost certainly possess powers relating to the formulation and scrutiny of proposals for changes in land use within its administrative area, including not only those which may originate from the operations of local authority departments, but also those arising from the activities of private developers.

The interaction of the internal and the wider aspects of the Council's developmental responsibilities may be particularly marked in relation to comprehensive schemes of urban renewal and 'three-dimensional' civic design, which may embrace the provision of several local authority services as well as the participation of private developers.

Among the possible models which Newbound might consider for the internal organization of its developmental services are the established precedents of the architecture/planning department, the engineer/planning department, and the option of separating the town-planning function from both architectural and engineering services; a further solution is the integration of all these functions within a single departmental unit. Our own perspective of the planning process suggests that, if there is to be any functional grouping within the wider field of activity concerned with the built environment, it should involve (a) a close integration between the architectural and engineering design services, with their parallel concern in effective uses of particular spaces and of materials within the priorities allocated by the Council's development programme, and (b) a separate focus related to the wider town and country planning responsibilities of the Council. There would of course have to be especially close liaison between these two aspects in the Council's developmental services where matters of urban renewal and civic design were involved.

A grouping along these lines would in effect mean that the Council's common service organization would include a separate focus related to each of the four types of resource-based planning activity we identified in Part I – these concerned the forward control of manpower, finance, developmental priorities, and land use, respectively. Of the types of internal service function we have so far considered there is in fact only one – the legal function – which does not have a direct association with the management of resources: in this case, the concern is not so much with the need to make effective use of limited resources as with the need to work within certain constraints of a more absolute nature.

Although the kinds of grouping we have suggested within the Council's internal service organization may be logical from the point of view of the planning process, they may not of course be equally rational from more technical or professional viewpoints. Newbound may therefore have to examine the case for various alternative groupings, perhaps involving direct linkages between particular internal service functions and other activities of a more operational nature.

The Council might also wish to consider whether certain other types of common service function – perhaps of a comparatively novel nature – might not be included as components of its internal service organization. For instance, the case is sometimes made for a service concerned with integration of a local authority's activities from a point of view which is community-centred and family-centred, rather than service-centred or resource-centred. This concept has been applied notably in the organization of New Town Development Corporations, where the wishes of the prospective population cannot be directly represented as in an established community; however, its application in an area where community pressures already make themselves felt through electoral and political channels may raise questions of a rather more controversial nature.

Perhaps the new local government structure within which Newbound is operating will limit the range of solutions which the Council is free to consider for the organization of its common service functions. Perhaps this structure will tend to encourage a grouping of some or all of these internal services within a unified 'administration'; or perhaps on the other hand it will lean towards the preservation of separate departments organized on functional or professional lines. It is nevertheless likely that there will be some scope for local choice, and that this choice will have to be made against a background of strong pressures from the various professional interests concerned. In such a situation we would not consider that our research experience gave us any special authority to advance firm opinions relating to matters of formal departmental structure. Our particular interest is in the relationship of the various common service functions to the processes of strategic choice and, provided these functions can be fulfilled in a way which can allow the necessary linkages to develop with other parts of the decision making system, the problems of incorporating them in a formal departmental structure need not concern us. However, for the purposes of this case example, we can postulate the existence of a small central nucleus of senior officers, almost certainly between three and six in number, each of whom will bear special responsibility for some particular group of common service functions. Whether these officers all head separate departments or whether some of them are grouped within a unified administrative structure, their relationship to the first officer of the Council will clearly be important and we will have more to say about this later in the chapter. For the time being, it is important to stress that the centrality of this particular set of officers within the Council's organization does not of itself imply that they should be accorded a higher status than other departmental heads, some of whom may be responsible for particularly far-reaching and important sectors of public service, and may have commensurate contributions to make to the formulation of the new Council's policies.

THE MECHANISMS FOR RESOURCE CONTROL

One of the first concerns of the new Council will almost certainly be to set up effective procedures for the allocation and forward planning of resources at an interdepartmental level. Experience will suggest that this requires the setting-up of certain common budgetary procedures associated with the various different categories of resource; in particular the drawing-up of a financial budget – equivalent to the traditional annual rate estimates but perhaps re-cast in a somewhat different form to take account of any new sources of local government finance – and a manpower budget to assist in the regulation of departmental establishments. Assuming that Newbound has been assigned certain land-use planning powers within its geographical area, it will also require some form of land-use budget, though probably this will take a more flexible form than the traditional Town or County Maps with their comparatively rigid zoning restrictions. Finally, we suggest Newbound will require a further type of budget in the shape of a capital works programme, as a basis for allocation of the associated 'scarce resource' of developmental priorities. These various budgetary instruments may during the course of time be expected to evolve in new and more flexible directions; but Newbound cannot expect to get off to a good start unless the Council is in a position to institute quickly a set of workable procedures which give at least some measure of budgetary control over the activities of all its departments.

The responsibility for developing each of these budgetary procedures will tend to devolve upon the appropriate specialist officer within the central nucleus which provides common services to all departments. Once set up, this group of four inter-related 'resource budgets' will serve initially as a framework for the scrutiny of claims submitted by particular operating departments, and subsequently also as a foundation for the development of the associated aspects of the interdepartmental planning process.

However, the question now arises as to how far, and through what channels, the elected members of Newbound should also be involved in these internal procedures of resource planning and control, and in particular whether the proposed 'central board' of members should concern itself directly with any of these activities. One extreme possibility is that the central board itself could assume full responsibility for the setting of resource budgets and the adjudication of all departmental claims against these budgets – although experience would suggest that such a solution might impose unrealistically heavy demands on the time of one limited group of members. Other possibilities include the delegation of responsibilities for adjudicating claims to specialist committees or sub-committees, to individual members of the central board, or to professional officers. Perhaps some combination of all these different options might be brought into play, based on some system of discrimination between claims of a more 'routine' nature and those

Figure 48

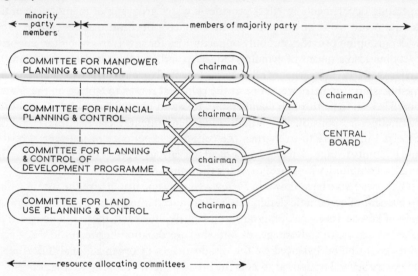

thought to raise questions of 'policy'; but this raises questions of definition which may not easy to resolve.

One further possibility that we would be prepared to suggest to Newbound is that they consider a solution based on a set of interlocking groups of members along the lines shown in *Figure 48*.

In this diagram, we have included a specific committee of members to look after the allocation and forward budgeting of each of the four basic types of resource. The chairman of each is shown also as serving on the central board itself, and as having *ex officio* membership of those other resource-allocating committees whose tasks are most closely related to his own; the pattern of cross-connection has been derived from the set of relationships between planning activities which we first identified in our analysis of the planning process in Coventry, and set out in *Table 5* (p. 62).

We would suggest that the minority party (assuming there to be one clearly identifiable group in Newbound which carries the status of 'the opposition') might be represented on each of the resource committees but not on the central board itself, on the argument that this would give the minority party the opportunity to keep abreast of Council affairs at an interdepartmental level, while preserving the central board as a forum where leading members of the majority party can meet to discuss major issues of policy in the presence of their advisers, but without the inhibiting presence of their political opponents.

THE DESIGN OF A CENTRAL CONTROL STRUCTURE

The formation of a set of linked committees to govern the allocation of resources to operating departments in effect provides a wider grouping of members than the central board alone at the 'core' of the Council's decision-making system. This wider grouping provides not only opportunities for involvement by the minority party but also a means of avoiding too sharp and invidious a cleavage within the majority party between an all-powerful central group and the rank-and-file membership; furthermore, if one of the principal routes to a place on the central board is seen to lie through membership, followed by chairmanship, of one of the committees responsible for adjudicating departmental claims, this might be expected ultimately to strengthen the collective experience of the central board, and its ability to take a balanced view of all the various services of the local authority and the community pressures to which they must respond.

The pattern we have shown in *Figure 48* is only one instance of the way in which an element of systematic design can be introduced into the interlocking membership of key decision-making groups. Obviously, however, there is a danger that, taken to excess, the advantages of built-in co-ordination between these key activities could be outbalanced by the disadvantages of organizational inflexibility. There are several options as to how the broad pattern of *Figure 48* might be interpreted in any local setting, depending on the members' judgements on such factors as the ideal size of committees, the extent to which tenure of chairmanships should be restricted, and the value of duplicating *ex officio* linkages by extension to include vice-chairmen in addition to the chairmen themselves.

For instance, the leading members of the new Council might consider that any committee should be restricted to not more than twelve members, that any chairmanship other than that of the central group should be restricted to some given number of years, and that any *ex officio* link involving the chairman should also involve the vice-chairman, from the point of view of cover against absence and also of continuity of succession. Given this information, the pattern of *Figure 48* could be interpreted more specifically as shown in *Table 37*.

This arrangement leaves a reasonable number of 'free' places to be allocated on each of the resource committees, but only two to be allocated on the central board itself; in practice, this could be expected to result in membership of the resource committees becoming regarded as a first objective for members with ambitions to fight their way upwards towards the key positions of power. Given a limited term for each chairmanship and vice-chairmanship of a resource committee, and therefore for each *ex officio* place on the central board, there is less risk of the board's membership becoming static – although, if the controlling party so desire, continuity can be maintained by a switching of roles between members, particularly if the cycles of appointment of new chairmen to the resource committees can be synchronized.

Table 37

Primary role of member		Status on central board	Status on resource committees			
			manpower	finance	programme	land use
Leader	) of majority	C				
Deputy	) group	V				
Chairman	) of manpower	E	C	E		
Vice-Chairman	) committee	E	V	E		
Chairman	) of finance	E	E	C	E	
Vice-Chairman	) committee	E	E	V	E	
Chairman	) of programme	E		E	C	E
Vice-Chairman	) committee	E		E	V	E
Chairman	) of planning	E			E	C
Vice-Chairman	) (land-use) committee	E			E	V
Total places on each committee reserved for chairman, vice-chairman, and *ex officio* members as specified above		10	4	6	6	4
Remaining places to be allocated assuming a total of twelve places for each committee		2	8*	6*	6*	8*
		12	12	12	12	12

Key: C = chairman
V = vice-chairman
E = *ex officio* member
* = including some representation of minority party.

It may be noted that the scheme shown in *Table 37* implies a somewhat larger board than the maximum of nine commended by the Maud Committee, unless some members are to be allocated dual roles. However, the question of whether a board of ten or twelve is 'too large' will depend on a definition of what its particular role should be, and we shall not be able to examine this question until later in this chapter when we have considered other possible components of the decision-making system.

Alternative arrangements of course become possible given different rules as to committee size and the degree of cross-connection, and the final choice must depend on local wishes. However, it is this general type of structure that we would commend to Newbound as the 'core' of its formal decision-making system; what further committees or other groupings of members the Council may require (if any) is a question we shall return to later. The basic pattern we put forward in *Figure 48* does, we suggest, have several important advantages: it ensures that there are several members of the central board who, through involvement in resource-allocation procedures, have a chance to keep their fingers on the pulse of each local authority service and to appreciate the social pressures underlying each department's claims for expansion or change; it provides, through the pattern of interlocking between the resource committees, for a measure of internal consistency in the way these claims are adjudicated; and furthermore, it relieves the central board of direct responsibility for the more routine mechanisms of control, so that it can concentrate on dealing with matters of a more strategic nature, in a way which we will come to consider later in the present chapter.

ELECTED MEMBERS AND THE MANAGEMENT OF DEPARTMENTS

Another question which requires early resolution in Newbound is that of the form of accountability for management of specific public services. Is the head of each operating department to be directly accountable to a controlling committee of elected members, or is he to be primarily responsible to the central board, either directly or through the medium of the co-ordinating first officer? It is only to be expected that the elected leaders of the Council will wish to give their departmental heads as wide a range of discretion as possible in the running of their own departments, so as to free both officers and members from the frustrations of 'committee-itis', which many of them will remember as one of the most inhibiting characteristics of the traditional system of local government.

Our analysis in Part I, however, suggests that even if the idea of the controlling committee is to be firmly rejected (possibly but not necessarily to be replaced by the 'deliberative and representative' committee of the Maud Committee's report) there is still an independent case to be made for the appointment of a particular member of the majority party to accept some degree of political responsibility for the work of each department, in that – like the traditional committee chairman – he is expected to develop a broad interest in the running of the service (or group of services) concerned, and thereby to provide the crucial link between the departmental chief officer, the majority party group, and the public at large. Such a member is always on tap to the departmental head when he requires advice as to whether or not a particular solution is likely to be politically acceptable to the majority party; he is also able to develop a whole range of informal contacts with other elected members who may have their own interests in particular issues that arise within the department concerned.

Conceivably, the member concerned can fulfil this kind of role at a purely un-official level, with each departmental chief officer having formal accountability only to the central board or to the Council itself; this would mean that any formal sanctions could be applied only at this level, and the responsible member could do no more than act as a channel for advance guidance as to the likely reactions of the management board or of the majority party group. An alternative is that the appointed member could carry some formal responsibility for the department (or departments) concerned, and perhaps be required, among other things, to defend the actions of his departmental manager in the Council Chamber; this is a role which he might fulfil either as an individual 'ministerial' spokesman or – as in the existing system in the United Kingdom – as the chairman of a committee carrying some degree of direct responsibility for this particular sector of public service.

We believe that a case can be made for retaining the idea of the responsible com-mittee carrying formal accountability for the work of one or more departments, but allowing a substantially increased degree of autonomy to the departmental manager or managers. However, this case will not emerge until later in this chapter, and for the time being we are solely concerned with the role of the appointed member of the majority party who, whether or not he fulfils the formal function of committee chairman, in practice assumes political responsibility for the work of a particular department or group of departments. For convenience, we will refer to this member as the 'chairman' without at this stage necessarily implying the existence of an associated committee.

THE MECHANISMS OF STRATEGIC CHOICE

If the number of departments in Newbound is kept small, following the recom-mendations of the Maud Committee's report, then the number of chairmen ap-pointed to take an interest in particular sectors of public service can also be kept restricted, and there is a possibility that they might then all be admitted to member-ship of the central board, in order to include a direct representation of each departmental interest – although it would be difficult to reconcile this requirement with the kind of structure proposed in *Table 37* without requiring at least some members of the central board to perform dual roles of a fairly demanding nature.

However, it is by no means inevitable that all problems of decision which cut across departmental boundaries and which require the involvement of elected members should be regarded as matters for resolution by the central board itself; the picture of many overlapping planning activities which we built up throughout Parts I, II, and III suggests a much more flexible approach, in which *ad hoc* groups of members are formed (and disbanded) as necessary to deal with particular stra-tegic problems which may arise, their membership being selected in each case to reflect the various different perspectives involved. For example, in the instance of our first case example in Part III, the combination of planning perspectives shown in *Figure 36* would suggest the need for the policy issues arising in relation to area A to be discussed by a group including the chairman of the 'resource' committee concerned with land-use planning, together possibly with other specialist 'chairmen' concerned with the management of the school service and with town centre development problems. Possibly, they would be accompanied by 'vice-chairmen' as well; certainly, they would expect to be attended by relevant departmental officers. In the second case example, policy discussions on the problem of priorities within area V might require the coming together of members and officers representing the operational perspectives of the drainage, housing, and school services, together with the resource-based perspectives of financial and developmental planning. Perhaps the perspective of manpower planning might also be represented as well – although this might be seen as of more marginal significance in relation to this particular problem area. At a later stage of the planning process, other groupings might of course become more appropriate, as the area of concern moved to other parts of the wider problem field shown in *Figure 44*. Because Fluxton is itself only one of several urban communities within the boundaries of Newbound, it might also be advisable for a policy group of this kind to include one or more representatives of the special local interests of the town. These might either be members of Newbound council itself, or perhaps representatives of a 'lower-tier' district council, depending on the general structure of local government within the area.

In the instance of the wider programme of sub-regional study and policy formation discussed in Case Three, a variety of different policy groups might be involved, meeting at key decision points throughout the co-ordinated programme of activities which we illustrated in part in *Figure 47*.

Certain policy groups of this kind might, over time, acquire a degree of permanence because of the continuing nature of the problems which they were set up to consider; for instance, the problem of traffic in and between towns might become the concern of a standing traffic policy group – on similar lines to the Traffic Policy Committee in Coventry – which might concern itself with the overall guidance of a continuing programme of research and consultation in the transportation planning field.

If it is accepted that the need for mechanisms for dealing with such problems of strategic choice is likely to be met more effectively through the medium of a series of interconnected policy groups than through referring all strategic issues to the central board itself, then the need for a grouping of all services within a strictly limited number of departments, watched over by a correspondingly limited number of specialist chairmen, becomes a much more debatable one: indeed, it is arguable that there may be positive advantages in separate departments of modest size for the operation of certain specialized services which are managerially self-contained, provided adequate mechanisms exist for co-ordinating their activities at a more strategic level. The chairman and chief officer responsible for direction of a specialized department of this kind might together expect to participate actively in the work of two or three different policy groups at any one time; and if these working groups provided adequate channels for the resolution of all problems of strategic choice which directly affected their departmental interests, the case for each specialist chairman to be a member of the central board itself would lose much of its force. An adequate level of communication between the specialist chairmen and the central board might then be achieved by stipulating that each policy group should be so constituted as to include at least one member of the central board. This member might then be regarded as the leader or chairman of the group concerned (in so far as such a leader may be necessary for an informal grouping which should require no formal rules of procedure); more significantly, he might also serve as the group's spokesman in the formal meetings of the central board itself.

THE ROLE OF THE CENTRAL BOARD

By this stage, we suppose that Newbound has agreed to set up, as components of its decision-making system grouped closely around a central board, first a limited set of resource controlling committees and then a flexible system of policy groups – some permanent, some ephemeral – designed to deal with particular areas of strategic choice. This means that the members of the Council are now in a position to review more clearly what might be the distinctive role of the central board itself in relation to these other decision-making groups.

There are a number of possible roles they may be able to envisage: the resolution of particular problems where two or more specialist policy groups or resource committees disagree; the consideration of any formal changes in the procedures of the council, as expressed in standing orders; and perhaps the periodic scrutiny of reports from departmental officers on the activities of their departments. However, our analysis in Part II also points to the need, at this central 'core' of the Council's organization, for a more forward-looking and exploratory function which we then called 'strategic control', concerned with the mobilization and scheduling of inter-group planning activities and depending for its effectiveness on a capacity to 'scan' all the current operations of the local authority and to learn about the needs for connection between them.

This mobilizing function is, we suggest, one to which both members and officers of the new Council should be prepared to give a good deal of attention. The need for mobilization of new groupings of officers and members can be seen to arise at many points in the case examples of Part III, and the need for co-ordinated scheduling of their activities appears particularly in the third case example; reference to *Figure 47* in particular will illustrate the kind of interlocking which may be necessary between several parallel activities at this strategic level of the decision process.

Closely linked with the problems of mobilization and scheduling is the problem of formal authorization of specific courses of departmental action based on the recommendations of the various policy groups. One would expect of course that, given a deliberate representation of all relevant interests on each of the policy groups concerned, there would be few instances in which the recommendations made would not be acceptable to the political leadership of the Council; however, some form of provision would have to be made for this contingency.

We will suggest to Newbound that the mobilization and scheduling of inter-group planning activities should become a direct responsibility of the central board itself, and that the board should be prepared to devote a high proportion of its time to this particular task. We will also suggest that the board should be re-quired to give its formal approval to any proposals for action emanating from these interdepartmental planning activities, as a prerequisite perhaps to their endorse-ment by the full Council.

So far as the procedures for strategic control are concerned, we suggest that the central board might meet regularly – perhaps a few days before each formal meet-ing of the Council, or perhaps at rather more frequent intervals – in order princip-ally to receive progress reports from specialist policy groups, to authorize any actions they may have proposed, and to decide what further mobilization or dis-bandment of policy groups might be necessary. So far as possible, the board should, we suggest, resist the temptation to become itself closely involved in the processes of strategic choice within fields already covered by the more specialized policy groups it had appointed, although it would expect sometimes to have to hear reasons why particular groups had failed to agree on particular issues within a pre-arranged period of time. The central board itself would then have the responsibility of deciding whether or not an extension of time was justifiable in order to permit further action to be taken to reduce the level of uncertainty and so improve the basis of choice; if so, a choice might then arise between the courses of initiating further departmental investigations, of enlarging the planning perspective of the group through introduction of new members, and of creating special opportunities for debate at party-political level.

The role we envisage for the central group in Newbound is therefore one of regulating all the more exploratory aspects of the Council's decision-making pro-cess – with particular reference to those aspects where more than one type of public service is involved – while allowing responsibility for regulating the continuing consumption of resources to devolve upon the specialist resource committees. We will consider later what aids might be made available to the central board to allow it to fulfil this, the most purposive and demanding aspect of its responsibilities, in an effective and discriminating way.

THE REPRESENTATIVE AND HIS INVOLVEMENT

Having now considered a number of groupings through which the councillors of Newbound might become involved in the decision-making process, we are in a position to consider whether these groupings are together likely to provide a suffi-cient framework within which every elected representative can hope to develop a meaningful sense of involvement in Council affairs.

Without the existence of further opportunities for participation than those we have so far allowed, it seems unlikely that this will turn out to be so. Unless the number of electoral districts within Newbound is so small as to restrict the total number of representatives on the Council to (say) two or three dozen, then not every councillor can expect to participate as a member of the central board, or as a member of a resource committee, or as a 'chairman' with interests in a particular operating department, even assuming him or her to be a member of the majority party; neither can every member of the minority party expect to have an opportunity to keep abreast of Council affairs through allocation of a seat on one of the four resource committees.

Newbound is therefore likely to be faced with the problem of how provision can be made for every member of Council to gain the experience which will allow him to carry out effectively his many responsibilities as representative of his own local electorate. This problem may create pressures which force the leading members of the majority group to overcome any personal antipathy they may have to the establishment of specialist committees for particular public services; and they may therefore wish to examine the possibility of establishing a sufficient number of committees of this kind to give every member the opportunity of identifying himself with the running of one or more of the Council's services.

Once this possibility is considered, a choice arises as to how far each specialist committee should act as a controlling body and how far it should be confined to acting in a 'deliberative and representative' capacity. Even if there is a firm intention in the first instance that the role of the committee should be no more than an advisory one, there are likely to be pressures from members for some degree of formal authority, and even the report of the Maud Committee itself (let alone the note of dissent by Sir Andrew Wheatley) envisaged that the specialist committee might be given some limited powers of decision taking in the formal sense (see paragraph 167). The problem therefore can be seen as one of selecting some point in the spectrum between the extreme solutions of the purely executive and the purely advisory roles, which will give the departmental manager an adequate level of responsibility yet satisfy the desire of elected members for some measure of direct involvement in the provision of public services.

A satisfactory point of compromise is only likely to be discovered through experience over time, but there will nevertheless be an initial choice to be made as to whether the primary emphasis is to be placed on the managerial independence of the chief officer or on the principle of committee control. To give the opportunity for a clear break with traditional attitudes in British local government, where by general agreement the principle of committee control had been taken to excessive lengths, we suggest that the initial emphasis in Newbound should be on the independence of the manager.

Initially, each specialist committee might meet – perhaps only three or four times a year – for the main purpose of receiving, and perhaps recommending for the approval of the central board or the full Council, a report by the departmental manager on the principal actions taken since the previous meeting; they would also be able to advise him on any of his current problems which he or the chairman judged to be of particular significance for the local electorate. Over the course of time, the committee might come to ask for certain particular classes of decision to be referred in advance for the approval of the members or – in order to avoid delay – for the approval of the chairman acting on their behalf; but it would always be up to the members themselves to make a case for encroaching further on the chief officer's discretion in matters affecting the management of his department. In this way, one would expect that an acceptable division of roles between the committee, the chairman, and the manager himself might ultimately be determined.

Even if, as one might expect, the formal role of the committee itself in the decision-taking process is to remain a very restricted one, this need not of course prevent its members from exerting a significant influence on the processes of decision-making at a less formal level. The manager of each operating department will be wise to be responsive to the views expressed in committee, as well as to the private advice of the chairman; and any committee member who has particularly strong views on matters which arise can always press them further through private discussions with his chairman – who has a much closer involvement in the continuing decision process – or as a last resort through submitting his views to the majority vote of his political party group.

It is only at this stage in our argument, therefore, that we find ourselves conceding the case in Newbound for the formal establishment of committees with direct interests in the running of particular public services – perhaps playing only a limited part in the council's formal machinery of decision-taking, but at the same time providing a channel for representation of community viewpoints, and allowing the rank-and-file councillors – of any political party – to acquire an understanding of what is involved in the management of particular services and in the competition for resources between services.

However, membership of committees concerned with the running of particular public services is by no means the only way in which the less senior councillors can develop an appreciation of the operations and problems of the local authority on which they serve. In particular, there is the possibility that councillors might also meet from time to time in consultative groups or committees convened not according to functional divisions but according to geographical ones, in order to learn about and give their views on the changing problems of the particular districts or towns they represent. Perhaps a set of separate consultative groups might be set up for Adminster, Fluxton, Brawley, Grumwich, and the rural areas; or perhaps it might be possible to develop a less rigidly defined system of interlocking groups whereby – for instance – those representing rural areas within the overlapping spheres of influence of Adminster and Fluxton would have an opportunity to give their views on new developments in either town.

It is difficult to put forward specific ideas as to how the Council might set about the formation of local consultative groups, without making assumptions as to the existence or otherwise of a second tier of district authorities within Newbound's geographical area, perhaps carrying special responsibility for some of the more personal services of local government. For the purposes of this case example, we will make no such assumptions either way, but simply suppose that Newbound Council agrees that each of its members should serve on one or more 'district consultative committees', which might or might not also have linkages with independently constituted district councils at another level of the local government system.

The task of each district consultative committee might be to meet, perhaps two or three times a year, in order to review actions taken by any of the departments of the Newbound local authority within its own district, and to express its opinions on any current problems of change or development. At times when particularly significant changes are afoot – for instance, when planning proposals are being formulated for a local 'action area' – the committee might of course be consulted more frequently, although in such a case the requirements for policy guidance to the planners might be met more fully by the mobilization of a special policy group on which local leaders were represented together with relevant chairmen of specialist committees.

PATTERNS OF PARTICIPATION BY COUNCILLORS

We are now in a position to review the overall pattern of participation in Newbound's affairs by the elected members of Council. We summarize this pattern in *Figure 49*.

The various types of grouping in which members may participate are here given

Figure 49

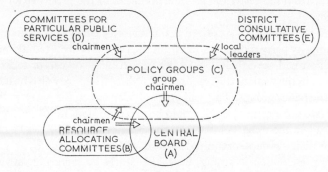

code letters from (A) to (E) according to the sequence in which we have introduced them. The policy groups are distinguished by a broken outline to stress that these will tend to meet irregularly as circumstances demand, and may sometimes be of an ephemeral nature, whereas the other groups are all more permanent and will expect to meet with some degree of regularity. In the diagram, we have indicated the pattern of interlocking which could be expected to arise from the participation in other related groups of chairmen of committees and perhaps also of 'local leaders' appointed to represent the interests of district consultative committees. Of course, some further interlocking between the memberships of different groups can be expected to arise by accident rather than design; but our aim in *Figure 49* is to bring out the existence of *planned* rather than unplanned overlapping between parts of the decision making system.

Our diagram is consistent with the recommendations of the Maud Committee, in so far as it incorporates the basic features of a 'management board' (A) and a set of specialist committees for different sectors of public service (D). However, the most crucial inference we draw from our research is that the requirements of an effective control system must extend beyond the specification of a hierarchical arrangement of management board and specialist committees, to the type of balanced, non-hierarchical structure of interlocking groups we show in *Figure 49*, in which the requirements for a continuing responsiveness of management to community pressures are met through different types of standing committee as at (B), (D), and (E), while the requirements for planned adaptation to change are met through a more flexible system of policy groups (C) as regulated through the control mechanisms of the central board (A).

Such a pattern allows all councillors to participate in settings (D) and (E) at least, and gives any new member of the majority party the opportunity ultimately to work his or her way up to membership of the central board, either through serving on a resource-allocating committee or perhaps through experience of contributing to policy groups either as spokesman for a particular public service or as leader of a district committee. In this way, we suggest it will be possible for Newbound to soften the sharp division between 'first-class' and 'second-class' councillors which might result from too restricted an interpretation of the proposals of the Maud Committee.

Although we will not be surprised if the majority party in Newbound wish to exclude minority party representation from the central board, leading members of the opposition will nevertheless have the opportunity to keep in touch through participation in the work of the resource committees, and may also be admitted to certain of the policy groups. This will probably depend on the party-political content of the issues concerned, and it would be presumptuous for us to suggest to the majority leaders the exact point where the balance should be drawn. However, wherever a policy group is required to deal with a local issue in an area where minority representation is strong, it would clearly be tactically unwise for the majority group to exclude any opposition members from its composition.

The test of success for this total pattern of involvement by councillors will be the extent to which it is accepted by the majority group as a framework for the exercise of strategic choice. If it is not so accepted, then decisions on matters of strategic importance to the community will tend to be resolved, as they often are in local authorities today, in the unofficial setting of the party political group, where access to technical advice is at best severely limited. There will always be a role for the party political group in resolving questions of broad objectives, of party discipline and of political tactics, but if the party group also becomes a recognized forum for the resolution of complex problems of strategic choice affecting the long-term development of the community, then the official organizational structure will have failed in one of its most important functions. This will provide a long-term challenge to the elected members of Newbound, but it will also provide a challenge to their official advisers, whose responsibilities we will now consider in relation to the basic control structure which we set out in *Figure 49*.

PATTERNS OF PARTICIPATION BY OFFICERS

Each group of members shown in *Figure 49* will, of course, require to be served by one or more professional officers, whose task will be to provide a sufficient level of information and advice to allow the group to carry out its allotted task. It is therefore appropriate for us at this stage to turn from the total pattern of participation by councillors to the equivalent pattern of participation by officers, and examine the ways in which the various categories of senior officer we have so far mentioned might expect to be involved.

So far, the officers we have introduced to the service of Newbound include an unspecified number of departmental managers concerned with the provision of particular public services, together with a 'first officer of the Council' whose responsibilities we have not yet fully defined, supported by a small central nucleus of senior officers responsible for certain broadly defined groups of internal service function.

Particular officers within this central nucleus will, as we suggested earlier, be particularly associated with the management of different types of resource, and will therefore be expected to play prominent roles in the provision of information to the corresponding committees within the resource-allocating group of *Figure 49* (group B). In *Figure 48*, we suggested that the four committees concerned might be linked to each other through cross-membership of chairmen; there is, of course, a similar case to be made out for cross-linkage at officer level so that – for instance – while the officer in charge of financial services would bear the primary responsibility of supplying information to the committee for financial planning and control, he would also play an active part in the parallel committee for manpower planning and control, and in the committee for planning and control of the development programme.

The officers within this central nucleus (or their more senior assistants) would also expect to participate actively in other types of interdepartmental planning activity, in association with specialist officers drawn from the various operating departments. In effect, each *policy group* of members, formed to deal with a particular issue which is seen to cut across departmental boundaries, will require to be served by a parallel *planning team* of officers, drawn from all relevant departments and perhaps meeting a good deal more frequently than the policy group itself, in order to carry out the groundwork required to prepare an adequate basis for strategic choice. Our distinction between 'planning teams' and 'policy groups' follows broadly the distinction between 'the planners' and 'the policy-makers' in Part III; most of the more analytical and time-consuming operations in the tackling of the three case examples of Part III would, we suggest, in practice be carried out by 'planning teams' of officers – whose composition might change over time as the area of choice was seen to expand or contract – while the 'policy groups' would be concerned only when some particularly significant point of choice was seen to have arisen. For instance, referring to the particular example given in *Figure 47*, the various activities indicated by rectangular blocks would probably involve the participation of officers only, perhaps working in small groups associated with the main sub-regional planning team, while the choices indicated by oval shapes might involve the participation of both officers and members in corresponding policy groups. Of course, occasions might arise when it would be advisable to draw elected members as well as officers into the day-to-day work of the planning teams, but this might be difficult because of the strictly limited amount of time that the members concerned would probably be able to afford for active participation in council affairs.

Both the managers of operating departments and the senior officers responsible for internal services would of course expect also to be represented in other kinds of meeting involving the elected representatives, including the periodic meetings of the specialist public service committees and the district consultative committees (as represented in blocks (D) and (E) of *Figure 49*). Inevitably, the volume of work involved would make necessary a degree of delegation by chief officers to their senior assistants or, where appropriate, to divisional managers responsible for work in particular towns or rural areas.

One important question to be resolved concerns the attendance of officers at the meetings of the central board itself. If the role of the central board is not to engage directly in the formulation of policy, but rather to mobilize and regulate the activities of a number of specialist policy groups, then there is no obvious case for regular attendance by the managers of particular public services. However, those officers who provide common services to the various departments of the Council, and particularly those concerned in the management of resources such as finance, manpower, and land, should be in a particularly good position to develop a broad understanding of the competing pressures for change in different public services, and therefore on occasion to provide advice of special relevance to the mobilization and regulation of the interdepartmental decision process.

This leads to the suggestion that they might be regarded as forming a team of advisers to the central board, under the general leadership of the first officer of the Council. Before examining this suggestion further, however, it will be advisable for us to pause to consider what the role of the first officer himself should be in relation to all the various aspects of the decision-making process.

THE ROLE OF THE FIRST OFFICER OF COUNCIL

If the role of the central board is to include the mobilization and regulation of interdepartmental planning activity, then we would suggest that a primary responsibility of the first officer of the Council should be to provide the machinery which will allow the board to fulfil this task to maximum effect.

In Chapter 7 we argued that this kind of task – which we called the function of strategic control – required above all a capacity to scan the operations of all specialist agencies and to learn about the needs for connection between them. We put forward the proposition that the effectiveness of any strategic control machinery was likely to depend not only on the flow of 'hard' information as to specific actions and commitments to future action in different sectors of the total organization, but also on the flow of 'soft' information as to currently perceived problems where the range of possible solutions might still be only in an early stage of formulation. Connection (or co-ordination) between departments at this stage may often, we suggested, be more effective and less frustrating to those concerned than connection at a stage where personal and group commitments have become more clear cut.

Those officers who are specially concerned with the management of resources, and with the initial scrutiny of departmental claims to be submitted to the four resource-controlling committees, are particularly well placed to scan the comparatively 'hard' information on specific departmental proposals and actions, and to bring to the attention of members any matters which appear to involve mobilization of joint planning activity. This means that the routine submission of such information to the central board itself should be unnecessary; this would tend merely to duplicate the work of the resource-controlling committees, and the strong representation of central board members on each of the four committees concerned – which is implicit in the pattern of cross-membership shown in *Figure 48* – should of itself be sufficient to allow the exploiting of any opportunities for connection arising from the flow of 'hard' information on departmental claims for resources.

It is when the need for 'soft' information is acknowledged that the resource committees become inadequate as channels through which needs for connection can be brought to the attention of the central board. It is here, we suggest, that the first officer of the Council will have a particularly demanding role to play, which is not related in any special way to any one of the internal service functions for which the other officers in the central team are responsible. The implications of this role will become clearer shortly when we examine the way in which systems for the flow of 'soft' information might be developed. Meanwhile, we can expect Newbound will be concerned more immediately with the need to clarify so far as possible the relationship of the first officer of their Council to the other members of the team of senior officers that advises their central board.

Our advice to the Council will be that it is inappropriate for the first officer himself to become identified in any special sense with any one of the internal service functions for which other members of the central team of officers have a direct responsibility, unless of course the form of local government constitution within which Newbound is required to operate makes this unavoidable. His role is not definable primarily in terms of financial co-ordination, of efficiency in administration and the use of manpower, of management of the development programme, of the land-use planning function, or of advice on legal powers and constraints. Rather, it is concerned with provision of the machinery through which the policy-makers can be enabled to deal more effectively with the challenges of strategic choice at an interdepartmental and inter-committee level.

This emphasis on strategic choice does not imply that the concern of the first officer should be exclusively with long-term problems, at the expense of decisions of a more immediate nature. As we stressed in Chapter 5, the value of any planning process must depend on the influence which it exerts on the actions taken to deal with current situations as they arise. It is therefore desirable that the first officer should maintain an interest in all the Council's processes of decision, both at the more formal and at the more informal level. At the more formal level, a case can be argued for a particularly close linkage between the first officer and the committee secretariat, which bears the responsibility for maintaining the machinery through which most of the more formal decisions of the Council must be taken; although it is of course debatable whether the relationship of the committee secretariat to the first officer need necessarily be one of direct departmental accountability.

It is likely to be crucial to the development of the role of first officer of Council that the individual appointed should be seen to stand apart from specific departmental or sectional interests. In particular, it will be important that each of the other senior officers should be able to feel that his prospect of ultimate succession to this position depends not on his particular departmental or professional background, but rather on his capacity to take a broad and discerning view of the Council's affairs. It is of course the members of the central team of advisers who are likely to have the fullest opportunities to develop and demonstrate such a capacity, although there might be particular circumstances where the board would prefer to fill the post of first officer from outside the existing team.

A FRAMEWORK FOR THE DEVELOPMENT OF LANGUAGE

At this point, we must turn from the problems of organizational form to the problems of communication and information flow which they imply, making particular reference to the flow of 'soft' information for which the central group and the associated team of senior officers must bear a special responsibility.

Examples of possible ways of communicating 'soft' information were in fact presented at several points in the discussion of case examples in Part III. For instance, in Case One we made use of outline maps of area A and its environs (*Maps 8* and *10*, pp. 143 and 153)in order to throw light on the scope for choice between alternative uses of land, while in Case Two we introduced, in *Table 13* (p. 166) and *Map 13* (p. 168) respectively, two different devices through which information on a set of development projects might be presented, with emphasis on opportunities for choice rather than specific proposals for timing or design. Some other examples of techniques for presenting information on fields of discretion were presented in Part I; for instance, we would suggest that the logarithmic chart of *Figure 3* (p. 13) can, once its meaning is understood, give a clearer view of the options for forward control of departmental expenditure than would be possible through the use of columns of figures alone; similarly, the use of structural block diagrams such as those presented in *Figures 14, 15,* and *16* (pp. 71, 72, 73) offers a means of exposing assumptions which is capable of revealing a good deal more than can a statement in conventional narrative form. The English language on its own, although a supremely adaptable instrument for most everyday purposes of expression, is at a disadvantage when it comes to the expression and exploration of problems of strategic choice, and it is for this reason that the need to develop new forms of language becomes a vital one so far as Newbound is concerned.

To the extent that some of these forms of language will involve symbolism and abstraction, they will lend themselves more immediately to communication between professionals than between professionals and lay representatives. For instance the option graph of *Figure 34* (p. 154), or the coded tabulation of costs and benefits in *Table 26* (p. 191) might not be immediately intelligible to the layman, and might have to be interpreted into some alternative form which brought out more dramatically its social and political implications. This might require some ingenuity on the part of the officers concerned; for instance, in the comparison of different solutions to the problem of area V, the information given in *Table 26* might possibly be transferred to a series of large display cards, one for each solution; each card would be so designed as to present the essential information on that particular solution in such a way that its significance for ratepayers, schoolchildren, tenants, and others could be more readily grasped. If a group of members (for instance, a policy group specially mobilized to consider the problem of area V) then wished to make comparisons between certain selected solutions, it could ask for particular 'solution display cards' to be drawn and compared, two at a time, gradually discarding those solutions they considered to be less desirable than others until they were finally left with a short-list of 'good' solutions from which they could proceed to agree on choice of a preferred action set.

These examples illustrate that the need is not so much for a new kind of jargon which would become the special province of a new kind of professional, but for ways of breaking down barriers of communication between existing professions and of promoting more meaningful dialogues with lay representatives. If, as in Case Two of Part III, a computer is used in order to assist the processes of strategic choice, then problems of communication between man and machine are involved as well. The problem is not simply to interpret the computer's output in such a way that the layman will understand it, but also to develop ways of ensuring that the layman has some means of influencing the information that is fed into the machine; unless the lay member has some opportunity to contribute to the choice of predictive assumptions, of assumptions of relative values, and of instructions as to 'what the computer should do next', then he is all too likely to feel that his prerogative of choice is becoming dangerously eroded by the computer and those who have the power to understand it. The need to find ways of bringing the councillor as well as the professional officer close to the input console of the computer is one of the many challenges of intercommunication within the decision-making system.

Although any developments in the system of internal communication must concern many different people in Newbound, they are not likely to come about spontaneously, and so we would suggest to the Council the formation of a small central task force which can devote all its energies to the practical development of new aids to decision and new channels of communication between the different sectors of the total decision-making system.

The qualifications required for membership of such a task force are unlikely to be found exclusively in any one professional discipline – the most important attributes are, we suggest, a degree of numeracy and capacity for logical thought, an ability to view complex systems as a whole rather than from any one limited specialist angle, and of course an ability to communicate effectively with the lay representative. If this task force is to be given any specific location in the organizational structure, then we would suggest it should report directly to the first officer of the Council, so as to detach it from any restricted departmental view. If it is to be given any formal title, we would suggest the *Communications Development Unit*, a phrase which comes as close as possible to describing the kind of role we have in mind. It might perhaps consist initially of only one individual, although we would suggest that, in an authority the size of Newbound, it would pay to have a small team, perhaps including members drawn from different sections of the organization and preserving explicit links with them. For instance, the need to develop methods for expressing problems involving multiple costs and benefits would suggest a special link with the officer responsible for financial services, while the need to develop ways of looking at many interrelated choices within a locality would suggest a special link with the officer responsible for the land-use planning function.

Members of the communications development unit, as we have now called it, would be expected to give active support to the various planning teams and to the central team of chief officers, by suggesting new forms of aid to decision, by assisting in their application, and by evaluating their degree of success or failure as practical means of improving communications between decision-makers, so that further modifications could be made as necessary. The ability to move freely within the organization would be essential to members of the new unit: much would be lost if the unit came to be regarded as part of a specially privileged department accountable only to the first officer of Council, rather than as a loose grouping of advisers who, like the first officer himself, deliberately cultivate an extra-departmental status and maintain a range of different linkages with officers and councillors throughout the total organization.

THE DEVELOPMENT OF AN EARLY WARNING SYSTEM

In Part III, we explored a number of ways in which information might be presented to planners and policy-makers to allow them to deal more effectively with particular problems of strategic choice once these had been identified. A related task for the communications development unit, however, must be to develop an 'early warning system' which will enhance the opportunities for any member of the central board – or for that matter, any other member of Council or any departmental officer – to scan the current activities of the council and spot any new needs for connection between different areas of choice at a formative stage in the decision-making process. Such a system will of course have to depend predominantly on 'soft' rather than 'hard' information; it will have to extend to any currently perceived areas of doubt or discretion where commitments have not yet begun to harden, and even perhaps to certain areas where no clear consideration of alternative lines of solution

Figure 50

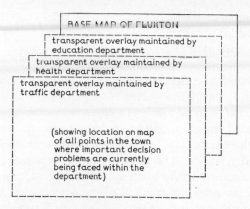

BASE MAP OF FLUXTON

transparent overlay maintained by education department

transparent overlay maintained by health department

transparent overlay maintained by traffic department

(showing location on map of all points in the town where important decision problems are currently being faced within the department)

has yet taken place. As we demonstrated in Part III, one of the ways of exposing relationships between different areas of doubt and discretion is by use of a geographical map, as for instance in *Maps 8, 10*, and *13*. In *Figure 50* we show how this principle might be extended to provide a constantly changing picture of all the more significant decision problems of a localized nature currently being faced by different departments in any particular zone of Newbound.

The system suggested in *Figure 50* involves a wall map displaying the main geographical features of a particular area (in this case Fluxton) which is designed to be used as a base for the superimposition – in any desired combination – of various transparent overlays, each of which picks out the existence of the more outstanding problems of a localized nature which are currently being faced by a particular operating department. In *Figure 50* we have included, for purposes of illustration, the overlays for only three of the many different departments which might exist within the local authority; these we suppose to be concerned with education, health, and traffic respectively. We suggest that each such overlay, while conforming to certain common conventions, can be regarded as the property of the department concerned and can be kept up to date as a by-product of its normal working. The overlay contributed by the education department might pick out not only the locations of all existing and proposed schools, but also – by the use of distinguishing symbols or colour codes – the locations of any existing schools where an element of discretion was currently seen to exist as to whether or not to carry out extensions to site or buildings, or as to the year in which a planned closure or alteration of age intake might take place. Other types of symbol might pick out the approximate locations of proposed new schools where problems of site selection, or of layout, or of programming were currently being faced. The overlay provided by the health department might use different but related sets of symbols to show locations where similar types of choice were seen to arise in relation to local clinics, health centres, and other facilities; while the overlay provided by the traffic department might show streets or junctions where choices were currently under consideration as to whether or not to limit parking, or to provide improved facilities for pedestrian crossings, or to install new traffic-control equipment.

The superimposition of any two or more such overlays, in any required combination, might be expected to help in illuminating, to lay representatives and perhaps even to the departmental specialists themselves, any points of possible interaction between problems currently facing different departments in the same or adjacent localities. In effect, the system of maps and overlays would provide a physical expression of the need to bring together many different planning perspectives in any one local setting; it could thereby assist the members of the central board – and all other councillors – in their task of scanning the ongoing activities of the local authority, and could result in the formation of new planning teams or policy groups in instances where needs for co-ordination might otherwise have passed unrecognized. After the required planning teams had been formed, the maps could then form a basis from which more specific option graphs could be derived (as in the derivation of *Figure 34* from *Map 10*, or the derivation of *Figure 37* from *Map 13*).

Not all departmental problems, of course, are of the type which can be pinpointed geographically, and the communications development unit might also be able to explore with relevant specialists the possibilities of similar 'mappings' of current problems using not a geographical base but perhaps a base of the Council's organizational structure, or its structure of cost code headings. For instance, overlays superimposed on a 'base map' of the Council's organization tree might draw councillors' attention to any departments or sections which currently faced severe problems of staff shortage, or situations of dispute over pay or conditions of service, or doubts as to possible changes in the definition of roles.

The set of all such maps and overlays using different types of base would then be seen as presenting a general picture of 'what is going on' at any given time, and what further problems are currently seen as likely to arise in future. While the overall co-ordination of an early warning system of this kind might be the special province of the communications development unit, reporting to the first officer of Council, we suggest it would be appropriate for the other officers in the team advising the central board to assume special responsibilities in relation to the up-keep of particular parts of the system, especially in so far as they relate to differing organizational perspectives such as those associated with the resources of land, manpower, and finance.

A PREDICTIVE REPORTING SYSTEM

There is one aspect of an early warning system which is of particular relevance to the task of the central board, and also to that of the 'resource' committee respon-sible for allocation of priorities on the development programme. This concerns the provision of early warning of difficulties that may be expected to arise in the execution of any programme of linked activities involving co-ordination between different parts of the overall organization.

A system for the flow of 'soft' information to provide early warning of difficulties of this kind has already been put into practical effect on a regional scale by a major public undertaking [10]. The principle which has been adopted is that, where a continuous process of management is characterized by the criticality of the time dimension and the need for co-ordination of many related tasks, it may be possible to enhance the level of control by requiring the various participants to feed in regularly, to a central information point, subjective estimates of the likelihood of meeting certain previously agreed target dates, and perhaps also of the likelihood that certain particular contingencies will arise.

Figure 51 shows how this principle might be used to help Newbound in control-ling the implementation of its development programme. This example relates to the development programme for area V, whose priorities we discussed in Chapter 10, and whose sequential relationships we indicated in network form in *Figure 38*.

Figure 51 shows the state of progress on the programme for area V as it might stand a year or two after completion of the exercise in reviewing priorities dis-cussed in Chapter 10. By this time, we will suppose that commitments have been made to the starting of preliminary work on the secondary school project and the drainage project (with construction due to start in year 3 in both cases) and also on the first housing project (with construction due to start in year 4).

This diagram shows how the use of a readily comprehensible system of coding, based on subjective estimates of degrees of difficulty in meeting planned target dates, can help in giving an immediate impression of the main points of pressure in the implementation of an agreed development programme. Although the assessments of 'difficulty' can be expected to vary from one reporter to another, the development of procedures for comparing predictive statements with what subsequently occurs should, over time, allow any consistent biases towards opti-mism or pessimism to be corrected.

This particular kind of 'soft' information system can, we believe, provide the foundation from which the committee responsible for planning and control of Newbound's development programme might develop the potential to monitor how far the priorities it allocates to the council's various development projects

Figure 51

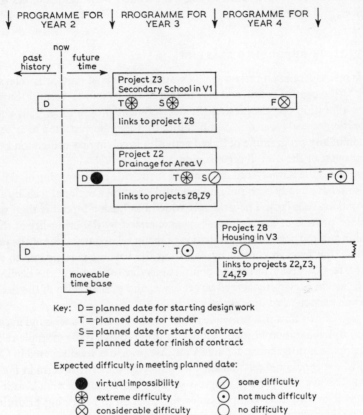

Key: D = planned date for starting design work
     T = planned date for tender
     S = planned date for start of contract
     F = planned date for finish of contract

Expected difficulty in meeting planned date:

⬤ virtual impossibility   ⊘ some difficulty
✳ extreme difficulty   ⊙ not much difficulty
⊗ considerable difficulty   ○ no difficulty

are in fact used effectively. This will bring the capital programme in line with the other resource budgets, by fulfilling a need we first spotlighted in *Table 5* (p. 62); the need that the procedures for judging claims against any resource budget should be balanced by procedures for ensuring that the resources allocated are likely to be put to good effect in practice.

PREDICTIVE REPORTING AND THE REGULATION OF THE DECISION PROCESS

Like the developmental process, the process of decision-making is itself, at the more strategic level, characterized by the criticality of the time dimension and the need to co-ordinate a set of many related tasks. We have already discussed in general terms the problem of regulating the activities of a set of interlocking policy groups; however, to more specific illustrations of the kind of scheduling and control problems which are likely to arise can be seen in the network diagram developed for Coventry's transportation study (*Figure 8*, p. 34) and in the somewhat less complex network of activities we drew up in connection with the third case example in Part III (*Figure 47*, p. 228).

This leads us to suggest to Newbound that the language of predictive reporting can provide the central board with a starting-point from which to develop systems of control over the progress of all the various planning teams which may at any time be accountable, through a network of interlocking policy groups, for elements of the total planning activity.

Of course, it is only to be expected that sometimes the leader of a policy group will have to inform the central board of 'extreme difficulty' in completing a particular stage of the decision process within the allotted time. For instance, in the example of *Figure 47*, the planning team responsible for activity 1 (exploration of the feasibility for Newbound of various novel systems of public transport) might find it extremely difficult to provide the necessary information to their particular policy group soon enough to enable them to formulate, by the agreed date, a clear set of alternatives in decision area T3. However, the group chairman – whom we would expect to be a member of the central board – would then have an opportunity to put his case to the board for an extension of the deadline to let his planning team take further actions to improve the basis for decision; the other board members would then have to weigh up the advantages to be gained from agreeing to such an extension against the penalties of any further delay in the present phase of the sub-regional planning programme.

Whereas one would expect that the establishment of a predictive reporting system for the development programme would be of special concern to the senior officer or officers responsible for Newbound's developmental services, one would expect the development of a similar system for the processes of strategic choice would be of special concern to the first officer of Council himself, as principal adviser to the central board. However, it is reasonable to expect that a good deal of the practical work of developing either system will fall to the specialist staff of the communications development unit.

THE ACCESSIBILITY OF INFORMATION

We have now given some more tangible indications of how we believe Newbound's communications development unit might be able to set up a system of 'soft' information, designed, first, to give early warning of the needs for co-ordinated planning between different sectors of the local authority, and, second, to assist in the regulation of interdepartmental planning activities after these have been initiated.

20

In discussing these aspects of an interdepartmental information system, we have so far paid special attention to its significance as an aid to those at the central 'core' of the decision-making system. However, there are, of course, many other people apart from the members of the central board and the central group of officers who will be actively concerned both in the provision of 'soft' information and in its subsequent use as a basis for decision. The inward flow of information on departmental problems still 'in the pipeline' will be dependent on the active participation of officers in many parts of the total organization, while the flow of information for any predictive reporting system will involve collaboration on the part of all the various specialist officers responsible for different aspects of the development programme, and also on the part of all the interdepartmental planning teams. These same officers would, of course, often themselves be dependent on information supplied by others to help them in fulfilling their own tasks, so would expect to obtain some direct return from whatever effort they were asked to expend in supplying information on their own current activities.

It is not, however, to be expected that Newbound will find itself able to introduce this concept of an interdepartmental 'information bank' smoothly and without opposition from any of the proposed participants. Our concept differs significantly from that of the local or regional 'data bank', which depends essentially on the collection of comparatively 'hard' information on the current state of the community and its environment [11]; what we are now considering is a pooling of information of a more intimate kind, relating to current areas of discretion and doubt, and it is only natural that the people concerned should sometimes feel reluctant to divulge such information to other parties, even in different departments of the same local authority.

There may therefore be certain forces within each department which will at first tend to resist the attempt to bring about a pooling of 'soft' information, particularly if it is envisaged that this information should be made widely available not only to other departments but also to elected members of Council. The idea of an interdepartmental 'information room', open at all reasonable times for casual visits by officers and members, has many attractions – particularly if a series of displays can be mounted, along the lines indicated in *Figures 50* and *51*, in order to give a broad perspective of 'what is going on' at the moment in question, and to allow any particular local or departmental problem to be appreciated in a broader setting. However, our own experience has indicated that departmental officers usually tend to have anxieties as to the effects of giving elected members too much uncontrolled access to information on current problems which are still undergoing departmental examination; and to the extent that such information can be only too easily misinterpreted or misapplied, this anxiety may indeed have a good deal of justification from the Council's point of view.

The existence of such anxieties suggests that Newbound's initial experiments in setting up a 'bank' of soft information will have to be carefully controlled. Initially, information on currently unresolved problems might have to be withheld from permanent display, and made available to members only at meetings of the various groups which make up the control structure indicated in *Figure 49*, so that appropriate specialist officers would always be available to interpret particular points in answer to members' questions; however, open access to the displays could perhaps be provided for an hour or so prior to the formal opening of each meeting, to give members an opportunity to scan the overall picture of 'what is going on' and pick out points of particular concern to them. As we argued in Chapter 7, the effectiveness of a strategic control group in detecting requirements for inter-group co-ordination must depend largely on the extent to which it can tap the individual scanning abilities of all elected representatives, with their many differing perspectives of the community which the local authority serves; and scanning is an activity which we suggest is more effectively carried out by individuals prior to a group meeting than in the context of the meeting itself.

Although Newbound's initial experiments in setting up an interdepartmental information system might be cautious, allowing only limited access and restricted to limited fields of information, one might expect – with experience and the passage of sufficient time to show whether the benefits of the system were sufficient to outweigh the risk of possible abuse – that pressures would begin to build up for a fuller coverage of current problem areas and for progressive extensions in levels of accessibility to officers and members of Council. It would be the task of the communications development unit to ensure that these pressures were not frustrated, and that the system continued to grow steadily, with due regard to whatever reservations might be expressed from time to time in particular quarters.

Perhaps the ultimate goal would be not so much the establishment of a single information room at one central point, accessible at all times to members and officers alike, but a readily demountable series of displays, parts of which could be transported to Fluxton, or Brawley, or Market Sheeping, whenever particular local consultations were scheduled to take place. Although we can probably assume that the administrative headquarters of Newbound will be located in the central city of Adminster, the leading members of the council may be only too ready to encourage the feeling that they are there to serve the area as a whole rather than merely its principal centre of population.

Ultimately, of course, developments in the field of information technology – and in the technology of data-transmission systems and computer graphics in particular – may make the principle of a decentralized, flexible information bank very much more easy to realize, with keyboard interrogation of a central store of 'soft' information, and selective display on a television screen of any required areas of a local map, or of the current status of any required set of projects within a development programme. However, we believe that there is a great deal that can be done in Newbound without this kind of advanced technical aid, and that the problems of internal co-ordination cannot be shelved until such time as more powerful tools become freely and economically available.

20*

THE EXTERNAL RELATIONS OF NEWBOUND

The concept of the information bank presents a number of questions relating to Newbound's external relations as well as to its internal organization. How far should information on 'what is going on' within the council be made accessible to the press, to representatives of local voluntary organizations and business firms, or indeed to individual members of the local electorate ? How far might the information bank be extended to include information about the current problems facing other public authorities within the same area ? For instance, might the system of overlays illustrated in *Figure 50* include contributions maintained by other public authorities such as those responsible for postal services or the services of gas and electricity supply ? Although they might be administratively independent of the local authority, such authorities might also have many points of functional interdependence, and have much to gain from a wider pooling of 'soft' information at local level.

There may be many planning tasks calling for the formation of joint planning teams, or at least for the initiation of informal joint consultations, between Newbound and other public bodies. This was illustrated by the third case example of Part III, where we saw that even the comparatively limited section of the subregional planning programme illustrated in *Figure 47* required consultations both with a regional rail authority and with the neighbouring local authority covering the city of Dockport. Other planning consultations might be required from time to time with departments of national government, with regional planning councils, with chambers of commerce and employees' organizations, or even with individual commercial firms whose corporate plans might impinge on public policies within the locality.

In any external consultations of this kind, there are likely of course to be organizational barriers to the free interchange of information, and equally there will be limits to the ability of the local council to mobilize any form of joint planning activity if the other party is not convinced of the need to do so. Having developed its own internal organization to be as responsive as possible to the challenges of strategic choice and strategic control, Newbound can at this stage do no more than exert whatever influence it has on the national and regional scene, in order to promote the formation of whatever kinds of mobilizing machinery at an interauthority level it sees to be necessary. It can also campaign at a national level for assistance in the development of new aids to decision, and of the technology to support its concept of an interdepartmental information bank. But these questions take us beyond our localized concern with the problems of Newbound, and we will defer them for more general discussion in the next and final chapter.

A REVIEW OF THE CASE EXAMPLE

Following the precedent of Part III, we will now conclude our case example of organizational choice in Newbound by reviewing how far we have succeeded in covering the brief for organizational choice that we set ourselves in Part II. We will therefore now summarize the main points emerging from the case example in relation to the six basic classes of organizational problem that we identified during the course of Chapter 7. These were defined as follows:

ORGANIZATIONAL PROBLEM 1
The problem of mechanisms for strategic control

including the development of processes for connecting, and sometimes disconnecting, different agencies which are seen to have related fields of decision, and for regulating the activities of the various planning frameworks so formed wherever these are seen to be interdependent.

ORGANIZATIONAL PROBLEM 2
The problem of authority for strategic control

including the question of where, within an organization, responsibility for the function of strategic control is to be located; and, in the multi-organizational case, the question of how to develop a nucleus for strategic control which is both effective and acceptable to all the agencies concerned.

ORGANIZATIONAL PROBLEM 3
The problem of sufficient information

embracing the questions of how much information is necessary to provide the requisite level of strategic control, how far for these purposes it is necessary to supplement 'hard' information by 'soft', and how the requisite level of information flow may be stimulated and maintained.

ORGANIZATIONAL PROBLEM 4
The problem of democratic guidance

including the questions of developing mechanisms for participation by representatives of the community system in the governmental planning process, and of exploring how far their participation can be supplemented by other forms of public involvement.

ORGANIZATIONAL PROBLEM 5
The problem of common language

including the question of developing languages for communication between different professions, and between professional and lay participants in the governmental system, which will provide a basis for clearer expression and wider comprehension of the implications of complex planning problems.

ORGANIZATIONAL PROBLEM 6
The problem of sufficient motivation

or the question of how the processes of strategic choice and control can be made to evolve in the direction of a more effective approach to the fundamental problems of public planning, while retaining a sufficient level of acceptability to all concerned in their operation.

In Newbound, we tackled the *problem of mechanisms for strategic control* by suggesting that the central board, as the body responsible for the strategic control function, should meet regularly to receive information on the progress of all policy groups and interdepartmental planning teams, to decide on the formation of any further groups, and to take action to deal with any likely delays in the decision-making process, in so far as these can be identified with the help of predictive reporting procedures. If the board was to be free to concentrate most of its energies on this task of strategic control, we stressed the need for it to limit severely its own interventions in the decision-making activities of any joint policy groups which it had established, while retaining the ultimate sanction of final authorization of any actions they proposed. In this interpretation of its role, the central board is not primarily a 'policy committee' in the sense that it sets out by itself to resolve major strategic issues as they arise; nor is it a 'management board' in the sense that it sets out to oversee all the day-to-day affairs of the council. Rather, it provides a driving force for the co-ordination of an interlocking and continually evolving system of decision-making groups, which together provide the council with a capacity to adapt to a rapidly changing environment.

We found that the *problem of authority for strategic control* was not difficult to resolve in Newbound in so far as it related to matters of internal connection within the council's own organization. The central board's powers of authorization in relation to the proposals of the policy groups, together with the interlocking of membership between the central board and those key committees which control the principal resource budgets, should together provide sufficient 'teeth' to allow the board to fulfil its strategic role effectively. However, once the perceived needs for connection extend beyond the boundaries of the local authority to other parts of the governmental system, the powers of Newbound's central board inevitably become more restricted, and it becomes much more difficult to see how the problem of authority for strategic control can be resolved. We will return to this question briefly in Chapter 15.

The *problem of sufficient information* was seen to relate not so much to 'hard' information on specific departmental actions and proposals (which can be kept track of by board members through their work on the resource committees), but to 'soft' information on areas of discretion where solutions have not yet been fully worked out within the departments concerned. In Newbound, we suggested that this problem should be approached through controlled experimentation leading to the development of an 'information bank' where each department would be asked to keep on deposit a limited amount of information, primarily in display form, giving an up-to-date picture of whatever current and anticipated problems of choice within the department were likely to have significant extra-departmental repercussions. The central board would then be able to rely, for its assessment of areas of relevant connection between departments, on periodic scanning of the information in the 'bank' not only by the board members themselves but by all members of council and all senior departmental officers.

The *problem of democratic guidance* was tackled in Newbound by making specific provision for councillor involvement at three different levels of the decision-making process. At the level of operational control, democratic guidance was provided through the service of elected representatives on specialist committees for different public services and on district consultative committees; at the level of strategic choice, through the involvement of key councillors in the activities of the interlocking policy groups; and at the level of strategic control, through the work of the central board itself.

At this last level, we argued that a degree of planned interlocking of membership with the resource-allocating committees could help to enrich the experience of the members concerned and so enhance their capacity to play an effective role. This capacity will, of course, depend to some extent on how much time they can afford to devote to council affairs. Although we have avoided giving any opinions on the question of remuneration for members of the board and for other key councillors, this is an important question which bears directly on the ability of elected members to achieve the degree of involvement which is required to ensure democratic guidance of the processes of strategic choice.

We were only able to touch briefly on the wider question of how far the involvement of councillors might be supplemented by other more direct forms of public participation; this raises a number of problems which come beyond the scope of our own research experience. Nevertheless, we did try to keep in mind the need for Newbound's control system not to inhibit the development of any arrangements for direct public participation which are consistent with the special responsibilities of the elected representatives.

The *problem of common language* we approached by a suggestion that Newbound should appoint a 'communications development unit', with a special interdepartmental status, charged with the responsibility of developing new forms of language which would assist the growth of more effective communication both between one profession and another, and between professional and lay participants in the total decision-making system. To the extent that computers may come to play a part in expanding the members' capacity to consider alternative courses of action, we suggested that the role of the communications development unit would have to extend to the development of languages for communication across the interface between man and machine. However, whether or not computers are to play a part in the decision-making processes of the council, we suggest that the most vital aspect of the communications problem is the need for clear presentation of information in terms (probably visual) which allow the lay representatives to appreciate the full range of options which may be open to them, rather than merely to vote for the acceptance or rejection of selected planning proposals.

The final problem, which we called the *problem of sufficient motivation*, we acknowledged to be a particularly difficult one in human terms, and one which would require much patience and dedication to resolve. So far as possible, we tried to build into our proposals for a control system certain factors designed to prevent the frustration of the legitimate ambitions and motivations of the various officers and elected members concerned. In regard to the councillors, we endeavoured to make sure that opportunities for working upwards to membership of the central board were always kept open, and that the system of interlocking groups would provide a workable instrument of control by the majority party, while allowing their opponents sufficient access to information to provide an effective opposition in the council chamber. So far as the officers were concerned, we regarded it as important that each participant in the team of advisers to the central board should feel that he had a real opportunity to succeed to the post of chief officer of the council, and to this end we argued that the post should not be identified primarily with the internal management of any particular department.

We anticipated difficulties in winning the acceptance of all departments for the idea that they should contribute 'soft' information on their current problems to a common information bank, particularly if it were proposed that this should be accessible to all elected members. We suggested therefore that a carefully controlled programme of experiment would be required, in which the communications development unit would have to work closely with individual departments in order to discover whether acceptable ways could be found of overcoming any reservations they might express from time to time.

A STRATEGY OF ORGANIZATIONAL CHOICE

Through the discussion of this case example, in which a new council is faced with the immediate problem of setting up a basic control structure which will allow it to respond effectively to the challenges of strategic choice, we have in fact arrived at the formulation of one particular 'action set' which, in the terminology of Part III, should be reasonably 'robust' in that it will allow those concerned to choose, over the course of time, between several alternative solutions to their internal problems of control and information flow. The action set we have proposed is, of course, by no means the only one which such a council might wish to examine in the crucial initial months of its existence.

To facilitate comparison with other alternatives, we summarize below the various types of action we would propose, within the framework of the organizational brief developed in Part II.

Problem of mechanisms for strategic control: periodic meetings of central board to regulate activities of specialist policy groups; setting-up of predictive reporting system.

Problem of authority for strategic control: formal powers of authorization of proposed actions vested in central board and resource-allocating committees.

Problem of sufficient information: principle of 'soft' information system with opportunities for scanning by all members and departments.

Problem of democratic guidance: councillor involvement at three levels of decision-making process: operational control, strategic choice, strategic control.

Problem of common language: formation of a communications development unit.

Problem of sufficient motivation: principle of cautious experimentation with emphasis on maintaining acceptability of system to all participants.

15. Prospects for public planning

Although we deliberately chose to set the case example of the previous chapter in the period of fundamental change in the structure of British local government that is expected to occur during the nineteen-seventies, we believe there is nevertheless a great deal that local authorities can do in the more immediate future to put the suggestions we have made in Parts III and IV to the test.

So far as the technological aspects of strategic choice are concerned, the guide-lines we developed in Part III can only be tested by being used as the basis for practical experiments in decision-making in different local settings, and at the time of writing some modest steps in this direction are already being taken. In each of our three case examples we set out to show what could be achieved without assuming the availability of any advanced technical aids; the first case example involved logical processes only, the second case example involved a level of computational power well within the compass of most existing electronic computers, and the third case example, although it raised some challenges of a particularly severe order, showed how the concepts of the proposed 'technology of choice' could be of value even when the problems concerned could not be formulated with any degree of precision. The future development of this kind of technology will, we suggest, require a sustained dialogue at two levels: between different groups of research workers who may have different approaches to offer, and between research workers and potential users in local authorities, some of whom will undoubtedly have highly significant contributions to make.

So far as the organizational problems are concerned, we believe again that many of the principles we have developed in the setting of a fictitious local authority of the future can form the basis of experiment in local authorities as at present constituted. Any council which feels it useful to do so can examine the existing role of its central committee (by whatever name it may be known) in the light of our definition of the function of strategic control, and can experiment in the setting-up of a network of interlocking policy groups whose progress can be regulated through this machinery. Experiment is also possible in the introduction of more deliberate interlocking between the membership of key committees, although this may in some cases impinge on the vested interests of individuals; and experiment is possible in loosening the reins by which committees control the actions of operating departments, provided means are sought of strengthening the participation of elected

287

members in other fields, for instance in *ad hoc* policy groups or in district consultative committees.

When it comes to the general problem of internal communications, it is open to any local authority to set up some form of communications development unit even if this may consist of one individual only, so as to explore the possibilities of building up a system for the flow of 'soft' information which will help the participants to discern new ways in which different parts of the decision-making system might be connected, and thus to establish a firmer basis for the processes of strategic choice. In our case example, we have deliberately focused on the possibilities of a relatively easily maintained set of visual displays, rather than on the longer-term possibilities which are opened up by the development of computer graphics and data-transmission techniques.

Clearly, any experiments of these kinds will be of greatest value if they can be conducted in many local settings, with free interchange of ideas and experience between them. Also, their success will depend on the extent to which support in the form of research, advice, and co-ordination can be provided at a national level.

CONNECTIVE PLANNING: A NATIONAL CHALLENGE

The challenge we have posed – in terms of the need to develop a more explicit 'technology of strategic choice', and the need for adequate organizational forms to support it – therefore concerns not only local government but national government itself. The challenge at national level does not, however, only concern the ability to give background support to the processes of experiment at local level; it also relates to the problem of mobilizing joint planning activities involving two or more local authorities, and of forming relevant connections between local authorities and other decision-making bodies within the total framework of a national planning activity.

At the heart of this problem lies the question of what forms of authority, either formal or informal, are to support the mobilization and regulation of such 'inter-corporate' planning activities. We are therefore brought back to the second of our six types of organizational problem, in a much wider context than we were able to consider through the Newbound case example. This problem of authority relates also to the problem of sufficient information, which is itself associated with the cybernetic problem of requisite variety. No national body will be able to use its authority to connect to good advantage unless it has the capacity to scan the whole vast range of activities which may at any time be expected to come within its field of interest. This problem might become somewhat more manageable if some part of the total scanning activity could be organized at regional rather than national level; however, any delegation of this kind would still leave problems of who is to have the authority to form relevant connections across regional boundaries, particularly if there are discrepancies between the geographical boundaries of administration for different public authorities.

Ultimately, one solution might lie in the development of a national 'grid' of information banks of the type we have proposed for Newbound, each using the same basic language for the expression of 'soft' as well as 'hard' information, and together providing a capacity for scanning the activities of government at local, regional, and national levels. Such a vision is likely to become more feasible technically over time, with the continuing development of computers and data-transmission techniques; but of course the human problems of motivation and accessibility, which we have already discussed in the local context, will then become even more acute. However, in the interests of democracy, we believe it is vital that these problems should be confronted so that eventually they may be overcome.

Our experience does not permit us to be specific as to the kind of machinery we think should be developed at a national level in order to work towards this aim. There is now in the United Kingdom an ever-growing number of agencies that set out to provide connective functions within and beyond the governmental system, or to scan the activities of different sectors of the national scene; some of the most significant include the National Economic Development Council with its specialist committees, the Prices and Incomes Board, the Industrial Reorganization Corporation, the Regional Economic Councils and Boards, and the various joint planning bodies that have been set up on a sub-regional basis. Perhaps, however, one of the most crucial needs of all is for some national equivalent of the 'communications development unit' we have suggested for Newbound, to address itself specifically to the task of developing methodologies for strategic choice, and languages through which public agencies of many different kinds may together reach a clearer appreciation of those problems which cross the boundaries between them.

We have not, of course, had the opportunity to observe at close quarters the processes of public planning at a national level, as we have been able to do at a local level in Coventry, and therefore we can do little more than speculate as to possible lines of approach. However, the challenge is essentially the same; to find means of coping with the increasing conflict between the sheer complexity of the problems with which the planners are faced, and the requirement for responsiveness to the pressures of the community which is the essence of a democratic society. The search for improvement in the processes of public planning must always be a difficult one for those who are in any way involved; but our work in Coventry leaves us with a firm belief that, provided sufficient of the nation's potential for scientific inquiry can be mobilized in this direction, there is real and substantial progress to be achieved.

References for Part IV

[1] Gowan, I. and Gibson, L.: The Royal Commission on Local Government in England: A Survey on Some of the Written Evidence. *Public Administration,* Spring 1968.

[2] The Basildon Experiment. *Public Administration,* Summer 1966.

[3] *Local Government Chronicle,* 3 December 1966, p. 1947.

[4] *Local Government Chronicle,* 12 March 1966, p. 437 and 19 March 1966, p. 485.

[5] Committee on the Management of Local Government: *Management of Local Government.* London: HMSO, 1967.

[6] *Report of the Committee on the Staffing of Local Government.* London: HMSO, 1967.

[7] Stringer, J., Luck, G. M., and Smith, B. W.: Decision Making and Adaptation to Change by Hospital Management. Paper to Operational Research Society Annual Conference, Exeter, 1967.

[8] Burns, T. and Stalker, G. M.: *The Management of Innovation.* London: Tavistock, 1961.

[9] Miller, E. J. and Rice, A. K.: *Systems of Organization.* London: Tavistock, 1967.

[10] Kidd, J. B. and Morgan, J. R.: The C.E.G.B. Midlands Region Information System. Paper to Operational Research Society Annual Conference, Exeter, 1967.

[11] Jay, L. S.: The Development of an Integrated Data System. Town Planning Institute, October 1966.

Index

Ackoff, R. L., xi, xvii, 103, 115, 136
action sets, 148–52, 192–7, 220–2, 237, 286
adaptive planning, 112–13
Adminster (fictional), 215–23, 226–7, 229–30, 250–1, 266, 281
agencies, 120–1
  connections between, 124–7, 129–30
agency-centred model, 122–4
AIDA, see Analysis of Interconnected Decision Areas
Airport Committee, 5
Airport Department, 5
aldermen, election of, 10
Alexander, Christopher, 126, 136, 238–9
alternative action sets, see action sets
Analysis of Interconnected Decision Areas (AIDA), 139–41, 143–4, 154–5, 160, 200, 208, 233, 238
Anglican Church, 31
annual rate estimates, 8, 12–14
Architecture and Planning, Department of, 5, 16, 18, 22–6, 39, 69, 78
Ashby, W. Ross, 130, 136, 239
Association of Education Committees, 45
Association of Municipal Corporations, 44–5
authority for strategic control, problem of, 129, 283–4, 286

Barratt, Sir Charles, xii, xvi
Basildon, 244–6, 252
Baths Department, 5
Battersby, A., 239
Beale, E. M. L., 239
Bedworth, 24
Beesley, M., 239
Bellman, R., 239
Berry, Granville, xvi
Birmingham, 4, 44
bounded interval scale, 221–2
Brawley (fictional), 215–17, 229–30, 266, 281
British Rail, 26, 40
Burns, T., 290

capital programme, 14–16, 39, 56–7, 61
  review of, 16–17

Carter, K. R., xvii
Catering Committee, 5
Catering Department, 5
central control structure (proposed), 258–60, 263–4, 284
chairmen, see under committee chairmen
Chamber of Commerce, 26, 74
Chermayeff, S., 239
chief officer, see departmental chief officer
Children's Committee, 5, 13
Children's Department, 5
Chinn, W. L., xvi
choice, see strategic choice, technology of choice
City Analyst's Department, 5
City Architect and Planning Officer (Coventry), xvi, 64, 65, 71
City Engineer and Surveyor, xvi, 64, 65
City Engineer's Department (Coventry), 5, 16–18, 24, 39, 78
City Estates Department, 5, 18, 39
City Treasurer (Coventry), xvi, 11, 14, 64, 65
Civil Defence Committee, 5
Civil Defence Department, 5
combined effect measure, 188–9, 193–4
commitment, 117–18, 232
  pressures for, 149–50
committee chairman, 51, 55–6, 262–3
committee meetings, 56–8, 246–7
  proposed role, 265–7
committee structure (Coventry), 5
common language, problem of, 132–3, 272–4, 283, 285–6
Communications Development Unit (proposed), 274–5, 279, 285–6, 288–9
community system, definition, 101
computer, electronic, 80, 181, 273–4
connective planning, 124–5, 288–9
Conservative Party, xv, 8–9, 23, 40, 50
context of operations, 105–7
contingency plan, definition, 112
conventions in local government, 47–8
co-ordination, 60, 64–5, 95–6, 124, 244–6, 252–3, 271
cost-benefit analysis, 116, 139–40, 185–8, 202–3, 234, 238

cost-effectiveness, 236
Council meetings (Coventry), 50–2
councillors
    election of, 9
    involvement of (proposed), 264–9, 284–6
Coventry, description of, 3–4
Coventry City Council
    elections to, 7–10
    interconnection of development projects, 18–19, 257
    internal organization, 4–6
    landmarks of planning (1963–67), 7–8
    relationship with research team, 66–8
'Coventry City Region' (report), 24–5, 28, 43, 72, 98
Coventry road system, see road system, planning of (Coventry)
'Coventry Road System, The' (report), 24, 80–2, 98
critical path analysis, 139, 172–3

data bank concept, 280
decision area, concept of, 144
decision field, perception of, 104
decision tree concept, 237
decision-making, processes of, 48–50, 52–4, 104–5
    role of committee meetings, 56–8, 265–7
    uncertainties in, 87–91, 95–7, 222–6
decision-taking, 56, 105
democratic guidance, problem of, 131–2, 283–6
departmental chief officer, 54–5
desire lines, 81
Development Plan (Coventry), 21–3, 33, 57, 70, 78, 98
Development Plan Review (Coventry), 22–8, 40, 56, 69–70, 76, 78–9, 86, 98, 235
developmental planning (Coventry), 17–21, 29, 46, 61–2
developmental services, 253–5, 279
'dialogue' model, 102–3
directed graph (example), 151
discounted cash flow, 203
discretion content of information, 87–8, 97
Dockport (fictional), 216–17, 227, 229, 282
dominance, 234–5
drainage, 16, 18, 39–40
    planning of (fictional case), 165, 169–79
dynamic programming, 237

early warning system, 275–7
Economic Affairs, Department of, 44
economic analysis, 203, 206
Economic Planning Councils, 44, 289
Education and Science, Department of, 30, 44

Education Committee, 5–6, 12–13, 18–20, 30–1
Education Department, 5
educational system, 29, 43, see also school system
effects, measurement of, 177–81, 201–5, 219–22
elected representatives, 6, 131–2, 264–7, see also councillors, aldermen
electoral cycle (local government), 7–10, 47
electricity boards, 247, 282
environmental uncertainties, see under uncertainties in planning
Establishment and General Administration Committee, 5, 29, 61–3
Estates and Parliamentary Committee, 5, 12–13
exploratory actions, methods of selecting, 232, 236, 238
expressing preferences, methods of, 232–5, 238

Feldstein, M. S., 136, 239
Finance Committee, 5, 11, 16–17, 49, 61–3
Finance Department, 5, 11, 18
financial planning, 208–9, 262
    in Coventry, 7, 10–11, 29, 46, 61–2
financial services, 253–5
finding solutions, methods of, 231–3, 238
Fire Brigade, 5
first officer of Council, role of (proposed), 271–2
Fishburn, P. C., 234, 239
flexibility, 117–18, 232, 237
flexibility criterion, 148–52, 160–1, 237
Fluxton (fictional), 162–213, 214–19, 227, 229–30, 262, 266, 275, 281
Fluxton bypass (fictional case), 146–8, 159–60, 164, 208–9, 214–16, 227–30
Foster, C. D., 239
Fox, Betty, xvii
Fox, Levi, 98
Friend, J. K., 98

games, theory of, 112, 237
gas boards, 41, 247, 282
General Works Committee, 5, 12–13, 18–19, 38
'generation zones', 79
Gibson, L., 290
governmental system, definition, 101
Gowan, Ivor, 290
grants from central government, 10
'Greater Warwickshire' concept, 28
Gregory, T. W., xvi
Griffith, Professor J. A. G., 30, 98
Grumwich (fictional), 215–17, 266
Gupta, S. K., 237, 239

Harris, Britton, 115, 136, 239
Health Committee, 5, 12–13
Health Department, 5, 39
Hender, J. D., xvi
Hertz, D. D., 90, 239
Higgin, G. W., 136
Hodgkinson, G. E., xvi
hospitals, 247
housing (Coventry), 10, 15–16, 18, 27–8, 39–40, 42–3, 46, 59
    planning of (fictional), 146–7, 162–3, 165, 169, 171–81, 189–92, 195–200, 208–11
Housing and Local Government, Ministry of, 22–3, 27–8, 246
housing associations, private, 40
Housing Committee, 5, 12–14, 18–19, 40
Housing Department, 5, 39

immediate commitments, methods of selecting, 232, 237–8
income, sources of (Coventry City Council), 10–11
indifference curves, 206
Industrial Reorganization Corporation, 289
information
    accessibility of, 279–81
    discretion content of, 87–8
    'soft', 130, 133–4, 271–3, 278–9, 288
information bank concept, 280–2, 289
information systems, predictive, 277–9
information technology, 281
integer programming, 233
'inter-corporate' planning, 288
interdependence (of planning activities), 72–3, 97
internal organization, 251–3
    of Coventry City Council, 4–6
internal services, organization of, 253–6

Jay, L. S., 290
Jessop, W. N., 98
joint effect tables, 198–201, 208, 227

Kenilworth, 24
Kidd, J. B., 290

Labour Party, xv, 8–9, 31, 40, 50
Lanchester College of Technology, xvii, 43
land-use planning
    in Coventry, 21–6, 28, 39, 46, 61–2, 255, 257
    fictional case, 142–61
latent uncertainty, 108, 116–8
    exposure of, 232, 235–6
latent urgency, 110
leading solutions' 182–5, 196, 210, 235

Leamington Spa, 24
legal services, 254
Levin, P. H., 87, 98
Libraries, Art Gallery, and Museums Committee, 5, 20
Libraries, Art Gallery, and Museums Department, 5
Lichfield, N., 239
Ling, A. G., xvi
local government
    in Coventry, 4
    experiments in (Basildon and Newcastle upon Tyne), 244–6
    in Great Britain, 4
    overseas, 247
    restructuring of, 243–4, 248–9
    Royal Commissions on, xvii, xxv, 243–4, 250
Local Government Operational Research Unit, 165, 243–4
local planners, definition, 142, 162, 270
local planning, relationship to national, 44–5
local taxation, see rate levy
London, 41
    third airport, 113
long-term capital programme (Coventry), see capital programme
Lord Mayor, see Mayor
Luce, R. D., 136, 239
Luck, G. M., 290
Luckman, John, xvii, 239

McDonald, N., xvi
McKean, R. N., 75, 98
Mallaby Committee (Local Government Staffing), 246
'management board' concept, 246, 252
manpower planning, 8, 29, 46, 61–2, 208–9, 262
manpower services, 253–5
Market Sheeping (fictional), 250–1, 280
Markets and Baths Committee, 5, 12–13
Markets Department, 5
Marshall, Dr A. H., xvi, 247
Maud, Sir John (Lord Redcliffe-Maud), 246
Maud Committee (Management of Local Government), 244, 246–7, 251–2, 259–61, 265, 268
Mayor, Lord, 4, 51
Merrett, A. J., 239
Miller, E. J., 290
'modal split', 225, 234
models
    behavioural, 233
    'dialogue', 102–3
    of planning process, 101–8, 121, 123, 125, 128
    predictive, 109, 123

'Monte Carlo' technique, 94
Morgan, J. R., xvii, 290
multi-organization, 121–2, 129
Murray, Dr Hugh, xvi, 136

National Coal Board, 41–2
National Economic Development Council, 78, 289
New Town Development Corporations, 255
Newbound (fictional), 250–85
Newcastle upon Tyne, 244–6, 252
Nuffield Foundation, xii, xv
Nuneaton, 24

objectives, 105–6
officers, local government, 6, 269–70
old people's homes, 40
operation, definition, 103
operational control, 128, 130
operational policies, definition, 105, 111
operational problems, xxiv, 115–19, 231–8
operational research, xi–xii, xx, xxii
Operational Research, Institute for, xi–xii, xv–xvi, 247–8
Operational Research Society, xi–xii, 87
option bar, 143–4, 155, 173–5
option graph, 143, 155, 170–1, 208
options, compatibility of, 173–4, 200–1
    definition, 218–9
    questioning of assumptions, 197–8
organization, definition, 121–2
organizational choice, 243–9, 282–3, 286
    scope for (internal), 251–3
organizational problems, xxiv, 127–35, 243, 249, 283–6
Osborn, E., xvi

Park, Councillor G. M., xvi
Parks and Allotments Committee, 5
Parks Department, 5
party politics, 7, 47, 58–9, 131, 251, 269
Passenger Transport Authorities, 247
'People and Housing' (report), 25, 98
perception
    of decision field, 104
    of uncertainties, 106
plan, definition, 111–12
planners, definition, 142, 162, 270
planning
    adaptive, 112–13
    improvement in, 113–14, 238
    and mechanisms of decision, 47–68
    models, 101–3, 109, 122–4
    nature of, 97, 101–13
    operational problems, 115–19, 231–8
    and organizational change, 66
    organizational problems, 127–35, 243, 249, 283–6

Planning—cont.
    perspectives, 45–6, 209–11, 216–18
    as process of strategic choice, xxiv, 97, 101–2, 110
    technology and technique, 139–40
    uncertainties, see uncertainties in planning
Planning Advisory Group, 22–3, 28, 44, 112–13
Planning and Redevelopment Committee, 5, 12–13, 18–21, 38, 61–3, 77
planning teams (concept), 269–70
police, reorganization of, 247
Police Force, 5
policy, definition, 111
Policy Advisory Committee, 5, 16–17, 38–40, 50, 59–65, 252
Policy Committee, see Policy Advisory Committee
policy group (concept), 269–70
Policy Map of Coventry, 22–3
'policy space', 115
policy trap, 113
policy-makers, definition, 142, 162, 270
political groups, 51–3, 58–9, 86
'political richness', 202, 220
Pollock, A. B., 136
population growth (Coventry), 27–8, 72
prediction, 71–3, 78–81
predictive reporting system, 277–9, 286
preferences, methods of expressing, 233–5, 238
preferred-full-solution criterion, 150–2, 161
press, local, 52, 78, 87
Prest, A. R., 239
Prest, John, 98
Prices and Incomes Board, 289
procedure (decision-making), 47–8
programme
    capital, see capital programme
    definition, 111
Programme Map, 21, 23
programming, mathematical, 233
Public Health Inspector's Department, 5
public transport (see also transportation system), 214, 218, 227
    in Coventry, 10, 32, 39, 41, 56, 59

questioning of assumptions (on options), 197–8

Raiffa, H., 136, 239
railways, 214, 217, 227
    in Coventry, 40–1
rate estimates, 12
rate levy, 177–80, 206, 211–12
    in Coventry, 11, 14, 57

ratepayers, 10–11, 177–91, 203–6
Rayman, N., xvi
Redcliffe-Maud, Lord, 246
Reece, M., xvi
Regional Economic Planning Councils, 44
Regional Hospital Boards, 40
regional planning, 43–4
related fields of choice, *see under* uncertainties in planning
rents, housing, 40, 170–2
representatives, *see* elected representatives
requisite variety, law of, 130, 132
research, demands for, 95–6, 107
resource control, mechanisms for, 256–8
resource-controlling committees, 60–4, 256–9, 263
resource planning, 45–6, 60–4, 256
response-to-pressure criterion, 149–51, 161, 237
Rice, A. K., 290
Richards, Councillor G. S. N., xvi
risk analysis, 91–5, 139–40, 235–6, 238
Rivett, B. H. P., xi
road system, planning of (Coventry), 24–5, 27, 41, 69–70, 74–5, 78–87, 90, 94–6
    fictional case, 146–8, 159–60, 164, 208–9, 214–30
    'robustness', 139, 159, 161, 193–5, 210, 229, 237–8, 286
Roman Catholic Church, 31
Rosenhead, J., 237, 239
Royal Commissions on Local Government, xvii, xxv, 243–4, 250
Rugby, 24

'saturated roads', 84–5
school system, planning of (Coventry), 18, 29–32, 42–4
    fictional case, 165, 168–9, 171–81, 189–92, 195–200, 207–11
selection of response, 103–5, 110
sensitivity analysis, 91, 200, 224, 225
Severn Valley, 32
Sharp, T., 136
shopping, planning of (Coventry), 25, 70–8, 88–93
    fictional case, 164–5, 169, 171–81, 185, 189–92, 195–200, 208–9
'Shopping in Coventry' (report), 25, 70, 98
Smith, D. W., xvii, 290
Smockley Parva (fictional), 250–1
social networks, xvii, 222
socio-technical system, 120
Solihull, 28
Spencer, Paul, xvi–xvii, 16, 77, 98, 222, 239
Stalker, G. M., 290
Stansted, proposed airport, 113

Stewart, J. D., xvii
Stoke district study (Coventry), 28
strategic choice, xix–xxv, 97, 101–2, 108, 110, 113, 139, 160, 213, 243–4, 272, 287–9
    definition, 97
    mechanisms of, 261–3
    operational problems (summary), 118–19, 231–2
    organizational problems (summary), 135, 283, 286
strategic control, 127–9, 131–2, 263–4, 271, 281, 287
strategy, definition, 112
strategy graph, 207–9
Stringer, J., xvii, 121, 136, 290
Stringer, S., xvi
sufficient information, problem of, 129–31, 283–4, 286
sufficient motivation, problem of, 133–4, 283, 285–6
Sykes, A. M., 239
systems approach, xxi, 101–2

Tavistock Institute of Human Relations, xi, xvi
technology of choice, xix–xx, 139, 144, 160
Town and Country Planning Act (1947), 21
Town Clerk, role of, 48, 64–5, 67, 244–7
Town Clerk's Department, 5, 18, 29
Town Map, 21, 23, 86, 112
trade-off curves, 205–6
trade-off rates, 186–91
traffic control (Coventry), 24, 27, 33
traffic flow, prediction of (Coventry), 78–81, 83, 96
    Fluxton (fictional case), 164, 214–15
Traffic Policy Committee, 38, 50, 59–60, 64, 67, 262
transparent overlays, use of, 275–7
Transport, Ministry of, 38–9, 41, 65, 67
Transport Committee, 5, 38
Transport Department, 5, 32–3
transportation system, Coventry, 24, 32, 40–1, 43, 279
    fictional case, 216–18
    planning of, 33–9, 46, 67
Transportation Study Plan, Coventry, 34–9
Treasurer, *see* City Treasurer
Trist, E. L., 136
Turvey, R., 239

uncertainties in planning, 69, 74–5, 78, 97, 116–17, 145–6, 191–3, 222–6, 230, 235–6
    components of, 88–90

uncertainties in planning—*cont.*
    environmental, 88–90, 92–4, 106–8, 116–17, 121–3, 152, 205–6, 224, 232, 236
    latent, 108, 116–18, 232, 235–6
    perceptions of, 106–9
    reduction of, 122–4, 225–6
    related fields of choice, 89–90, 92–7, 106–7, 116–19, 121–5, 146, 152, 205–6, 225, 232, 236
    value judgements, 89–90, 92–7, 106–8, 116–17, 121–3, 131, 145, 159, 161, 202, 205–6, 225, 232, 236
University of Warwick, 42
urban renewal, xxiv–xxv, 18, 27, 254
Urban Structure Map (Coventry), 22

Vajda, S., 239
value judgements, *see under* uncertainties in planning
Vickers, A. J., xvi
Vickers, Sir Geoffrey, 101, 110, 136

Wagle, B., 239

Ward, R. A., xvii
Wards, electoral, 9
Warwick, 24
Warwick, University of, *see* University of Warwick
Warwickshire County Council, 4, 24, 26, 28
Watch Committee, 5, 12–13, 38
Waterworks and Fire Brigade Committee, 5
Water Department, 5, 32
Weights and Measures Department, 5
Welfare Committee, 5, 20, 40
Welfare Department, 5
West Midlands Economic Planning Council, 44
West Midlands Gas Board, 41
West Midlands Region, 42, 44
West Midlands Study (report), 44, 98
Wheatley, Sir Andrew, 246, 265
Williams, Elizabeth, xvii
'Work in Coventry' (report), 24, 98

zoning, 26, 142–3, 149, 152, 159